JAIRUS'S DAUGHTER
AND THE FEMALE BODY IN MARK

EARLY CHRISTIANITY AND ITS LITERATURE

Emerson B. Powery, General Editor

Editorial Board:
Ronald Charles
Mary F. Foskett
Jennifer A. Glancy
Joseph A. Marchal
Anders Runesson

Number 33

JAIRUS'S DAUGHTER
AND THE FEMALE BODY IN MARK

Janine E. Luttick

SBL PRESS
Atlanta

Copyright © 2023 by Janine E. Luttick

All rights reserved. No part of this work may be reproduced or transmitted in any form or by any means, electronic or mechanical, including photocopying and recording, or by means of any information storage or retrieval system, except as may be expressly permitted by the 1976 Copyright Act or in writing from the publisher. Requests for permission should be addressed in writing to the Rights and Permissions Office, SBL Press, 825 Houston Mill Road, Atlanta, GA 30329 USA.

Library of Congress Control Number: 2023948294

Contents

Acknowledgments vii
Abbreviations ix

Jairus's Daughter: Dead and Buried? 1

1. The Raising of Jairus's Daughter and the Healing of the
   Bleeding Woman: Parallels and Contrasts 9
   1.1. Parallels   10
   1.2. Contrasts   25
   1.3. Shifts in the Focus: The Particularity of Jairus's Daughter   30
   1.4. Summary   41

2. The Body in the Gospel of Mark 43
   2.1. Ill Bodies   47
   2.2. Suffering, Violence, and Death   51
   2.3. The Body and Emotion   57
   2.4. Sensory Functions   61
   2.5. Summary   74

3. The Landscape of the Hearer in the First Century CE 77
   3.1. The World of a Hearer   77
   3.2. Voices That Sound in the Landscape of the First Century CE   91
   3.3. Working with the Voices of the First Century CE   102

4. Images of Female Bodies in the Greco-Roman Landscape 109
   4.1. The Family as a Central Image in the Early Empire   111
   4.2. Images of Adult Females within the Family   115
   4.3. Images of Children within the Family   124
   4.4. The Young Female in the Context of the Family   134
   4.5. Depictions of Dying and Deceased Girls   139

4.6. Summary	145

5. Images of Female Bodies in the Landscape of Late
   Second Temple Judaism 147
5.1. The Image of the Family in Late Second Temple Times	148
5.2. Images of Women	153
5.3. The Bodies of Children	164
5.4. Daughters and Virgins	183
5.5. Summary	194

6. Raising Jairus's Daughter 197
6.1. The Function of Location	198
6.2. The Representations of Father, Daughter, and Mother	203
6.3. The Restoration of a Child	210
6.4. The Interaction of Bodies to Restore a Daughter's Life	212
6.5. The Representation of Jesus as a Figure of Authority	213
6.6. The Notion of Family	224
6.7. Summary	251

7. Conclusions 255

Bibliography 271
Ancient Sources Index 293
Modern Authors Index 304
Subject Index 308

Acknowledgments

This book has its roots in a summer course some years ago at the Centre for Biblical Formation in Jerusalem, in which I studied the Gospel of Mark with David Neuhaus, SJ. The questions that were sparked at the time, along with those that had also been prompted in years of undergraduate study and lively discussions with others who studied the Bible, brought me to postgraduate studies and a world of new inquiries. Many have nurtured me along the way, not least Amy-Jill Levine and past mentors Peter Howard and Michael Fagenblat at Monash University. Many others have supported me since. I now name but a few.

Wishing to develop my thinking further, I undertook a PhD under the supervision of James McLaren, to whom I owe a great debt of gratitude. I am thankful for his generosity, rigor, understanding, and care. He has read many iterations of this work and has been generous in feedback. I also thank others at Australian Catholic University who have read parts of my work and provided feedback: David Sim, Michael Champion, and Emmanuel Nathan. I enjoyed the privilege of discussing my work while in its infancy with John Barclay and Francis Watson for which I am very grateful. Early in the project, Mary Coloe also provided great encouragement.

I owe further debts to Janina Hiebel, who supported me in my translation of German scholarship, and Robyn Horner, who checked the instances in which I refer to French scholarship. Any errors are mine. Australian Catholic University generously provided me with an Australian Postgraduate Award. The Sisters of Our Lady of Sion/Notre Dame de Sion have also given me great financial and personal support, along with the Loreto sisters, who provided me with a Mary Ward grant. The Faculty of Theology and Philosophy provided a space for me to research and to engage with the faculty. I am indebted to the dean, Dermot Nestor, who has made me feel welcome in the faculty. Equally, I am thankful for the scholarly support of Wojciech Kaftanski, Gareth Wearne, and Blake Wassell. For the friendship of Linda Tracey throughout the project—thank you. Likewise, I am grateful for the opportunities to gather with members of the Fellowship of Biblical Scholars and the Australian Catholic Biblical Association. The latter have supported me financially to attend their conferences.

Personally, I have been sustained by dear friends. There are too many to name but I make note of Vania Tiatto and Jayne-Louise Collins. And, of course, Debra Snoddy.

I dedicate this study to my parents, Ray and Dorothy.

Abbreviations

A.J.	Josephus, *Antiquitates judaicae*
AB	Anchor (Yale) Bible
ABD	Freedman, David Noel, ed. *Anchor Bible Dictionary*. 6 vols. New York: Doubleday, 1992.
ABRL	Anchor (Yale) Bible Reference Library
Aen.	Vergil, *Aeneid*
AGJU	Arbeiten zur Geschichte des antiken Judentums und des Urchristentums
AJA	*American Journal of Archaeology*
Am.	Ovid, *Amores*
Ann.	Tacitus, *Annales*
Ant	Sophocles, *Antigone*
AOTC	Abingdon Old Testament Commentaries
Att.	Cicero, *Epistulae ad Atticum*
B.J.	Josephus, *Bellum judaicum*
BASOR	*Bulletin of the American Schools of Overseas/Oriental Research*
BBB	Bonner biblische Beiträge
BCAW	Blackwell Companions to the Ancient World
BECNT	Baker Exegetical Commentary on the New Testament
Bell. civ.	Lucan, *De bello civili* (*Pharsalia*)
BETL	Bibliotheca Ephemeridum Theologicarum Louvaniensium
BibInt	*Biblical Interpretation*
BibInt	Biblical Interpretation Series
BJS	Brown Judaic Studies
BLS	Bible and Literature Series
BMC	*British Museum Collection*
BNP	Cancik, Hubert, ed. *Brill's New Pauly: Encyclopaedia of the Ancient World*. 22 vols. Leiden: Brill, 2006–2011.

BNTC	Black's New Testament Commentary
BRev	Bible Review
Brut.	Cicero, *Brutus*
BSac	*Bibliotheca Sacra*
BTB	*Biblical Theology Bulletin*
BZ	*Biblische Zeitschrift*
BZNW	Beihefte zur Zeitschrift für die neutestamentliche Wissenschaft
C. Ap.	Josephus, *Contra Apionem*
CAH	Cambridge Ancient History
Cal.	Suetonius, *Gaius Caligula*
CBQ	*Catholic Biblical Quarterly*
Chaer.	Chariton, *De Chaerea et Callirhoe*
CIIP	Cotton, Hannah M., Leah Di Segni, Werner Eck, Alla Kushnir-Stein, Haggai Misgav, Jonathan Price, Israel Roll, and Ada Yardeni, eds. *Inscriptionum Iudaeae/Palestinae: A Multi-Lingual Corpus of the Inscriptions from Alexander to Muhammad; Jerusalem, Part 1: 1–704.* Berlin: de Gruyter, 2010.
CIJ	Frey, Jean-Baptiste, ed. *Corpus Inscriptionum Graecarum.* 2 vols. Rome: Pontifical Biblical Institute, 1936–1952.
CIL	*Corpus Inscriptionum Latinarum.* Berlin, 1862–.
Claud.	Suetonius, *Divus Claudius*
CLE	Beucheler, Franz, ed. *Carmina Latina Epigraphica.* 2 vols. Leipzig: Teubner, 1895–1987.
Clu.	Cicero, *Pro Cluentio*
Comp. Lyc. Num.	Plutarch, *Comparatio Lycurgi et Numae*
Comp. Per. Fab.	Plutarch, *Comparatio Periclis et Fabii Maximi*
ConBNT	Coniectanea Biblica: New Testament Series
Congr.	Philo, *De congressu quaerendae eruditionis gratia*
Cons. Helv	Seneca, *De consolatione ad Helviam*
Cons. ux.	Plutarch, *Consolatio ad uxorem*
CurBR	*Currents in Biblical Research*
EJL	Early Judaism and Its Literature
Enc	*Encounter*
Ep.	Pliny the Younger, *Epistulae*
Epig.	Martial, *Epigrams*
Fact.	Valerius Maximus, *Facta et Dicta Memorabilia*

Fam.	Cicero, *Epistulae ad familiares*
FB	Forschung zur Bibel
FJTC	Flavius Josephus: Translation and Commentary
Flacc.	Philo, *In Flaccum*
GBS	Guides to Biblical Scholarship
Germ.	Tacitus, *Germania*
Gyn.	Soranus, *Gynaecology*
HCS	Hellenic Culture and Society
Hen	Henoch
HeyJ	Heythrop Journal
Hist.	Tacitus, *Historiae*
HThKNT	Herder Theologischer Kommentar zum Neuen Testament
HTR	Harvard Theological Review
HvTSt	Hervormde teologiese studies
IBC	Interpretation: A Bible Commentary for Teaching and Preaching
IDS	*In die Skriflig*
IJST	*International Journal of Systematic Theology*
IK	Inschriften griechischer Städte aus Kleinasien. Bonn, Habelt, 1972–.
Il.	Homer, *Iliad*
Inst.	Quintillian, *Institutio oratoria*
Int	*Interpretation*
ITQ	Irish Theological Quarterly
JBL	Journal of Biblical Literature
JCR	Journal of Childhood and Religion
JFSR	Journal of Feminist Studies in Religion
JJS	Journal of Jewish Studies
JR	Journal of Religion
JRS	Journal of Roman Studies
JSJ	*Journal for the Study of Judaism*
JSJSup	Journal for the Study of Judaism Supplement Series
JSNT	*Journal for the Study of the New Testament*
JSNTSup	Journal for the Study of the New Testament Supplement Series
JSOTSup	Journal for the Study of the Old Testament Supplement
JSP	*Journal for the Study of the Pseudepigrapha*
JSPSup	Journal for the Study of the Pseudepigrapha Supplement Series

JTSA	*Journal of Theology for South Africa*
Jub.	Jubilees
LAB	Liber Antiquitatum Biblicarum/Biblical Antiquities
LCL	Loeb Classical Library
Leg.	Cicero, *De legibus*
Legat.	Philo, *Legatio ad Gaium*
LNTS	Library of New Testament Studies
LSJ	Liddell, Henry George, Robert Scott, and Henry Stuart Jones. *A Greek-English Lexicon*. 9th ed. with revised supplement. Oxford: Clarendon, 1996.
LSTS	Library of Second Temple Studies
Mor.	Plutarch, *Moralia*
Mos.	Philo, *De vita Mosis*
NA^{28}	*Novum Testamentum Graece*, Nestle-Aland, 28th ed.
Nat.	Pliny the Elder, *Naturalis historia*
NIGTC	New International Greek Testament Commentary
NovT	*Novum Testamentum*
NovTSup	Novum Testamentum Supplements
NRSV	New Revised Standard Version
NTAbh	Neutestamentliche Abhandlungen
NTL	New Testament Library
NTOA	Novum Testamentum et Orbis Antiquus
NTS	*New Testament Studies*
Num.	Plutarch, *Numa*
Opif.	Philo, *De opificio mundi*
OTL	Old Testament Library
OTP	Charlesworth, James, ed. *The Old Testament Pseudipigrapha*. 2 vols. New York: Doubleday, 1983, 1985.
PACS	Philo of Alexandria Commentary Series
Phil.	Cicero, *Orationes philippicae*
P.Mich.	Papyri in the University Michigan Collection
Pomp.	Plutarch, *Pompeius*
PRSt	*Perspectives in Religious Studies*
PrT	*Practical Theology*
Ps.-Philo	Pseudo-Philo
QG	Philo, *Questiones et solutiones in Genesin*
Quint. fratr.	Cicero, *Epistulae ad Quintum fratrem*
Rab.	Rabbah
Rep.	Cicero, *De republica*

RIC	Sutherland, C. H. V., and R.A. G. Carson. *Roman Imperial Coinage*. 2 vols. London: Spinks, 1948.
RRC	Crawford, Michael H. *Roman Republican Coinage*. London: Cambridge University Press, 1974.
RW	*Reformed World*
Sat.	Juvenal, *Satirae*
SBLDS	Society of Biblical Literature Dissertation Series
SHBC	Smyth & Helwys Bible Commentary
SNTSMS	Society for New Testament Studies Monograph Series
SP	Sacra Pagina
Spec.	Philo, *De specialibus legibus*
SPhA	*Studia Philonica Annual*
SR	*Studies in Religion*
StBibLit	Studies in Biblical Literature (Lang)
T. Ab.	Testament of Abraham
TAPA	*Transactions of the American Philological Association*
Thf	*Theoforum*
ThTo	*Theology Today*
TSAJ	Texte und Studien zum antiken Judentum/Texts and Studies in Ancient Judaism
Tusc.	Cicero, *Tusculanae disputationes*
Verr.	Cicero, *In Verrem*
Vit. Apoll.	Philostratus, *Vita Apollonii*
Vita	Josephus, *Vita*
WBC	Word Bible Commentary
WUNT	Wissenschaftliche Untersuchungen zum Neuen Testament
WW	*Word and World*
ZECNT	Zondervan Exegetical Commentary on the New Testament
ZPE	*Zeitschrift für Papyrologie und Epigraphik*

Unless indicated otherwise, Scripture quotations are from the New Revised Standard Version (NRSV). Quotations from other ancient texts are from the Loeb Classical Library. Quotations from the pseudepigrapha are from *OTP*. Scripture quotations and references in Greek are from NA^{28}.

Jairus's Daughter: Dead and Buried?

In this book I argue that, through the representation of Jairus's daughter in the narrative of Mark's Gospel, a hearer is aware that bodies in their most liminal states are sites of life and signs of future hope. Over the centuries, the image of the girl who was raised to life by Jesus (Mark 5:21–24, 35–43) has singularly inspired the imagination of various artists. Depictions of Jairus's daughter grace the canvasses of artists such as William Blake and Giovanni Tiepolo, while in recent decades she has been portrayed in works by Stanley Spencer and Noel Connor.[1] In the world of biblical studies, however, the story of the restoration of the child and daughter is seldom the subject of its own in-depth study.[2] This book addresses that gap

---

1. William Blake, *Christ Raising Jairus' Daughter*, 1799–1800; Giovanni Tiepolo, *Jesus in the House of Jairus*, ca. 1790–1804; Stanley Spencer, *Resurrection with the Raising of Jairus' Daughter*, 1947; Noel Connor in David Constantine et al., *Talitha Cumi* (Newcastle Upon Tyne: Bloodaxe, 1983). These works are cited in Christine E. Joynes, "Still at the Margins? Gospel Women and Their Afterlives," in *Radical Christian Voices and Practice: Essays in Honour of Christopher Rowland*, ed. Zoë Bennet and David B. Gowler (Oxford: Oxford University Press, 2012), 129–32.

2. Works that are solely devoted to Mark 5:21–24, 35–43 include Mary Ann Beavis, "The Resurrection of Jephthah's Daughter: Judges 11:34–40 and Mark 5:21–24, 35–43," *CBQ* 72 (2010): 46–62; Donald Capps, "Curing Anxious Adolescents through Fatherlike Performance," *Int* 55 (2001): 135–47; Charles W. Hedrick, "Miracle Stories as Literary Compositions: The Case of Jairus's Daughter," *PRSt* 20 (1993): 217–33; Mercy A. Oduyoye, "*Talitha qumi*: Celebrating Africa's Struggles against Structures and Cultures That Legitimize Exclusion and Inequalities; A Study of Mark 5: 21–24, 35–43," *RW* 58 (2008): 82–89; Rudolf Pesch, "Jaïrus (Mk 5:22/Lk 8:41)," *BZ* 14 (1970): 252–56; Leopold Sabourin, "The Miracles of Jesus (III): Healings, Resuscitations, Nature Miracles," *BTB* 5 (1975): 146–200; Martijn Steegen, "'Little Girl, Get Up!': The 'Perspective of the Impossible' as Inspiration for Health Care Chaplains" (paper presented at the Annual Meeting of the Society of Biblical Literature, San Antonio, TX, 20 November 2016); Max Wilcox, "Talitha Koum(I) in Mk 5:41," in *Logia: Les paroles*

by providing an in-depth examination of the account of Jairus's daughter as it may have been heard by a person in the first century CE.

At first glance, it may appear that Mark 5:21–24, 35–43 receives extensive treatment in commentaries and studies. The story of the synagogue leader and his daughter is examined in the numerous commentaries on Mark's Gospel. It also appears in various thematic studies related to Mark or to broad biblical themes.[3] Upon closer inspection, it becomes evident, however, that the passage is generally analyzed in relation to the story of the bleeding woman (5:25–34).[4] The episode concerning Jairus's daughter is understood to form the outer layers of one of Mark's signature literary techniques, the so-called Markan sandwich. As such, the intercalated story of the woman constitutes the inner layer, the key component, and Mark 5:21–24, 35–43 is routinely examined in relation to this structure.

As a result of this treatment, two patterns generally emerge in the scholarship. First, scholars observe numerous parallels between both

---

de Jésus = The Sayings of Jesus; Mémorial Joseph Coppens, ed. Joël Delobel, BETL 59 (Leuven: Leuven University Press, 1982), 469–76.

3. E.g., Sharon Betsworth, *Children in Early Christian Narratives*, LNTS 521 (London: Bloomsbury, 2015), 47–52; Betsworth, *The Reign of God Is Such as These: A Socio-literary Analysis of Daughters in the Gospel of Mark*, LNTS 422 (London: T&T Clark, 2010), 107–15; Peter Bolt, *Jesus' Defeat of Death: Persuading Mark's Early Readers*, SNTSMS 125 (Cambridge: Cambridge University Press, 2003), 158–90; Stephanie M. Fischbach, *Totenerweckungen: Zur Geschichte einer Gattung*, FB 69 (Würzburg: Echter, 1992), 155–96; Tinyiko Sam Maluleke, "Bible Study the Graveyardman, the 'Escaped Convict' and the Girl-Child: A Mission of Awakening, an Awakening of Mission," *International Review of Mission* 91 (2002): 550–57; Elizabeth Struthers Malbon, "Echoes and Foreshadowings in Mark 4–8: Reading and Rereading," *JBL* 112 (1993): 211–30; Susan Miller, *Women in Mark's Gospel*, JSNTSup 259 (London: T&T Clark, 2004), 52–72; Dagmar Oppel, *Heilsam erzählen—erzählend heilen: Die Heilung der Blutflüssigen und die Erweckung der Jairustochter in Mk 5,21-43 als Beispiel markinischer Erzählfertigkeit*, BBB 102 (Weinheim: Beltz Athenäum, 1995); Gérard Rochais, *Les Récits de Résurrection des Morts dans Le Nouveau Testament*, SNTSMS 40 (Cambridge: Cambridge University Press, 1981), 39–48, 54–73, 100–112, 197–202; Steven Richard Scott, "Raising the Dead: Finding History in the Gospel Accounts of Jesus's Resurrection Miracles, Part One: The Synoptic Tradition" (PhD diss., University of Ottawa, 2010), 164–69; Willard M. Swartley, "The Role of Women in Mark's Gospel: A Narrative Analysis," *BTB* 27 (1997): 16–22; Elaine M. Wainwright, *Women Healing/Healing Women: The Genderization of Healing in Early Christianity*, Bible World (London: Acumen, 2006), 112–23.

4. Throughout this work I will generally designate Mark 5:25–34 as the story of the bleeding woman, and 5:21–24, 35–43 as the story of Jairus's daughter.

stories. These commonly include notions relating to gender and disease, faith and fear, the ritual impurity of both females, and the power of Jesus to restore illness and death. Second, scholars discern contrasts between both episodes. These contrasts are frequently constructed along social and religious lines, with sharp distinctions drawn between the status of the synagogue leader and his daughter and that of the woman. Discussions of these differences often result in the bleeding woman being cast as the superior figure in 5:21–43. Another consequence of this treatment is that the interpretation of the story of Jairus's daughter is frequently controlled and limited by the readings of the bleeding woman's account.

Among those who examine the story of Jairus's daughter according to the Markan sandwich technique, some identify distinctive elements in the story. That is, they do not attempt to correlate each detail in the girl's story with the details of the bleeding woman's account. This often leads to questions concerning the significance of the girl being raised from the dead. Scholars, for instance, deliberate over what is meant by the reference to Jairus's daughter as not dead but sleeping (5:39), or questions of whether she is resuscitated or resurrected (5:41–42).[5] Some scholars assert that the ways for addressing these questions are not necessarily contingent on the reading of the story of the bleeding woman. Instead, they look for lines of correspondence in other parts of the gospel, including the resurrection of Jesus. The ongoing discussion across commentaries and studies concerning the significance of the dying-deceased-restored girl suggests that new approaches to examining the story ought to be explored.

While the dominant paradigm for reading 5:21–24, 35–43 is through the lens of the sandwich technique, some scholars draw on alternative frames of reference. These include other passages or sections in the Markan narrative, as well as references to the wider biblical tradition and/or the broader sociocultural context. In shifting the interpretive frame of

---

5. E.g., R. T. France, *The Gospel of Mark: A Commentary on the Greek Text*, NIGTC (Grand Rapids: Eerdmans; Carlisle: Paternoster 2002), 239–40; Robert H. Gundry, *Mark: A Commentary on His Apology for the Cross* (Grand Rapids: Eerdmans, 1993), 274–84; Morna D. Hooker, *The Gospel according to Saint Mark*, BNTC (Peabody, MA: Hendrickson, 2009), 147; Joel Marcus, *Mark 1–8: A New Translation with Introduction and Commentary*, AB 27A (New York: Doubleday, 2000), 371–73; Rudolf Pesch, *Das Markusevangelium*, HThKNT 2 (Freiburg im Breisgau: Herder, 1977); Robert H. Stein, *Mark*, BECNT 2 (Grand Rapids: Baker Academic, 2008), 273–74.

5:21–24, 35–43, new perspectives are opened up for reading the account.[6] In recent decades, this move has prompted discussion concerning the status of Jairus's daughter as a child and/or daughter.[7] In addition, it has further opened up the deliberations concerning the possible significance of her dying, death, and restoration.[8]

To date, however, no attempt has been made to understand the story of Jairus's daughter in light of the depictions of the body in the Markan narrative. It is my observation that throughout the narrative the body functions as a vehicle for communicating ideas and attitudes. The representations of particular bodies and the descriptions of what they do and what others do to them mediate meaning. This insight drives the aim of this study: to interpret the story of Jairus's daughter with an awareness of the role and function of representations of the body in the first century CE. In line with recent studies that widen the vantage point from which Jairus's daughter is examined, I argue that we need to open up further ways of considering the story of Jairus's daughter, rather than continuing to limit our analyses to the current parameters that generally dominate how the passage is read.

This study takes the body of Jairus's daughter—the body of a dying, deceased, and restored female—as its focus. In so doing, I pose the question: What is the significance of the body in the raising of Jairus's daughter and how might a hearer in the first century CE have constructed meaning about this story? In asking this question, I am interested in understanding

---

6. E.g., Elizabeth Struthers Malbon, "The Jewish Leaders in the Gospel of Mark: A Literary Study of Marcan Characterization," *JBL* 108 (1989): 259–81. Other than a brief mention, the story of Jairus's daughter is not treated in relation to the bleeding woman in Mark Kiley, "Marcan Love, Sotto Voce," *BTB* 39 (2009): 71–76.

7. E.g., Beavis, "Resurrection of Jephthah's Daughter," 46–62; Judith M. Gundry, "Children in the Gospel of Mark, with Special Attention to Jesus' Blessing of the Children (Mark 10:13–16) and the Purpose of Mark," in *The Child in the Bible*, ed. Marcia C. Bunge (Grand Rapids: Eerdmans, 2008), 143–76; James Murphy, *Kids and Kingdom: The Precarious Presence of Children in the Synoptic Gospels* (Eugene, OR: Pickwick, 2013), 71–72, 121–22. Betsworth includes Jairus's daughter in relation to 5:25–34 in her recent study of children (*Children in Early Christian Narratives*, 47–53).

8. E.g., Kasper Dalgaard, "The Four Keys of God: Mark 4:35–6:44 and the Midrash of the Keys," *Hen* 33 (2011): 238–49; Paul M. Fullmer, *Resurrection in Mark's Literary-Historical Perspective*, LNTS 360 (London: T&T Clark, 2007), 172; Murray J. Harris, *From Grave to Glory: Resurrection in the New Testament; Including a Response to Norman L. Geisler* (Grand Rapids: Zondervan, 1990), 86–87; Hedrick, "Miracle Stories as Literary Compositions," 233.

the imagery and language of women's and female children's bodies that was operative in the first-century landscape and how it may be brought into dialogue with the story of Jairus's daughter. In particular, I am interested in how the imagery and language associated with dying and deceased females might have intersected with 5:21–24, 35–43.

In order to pursue these questions, the study takes the form of a historical investigation into the world that hearers of Mark inhabited. The investigation proceeds in three steps. The first step is to locate the world of the first-century hearer. How we go about such a task is a vexed issue. Currently, there is neither a consensus nor conclusive evidence for the provenance of Mark. One option is to choose one of the proposed locations (Rome, Syria, Galilee) and to anchor the analysis in that place. While certainly legitimate and common, such a course runs the risk of applying a predetermined theology or set of assumptions to the findings, potentially curbing the possibility of gaining new insights.

An alternative is to locate the hearer along the lines of what *is known* about Mark's narrative: it is written in the first-century CE. It is set geographically in the Jewish homeland of the first century CE, while concomitantly possessing traces of Greco-Roman culture. In other words, it bears the imprint of an awareness of a construct of both late Second Temple Judaism and Greco-Roman society in the early Roman Empire. The latter approach is the one taken in this study. I locate the hearer in the temporal reality of Mark, rather than one specific geographical context. The focus on the temporal context recognizes that those who encountered Mark's story inhabited a milieu in the first century CE that comprised a complex system of texts, images, and practices. Within that system, some hearers would have been cognizant of Jewish thought and customs, while others would not. Situated in the Greco-Roman world, all would have been engaged in a process of what is generally described as hellenization. This context influenced both how a story was constructed and how it was encountered by various hearers depending on their circumstances.

The approach I take has two advantages. First, it creates an opportunity to examine the images of women and female children that were broadly operative in the literary and material data in both late Second Temple Judaism and the early Roman Empire. This analysis will provide an insight into how dying and deceased women and female children were depicted in visual and written forms. Such a wide-ranging examination of this particular subject has not been brought to bear on Mark 5:21–24, 35–43 to my knowledge. Second, broadening the scope for understanding the influences on people who heard the story of Jairus's daughter in the first century CE provides a new entry point into the analysis of the story. This positions us to offer a new perspective to the current conversations among biblical scholars concerning the import of the girl's status as a child and the representation of her death and restoration.

The second step in the investigation is to undertake an analysis of the images and language of late Second Temple Judaism and the early Roman Empire. This examination is guided by the question: How were the bodies of women and female children, particularly dying and dead bodies, represented in the first century CE? In asking this question, I am interested in understanding how the interrelated elements of gender, age, and ethnicity may have had a bearing on the construction of people's bodies in textual and visual imagery. Each of these elements relates to markers in 5:21–24, 35–43, given that a twelve-year-old daughter of Jewish ancestry is one of its main protagonists.

In the third step, I bring the images and ideas that are generated in step two into dialogue with the story of Jairus's daughter. On the basis of this analysis, I am able to make the case for the central argument of this study. By widening the interpretive vista of 5:21–24, 35–43, the story of Jairus's daughter can be understood to make a distinctive contribution to notions concerning who and what constituted the household and family. Indeed, the analysis of representations of the body in the story of Jairus's daughter points toward the observations about the importance of household and related expectations of hope, continuity, and generativity.

The study unfolds over the following chapters. In chapter 1, I analyze how the story of Jairus's daughter is treated in modern scholarship. The examination demonstrates that the account is often limited by readings of the intercalated story of the bleeding woman. This observation leads me to make a case for broadening the perspective from which we read the passage. Chapter 2 lays the initial groundwork for widening the interpretive vista. I discuss my observation that representations of the body are significant throughout the entire narrative of the gospel, functioning as vehicles for conveying meaning. This finding leads me to propose that a study of the story of Jairus's daughter—a dying, deceased, and restored daughter—with the role of the body at the forefront of the analysis, will be instructive for opening up new ways of thinking about the passage.

Having established what I observe to be the import of the body in Mark's narrative, the study turns toward the first century CE. I investigate some of the perspectives and mindsets a hearer in the first century

CE would have brought to their encounter with the story. Depictions of women and children were fundamental elements of the material and literary landscapes of both late Second Temple Judaism and the early Roman Empire. There is a broad range of source material from which to draw. To begin, therefore, I outline in chapter 3 the scope of the primary sources that will be used to examine the temporal context of Mark, and how these sources will be used. In chapters 4 and 5, I examine the import of images of women and female children among various voices associated with Greco-Roman culture and late Second Temple Judaism respectively. In chapter 6, the insights that are gleaned from these latter two analyses are each brought into dialogue with the story of Jairus's daughter to discuss how a hearer may have approached the story. After proffering several insights into the passage, I examine how a hearer may have situated the story of Jairus's daughter within the broader narrative of Mark. I demonstrate it is plausible that the passage illuminated ideas about the family and household, paying particular attention to the membership of children. The discussion also considers the relationship between the stories of Jairus's daughter and the bleeding woman with a focus centered on the family and household.

In the final chapter, I draw conclusions from the analysis that has been undertaken. In particular, I highlight the significance of the study for expanding the vantage point from which to read the passage of Jairus's daughter in light of the new perspectives that have been opened up. I then draw the study to a close by setting out the possible significance of the story for some who may encounter it in the twenty-first century CE.

A few words about the structure of the book are necessary. Some readers may approach this book expecting first to read an exegesis of the passage followed by comparisons to Greco-Roman and Hellenistic Jewish literature, as well as the Synoptic parallels in Matt 9:18–26 and Luke 8:40–56. The organization of the book does not fall into this approach. Instead of building on well-milled methods in biblical studies, the purpose of the book is to widen the vantage point from which the story of Jairus's daughter has been read in scholarship to date (ch. 1). In the ensuing sequence of chapters, you will trace a historical investigation into how images of female children influenced the reception of the story of Jairus's daughter in the first century CE by understanding how representations of female children functioned in the first century (chs. 4 and 5) and then considering how these patterns of thought shaped a person's encounter with Mark 5:21–24, 35–43 (ch. 6).

Given that representations of the body provide the entry point to the inquiry, it is necessary early in the book to paint a broad picture of how images of bodies functioned in the narrative of Mark. Joan Taylor has observed how ideologies and emotions were projected onto representations of the body in the ancient world.[9] From the outset, therefore, I illustrate how issues of power, authority, gender, social structures, and emotions emerge through the depiction of bodies throughout the narrative (ch. 2). This discussion provides a necessary frame of reference for us then to examine some of the religious, social, and political ideas that populated the broader milieu of the hearer of Mark's Gospel and were conveyed specifically through the images of females.

Methodologically, the book reveals how new insights emerge when we evaluate how the story relates to patterns of thought in the broader social context. It is necessary, therefore, to describe this context before considering the passage in the gospel. To chart how hearers' understandings of female children's bodies were formed, the book provides an analysis of ideas (chs. 4 and 5) that were conveyed through representations of female bodies in the early Roman empire via a variety of media (identified in ch. 3). The purpose of the discussion in chapters 3–5 is to reveal how the understandings of everyday people were influenced by the architecture and monuments, coins, and funerary monuments, that were encountered daily in the public spaces of the early empire. Insights from material culture are also compared to ideas that emerge in literary representations to describe mindsets concerning female children that were brought to bear on the reception of the story of Jairus's daughter. This discussion creates the map by which to finally consider how the story of Jairus's daughter was heard.

Having described the experiences and existing thought patterns concerning representations of female children, the climax of the book is a return to the narrative of Mark to discuss the interaction between these mindsets and the narrative of Mark 5:21–24, 35–43 (ch. 6). What emerges from this investigation is a new reading of the story of Jairus's daughter that reveals how hearers were formed by the worldviews of their time to make sense of the passage (and, indeed, the whole narrative of the gospel) and how, through engagement with the passage, hearers may have reformed these worldviews in light of beliefs in Jesus, the Messiah.

---

9. Joan Taylor, ed., *The Body in Biblical, Christian and Jewish Texts*, LSTS 85 (London: Bloomsbury, 2014), xv–xvi.

1

The Raising of Jairus's Daughter and the Healing of the Bleeding Woman: Parallels and Contrasts

Before we undertake an analysis of the story of Jairus's daughter in light of the reality of a hearer in the first century CE, it is necessary first to consider the influences on the interpretation of this passage in modern scholarship and the readings they subsequently generate. The observations I draw from such a survey lead me to argue that we need to open up new ways of considering the story of Jairus's daughter, rather than limiting our analyses to the current parameters that define how the account is interpreted.

Across a breadth of disparate methodologies and approaches, the story of Jairus's daughter is predominantly read within the context of Mark 5:21–43, with interpretations of the intercalated story of the bleeding woman (5:25–34) often controlling the analysis of 5:21–24, 35–43. In the most recent monograph concerning this pericope, for instance, Arie Zwiep thoroughly examines the story of Jairus's daughter and its intertwining with the story of the bleeding woman using both synchronic and diachronic approaches.[1] While treating 5:21–43 as a whole has yielded exegetical fruit, a common characteristic of this produce is the privileging of the woman's story over that of the little girl's. Moreover, the woman is often depicted as the superior character in comparison to the synagogue leader and his daughter. Criticisms of some of these comparisons, as well insights derived from studies of how 5:21–24, 35–43 relates to broader themes in Mark and the biblical tradition, indicate that widening the van-

---

1. Arie Zwiep, *Jairus's Daughter and the Haemorrhaging Woman: Tradition and Interpretation of an Early Christian Miracle Story*, WUNT 421 (Tübingen: Mohr Siebeck, 2019).

tage point from which to read the story of Jairus's daughter is appropriate and can produce new insights into this story.

1.1. Parallels

Much of the scholarship and popular writing on Mark 5:21-24, 35-43 has treated this story in the context of the account of the healing of the bleeding woman, 5:23-34. There is a scholarly consensus that both 5:21-24, 35-43 and 5:25-34 form a narrative whole. The episode in which the bleeding woman is healed is widely understood to be an intercalated text, revealing an A-B-A structure that commentators often refer to as the Markan "sandwich technique." In this technique, two stories are related as follows: (1) together they illustrate an A1-B-A2 structure; (2) the B episode comprises one story only; (3) the A2 section refers back to the A1 section with the former needing the latter to be completed; (4) the A2 section is delayed by the insertion of the B episode.[2] Both episodes in the Markan sandwich technique are considered to be "mutually interpretative."[3] Addressing a "common theme," both stories "enrich" and "illuminate" each other, or "comment on each other by contrast."[4] The reader is invited to "read this episode specifically in light of that one, and that one in light of this one."[5]

The full account of 5:21-43 is commonly identified as a typical example of Mark's ubiquitous use of this structure. Just as ubiquitous is the scholarly examination of Jairus's daughter primarily in terms of this structure. This way of understanding the story of Jairus's daughter is found among a diversity of approaches and methodologies, spanning historical, redaction, form, narrative, and literary criticism. It also emerges in intertextual,

---

2. Scott G. Brown, "Mark 11:1–12:12: A Triple Intercalation?," *CBQ* 64 (2002): 78–79, 87.

3. Brown, "Mark 11:1–12:12," 79. See also William R. Telford, *The Barren Temple and the Withered Tree*, JSNTSup 1 (Sheffield: JSOT Press, 1980), 48.

4. David Rhoads, Joanna Dewey, and Donald Michie, *Mark as Story: An Introduction to the Narrative of a Gospel*, 3rd ed. (Minneapolis: Fortress, 2012), 51–52. Brown also quotes an earlier edition of this publication ("Mark 11:1–12:12," 79).

5. Robert M. Fowler, *Let the Reader Understand: Reader-Response Criticism and the Gospel of Mark* (Minneapolis: Fortress, 1991), 144. For another definition, see Mary Ann Tolbert, *Sowing the Gospel: Mark's World in Literary-Historical Perspective* (Minneapolis: Fortress, 1989), 197.

reader-response, psychological, and feminist approaches, as well as in the areas of healthcare and postcolonial studies.[6]

When scholars examine both stories in light of the Markan sandwich technique, they regularly identify parallels between both accounts. Numerous themes routinely emerge through this approach, notably: the focus on females, the namelessness of both female characters, the hopelessness and desperation of the woman's and Jairus's daughter's situations, the references to "twelve years," the uses of the term *daughter*, the significance of ritual impurity, the gestures of touch, the desire for salvation and healing, and notions of death and of Jesus's power over death.[7] Three themes that

---

6. Commentaries that employ historical and literary methods include M. Eugene Boring, *Mark: A Commentary*, NTL (Louisville: Westminster John Knox, 2006), 155–63; France, *Gospel of Mark*, 233–40. Examples of narrative criticism include Normand Bonneau, "Suspense in Mark 5:21–43: A Narrative Study of Two Healing Stories," *ThJ* 36 (2005): 131–54; Brigitte Kahl, "Jairus und die verlorenen Töchter Israels: Sozioliterarische überlegungen zum Problem der Grenzüberschreitung in Mk 5, 21–43," in *Von der Wurzel getragen: Christlich-feministische Exegese in Auseinandersetzung mit Antijudaismus*, ed. Luise Schottroff and Marie-Theres Wacker, BibInt 17 (Leiden: Brill, 1996), 61–78. For literary criticism, see, e.g., Tolbert, *Sowing the Gospel*, 164–72. For narrative and historical criticisms, see, e.g., Francis J. Moloney, *The Gospel of Mark: A Commentary* (Peabody, MA: Hendrickson, 2002), 106–11. Expanding on these methods to include the social sciences is Mark L. Strauss, *Mark*, ZECNT 2 (Grand Rapids: Zondervan, 2014), 24–237. Commentaries that draw on redaction and historical criticisms include Robert A. Guelich, *Mark 1–8:26*, WBC 34a (Dallas: Word, 1989), 289–305; Marcus, *Mark 1–8*, 354 73. For literary and feminist approaches, see, e.g., Miller, *Women*, 52–72. For reader-response, see,. e.g., Bas M. F. van Iersel, *Mark: A Reader-Response Commentary*, trans. W. H. Bisscheroux, JSNTSup 164 (Sheffield: Sheffield Academic, 1998), 203–12. For a psychological approach, see Rodney Bomford, "Jairus, His Daughter, the Woman and the Saviour: The Communication of Symmetric Thinking in the Gospel of St Mark," *PrT* 3 (2010): 41–50. For an intertextual approach, see, e.g., Rikki E. Watts, "Jesus and the New Exodus Restoration of Daughter Zion: Mark 5:21–43 in Context," in *The New Testament in Its First Century Setting: Essays on Context and Background in Honour of B. W. Winter on His Sixty-fifth Birthday*, ed. Peter J. Williams et al. (Grand Rapids: Eerdmans, 2004), 13–29. For the entire episode in healthcare studies, see Robin Gill, "Health Care, Jesus and the Church," *Ecclesiology* 1 (2004): 37–55. Oppel employs A. J. Greimas's approach to structural semantics (actantial model) and North American narrative criticism in Oppel, *Heilsam erzählen*, 97. Zweip has recently undertaken a history of the interpretation of Jairus's daughter. Arie W. Zwiep, "Jairus, His Daughter and the Haemorrhaging Woman (Mk 5.21–43; Mt. 9.18–26; Lk. 8.40–56): Research Survey of a Gospel Story about People in Distress," *CurBR* 13 (2015): 351–87.

7. Examples of these themes can be found in Betsworth, *Children in Early Chris-*

often appear in the discussion of parallels are: (1) notions of gender and disease; (2) notions of faith and fear; and (3) the impurity of both females. Each of these warrants further discussion as an example of how the story of Jairus's daughter is interpreted through its relationship with the account of the bleeding woman. The discussion concerning the impure status of both females, in particular, illustrates the need to be open to further ways of studying the passage.

1.1.1. Notions of Gender and Disease

Of the similarities that are identified between both stories by scholars, the understanding that both females suffer from an illness is considered a major link. A strong theme that runs through the interpretations of these stories is the gendered nature of the female protagonists' illnesses. Mary Rose D'Angelo, for example, brings theories of the body, especially women's bodies, and beliefs about disease and gender-based cures in antiquity to her study of 5:21–43. Drawing on the work of the ancient medical writer Soranus as well as the writing of Philostratus, she observes that early audiences would have understood a relationship between the two stories.[8] She states,

> The two stories belong together because they record healings/wonders that offset two opposing dangers to the female body. The woman with a flow of blood for twelve years suffers from a womb that is inappropriately open. The twelve-year old girl may well represent the young girl who dies because her womb is closed; at twelve, she is just at the age for mar-

---

tian Narratives, 48–49; Boring, *Mark*, 158; R. Alan Culpepper, "Mark," SHBC 20 (Macon, GA: Smyth & Helwys, 2007), 171; James R. Edwards, "Markan Sandwiches: The Significance of Interpolations in Markan Narratives," *NovT* 31 (1989): 204; Susan Haber, *"They Shall Purify Themselves": Essays on Purity in Early Judaism*, EJL 24 (Atlanta: Society of Biblical Literature, 2008), 137–39; Miller, *Women*, 54–72; Stein, *Mark*, 262; Strauss, *Mark*, 158; van Iersel, *Mark*, 211. France, on the other hand, sees few links between both stories except that both recipients of healing are women and are unclean (*Gospel of Mark*, 235). For a detailed summary of these themes, see Zwiep, *Jairus's Daughter*.

8. Mary Rose D'Angelo, "Gender and Power in the Gospel of Mark: The Daughter of Jairus and the Woman with the Flow of Blood," in *Miracles in Jewish and Christian Antiquity: Imagining Truth*, ed. John C. Cavadini, Notre Dame Studies in Theology 3 (Notre Dame: University of Notre Dame Press, 1999), 83–109. Philostratus, *Vit. Apoll.* 4.45; Soranus, *Gyn.* 3.26, 28.

riage in Roman law.... [Together, they] may have represented the poles of danger and debility for the female body to the audiences of Mark and/or Mark's predecessors.⁹

D'Angelo's focus on the female body, specifically diseases associated with the womb, suggests that notions concerning female infertility link both stories. Others also argue along similar lines that both stories are linked in terms of female (in)fertility and the (in)capacity to enter into what are deemed the hallmarks of womanhood in antiquity: marriage and childbearing.¹⁰ Much of this interpretation rests on two indicators in the episode: the reference to the woman suffering under physicians for twelve years and the little daughter being twelve years old (5:25, 42); and the description of the woman as having a flow of blood (5:25). The woman's flow of blood is commonly understood to be a form of gynecological bleeding, typically menstrual (or some abnormal form of menstruation) based on a linguistic similarity to a description of menstrual bleeding in Lev 15:25, 33 LXX.¹¹ As a result, this continuous bleeding—for at least twelve years—is generally interpreted as rendering her infertile and prohibited from engaging in sexual relations. Concomitantly, the young girl, labeled as twelve years old, is commonly read as being of marriageable age; her life is thus ending at the borders of entering womanhood and what was considered the onset of childbearing. As Miller notes, "The woman's condition of constant menstrual bleeding would make her infertile, and the girl dies at the age of physical maturity."¹² In a state of being unmarried

---

9. D'Angelo, "Gender and Power," 95–96.

10. E.g., Boring, *Mark*, 158; Robin Gallaher Branch, "Literary Comparisons and Contrasts in Mark 5:21–43: Original Research," *IDS* 48 (2014): 4–7; Donald Capps, "Jesus the Village Psychiatrist: A Summary," *HvTSt* 66 (2010): 3; Frank England, "Afterthought: An Excuse or an Opportunity?," *JTSA* 92 (1995): 56–59; Haber, *They Shall Purify Themselves*, 139; Miller, *Women*, 55–56; Moloney, *Gospel of Mark*, 111. I note Strauss's rejection of the idea that "twelve years old" denotes marriageable age (*Mark*, 285).

11. The term ῥύσει αἵματος, "flowing blood" (Mark 5:25), also appears in Lev 15:25 LXX. The terms αἱμορροέω and ῥύσει are used in Lev 15:33 LXX.

12. Miller, *Women*, 56. Various meanings are attributed to the descriptor "twelve years." While this designation may link notions of the girl's sexuality, fertility, and social status to that of the woman's, for some scholars the descriptor also connotes the twelve tribes of Israel, the twelve who feed the crowd, and the number of baskets of food left over after the feeding of the five thousand (6:30–44). See Miller, *Women*, 68; Ched Myers et al., *Say to This Mountain: Mark's Story of Discipleship* (Maryknoll,

(or perhaps married) and childless, neither female is of great value in the broader Greco-Roman culture.[13]

As a twelve-year-old female, Jairus's daughter is considered to be prepubescent, perhaps betrothed, although she would not have been necessarily married for a couple of years.[14] Elaine Wainwright notes that the girl would have been approaching an age of physical transition, bringing with it possibilities of disease.[15] It is the gendered nature of disease that is the focus of Wainwright's attention. Drawing on the Hippocratic corpus, she suggests that *The Diseases of Young Girls* and *Diseases of Women* may have been an intertext for Mark 5:21–43, in which case what the girl possibly suffered was the retention of menstrual bleeding, a condition mostly described of unmarried young women. Manifestations of the disease included loss of appetite and even the appearance of being dead.[16] Interpreted in this diagnostic way, Wainwright reads the bleeding woman as a "mirror image" of the young girl, "her blood flowing too profusely than refusing to flow."[17]

1.1.2. Faith and Fear

A second theme linking the two stories is the centrality of faith to healing.[18] In Robert Gundry's view, faith is concerned with a belief in Jesus's ability to save. This is exemplified in the characters of both the woman and

---

NY: Orbis Books, 1996), 66; Scott, "Raising the Dead," 168–69; Watts, "Jesus and the New Exodus Restoration," 22, 23, 29. Zwiep notes that the repetition of twelve in both accounts may have been a rhetorical device to aid memorization in an oral setting (*Jairus's Daughter*, 212).

13. Betsworth, *Reign of God Is Such as These*, 115.

14. Judith Evans Grubbs, *Woman and the Law in the Roman Empire: A Sourcebook on Marriage, Divorce and Widowhood* (London: Routledge, 2002), 88; Michael Satlow, *Jewish Marriage in Antiquity* (Princeton: Princeton University Press, 2001), 105–11.

15. Wainwright, *Women Healing/Healing Women*, 114–15.

16. Wainwright, *Women Healing/Healing Women*, 114–16.

17. Wainwright, *Women Healing/Healing Women*, 116. For commentary on the "drying up" of the woman's "flow of blood" and perceptions of infertility in early Christianity, see Candida R. Moss and Joel S. Baden, *Reconceiving Infertility: Biblical Perspectives on Procreation and Childlessness* (Princeton: Princeton University Press, 2015), 200–206.

18. E.g., Betsworth, *Reign of God Is Such as These*, 109, 14; Moloney, *Gospel of Mark*, 106–9; Oppel, *Heilsam erzählen*, 117–18; Strauss, *Mark*, 227; Zwiep, *Jairus's Daughter*, 280.

Jairus. The Markan Jesus identifies that it is the faith of the woman that has saved her (5:34). Likewise, it is Jairus's faith that will save his daughter, even when surrounded by the unbelief of others.[19] Indeed, the time lapse occasioned by the interruption of the bleeding woman can be interpreted as heightening the sense of suspense in Jesus's response to Jairus, thereby "accenting the call to faith."[20] Taken as a whole, the episode illustrates that faith is the prerequisite to healing and even to overcoming death.[21]

The interconnectedness of the notions of faith, death, and life in 5:21–43 is examined by various scholars. Reading the episode from narrative, postcolonial, feminist, and HIV/AIDS perspectives, Musa W. Dube Shomanah echoes an often-noted description that faith is able to defeat death in Mark's Gospel. For Dube Shomanah, both stories in 5:21–43 reveal that even in the most liminal of states—the spaces between life and death—faith ensures that death does not have the final word. Indeed, faith is to be found among those who dwell in the places of extreme hopelessness.[22] Likewise, in his comments on the interrelationship between faith, death, and life in 5:21–43, R. Alan Culpepper understands each story to be concerned with the restoration of life, "Blood, the life force, was restored to the hemorrhaging woman, and life was restored to the dead girl."[23] Together, the pericopes reveal a sense in which the divine power that grants life beyond death is understood to be operative in Jesus and promised to those who have faith.[24] Mark is understood to summon his readers/hearers not to fear, according to Thomas Kazen, but to preserve their faith in the rising of Jesus and therefore to have faith in their own "new life" as believers.[25] For Gérard Rochais, the summons is to have faith in the God who raised Jesus, in the face of death.[26]

---

19. For Jairus's faith, see Gundry, *Mark*, 273; for the unbelief of others, see Branch, "Literary Comparisons," 7.

20. Stein, *Mark*, 262.

21. Malbon, "Jewish Leaders in the Gospel of Mark," 170.

22. Dube Shomanah, "Talitha Cum! A Postcolonial Feminist and HIV/AIDS Reading of Mark 5:21–43," in *Grant Me Justice! HIV/AIDS and Gender Readings of the Bible*, ed. Musa W. Dube Shomanah and Rachel Angogo Kanyoro (Pietermaritzburg, South Africa: Cluster; Maryknoll, NY: Orbis Books, 2004), 122–23.

23. Culpepper, *Mark*, 179.

24. Culpepper, *Mark*, 183.

25. Thomas Kazen, *Jesus and Purity Halakhah: Was Jesus Indifferent to Impurity?*, ConBNT 38 (Winona Lake, IN: Eisenbrauns, 2010), 172.

26. Rochais, *Les récits de résurrection*, 201–02.

Alongside the notion of faith lie references to fear. The relationship between both attracts comment among scholars. The experience of fear in 5:21–43, according to Robert Stein, denotes a shortage of faith. In his words, fear is about "being frightened and lacking faith."[27] For Elizabeth Struthers Malbon, fear is the enemy of faith.[28] While the Markan Jesus applauds the woman's faith and requests faith from Jairus (to which he unquestioningly accedes), Mark also depicts both characters with reference to having fear. While Jairus fears for his daughter, the woman's fear, coming to the fore after she has been healed, can be read as a form of reverential awe.[29]

More broadly, the faith of Jairus and the bleeding woman are contrasted with the fear of the disciples in the larger narrative. Stein, for example, contrasts Jairus and the bleeding woman with the lack of faith displayed by those in Nazareth (6:1–6a) and in Gerasa (5:17).[30] Mary Ann Tolbert takes the episode, along with the healing of the Gerasene demoniac (5:1–20), and contrasts the descriptions of faith with the fear of the disciples in the calming of the storm (4:35–41).[31] Susan Miller expands the interpretive context, reading the relationship between faith and fear within the broader setting of Mark. She is of the view that the tension between fear and faith represented in 5:21–43 correlates with the experience of the Markan audience. For the "suffering and persecuted" community that encounters Mark's narrative, 5:21–43 reassures that God will prevail over evil.[32]

1.1.3. The Impurity of Both Females

The ritual status of both females provides another link between the two stories in some of the scholarship. In the biblical tradition, corpses and bodily discharges—menstruation, irregular gynecological bleeding, and semen emissions—were considered to be sources of ritual impurity.[33]

---

27. Stein, *Mark*, 272.
28. Malbon, "Jewish Leaders in the Gospel of Mark," 277–79.
29. Gundry, *Mark*, 273; Robin Gallaher Branch, "A Study of the Woman in the Crowd and Her Desperate Courage (Mark 5:21–43)/'n studie van die vrou tussen die menigtes en haar desperate dapperheid (Mark 5:21–43)," *IDS* 47 (2013): 6.
30. Stein, *Mark*, 272.
31. Tolbert, *Sowing the Gospel*, 170–71. Adela Yarbro Collins also notes that the faith of the bleeding woman stands out against the fear of the disciples in the storm. (*Mark: A Commentary*, Hermeneia [Minneapolis: Fortress, 2007], 284).
32. Miller, *Women*, 68.
33. For the biblical origins of the states of impurity of human corpses, Lev 19:10–

Building on the idea that the woman suffers from a form of gynecological bleeding (ῥύσις αἵματος, 5:25) grounded in a linguistic link with Lev 15:25, 33, the woman is often understood to be ritually unclean on the basis that she is affected by a form of menstrual bleeding.[34] In parallel with the woman, Jairus's daughter is interpreted as being in a state of corpse impurity in view of Mark's identification of the child as dead in 5:35.[35]

The significance of being ritually unclean is an interpretive interest in much of the scholarship on the passage. While Mark makes no explicit reference to the purity laws or to any protagonist being in an unclean state, there are many instances in which scholars develop their readings of the episode along this line.[36] As will be illustrated in the discussion that follows, Malbon typifies this kind of development. Approaching the episode from the perspective of narrative criticism, she exemplifies a view held more broadly in the literature when she asserts, "according to Jewish law, the continual uncleanness of the hemorrhaging woman made her a social and religious outcast, as dead socially as Jairus's daughter was physically."[37]

22; Num 19:11; of childbirth, Lev 12:1–8; of leprosy, Lev 13:1–14.32; of genital discharges, Lev 15:1–33; and of the carcasses of some impure animals, Lev 11:1–47.

34. For my comments on the linguistic link, see n. 11.

35. For examples of this treatment, see John R. Donahue and Daniel J. Harrington, *The Gospel of Mark*, SP (Collegeville, MN: Liturgical Press, 2002), 175, 181; Haber, *They Shall Purify Themselves*, 125–41; Miller, *Women*, 57; Moloney, *Mark*, 110; Charles E. Powell, "The 'Passivity' of Jesus in Mark 5:25-34," *BSac* 162.645 (2005): 66–75; Strauss, *Mark*, 224. Marcus draws on fourth century CE rabbinic material, Hekhalot Rab. 18, to explain the isolation of the woman but does not refer to corpse impurity (*Mark 1–8*, 357). See also Bruce Chilton, Darrel L. Bock, and Daniel M. Gurtner, eds., *A Comparative Handbook to the Gospel of Mark: Comparisons with Pseudepigrapha, the Qumran Scrolls, and Rabbinic Literature*, New Testament Gospels in Their Judaic Contexts 1 (Leiden: Brill, 2010), 195–203.

36. Kahl finds evidence of the use of Jewish purity laws for menstruation as an interpretive lens as early as the third century CE in the Didascalia Apostolorum and the writings of Dionysius of Alexandria in his letter to Basilides ("Jairus und die verlorenen Töchter Israels," 62).

37. Elizabeth Struthers Malbon, *In the Company of Jesus: Characters in Mark's Gospel* (Louisville: Westminster John Knox, 2000), 27. Hooker also reads the bleeding woman as outcast from the whole of society as a result of ritual impurity and thus prohibiting her from being in a crowd or touching others (*Saint Mark*, 148–49). See also Ched Myers, *Binding the Strong Man: A Political Reading of Mark's Story of Jesus* (Maryknoll, NY: Orbis Books, 1988), 201; Marla J. Selvidge, *Woman, Cult, and Miracle Recital: A Redactional Critical Investigation on Mark 5:24–34* (Lewisburg, PA: Bucknell University Press; London: Associated University Presses, 1990); Elaine J. Lawless,

Moreover, Malbon represents a common attitude to ancient Jewish purity law in the commentaries on this episode by conceiving of them pejoratively, considering them to have been stigmatizing, marginalizing, and oppressive in the first century CE.[38]

Following along this trajectory, in much of the commentary this passage is seen to depict Jesus as subversive. The notion of the physical touch between the woman and Jesus, and Jesus and the dead child, often forms the basis of this reading. R. T. France, for example, notes that Jesus's touch of two defiled persons—one with a menstrual disorder and the other (presumably) a corpse—is a thematic connection between the two stories.[39] Francis Moloney takes the reading further, viewing Jesus's touch of the impure menstruating woman and the impure corpse of the child as a sign of the Markan Jesus ignoring the taboo of ritual impurity.[40] Terms such as "crossing boundaries," "breaking down" barriers and boundaries, and "challenging" religious and social norms appear in studies of 5:21–43 to describe the gestures of touch between Jesus and the two impure females.[41] John Donahue and Daniel Harrington use the language of Jesus violating purity codes in their commentary on the passage. They state:

"Transforming the Master Narrative: How Women Shift the Religious Subject," *Frontiers: A Journal of Women Studies* 24 (2003): 67–68.

38. A slightly different reading is proffered by Sibeko and Haddad. They use purity law and the gesture of touch as an interpretive lens but the ancient Jewish laws are not the focus. Instead, their experiences of modern clerics in the African Independent Church using the purity laws of Leviticus to restrict women from domestic, social, and ecclesial activity on the basis of menstruation and touch are the lens through which they view the story. Malika Sibeko and Beverley Haddad, "Reading the Bible 'with' Women in Poor and Marginalized Communities in South Africa," *Semeia* 78 (1997): 85, 87, 88.

39. France, *Gospel of Mark*, 235. Indeed, France asserts that there are very few thematic connections between the stories. One connection is the presentation of the victims as females. The other is Jesus's touch of two defiled persons. See also Marcus, *Mark 1–8*, 364–65.

40. Moloney, *Mark*, 110. See also Joanna Dewey, "Jesus' Healings of Women: Conformity and Nonconformity to Dominant Cultural Values as Clues for Historical Reconstruction," *BTB* 24 (1994): 122–31.

41. For crossing boundaries, see Charles L. Campbell and Johan Cilliers, *Preaching Fools: The Gospel as a Rhetoric of Folly* (Waco, TX: Baylor University Press, 2012), 108–9. Against using the idea of transcending boundaries imposed by purity codes to describe the dynamics of Mark 5:21–43, see Mary Ann Beavis, *Mark*, Paideia (Grand Rapids: Baker Academic, 2011), 98. For breaking down barriers, see Branch, "Study

"Since corpse impurity was the most severe of all impurities, this touch is another instance of Jesus violating cultural codes for the greater good of humanity."[42] Similarly, J. Lyle Story observes that Jesus is indifferent to any objections about the religious and social taboos concerning the two unclean females. Indeed, Jesus "abrogates such distinctions and critiques."[43] This act of abrogating the purity codes is thus viewed as the means by which both females reclaim their dignity and take their place within the new community inaugurated in Jesus.

Jesus's touch of the defiled woman and child is rendered as a sign that he rejects the negative taboo of Jewish purity codes that saddle humanity. In contrast, according to this interpretation, the reign of God enacted in Jesus's healing relieves a suffering humanity. The compassion of Jesus is understood to stand in stark contrast to the prejudice that characterizes what is perceived as the systemic discrimination of Jewish ritual purity.[44] Jesus's healing, therefore, not only challenges this system but also reveals a view of the reign of God that is inclusive of those whom the Jewish system is understood to exclude. Mark Strauss uses the language of "breaking down barriers that divide and alienate" to articulate one of the challenges presented to the reader today through this passage.[45] This terminology indicates how Jesus's actions (and the reign of God) are understood not only to oppose the purity system but, in so doing, to embody a way of living that embraces all people. In this reading, Judaism is viewed as exclusive while the activity of Jesus is depicted as radically inclusive.

Jesus's subversive touch of the girl's corpse is linked with the previous gestures of the bleeding woman in the intercalated story. Like Jesus, the woman is also routinely depicted as violating the taboos of ritual purity. Donahue and Harrington exemplify this interpretation: "Once she breaks through the physical barrier of the crowd and the religio-social barrier of her ritual impurity and touches Jesus, her illness ceases and she senses the

---

of the Woman," 7; Strauss, *Mark*, 237; Boring, *Mark*, 158. For challenging norms, see Strauss, *Mark*, 237.

42. Donahue and Harrington, *Mark*, 177.

43. J. Lyle Story, "Four Females Who Encounter Jesus," *Priscilla Papers* 23 (2009): 14. See also Campbell and Cilliers, *Preaching Fools*, 108.

44. A. Edward Gardner, "Reading between the Texts: Minor Characters Who Prepare the Way for Jesus," *Enc* 66 (2005): 58.

45. Strauss, *Mark*, 237.

cure in her body."[46] In this reading, the woman's actions are considered subversive and courageous. Likewise, Teresa Okure uses the language of breaking taboos to explain the woman's courage. This is evident in her appraisal of fellow scholars Elizabeth Amoah and Musimbi R. A. Kanyoro. She writes, "Both works emphasize the woman's courage in breaking the crippling cultural taboos imposed on her so as to reach Jesus directly and be fully restored and integrated as a person with full rights in her society."[47] In a further example of this approach, Culpepper also links both stories through the notion of the subversive touch of the woman and Jesus in his commentary on the episode. He observes that while the female protagonists are ritually unclean through a menstrual disorder and death, this status is "boldly ignored" by the woman who touches Jesus's garment and by Jesus who touches the girl's corpse.[48]

In Rikki Watts's analysis, the raising of Jairus's daughter unifies an Israel characterized by impurity and death. Taking up the allusions to "twelve years" (5:25, 42), Watts views the number twelve as symbolic of Israel. The woman who has been bleeding and impure for twelve years represents an exiled Israel. The raising of the twelve-year-old daughter of Jairus signifies what Jesus offers to an exiled Israel: purity and resurrection. Jairus's daughter is a symbol of life for an Israel that is separated by impurity and death.[49]

---

46. Donahue and Harrington, *Mark*, 180.

47. Teresa Okure, "Feminist Interpretation in Africa," in *Searching the Scriptures: A Feminist Introduction*, ed. Elisabeth Schüssler Fiorenza (New York: Crossroad, 1993), 82.

48. Culpepper, "Mark," 171. Further evidence of the link between the two stories along the lines of purity law is provided in the interpretation of the character of Jairus. In Storey's view, the synagogue leader transcends the oppressive laws—which presumably a person in such a role ought to be preserving—in order to relieve his daughter's suffering and realize her restoration to health. While not a scholarly article, Storey reveals the uptake of this kind of reading in modern apologetic materials. He bluntly states in a sermon published in the social justice magazine, *Sojourners*, "Jairus' pain enables him to step over the long-held prejudice hidden beneath his purity code observance. He breaks his cultural laws … forsakes his religious heritage. Oh, how prejudice can be hidden in religious rituals that look virtuous on the surface. Sometimes if we want Jesus to come into our home and touch us and our sick family, we may be asked to give up our religious heritage." See Alan Storey, "For the Healing of the Nation," *Sojourners Magazine* (May 2011): 30.

49. Watts, "Jesus and the New Exodus Restoration," 22, 23, 29.

While the theme of ritual impurity and its perceived stigma has held sway in a wide range of examinations that treat both stories together, the validity of the grounds for this parallel is now questioned. In her assessment of the significance of the purity laws in Mark 5:24–34, Susan Haber, for example, contends that the theme is implicit rather than explicit in Mark's telling of the episode. Based on her observation that Mark focuses solely on descriptions of the woman's physical condition, Haber argues that the episode deals primarily with the woman's illness and health, although her hemorrhage would have carried an impurity that Mark's audience and broader society would not have ignored. She rejects the idea, however, that Jesus abrogates the purity laws. Instead, she contends that Mark's story is essentially concerned with faith that brings about healing, thus enabling the woman to undergo ritual purification and therefore to reclaim her place in society and have children.[50] Similarly, Adela Yarbro Collins rejects a reading in which purity is an explicit theme. She argues that if the woman is suffering from gynecological bleeding she would have been ritually unclean. In her view, however, the Markan Jesus appears indifferent to this particular impurity.[51]

Another group of scholars refutes outright that the episode bears any testimony to a notion that Jesus abrogated purity law on the grounds that the laws were oppressive and ostracizing for Jews in the first century CE. For at least twenty years, the casting of purity laws in this negative light has been a target of growing criticism, not least among historians of first-century CE Judaism and scholars of the religious literature of ancient Judaism. Notable among these are E. P. Sanders, Paula Fredriksen, Amy-Jill Levine, Shaye J. D. Cohen, Charlotte Elisheva Fonrobert, and Jonathan Klawans, all of whose opposition to the pejorative readings of ancient purity laws is well documented.[52] They argue that the approach to Jewish

---

50. Haber, *They Shall Purify Themselves*, 125–41.
51. Yarbro Collins, *Mark*, 284. See also Strauss who notes that Mark does not explicitly refer to impurity (*Mark*, 221). For further discussion of Jesus's seemingly indifferent attitude to ritual impurity in the story of Mark's Gospel, see Kazen, *Jesus and Purity Halakhah*, 169–74, 198.
52. Shaye J. D. Cohen, "Menstruants and the Sacred in Judaism and Christianity," in *Women's History and Ancient History*, ed. Sarah B. Pomeroy (Chapel Hill: University of North Carolina Press, 1991), 273–99; Charlotte Elisheva Fonrobert, *Menstrual Purity: Rabbinic and Christian Reconstructions of Biblical Gender* (Stanford, CA: Stanford University Press, 2000); Paula Fredriksen, "What You See Is What You Get: Context and Content in Current Research on the Historical Jesus,"

purity law in the first century CE was complex, varied, and widespread, and challenge the position it necessarily created a stigma or led to oppression and marginalization. Levine, who has engaged for well over a decade with this issue, critiques the readings of Jairus's daughter and the bleeding woman:

> Although no version cites Leviticus, mentions impurity, expresses surprise at a bleeding woman in public, finds odd Jesus' touching of a corpse, or portrays Jesus as abrogating any law, Western critics and their postcolonial counterparts import all this and more. [They] misrepresent and ridicule cultural practices.... It would be helpful for all feminist readers to provide specific examples of Jesus' dismantling the "patriarchy of Judaism" or its "cultural taboos" concerning women. It may even be that, when it comes to release from "crippling taboos," women's experience itself, rather than some quasi-historical anterior model such as faulty recreation of first-century Judaism and the divorcing of Jesus from it, is the better mechanism.[53]

Of the specific treatment of purity laws, Levine argues,

> Not all purity laws have the same effect. What is relevant to the Temple may not be of import to the home. Thus, menstruating Jews have never been forbidden to attend synagogue, let alone to appear in public.... Purity is not equivalent to social marginalization or internalized shame,

---

ThTo 52 (1995): 75–97; Fredriksen, "Did Jesus Oppose the Purity Laws," *BRev* 11.3 (1995): 19–25; Fredriksen, "Compassion Is to Purity as Fish Is to Bicycle and Other Reflections on Constructions of 'Judaism' in Current Work on the Historical Jesus," in *Apocalypticism, Anti-Semitism and the Historical Jesus: Subtexts in Criticism*, ed. John S. Kloppenborg and John W. Marshall, JSNTSup 275 (London: T&T Clark, 2005), 55–67; Jonathan Klawans, *Purity, Sacrifice, and the Temple: Symbolism and Supersessionism in the Study of Ancient Judaism* (Oxford: Oxford University Press, 2006); Klawans, *Impurity and Sin in Ancient Judaism* (New York: Oxford University Press, 2000); Amy-Jill Levine, *The Misunderstood Jew: The Church and the Scandal of the Jewish Jesus* (New York: HarperOne, 2007); Levine, "The Disease of Postcolonial New Testament Studies and the Hermeneutics of Healing," *JFSR* 20 (2004): 91–132, (including responses by Kwok Pui-lan, Musimbi Kanyoro, and Adele Reinhartz); E. P. Sanders, "Jesus, Ancient Judaism, and Modern Christianity: The Quest Continues," in *Jesus, Judaism, and Christian Anti-Judaism: Reading the New Testament after the Holocaust*, ed. Paula Fredriksen and Adele Reinhartz (Louisville: Westminster John Knox, 2002), 35–38.

53. Levine et al., "Disease of Postcolonial New Testament Studies," 94, 127.

for men or for women. To the contrary, a woman who observes the laws of family purity may just as easily boast in her piety as feel shamed by it.[54]

The perspectives that Levine offers resonate among other scholars working specifically with the episode of Jairus's daughter and the bleeding woman in Mark's Gospel. D'Angelo observes how the use of purity law in the treatment of these two stories often results in "inappropriate generalizations" about Jews and Judaism, "extravagant rhetoric," and "naïve or specious use of language."[55] These elements thus enable scholars to establish a dichotomy in which the openness of the Markan Jesus stands out against the oppressiveness of Judaism.[56] In contrast, D'Angelo demonstrates that it is improbable that Mark viewed this particular story as challenging purity laws on numerous grounds. First, she emphasizes that the story is not concerned with menstrual impurity; it is concerned with a disease that troubles the woman. Second, Mark reveals no interest in purity issues in 5:21–43, unlike clear instances such as 1:40–44 and 7:1–23.[57] Third, the story's setting in Galilee, some distance from the temple in Jerusalem where ritual purity was highly significant, makes issues of purity less relevant. Moreover, it is generally very difficult to know definitively how purity laws were applied in the first century CE.[58]

In D'Angelo's view, the interpreter is better served by turning their attention to notions of disease and healing. She shifts her analysis, therefore, to the contexts of medical and miraculous healing in antiquity and the theology of Mark's broader narrative. This enables her to explore, as do other scholars that I have previously noted, connections between Mark's story and accounts of cures and gendered diseases: the child with a form of the disease "hysteria," and the woman with a female manifestation of "flux."[59] Within the context of Markan Christology, D'Angelo puts for-

---

54. Levine et al., "Disease of Postcolonial New Testament Studies," 127–28. In relation to menstrual impurity in Judaism, Fonrobert provides a critical analysis of rabbinic notions of menstrual impurity within the context of early Judaism and Christianity (*Menstrual Purity*).

55. D'Angelo, "Gender and Power," 84. Her criticism is chiefly aimed at feminist scholars, although the use of purity laws in this way is found in literature other than feminist, as I demonstrate.

56. D'Angelo, "Gender and Power," 84.

57. See also Kahl, "Jairus und die verlorenen Töchter Israels," 66.

58. D'Angelo, "Gender and Power," 91.

59. D'Angelo, "Gender and Power," 96.

ward the idea that the episode is concerned with the "transfer of power."[60] Together, the woman and those present with the child share in the power and spirit that bring about healing, restoration, and life. From a feminist perspective, she suggests that this could offer ways of contemplating how "Jesus' power is active through the participation of others.... Through [a revision of] gendered arrangements of Christian power [instead of] creating a Jesus who saves women from Judaism."[61]

In a similar vein, Wendy Cotter disputes the idea that the episode is concerned with Jesus's lack of observance of Jewish purity codes. To widen the interpretive vista, she turns her attention to the literature of miracles in Greco-Roman and Jewish contexts, as well as the Christology of Mark's Gospel. She concludes that the episode reveals the cosmic, divine power of Jesus as well as his concern for ordinary, sick people, including women and children. She regards the intercalation as amplifying the pathos of the gospel as Jesus advances to the cross.[62]

Brigitte Kahl, too, critiques the use of purity laws as a lens through which to read the entire episode, particularly in light of the antithetical discourse of church versus synagogue to which she understands such a reading to contribute. Instead, using the tools of narrative analysis, she builds her reading by identifying sets of contrasting characters and groups in Mark's narration. From this, she concludes that the "old household" of Jairus is concerned with the destructive forces of death. In contrast, a new household arises through the faith of Jairus the synagogue leader that

---

60. D'Angelo, "Gender and Power," 99.

61. D'Angelo, "Gender and Power," 101, 104.

62. Wendy Cotter, "Mark's Hero of the Twelfth-Year Miracles: The Healing of the Woman with the Hemorrhage and the Raising of Jairus' Daughter," in *A Feminist Companion to Mark*, ed. Amy-Jill Levine and Marianne Blickenstaff (Sheffield: Sheffield Academic, 2001), 54–78. Beavis also rejects the reading of this episode as concerned with ritual impurity, the notion that purity laws were religiously and socially stigmatizing, and the portrait of Jesus as the breaker of religious boundaries. She argues, "the point is not that Jewish boundaries have been transgressed or transcended but that the sick woman is healed and a dead girl has been raised" (*Mark*, 98). See also Stein's rejection of purity as an issue in the episode in his commentary (*Mark*, 263). While Wainwright argues that the diseases of both women may be concerned with female bleeding (and that Mark emphasizes physical touch in the episode), she too critiques the application of purity laws as an interpretive lens (*Women Healing/Healing Women*, 117–18).

recognizes the life-giving power of the resurrection; the same power that works in the healing of the bleeding woman.[63]

In sum, the healing of the bleeding woman is routinely viewed through the lens of ancient Jewish ritual purity law. This, then, becomes an optic through which the story of the raising of Jairus's daughter is seen. Despite the prevalence of this approach, criticisms regarding its validity have prompted new ways of looking at the passage. We observed that some scholars, for instance, have shifted their analyses to other contexts, with the literature of miracles and the diagnostic writings of ancient medicine being read in dialogue with the Markan narrative.

1.2. Contrasts

Another outcome of examining together the story of Jairus's daughter and the interpolated account of the bleeding woman is that the story of the woman frequently dominates the analysis. Miller, for example, devotes a chapter to the entire episode in her work on women in Mark's Gospel. While the chapter is entitled "The Healing of the Woman with the Flow of Blood and the Raising of Jairus's Daughter (5:21–43)," the two-page introduction to the chapter deals only with the story of the bleeding woman.[64]

Moreover, when the story of the dying girl is read in light of the Markan sandwich technique, it is the story of the bleeding woman that often becomes the key to interpreting the entire episode. Willard Swartley, for instance, treats both accounts in his work on women in Mark's Gospel and recognizes that, taken together, they progress the broader Markan narrative. While he regards the raising of Jairus's daughter proleptically of Jesus's resurrection, he nonetheless argues that the role of this story is "secondary" to the "prominent and positive narrative role" of the bleeding woman. She is the leading lady in this entire episode. Perceived as a role model, it is her faith that trumps that of the synagogue leader, Jairus.[65] In a similar vein, James Edwards contends that it is the middle story in a Markan sandwich that provides the key to understanding the theologi-

---

63. Kahl, "Jairus und die verlorenen Töchter Israels," 61–78.
64. Miller, *Women*, 52–53. Women identify with the story of the bleeding woman while the story of Jairus's daughter is considered "incidental" in Sibeko and Haddad, "Reading the Bible," 89.
65. Swartley, "Role of Women in Mark's Gospel," 17–18.

cal purpose of the author.[66] In his analysis of the passage, therefore, he describes 5:21–43 thus, "the woman's faith forms the center of the sandwich and is the key to its interpretation. Through her Mark shows how faith in Jesus can transform fear and despair into hope and salvation. It is a powerful lesson for Jairus, as well as for Mark's readers."[67] This privileging of the image of the bleeding woman over against Jairus and his daughter pervades much of the commentary.

When the role of the bleeding woman provides the hermeneutical key to the whole episode, she is often depicted as the superior character. This is illustrated in the words of Ched Myers and colleagues in their liberationist study of the passage:

> Within the "family" of Israel, these "daughters" represent the privileged and the impoverished, respectively. Because of such inequity, the body politic of the synagogue is "on the verge of death…." Only when the outcast woman is restored to true daughterhood can the daughter of the synagogue be restored to true life. That is the faith the privileged must learn from the poor…. "The last will be first" and "the least will be greatest."[68]

In this analysis, we see contrasts applied to the reading of the bleeding woman and Jairus's daughter: the privileged and the impoverished; the outcast woman and the daughter of the synagogue; the privileged and the poor; the last and the first, and the least and the greatest. In each contrast, it is the bleeding woman who is deemed the better. She is the first and greatest due to her status as impoverished, which has previously rendered her last and least.[69]

The woman is commonly characterized as the Markan priority in the episode through a similar application of contrasts to describe the statuses of the woman, and Jairus and his daughter. These contrasts emerge from interpretations of the social, religious, and familial settings within the Markan narrative and the broader milieu of the first century CE, and are often broken down further along lines of gender, economic, marital, health, and ritual inequalities. Robin Gallaher Branch, for example, notes of Jairus

---

66. Edwards, "Markan Sandwiches," 196.
67. Edwards, "Markan Sandwiches," 205.
68. Myers et al., *Say to This Mountain*, 66.
69. Miller also discusses the priority of the woman in terms of the Markan notion of the first will be last and the last will be first (*Women*, 67).

and the woman, "[Jairus] is a wealthy and influential ruler, and she is an unclean and probably poor outcast [indicating] that they moved in different social and economic circles.... Their point of meeting is their point of need: Jesus."[70] Similarly, for Miller, the anonymity, poverty, and impurity of the woman contrasts with Jairus who is named, wealthy, and respected religiously. The woman approaches Jesus secretly and her healing is public while Jairus's approach is public and the healing of his daughter is carried out privately.[71]

Bas M. F. van Iersel, on the other hand, contrasts the bleeding woman with the figure of Jairus's daughter in his commentary on the passage. He outlines how the girl possesses a greater status than the woman does: She has a father who advocates for her and her cure is easily obtained. Her father's status as a local dignitary ensures that Jesus requires no persuading to come to her house. In addition, Jairus's daughter belongs to a respectable family. At twelve years old, she has enjoyed her youth and is now of marriageable age and thus able to participate in her social world. Conversely, the woman is of a lower status: She is depicted as fending for herself in a situation for which it has been impossible to obtain a cure among physicians.[72] Christine Amjad Ali also notes that the woman has no family to support her, never having been married or no longer with a husband due to her illness. The illness has further implications for her sexuality: Her state of uncleanness renders her unable to have sexual relations and therefore unable to produce children.[73] She has wasted a significant portion of her life—twelve years—in this impure state. Moreover, unlike the positive response to the esteemed Jairus's request for his daughter, the

---

70. Branch, "Literary Comparisons," 3.

71. Miller, *Women*, 57. Citing Christopher D. Marshall, *Faith as a Theme in Mark's Narrative* (Cambridge: Cambridge University Press, 1989), 104. See also Bomford, "Jairus, His Daughter, the Woman and the Saviour," 46–47; Martin Fassnacht, "Konfrontation mit der Weisheit Jesu: Das Verhältnis von Wissen und Rettung dargestellt an der Wundergeschichte Mk 5,21–43," in *Die Weisheit—Ursprünge und Rezeption: Festschrift für Karl Löning zum 65. Geburtstag*, ed. Karl Löning et al., NTAbh 44 (Münster: Aschendorff, 2003), 115; Ben Witherington III, *The Gospel of Mark: A Socio-rhetorical Commentary* (Grand Rapids: Eerdmans, 2001), 186.

72. Van Iersel, *Mark*, 211.

73. Amjad Ali, "Faith and Power in the New Community: Jairus' Daughter and the Woman with the Haemorrhages," in *Affirming Difference, Celebrating Wholeness: A Partnership of Equals*, ed. Ranjini Rebera (Hong Kong: Christian Conference of Asia Women's Concerns, 1995), 132.

disciples indirectly oppose the woman in their reaction to Jesus's question about touch (5:30, 31).[74]

According to van Iersel, the crux of these polarizing descriptions lies in the actions and words of Jesus who reverses the binary opposition. This is evident when the healing of the woman takes precedence over that of the child in the movement of the episode (5:30). The priority of the woman is further recognized in the language that the Markan Jesus uses when he speaks to both females: the woman is called "daughter," a member of the family of Jesus who does the will of God, while the child is addressed in the nonfamilial language of *talitha* or "girl."[75] Or, in Amjad Ali's view, this is the story of a "mature woman" and a "little girl." Resisting how women are treated in her own ecclesial context today, it is the image of the mature woman that is the key interpretive figure in the episode, "We are not little girls, we are mature women. Therefore, our model should be the model of the mature woman.... We can use power to bring about change."[76]

We have observed that the theme of faith (and fear) emerges widely in the commentary on this episode. Progressing further along the trajectory of contrasting descriptors, the woman is often depicted in scholarship as the better model of faith. Scholars commonly observe that Jesus affirms her existing faith (5:34) while he instructs Jairus to have faith (5:36). Indeed, she is the model of faith for Jairus.[77] Marla Selvidge's analysis of 5:24–34 has been influential in recent readings of this pericope. She asserts that the woman possesses an internal faith that needs no external support from Jesus, unlike Jairus who relies on external affirmation. In this way, the woman is cast by Mark as the exemplar of faith in comparison to the depiction of Jairus.[78] Timothy Dwyer, too, reinforces the contrasts between the two characters in his observations on faith. He notes, "the synagogue ruler also needs the faith of an unclean woman from the margins of society, who is not even given the dignity of

---

74. Van Iersel, *Mark*, 211.

75. Van Iersel, *Mark*, 211–12. Note, however, Betsworth's discussion on how the term *daughter* may also render the woman subordinate to Jesus when it is used instead of the term *sister*, which may have denoted a more equal standing between the two characters (*Children in Early Christian Narratives*, 49).

76. Amjad Ali, "Faith and Power in the New Community," 134–35.

77. Betsworth, *Children in Early Christian Narratives*, 49; Fassnacht, "Konfrontation mit der Weisheit Jesu," 119–20, 122; Swartley, "The Role of Women in Mark's Gospel," 18.

78. Selvidge, *Woman, Cult, and Miracle Recital*.

a name."[79] In this approach, Mark upends social and religious expectations by depicting the outcast woman as the paradigm of faith for the distinguished synagogue leader.

Another interpretive layer is added to the significance of the contrasts when scholars use Judaism as an optic through which to read the episode. In this approach, Jairus and his daughter become synonymous with Judaism while the woman represents a new order that is associated with Jesus. This contrast then becomes a means by which to argue that Mark rejects what is associated with Judaism in order to proclaim the good news enacted in Jesus. This theme was noted above in the earlier discussion on Jewish purity law. Dwyer illustrates how the theme is expanded further by considering a correlation between the dying girl and the dying of Jewish religious life. He contemplates that Jairus's daughter possibly "becomes a cipher, suggesting the death of the synagogue for Mark."[80] Myers also advances this theme, stating:

> Mark shapes this story to ... juxtapose the two extremes of the Jewish social scale. The little girl had enjoyed twelve years of privilege as the daughter of the synagogue ruler.... Indeed, as far as Mark's Jesus is concerned, the social order represented by the synagogue ruler's Judaism is on the verge of collapse. The statusless woman has suffered twelve years of destitution at the hands of the purity system and its "doctors"; yet she still took initiative in her struggle for liberation. The object lesson can only be that if Judaism wishes to "be saved and live" (5:23), it must embrace the "faith" of the kingdom: a new social order with equal status for all. This alone will liberate the lowly outcast and snatch the "noble" from death.[81]

In this political reading of Mark's Gospel Myers asserts that, not only is the Judaism of the synagogue collapsing and near death—signified in Jairus's daughter's death—it is the impoverished, outcast, impure bleeding woman seeking liberation from the strictures of Jewish ritual life who, paradoxically, reveals how Judaism may be saved from itself.

---

79. Timothy Dwyer, "Prominent Women, Widows, and Prophets: A Case for Midrashic Intertextuality," *Essays in Literature* 20 (1993): 26. See Joynes's comments on similar themes in the writings of Jerome ("Still at the Margins?," 128).
80. Dwyer, "Prominent Women, Widows, and Prophets," 26.
81. Myers, *Binding the Strong Man*, 201–2.

It is clear that when the raising of Jairus's daughter is read within the context of the Markan sandwich technique, it is the healing of the bleeding woman that often dominates the analysis and controls how the story of Jairus's daughter is treated. This has been revealed across an assortment of approaches and methodologies. While prevalent, this is not the only interpretation to be found and neither are the themes that we have observed the only ones to be revealed. There is a seam within the deposit of scholarship where we find evidence of how the raising of Jairus's daughter is interpreted without necessarily treating the bleeding woman as the hermeneutical key to the episode. This brings to the fore a different set of themes. It is to these that we now turn.

1.3. Shifts in the Focus: The Particularity of Jairus's Daughter

As we have observed, the story of the bleeding woman bears a significant influence on the reading of the raising of Jairus's daughter in modern scholarship. The interpretation of 5:21–24, 35–43 is routinely defined by the parallels and contrasts that it is understood to bear in relation to 5:25–34. While this is the dominant interpretive paradigm, some commentators who primarily use the sandwich technique desist from necessarily correlating each element of Jairus's story with the story of the bleeding woman. In fact, Zwiep asserts that it is arguable if the binary oppositions that emerge in scholarship can be supported with textual data. Instead, they are a result of interpreters "filling in the gaps" where precise details are absent.[82] In addition to highlighting parallels and contrasts, some scholars identify elements of the story that appear to have little overlap or strategic contrast with that of the bleeding woman. Their comments enable us to observe motifs whose meanings can be understood to function independently of the bleeding woman's story. These motifs concern the depiction of Jairus, as well as the representation of the dead girl being raised. These observations suggest further ways of looking at 5:21–24, 35–43 that are not bound to readings of the bleeding woman.

Other studies make no reference to the story of the bleeding woman at all. They shift the hermeneutical focus by examining the passage in light of the broader Markan narrative or use other biblical themes and ancient texts as their main reference points. Studies that concentrate on the repre-

---

82. Zwiep, *Jairus's Daughter*, 242.

sentations of children in the biblical tradition, as well as examinations of the notions of death and resurrection, for instance, draw on Mark's story of Jairus's daughter in their analyses. These shifts in the interpretive vista allow us to see new points of interest that are not necessarily visible when the story is read within the frame of the sandwich technique.

Taken together, both approaches reveal how further insights into the story, and into Mark's Gospel as a whole, are possible when the story of the bleeding woman does not control the interpretation of Jairus's account. Along with providing new insights, the shifts in focus also generate new questions concerning the possible meaning attached to the figure of the dying, dead, and raised daughter of Jairus. Furthermore, a change in the vantage point from which we read the passage moves the image of the little girl further into the foreground and subsequently opens up new perspectives and questions.

1.3.1. Images of Jairus

When commentators refrain from correlating all the elements of 5:21– 24, 35–43 and 5:25–34, new pictures of the character of Jairus form. Not all commentators on Mark 5:21–43 cast this character in a negative light. The conversations generally center on his roles as synagogue leader and father. In the case of the former, Jairus generally remains firmly associated with Judaism on the grounds of his name and his designation as the synagogue leader.[83] What is articulated, however, is the portrait of a positive authority figure within Judaism.[84] Contrary to an unsympathetic picture of Jewish officials, depicted as generally unreceptive to Jesus, the synagogue leader is perceived as brave for approaching Jesus when all hope appears lost and for placing himself in an undignified position at the feet of Jesus.[85] Rather than being a representative of a dying synagogue or a repressive purity code, he stands as one who rejects the Pharisees and instead seeks assistance from Jesus.[86] Of all those asso-

---

83. The name Jair appears in Num 32:41, Judg 10:3–5, Esth 2:5, 1 Chr 20:5. See France, *Gospel of Mark*, 235, including n. 22. Pesch asserts that "Jairus" and "synagogue leader" were elements of an original healing account (*Das Markusevangelium*, 313).
84. Yarbro Collins, *Mark*, 279; Marcus, *Mark 1–8*, 355.
85. Hooker, *Saint Mark*, 148.
86. Martha Driscoll, *Reading between the Lines: The Hidden Wisdom of Women in the Gospels* (Liguori, MO: Liguori, 2006).

ciated with the Jewish establishment in Mark, Malbon identifies Jairus as one of three "exceptional characters."[87] She observes that it is in the synagogue leader's house that Jesus exercises the only act of resuscitation narrated by Mark. This portrait of Jairus, in Malbon's view, demonstrates that characters are not categorized as opponents because of their status within Judaism but, rather, on the basis of their response to Jesus: "being a foe of the Markan Jesus is a matter of how one chooses to relate to him, not a matter of social or religious status and role."[88]

While the conversation is different, the overarching theme nevertheless remains loosely similar to that observed in the previous discussion: it is broadly continuous with an understanding of Mark's critique of the Jewish establishment except Jairus is now extricated from that regime. He no longer represents the regime but is an exception.

The second conversation concerns Jairus's depiction as a parent. In her recent work on children in the New Testament, Sharon Betsworth paints a picture of Jairus as the positive parent. Indeed, standing alongside two other parents who advocate on their sick children's behalf—the Syrophoenician woman (7:25) and the father of the boy with the unclean spirit (9:17)—Jairus is the antithesis of the stereotypical Hellenistic father figure, the paterfamilias, who viewed children as disposable.[89] The distinctive image of Jairus, according to Betsworth, unfolds in three actions that could be considered atypical of a man in his role. First, he seeks assistance from the very person to whom his peers have shown opposition. Second, he places himself in a position of humility at the feet of Jesus. Third, he refers to his daughter in what Betsworth interprets as a term of endearment, θυγάτριον, or "little daughter," in 5:23.[90] Martha Driscoll, who also pays attention to the paternal role of Jairus, gleans a similar reading. She argues that the story reveals the love between a father and daughter and affirms the role of parents to protect their chil-

---

87. The scribe (12:34); Joseph of Arimathea (15:43); Jairus (5:22).

88. Elizabeth Struthers Malbon, "Jewish Leaders in the Gospel of Mark," 276. Marcus notes Mark's use of the phrase "one of" in 5:22 to denote Jairus. It is also used to delineate the scribe in 12:28 and Judas in 14:10. He suggests it may have functioned to isolate the particular characters from the general portrait of the Jewish authorities and, in Judas's case, the Twelve (*Mark 1–8*, 355).

89. Betsworth, *Children in Early Christian Narratives*, 48.

90. Betsworth, *Children in Early Christian Narratives*, 48.

dren.[91] Again, Mary Ann Beavis notes the image of a father begging for the life of his daughter in her intertextual analysis of Jairus's daughter and the sacrifice of the daughter of Jephthah (Judg 11:34–40).[92]

1.3.2. Images of Jairus's Daughter

As we have observed, the portraits of Jairus's daughter are significantly influenced by the interpretations of the role of the bleeding woman on a regular basis. As such, in much of the analysis of these female figures, there are discussions of sexuality, fertility, marital status, and gendered illness and/or disease. James Murphy questions this widely embraced paradigm, however, in his recent study of children in the Synoptics. He asserts that the lack of clues provided by Mark to understand what causes the female child to be close to death opens up possibilities for understanding her condition beyond disease. In the absence of clear markers in 5:21–24, 35–43, one of the options he raises is the possibility of child abuse, "a poorly directed backhand—a reprimand gone wrong." Murphy also imputes a possible neglectful attitude to Jesus. While the girl's father appears desperate for the girl to be saved, Jesus does not rush to the dying child but allows the "young girl's life [to] get 'interrupted' by a seemingly less pressing problem than death."[93] A conversation with a healed woman is more worthy of Jesus's time than the state of a dying child. Murphy's speculation about the possible cause of the child's condition is unique in the scholarship. It is not without merit given the various causes of child mortality in the first century CE.[94] Moreover, while Mark's narrative is filled with stories of the sick being restored, it is also a gospel of violence and death, suggesting that Murphy's proposition is not entirely

---

91. Driscoll, *Reading between the Lines*, 34–38.
92. Beavis, "Resurrection of Jephthah's Daughter," 54.
93. Murphy, *Kids and Kingdom*, 121.
94. Parkin lists the following as contributing to the high rates of children's deaths: the level of urbanization and gender (infant girls more vulnerable); sanitation and hygiene; medical care; nutrition; no quarantine so infections related to fevers, pulmonary complaints, dysentery and diarrhea, cholera, scurvy, rabies, etc. took a toll. Childhood mortality was also influenced by rearing practices, levels of poverty, and seasonal or ecological changes, e.g., drought or famine. Tim Parkin, "The Demography of Infancy and Early Childhood in the Ancient World," in *The Oxford Handbook of Childhood and Education in the Classical World*, ed. Roslynne Bell, Judith Evans Grubbs, and Tim Parkin, Oxford Handbooks (New York: Oxford University Press, 2013), 46–48.

without a basis in the narrative. Murphy's deliberations not only highlight the assumptions that are shaped by the interpretation of the bleeding woman's story, but also reveal the new perspectives and questions that potentially arise with a change in the frame of reference for reading 5:21–24, 35–43.[95]

Another distinctive element of the story is the application of diminutives and a chronological age to describe Jairus's daughter. This is the only time this dual usage appears in Mark's Gospel. The labels θυγάτριον (5:23), παιδίον (5:39, 40, 41), κοράσιον (5:42), and ταλιθά (5:41) are all used to characterize the girl, in addition to Mark's identification of her as twelve years old (5:42).[96] While these terms may translate as *little daughter, little child, little girl,* and *lamb* respectively, for some scholars these diminutives do not indicate that she is particularly young or little.[97] Instead, coupled with Mark's description of the girl as twelve years old, scholars identify her as on the cusp of puberty rather than as a little girl.[98] Essentially, the descriptor of chronological age is thought to determine how the diminutives are read. In this way, Mark is understood to have used the diminutives as terms of endearment, rather than to signify her status as a little child.[99] As such, the diminutives function to underscore the portrait of Jairus as a devoted father and the girl as a valued daughter. Understanding Jairus's daughter as nearing puberty, rather than being a little girl, reinforces nonetheless the opinions of those scholars who discuss her restoration in terms of a transition to womanhood and its concomitant associations with fertility, marriage, and childbearing.[100]

---

95. Murphy further questions whether the story is even concerned with the corporeal life of the girl, regardless of the cause of her terminal state. In his view, the ambiguities concerning the translations of ἐσχάτως ἔχει (5:23) and σωθῇ (5:23) call into question whether the author is concerned with Jairus's daughter's physical restoration, or her eternal existence or, perhaps, both (*Kids and Kingdom*, 122).

96. Boring notes that the use of the term κοράσιον is not used in the New Testament except in this pericope (5:41) and when referring to Herod's daughter (6:28; Boring, *Mark*, 156).

97. The term ταλιθά, "lamb," was used to denote children (Zwiep, *Jairus's Daughter*, 71).

98. Betsworth, *Children in Early Christian Narratives*, 52; James M. M. Francis, *Adults as Children: Images of Childhood in the Ancient World and the New Testament*, Religions and Discourse 17 (Bern: Lang, 2006), 39–40; Stein, *Mark*, 266.

99. Gundry, *Mark*, 267, 275.

100. Betsworth, *Children in Early Christian Narratives*, 52.

1. Jairus's Daughter and the Bleeding Woman 35

With the emergence of scholarship on the representations of children in the biblical tradition, the focus shifts to the status of Jairus's daughter as a child rather than her identity as a female moving into womanhood. James Francis explains the use of diminutives as denoting a period in a person's life that is situated between being an infant or toddler and an adult.[101] The nuance in this case centers on the situation of the girl as a child, rather than her transition to womanhood. Judith Gundry observes that Mark uses diminutives in the gospel to denote young children, although she acknowledges that the additional reference to the girl's age is unique to the passage.[102] Identified as a child, Gundry locates Jairus's daughter alongside the other children in Mark's Gospel who are regarded as worthy of Jesus's concern.[103] Mercy Oduyoye, Christine Amjad Ali, and Tinyiko Sam Maluleke also emphasize the girl's identity as a child. In so doing, they characterize her as a person of low social status, an image Mark reworks in order to promote Jairus's daughter as a model of liberation.[104] Her social status as a child is critical for those scholars concerned to show evidence of Jesus's positive—even liberating—relationships with children and Mark's vision of the inclusive reign of God in an environment that is understood to have devalued female children.[105]

Not all who read the story of Jairus's daughter with the image of the child in view conclude that Mark's attitude to childhood is completely positive. While Murphy observes that the girl's account can be seen to demonstrate the in-breaking of God's reign, he questions the assertion that Jesus "displays particular concern" per se for children.[106] To the contrary, Murphy observes that very little detail is given about the girl in the passage. She is given no name, no speech, and nothing is asked of her as a response to her restoration. In this way, she takes her place alongside the rest of Mark's representations of children, with the exception of Herodias's daughter. Murphy suggests that Mark may be more interested in how chil-

---

101. Francis, *Adults as Children*, 98.
102. Gundry, "Children in the Gospel of Mark," 148.
103. Gundry, "Children in the Gospel of Mark," 146–76. See also Betsworth, *Children in Early Christian Narratives*, 66–69.
104. Amjad Ali, "Faith and Power in the New Community," 132–35; Maluleke, "Bible Study the Graveyardman," 556; Oduyoye, "*Talitha qumi*," 82–89.
105. Strauss, *Mark*, 237.
106. Murphy, *Kids and Kingdom*, 120.

dren function as part of the literary motif concerning the in-breaking of the reign of God, than the role of actual children as disciples.[107]

The discussion concerning the possible identity of Jairus's daughter as a child is significant for two reasons. First, it reveals a shift in the scholarship whereby the passage concerning Jairus's daughter can be approached from a different frame of reference than that of the account about the bleeding woman. Second, the insights that are produced through such a shift, while demonstrating how the passage may support some important Markan ideas, do not lead to a consensus on the significance of Mark's depiction of the girl, but instead open up questions for further deliberation.

1.3.3. Death, Restoration, and Resurrection

A third area of conversation specific to the story of Jairus's daughter concerns what is meant by her death and restoration. The issue is approached from two angles. First, scholars deliberate over whether or not the girl is understood to be dead. Second, they discuss questions of whether the story is about restoration, resuscitation, or resurrection. Indeed, few commentators examine this pericope without drawing attention to the acknowledgment of the girl's death (5:35) and Jesus's subsequent ignoring of this by claiming that the girl is sleeping (5:39). There are multiple options raised in the scholarship for interpreting Mark's language and message in this instance.

Some scholars view the death as real but temporary. In France's view, there is no finality to her death as Jesus is about to reverse her state, as if she were sleeping. This is indicated in the use of the term καθεύδω, "to sleep," which is unique in Mark to the story of Jairus's daughter.[108] Others share the view that Mark uses the term καθεύδω as a euphemism for death and draw on its usage in the biblical traditions to substantiate their claim.[109]

---

107. Murphy includes the healing of the Syrophoenician woman's daughter (7:25–30) and the boy suffering from possession (9:14–29) in his analysis. His assertion also extends to all three synoptics (*Kids and Kingdom*, 123–24).

108. France, *Gospel of Mark*, 239. See also Boring, *Mark*, 162; Harris, *From Grave to Glory*, 87; Pesch, *Das Markusevangelium*, 307; Rochais, *Les récits de résurrection*, 202.

109. Culpepper, *Mark*, 178; Gundry, *Mark*, 273; Sabourin, "Miracles of Jesus (III)," 174; Stein, *Mark*, 273.

Joel Marcus describes Jesus's words as an instance of "eschatological irony" whereby Mark uses biblical metaphors of death as a form of sleep to communicate that, "death ... is not the end of life but only an interim state of waiting before the final resurrection as the end of time."[110] Still others, such as van Iersel, use the Elijah and Elisha cycle as a parallel to Mark's pericope (obviously recognizing the differences between the narratives) to argue that an awareness of this cycle would have influenced the reception of the story by Mark's audience.[111] Max Wilcox, on the other hand, asserts that the girl is raised from sleep not death, which reinforces the portrait of Jesus as the great physician.[112]

Other scholars present further perspectives on the issue. Myers and colleagues shift the interpretation of sleep from an emphasis on a physical state to a metaphor for having no faith (cf. 13:36; 14:32–42).[113] Dagmar Oppel explains that in the death and subsequent command to the girl to get up, the Markan Jesus is understood to blur the conventional notions of what constituted life and death. What people believed to be the limits of life and of death were being redefined by Jesus.[114] Despite the various views that are raised, Charles Hedrick posits that uncertainty persists, nevertheless, regarding what is meant by the girl as dead or sleeping or even being near death.[115] Morna Hooker is of the view that it is no longer even possible to deduce conclusively whether or not the child was understood to be literally dead.[116] The broad array of views indicates that the possible import of Mark's reference to the dead daughter is an on-going source of inquiry.

Ambiguity also surrounds whether or not Mark depicts Jairus's daughter as resuscitated or resurrected. While Stein and Paul Fullmer, for instance, regard the story as depicting a resurrection, others discuss the story in terms of resuscitation.[117] Proponents of the latter position

---

110. Marcus, *Mark 1–8*, 371. He cites Dan 12:2; 1 Cor 15:6; 1 Thess 5:10.
111. Van Iersel, *Mark*, 210–11. Also Pesch, *Das Markusevangelium*, 300, 301, 308–9, 311–12, 313. The influence of the Elijah-Elisha cycle is refuted by France, *Gospel of Mark*, 239.
112. Max Wilcox, "Talitha Koum (I)," 469–76.
113. Myers et al., *Say to This Mountain*, 66.
114. Oppel, *Heilsam erzählen*, 105.
115. Hedrick, "Miracle Stories as Literary Compositions," 233.
116. Hedrick, "Miracle Stories as Literary Compositions," 227; Murphy, *Kids and Kingdom*, 121; Hooker, *Saint Mark*, 147.
117. Indeed, Fullmer sees this pericope as the first resurrection story in the gospel

distinguish between the resurrection of a person who has died and the restoration of a corpse to its former bodily state. According to Robert Guelich, "There is no evidence that the story or the early church confused what transpired in this account with the resurrection which connoted a different kind of life. Jairus's daughter simply returned to life as usual with her family as seen by her walking about and eating."[118] In this view, the resuscitation of a corpse is not synonymic for resurrection.

Building on the discussion of resurrection or resuscitation is a further debate on the significance Mark attributes to the girl's transition from a deathly state to one of living. Essentially, the argument concerns questions of whether or not Mark depicts the girl as prefiguring the death and resurrection of Jesus. On the one hand, across various approaches and methodologies, the raising of Jairus's daughter is understood to foreshadow the death and resurrection of Jesus.[119] Betsworth explores the language that associates the raising of the girl with the resurrection of Jesus, noting the use of the term ἔγειρε (5:41) which in the passive form—ἐγείρονται—is used for the raising of the dead.[120] Wainwright notes in her discussion of this story the term ἀνίστημι, used to describe the girl's restoration in 5:42 (and the boy's restoration in 9:27), and also employed in Jesus's passion predictions as well as other references to resurrection (8:31; 9:9, 10, 31; 10:34; 12:23, 25), albeit not directly of Jesus's resurrection.[121]

On the other hand, while calling attention to the usage of the term ἀνίστημι, Wainwright is wary to draw hard conclusions concerning the theme of resurrection in the pericope and its relationship to the resur-

---

(*Resurrection*, 172; Stein, *Mark*, 262). For an analysis of modern and premodern approaches to the issue of resuscitation and resurrection, see Steven Edwards Harris, "On Three Kinds of Resurrection of the Dead," *IJST* 20 (2018): 8–30. For resuscitation, see Sabourin, "Miracles of Jesus (III)," 174. Amerding argues it is a restoration or revival but not a resurrection. Carl E. Amerding, "The Daughter of Jairus," *BSac* 105 (1948): 56–58.

118. Guelich, *Mark 1–8:26*, 304. Or, as Schweizer explains in an earlier commentary, resurrection is concerned with the "re-creation by God to an existence which is entirely new." See Eduard Schweizer, *The Good News according to Mark*, trans. Donald H. Madvig (Richmond, VA: John Knox, 1970), 121.

119. Betsworth, *Reign of God Is Such as These*, 114; Branch, "Literary Comparisons," 8; Culpepper, "Mark," 179; Marcus, *Mark 1–8*, 372–73; Miller, *Women*, 64; Strauss, *Mark*, 236; Swartley, "Role of Women in Mark's Gospel," 17.

120. Betsworth, *Reign of God Is Such as These*, 113.

121. Wainwright, *Women Healing/Healing Women*, 116.

rection of Jesus. France also has reservations, stating that the significance of Jairus's daughter's transformation is unclear. Given they are common words, Mark gives no indication he is suggesting a resurrection typology in the uses of ἔγειρε and ἀνέστη, according to France. Moreover, the girl's return to her former earthly life that is demonstrated in her walking and eating confirms there is no resurrection.[122]

Locating the story more broadly within the context of the preceding miracles of 1:14–4:34, Peter Bolt explains that the raising of Jairus's daughter from death can be seen as the culmination of numerous healing activities in which Jesus had enabled people to recover their lives.[123] He observes that in the latter half of the pericope (5:35–43), Mark shifts the focus from Jairus to Jesus: not only is Jesus the subject of all the verbs in this section but additionally, after 5:36, Jairus is no longer referred to by name or as the synagogue leader. In other words, in Bolt's view, as the story progresses it no longer deals primarily with Jairus's faith but with the portrait of Jesus as one who raises a dead child to life. In this way, Mark conveys his understanding of Jesus's identity: the one who defeats death.[124]

In some studies, the transition of Jairus's daughter from death to life is understood to communicate ideas about the fate of the community. Stephanie Fischbach examines the story from the perspective of the Markan and pre-Markan redactors.[125] She argues that the pericope is most likely derived from an act of the historical Jesus in which an ill girl was healed.

---

122. France, *Gospel of Mark*, 240; Rikki E. Watts, *Isaiah's New Exodus and Mark*, WUNT 2/88 (Tübingen: Mohr Siebeck, 1997), 175.

123. Bolt, *Jesus' Defeat of Death*, 190.

124. Bolt, *Jesus' Defeat of Death*, 178. Maluleke reads 5:21–24, 35–43 within the context of the whole of Mark 5, arguing that each of the healing accounts reveals Jesus's power over death, "The narrative starts in a graveyard … and ends a few inches from the grave as the girl-child is raised from the dead.… Jairus knew only too well the smell of death that hovers over graveyards, for in his own house lay a young girl whose life was slipping away.… Jesus leads all three characters out of the area of the graveyard to life. All three were 'dead' but Jesus awakens all three and causes them to rise from death to life" ("Bible Study the Graveyardman," 551, 556). Dalgaard also argues that it is a story about Jesus's power over death ("Four Keys of God," 244).

125. Fischbach, *Totenerweckungen*. According to Fischbach's analysis, the evangelist subsequently embellished the account by inserting details pertaining to the so-called secrecy motif and the exclusive presence of the three disciples at the raising of the girl. Mark included Peter, James, and John in order to give the story credibility in a context in which eye-witnesses no longer existed (193–96).

The pre-Markan redactor took up the healing story, drawing on Jewish and Hellenistic ideas about healing, death, and restoration, to transform it into an account that deals with restoring the girl to life. Jesus is thus no longer portrayed as only a healer but as one who raises people from the dead.[126] In Fischbach's view, the pre-Markan redactor's transformation of the story to one that concerns resurrection reflects debates within the post-Easter community about the fate of those who died after the death of Jesus had occurred.[127] For pre-Mark, faith enables the person who is dead to be understood as sleeping. The story thus provides hope in the resurrection, including individual resurrection.[128]

Alternatively, the girl's transformation is understood to concern the restoration of Israel. This reading is promoted by Steven Richard Scott, who considers the significance of Jairus's daughter being identified as twelve years old. Scott suggests that the number twelve, which evokes images of the twelve apostles, twelve baskets of leftover food, and the twelve tribes of Israel, is presented to the fearful disciples (4:35–41) as a sign of the gathering of the new Israel. These faithful, righteous ones, including Jairus and in contrast to the Nazarenes and Herod, will constitute the resurrected Israel.[129]

Finally, Mark's reference to the mourners in 5:38–40 also draws various interpretations among scholars. Some posit that the scene painted by Mark is typical of ancient mourning rites. For example, Strauss asserts that Mark's description reflects the practice of employing paid mourners.[130] Francis, in his study of images of childhood in the ancient world and New Testament, argues that Mark's picture of the mourners provides evidence of the sorrow that accompanied the death of a child and how deaths of children could be mourned in the first century CE.[131] Others depict the

---

126. See also Pesch who argues that pre-Mark transforms a healing story into a resurrection story (*Das Markusevangelium*, 296–314).

127. Fischbach, *Totenerweckungen*, 155–96. Rochais also argues that 5:21–24, 35–43 was written for a post-Easter community. Using form and redaction criticism, Rochais argues that the passage was transformed from a healing story into an account concerning a raising from the dead. The story functioned to give hope to those in the community who were anxious for members who had died before the return of the Lord (*Les récits de résurrection*, 110–11, 199–202).

128. Fischbach, *Totenerweckungen*, 191–92.

129. Scott, "Raising the Dead," 169.

130. Strauss, *Mark*, 233.

131. Francis, *Adults as Children*, 28 n. 6.

mourners negatively. Their grief is understood to be superficial and misplaced, demonstrated in their laughter at Jesus's statement that the girl is sleeping. Murray Harris uses the terms "disorderly," "simulated grief," and "callous" to describe the grieving group.[132] Eugene Boring views them as representing the "misplaced scorn of early Christianity."[133] In a similar vein, Scott regards the commotion and wailing of the mourners as representing evil and chaos, and Jesus as the master of this chaos.[134] In Gundry's view, their unbelief is a foil to the faith of Jairus.[135]

1.4. Summary

Mark's story of the raising of Jairus's daughter is routinely examined in relation to the account of the bleeding woman in 5:25–34 through the lens of the Markan sandwich technique. This treatment of the story elicits themes across a span of methodologies and approaches that can be understood to relate to ideas concerning sexuality, (in)fertility, disease, and healing, issues concerning social and ritual status, and notions of faith and fear. A consequence of this treatment is that interpretations of the account of the bleeding woman often influence how the raising of Jairus's daughter is understood. Indeed, readings of the story of the girl are often controlled by the interpretations of the woman's story. At their extreme, these analyses establish polarizing portraits of the woman and the synagogue leader and his daughter. In identifying contrasts, the bleeding woman is often cast as the superior character to Jairus and his daughter, in a Markan reversal of the perceived norms that defined a person's status. These perspectives, while pervasive in the scholarship, are not without their critics, particularly those views that regard ancient Jewish ritual purity codes as marginalizing and oppressive. Scholarship on ancient Jewish purity law calls into question the validity of these assumptions and opens up the possibility for further ways of reading the raising of Jairus's daughter.

While the discussion of parallels and contrasts with 5:25–34 is the dominant way of approaching the story of Jairus's daughter, not all analyses of 5:21–24, 35–43 according to the sandwich technique are limited to

---

132. Harris, *From Grave to Glory*, 86.
133. Boring, *Mark*, 162.
134. Scott, "Raising the Dead," 178.
135. Gundry, "Children in the Gospel of Mark," 161.

this conversation. Some commentators identify distinctive elements in the story of Jairus's daughter, and do not attempt to correlate them with the bleeding woman's account. Moreover, there are studies that do not treat the story of Jairus's daughter within the context of the sandwich technique at all. Instead, the account is examined by drawing on alternative frames of reference in Mark, the wider biblical tradition, or the broader sociocultural context.

These latter studies reveal that when the story of Jairus's daughter is not confined to interpretations of the bleeding woman, further insights come to the fore. Shifts in the interpretive frame allow us to see the significance of the story of Jairus's daughter in new ways. The conversation moves to the consideration of the status of Jairus's daughter as a child. There are also further deliberations about the possible significance of her dying, death, and restoration. As we have observed, there is no consensus currently on the significance of the image of the dying, deceased, and raised child. To the contrary, the wide-ranging possibilities and on-going discussions suggest that a further exploration of the story of Jairus's daughter from a new vantage point could be enlightening.

I am of the view that there are further ways of reading the story of Jairus's daughter that build on the current discussions of the girl's status as a child and the meanings that may be attributed to her death and restoration. Following the line of those studies that use alternative frames of reference to analyze the passage, I believe that concentrating on the depiction of Jairus's little daughter as dying and deceased is one way of widening the vantage point by which the episode can be viewed. Given the role that depictions of the body play in the narrative of Mark's Gospel, analyzing the story of Jairus's daughter with an awareness of the representations of bodies, particularly the bodies of dying and deceased women's and female children's bodies, can open up the interpretive vista further. In order to carry out this analysis, it is essential first to set out my observations of how depictions of the body function in the narrative of Mark's Gospel. I undertake this task in the following chapter.

2
The Body in the Gospel of Mark

> And he said to them, "Truly I tell you, there are some standing here who will not taste death until they see that the kingdom of God has come with power."
>
> —Mark 9:1

In my reading of Mark, representations of the body are a fundamental element of the narrative. Stories abound in which Jesus comes across sick and suffering bodies that are healed largely through physical interaction. Similarly, throughout the gospel we observe images of bodies that are marked by violence, some of whom are saved, others that are not. Images and teachings appear that convey an ambiguity concerning physical life after death. The quotation that heads this chapter provides a snapshot of some of the ideas that, in my assessment, are apparent throughout the narrative of the gospel: proximity to the experience of physical death, and the centrality of the body in coming to an understanding of the reign of God. These notions are particularly evident when the narrative is read with an awareness of the role and function of the body. There are references to emotions that are experienced in the body, as well as ways of knowing that are experienced through the body, with both direct references and allusions to senses related to sight, speech, hearing, touch, smell, taste, movement, and kinesthesia.[1] A person also encounters an abundance of instances in which characters embody authority through their voice and physical actions, most notably Jesus. The body is an integral part of the unfolding story.

---

1. Louise J. Lawrence, *Sense and Stigma in the Gospels: Depictions of Sensory-Disabled Characters*, Biblical Refigurations (Oxford: Oxford University Press, 2013), 13.

As discussed in the previous chapter, ideas about bodies are contained in many of the modern approaches to the raising of Jairus's daughter. As we observed, the commentary often concerns Jesus's touch of the girl's corpse in relation to notions of Jewish corpse impurity. While moving away from this particular optic, other scholars continue to concentrate on the bodily dimensions of the episode. They discuss the role of touch and the use of hands in the pericope of Jairus's daughter in light of ancient activities involving touch. There is recognition that the hands were a constituent element in a number of common gestures in the ancient world, such as the performance of sacrifices, the punishment of criminals, blessings, acts of healing, commissioning, and ordination.[2] More specifically, they take into account the imagery of hands and touch in the Jewish and Greco-Roman worlds of healing. Gundry, for example, cites 4 Kgdms 5:11 to evoke descriptions of hands moving over an affected area to cure leprosy.[3] Culpepper and Stein both cite 1QapGen XX, 22, 29 as evidence of belief in laying hands on a person to heal them.[4] Yarbro Collins, Culpepper, and D'Angelo bring Greek literature to the conversation, citing the healing of a dead or death-like young woman before her marriage through touch and the whispering of a spell to her in Philostratus's *Life of Apollonius of Tyana*.[5] Together, they demonstrate that understandings of bodily interaction through the hands and voice, between the healer and the sick person, including dying young women, were part of the landscape of antiquity.

Donald Capps also takes the notions of touch and hands, and their intersection with the image of a young girl as a focal point. In his interpretation, the girl's illness—a condition in the ancient world called *hysteria* that was understood to be caused by a restless womb—is related to the anxiety and misunderstanding created in the intergenerational responses to a girl's emerging sexuality as a young woman.[6] In this reading, Jesus's touch of the young woman is a physical means of bridging the distance between generations. He explains that Jesus offers a "non-anxious presence

---

2. Schweizer, *Mark*, 117.
3. Gundry, *Mark*, 267.
4. Culpepper, *Mark*, 178; Stein, *Mark*, 266.
5. Yarbro Collins, *Mark*, 278–79; Culpepper, *Mark*, 179; D'Angelo, "Gender and Power," 92, 96. Philostratus, *Vit. Apoll.* 4.45.
6. Capps, "Curing Anxious Adolescents," 142–43. See also Capps, "Jesus the Village Psychiatrist," 1–5.

together with the empowerment of a father-like performance through the physical action of an extended hand."[7]

Wainwright also notes the importance of the body for understanding Mark's story of Jairus's daughter. She argues that the somatic restoration of Jairus's daughter, along with other episodes in which the storyteller narrates healing, reveals how healing in Mark was understood in material, bodily terms. Markan acts of healing involve the interaction of both the bodies of the healer and of the one being healed.[8] In Wainwright's own words, "Word and flesh on flesh together bring wholeness. The materiality of flesh is restorative."[9] Jesus's grasping of the girl's hands and his words to her reveal a belief in the capacity of bodies to restore each other. Moreover, it is a female's body that is the locus of corporeal transformation and, as we observed in our earlier references to Wainwright's study, she considers the young woman's disease to be gendered. The bodily restoration of the girl, therefore, symbolizes her restoration to the household and thereby creates possibilities for the inclusion of young women within the communities of the *basileia* who engage with the story.[10]

While the image of a sick female undergoing healing through touch and the hands is not unique to this pericope, when it intersects with the image of a child, rather than a young woman, a new awareness is brought to the conversation. Murphy deems physical closeness to Jesus positively. He contends that the "spatial and proximal location of children with or near Jesus" indicates that they are included in the reign of God.[11] This may imply that Jesus's physical interaction with the girl embodied a meaning that was broader than simply a physical healing. In other words, the child's proximity to Jesus and location with him in the house may have carried a symbolic relevance in the gospel. Murphy, however, does not explore the possibilities of this line of investigation. Instead, he contends that the inclusion of a child *as a child* in what he deems to be a resurrection narrative might suggest that children were to be included in the kingdom of God. In his words, "They are presented as characters in the vanguard

---

7. Capps, "Curing Anxious Adolescents," 147. Capps reads the story in dialogue with the experience of intergenerational conflict among adolescents and adults in the twenty-first century.

8. Wainwright, *Women Healing/Healing Women*, 102–3.

9. Wainwright, *Women Healing/Healing Women*, 116.

10. Wainwright, *Women Healing/Healing Women*, 116.

11. Murphy, *Kids and Kingdom*, 101.

of the in-breaking of the kingdom, demonstrating its power to others.... They ... are ascribed social parity with adult members."[12] Thus, the story becomes a vehicle for conveying notions of equality in Mark's vision of the kingdom of God.

Beyond the themes of touch and hands, and the notions of gendered disease and healing, there is little other development of ideas concerning the body in this story. Eduard Schweizer suggests possible corporeal dimensions in his comments, "When Jesus heals ... it does not merely affect the thoughts and feelings but the body also."[13] But these comments are not developed further. Likewise, Elaine Lawless observes that the story of Jairus's daughter and the bleeding woman equally concern embodiment. But she too does not develop this idea to any significant degree in the story of the young woman, preferring to concentrate on the healing of the bleeding woman.[14] Applying what he classes as "embodied performance," Richard Swanson undertakes a physical translation of 5:21–43.[15] Yet again, much of the attention is directed at the character of the bleeding woman, although Swanson's reading does bring into view the image of the girl's dead body that lies "eerily inert" and in which "life-giving blood no longer flows."[16] In addition, although his embodied translation generates comments concerning the girl's fertility, corpse impurity, and touch, he offers little development of these corporeal dimensions.

Another facet to the account of Jairus's daughter that is presented by scholars is the story's association with notions of suffering and death in Mark's Gospel. Miller contends that both females in 5:21–43 are identified through suffering and death and that, through them, Mark conveys the notion that suffering signifies the nearness of God's reign, and the capacity of that reign to overcome suffering and death.[17] In her study of children in Mark's Gospel of which the "child of Jairus" is a part, Betsworth acknowledges that suffering is a key Markan motif but concedes that she has chosen

---

12. Murphy, *Kids and Kingdom*, 101–2.
13. Schweizer, *Mark*, 117.
14. Lawless, "Transforming the Master Narrative," 67.
15. Richard Swanson, "Moving Bodies and Translating Scripture: Interpretation and Incarnation," *WW* 31 (2011): 271–78. Embodied performance is a method of exploring biblical texts in which persons interpret written texts by physically performing the stories.
16. Swanson, "Moving Bodies and Translating Scripture," 278.
17. Miller, *Women*, 71.

not to explore the theme in relation to the depiction of Markan children in favor of other equally illuminating themes.[18] As we shall observe, Mark presents a hearer with a plethora of corporal images that concern suffering and death. The remarks of Miller and Betsworth suggest that analyzing the episode of Jairus's daughter from the perspective of bodies, particularly suffering, dying, and dead bodies, may prove fruitful in understanding the role of the story in Mark's overall narrative in a new way.

What will be discussed in the remainder of this chapter is not an analysis of all of the representations of the body throughout Mark's Gospel, a task that is beyond the scope of this study. Rather, we will concentrate on the dominant images of the body that will have a direct bearing on the analysis of the story of Jairus's daughter.[19] I will make observations of what I understand the Markan author to be doing in depicting the body throughout the narrative. Grounded in these observations, I will argue that the body is a vehicle for communicating notions about sickness, violence, suffering, death, and transformation. It will be evident that emotions are often depicted as having a corporeal association that functions to interpret the actions of particular characters. In addition, the senses—orality, aurality, sight, touch, and movement—become a further means for communicating attitudes and ideas. These themes form the basis of the following discussion.

2.1. Ill Bodies

People who were ill form a dominant group in Mark's Gospel. This broad group takes in those who were sick (e.g., 5:25–34), disfigured (e.g., 3:1–6), and physically impaired (e.g., 8:22–26).[20] The types of conditions that are represented are diverse but most are described in physical terms.[21] Conditions relate to the organs and limbs, that is the skin, hands, eyes, ears, and

---

18. Betsworth, *Children in Early Christian Narratives*, 44, 48.

19. Other themes include: the language of the body to describe temperament (3:5; 6:52; 7:6; 10:5); images of hunger, food, and being fed; the head as a site of violation or honor; clothing and identity; bodily positioning and gestures to embody identity; bound and released bodies.

20. Each of these may be seen as a discrete sphere of illness. Given that each may also be understood as an expression of illness, however, I group them into one general category.

21. The daughter of the Syrophoenician woman is described as having an unclean spirit but there is no physical description of this condition (7:25).

tongue, and to the body more broadly in terms of bleeding, fever, and kinesthesia and mobility in the case of the paralytic. Physical illnesses affect men and women, and appear in both the Jewish and non-Jewish territories that Jesus traverses.

Of these characters, some are overtly depicted as suffering. In the account of the bleeding woman (5:24b–34), for instance, the term πάσχω is used to indicate explicitly that the woman has suffered at the hands of physicians treating her bleeding body (5:26). When describing the condition of those who possess unclean spirits (1:24, 26; 9:18, 20, 22, 26), graphic language is utilized to depict how the spirits manifest themselves in the bodies they inhabit. In the case of the Gerasene demoniac, for example, we find descriptions of bodily sound and volume to convey the spirit's corporeal presence: the man makes "howling" sounds (κράζω, "crying out or screaming wordlessly") as he traverses the tombs and mountains relentlessly, night and day (5:5). In terms of physical actions, he is described as "bruising himself with stones" (5:5). The term κατακόπτω connotes images of the man cutting, bruising, or beating himself. Pictures of shackles and chains are conjured up to depict what others have done to restrain the man. The man's resistance to this restraint is physical; the man is described as wrenching apart the chains and breaking into parts the shackles (5:4). While strong enough to break the chains that bind him, the man is nonetheless a picture of physical suffering.

Likewise, the physical suffering of the possessed boy is brought up close to the reader/hearer through the use of graphic corporeal language to describe the effect of the unclean spirit. When the spirit seized him, it took away his capacity for speech (ἄλαλος) and "dashed him down." He foamed, ground his teeth, and became rigid (9:18). The graphic depiction of the spirit through the boy's body is articulated four times. After 9:18, it reappears in 9:20 in a description of what the spirit does to the boy when it sees Jesus. The spirit convulses the boy so that he falls to the ground and rolls about foaming (9:20). Again, in 9:22 the boy's father describes what the spirit does to the boy. It often casts (βάλλω) him in the fire and into the water to destroy (ἀπόλλυμι) him (9:22). Finally, in 9:26, as the spirit leaves the boy's body it is depicted as crying out (κράζω), convulsing him again (σπαράσσω) and leaving the boy in a corpse-like state (νεκρός). The body of the male child becomes a means by which to mediate ideas about the violent presence of unclean spirits and their capacity for destruction.

While ill bodies are prominent in the gospel, they are not necessarily desirable. Instead, there is ambiguity in how they are approached. On the

2. The Body in the Gospel of Mark

one hand, ill bodies elicit pity from those around them, including Jesus. The depiction of his response to the person with leprosy is a case in point. Mark describes Jesus as feeling compassion for the man with the diseased skin (σπλαγχνίζομαι, 1:41).[22] On the other hand, they also arouse anxiety.[23] Those who are ill, or their family and friends, desire that their ill body is changed. Sick men and women who have bodily agency and voice pursue changes to their conditions (1:40-45; 5:3-20, 25-34; 10:46-52). Others are depicted as having advocates who approach Jesus on their behalf (1:29-31; 2:13; 5:21-24, 35-43; 6:56; 7:25-30, 32-37; 8:22-26; 9:17-27). All children who are ill have parents who advocate for them (5:21-24, 35-43; 7:25-30; 9:17-27). At least in the cases of 5:21-24, 35-43 and 9:17-27, the descriptions of the children's physical conditions—dying and severely incapacitated by unclean spirits respectively—imply that they would not be capable of approaching Jesus of their own volition. In all cases, people seek the transformation of these conditions.

Given the desire for the curing of ill bodies, the body can be understood to function as a site of transformation. Bodies are sites in which sickness and suffering are healed and life is preserved. In various instances, there are signals that the healings of people are physical. The term θεραπεύω appears on several occasions to denote the action that Jesus carries out (1:34; 3:2, 10; 6:5, 13). The NRSV translates the term as "cure," but the term can mean "to care for, heal," or "to restore." It can also connote being treated medically. While the transformation of ill bodies may have had social implications, as scholars often explain, healing nonetheless clearly has a practical, physical dimension in the narrative.

At the center of many of the healing accounts is the interaction of bodies. Physical contact between the body of Jesus and that of other people becomes the locus of transformation for those who are ill or have malfunctioning bodies. The dominant forms of interaction are touch and speech. Jesus touches the bodies of others predominantly with his hands (1:31, 41; 5:23, 41; 6:2, 5; 7:32), although his fingers and saliva also bring about corporal healing (7:33; 8:23). Indeed, in 6:2 Jesus's own kin are described as recognizing the power (δύναμις) that is associated with the deeds accomplished through Jesus's hands. Others touch him also (3:10), or touch his clothing to gain healing (5:27, 28; 6:56).

---

22. Another example, 3:1-5. Here I follow NA[28], which goes with the majority reading, but note that the SBLGNT adopts the reading in D: ὀργισθείς ("to anger").

23. Lawrence, *Sense and Stigma in the Gospels*, 50.

In other instances, it is the voice and spoken words of Jesus that trigger healing (1:25; 2:5; 3:5; 5:8, 41; 7:34; 9:25). When people are possessed by unclean spirits, it is the voice and words of Jesus addressed to the spirits that effects healing.[24] In the examples of the Gerasene demoniac and the boy with an unclean spirit (5:1–20; 9:17–27), it is the voice and words of Jesus to the spirit that bring about the physical restoration of both males. In 7:34, it is the speech of Jesus accompanied by another bodily sound that generates speech and hearing in a man. Jesus utters the Aramaic ἐφφαθά, which is then translated as the command, "be opened!" The healing activity includes a further vocalization—a deep sigh or inner groan or moan (στενάζω, 7:34). Jesus's capacity to heal another is predominantly centered in his body. The healing of another person becomes possible when Jesus physically engages with the person's body through voice or touch.

The transformation of people as a result of their engagement with Jesus also has a strong corporeal dimension. Scholars commonly note the possible social or religious consequences of healing, as we observed in the previous chapter's discussion of 5:21–43. An equally important feature of the narrative is the descriptions of the changes in people's bodies after they have engaged with Jesus. The bleeding woman, for instance, has a corporeal knowledge of her own healing, which is reinforced with the description that the source of bleeding had dried up (5:29). The dispossession of the Gerasene demoniac is clearly signified in his physical transformation: He physically relocates from the tombs to the home (οἶκος) with friends and into the Decapolis. He is transformed from wearing shackles and chains to wearing clothes; from bruising himself and breaking his chains to sitting quietly; from howling and shouting to proclaiming. In 5:15, the people are described as seeing (θεωρέω) these alterations in the man's appearance. The transformation is physically perceptible and indicates that he is in a right mind (σωφρονέω).[25]

In some healing accounts, specific verbs are used in relation to the transformation of a person's physical state. In 10:52, the verb σῴζω ("being saved from death") is taken up in relation to the blind man regaining

---

24. The instances in which there are no signs of interaction are the healing of the Syrophoenician woman's daughter, 7:24–31, and the healing of the sick and possessed in 1:32–34.

25. A withered hand is labeled as restored (ἀποκαθιστάνω, 3:5). Blind men regain sight (8:24–25; 10:52). Ears are opened and a tongue released so that a man can speak plainly (7:35).

sight.[26] It is the man's faith that has saved him, resulting in the restoration of his vision. Being able to see therefore is an expression of being saved. In other cases, the physical transformation of a person is further indicated by the use of ἐγείρω to describe the action either done to the healed character (1:31; 9:27) or that the character performs as a consequence of their healing (2:11–12). The verb ἀνίστημι is employed twice: to denote Jairus's daughter getting up (5:42) and the once-possessed boy as having the capacity to stand (9:27).[27]

In summary, bodies in the narrative of Mark's Gospel convey the idea that physical sickness, malformation, and suffering, while eliciting compassion, were not the ideal state. However, the fate of those who were ill or malformed was not sealed; transformation was possible through interaction with Jesus's own body. His body was depicted as a source of healing, and direct contact with his body transformed a person to a preferred physical state. This state was embodied in a person who was healthy, without impairment or disfigurement. It was personified in a woman whose source of bleeding had dried up and lived in peace and health, a man whose skin was healed, and a once paralyzed body that could move and feel. It was embodied in men who could hear, see, and speak plainly and proclaim, and men and children no longer possessed by unclean spirits, or living violently with the dead among the tombs, but sitting quietly, clothed and of a right mind, restored to families, friends, and homeland.

2.2. Suffering, Violence, and Death

In addition to the sick, another type of body that dominates the narrative is that characterized by violence, suffering, and death. The gospel contains images of people either meting out physical violence or those who were marked by violence. Graphic descriptions of violated bodies and the treatment of dead bodies, as well as accounts concerning who was to be saved and not to be saved bring ideas concerning suffering, violence, and death

---

26. In 5:23, the verb is used in anticipation of a restoration. In 6:56, the verb is used to signal the healing of those in the crowd but there is no description of the changes to bodies.

27. Two instances in which ἐγείρω is used in Jesus's command to an ill person to come forward appear in 3:3 and 10:49. Other instances in which the term is used but not in the context of physical restoration of the ill are 4:39; 14:42. In 14:28 the term is used to denote what will happen to Jesus postdeath.

up close to a hearer. The death of Jesus is a case in point, whereby graphic imagery is used to explain the actions carried out on Jesus, and the subsequent treatment of his body.[28]

While the treatment of Jesus's body may be classified loosely into three phases—his arrest, death, and burial—the narration of each phase contains details pertaining to the body. At his arrest, he is identified by means of a kiss from Judas. A gesture of intimacy becomes an embodiment of betrayal.[29] The violent overtones of the arrest are signaled in the details of the materiality of violence, "swords and clubs" (14:48), and the mutilating of the ear of the high priest's slave (14:47).

Following the arrest, graphic language is used to describe the violence inflicted on Jesus's body by both the Jewish religious leaders and the Roman leaders. While appearing before the high priest, "some" are depicted as spitting on him, blindfolding him, and striking him, followed by a beating by the guards. The fluid of others' bodies is projected onto his body and his sight is limited while others view the spectacle being performed. After he is bound and handed over to Pilate (15:1–5), his body is further violated by Pilate who flogs him before handing him over to be crucified (15:5). As the narrative progresses, the picture of Jesus's passion is intensified through eight successive verses of corporal violence and mockery that depict the Roman soldiers' treatment of him (15:16–24): clothing him in purple cloth; twisting thorns into a crown that they place on him; saluting him as "king of the Jews"; striking his head with a reed; kneeling before him in mock homage; stripping him of the purple cloth and dressing him in his own clothes; offering wine mixed with myrrh; and finally crucifying him.[30] The soldiers are the perpetrators of the action while Jesus is portrayed as the silent object. Despite the graphic detail, Jesus's reaction

---

28. There are other instances whereby the author takes up the imagery of physical violence, suffering, and/or death: 6:27; 8:34–37; 9:31, 42–50; 12:1–12; 13:7–9, 12–19; 14:27. Mark 11:15 depicts the physical aggression of Jesus, but this is not presented as being taken out on people's bodies.

29. In 13:13–19 Judas is identified as the one who will betray Jesus, signaled by the use of the term, παραδίδωμι.

30. For observations on Jesus's passion and sexual violence, see Manuel Villalobos Mendoza, *Abject Bodies in the Gospel of Mark*, Bible in the Modern World 45 (Sheffield: Sheffield Phoenix, 2012). See also Choi's observations about violence in the passion narrative and acts of sexual penetration: Jin Young Choi, *Postcolonial Discipleship of Embodiment: An Asian and Asian American Feminist Reading of the Gospel of Mark* (New York: Palgrave Macmillan, 2015), 49.

2. The Body in the Gospel of Mark 53

escapes description. The focus rests on the violence enacted on him and the picture of humiliation it creates.

Having been taken to a place of death denoted by its corporeal reference to Γολγοθᾶ—the place of a skull—Jesus's death is presented as a public spectacle of humiliation and violence. He is crucified between two bandits, and attracts the mockery of those who pass by, including the chief priests and scribes (15:29–31). His death is described in terms of crying out loudly and breathing his last breath (15:37). Images of physicality and pain—the vocalization of a cry, accentuated through the element of volume, at the final movements of breath—convey the end of Jesus's life.

After the death of Jesus, the sense of the bodily is particularly evident in the details concerning funerary rites. An emphasis in the narrative lies with the dead body of Jesus—the cadaver—and its treatment.[31] The term σῶμα in 15:43 is used to identify that for which Joseph of Arimathea asks Pilate. Joseph is the only person involved in the narration of the burial of Jesus. A named character, he is also identified as a Judean, an Arimathean, and a prominent member of the Jewish council. Having access to a tomb, he is also possibly wealthy. No family members or paid mourners, *libitinarii*, perform the funerary rites.[32] Indeed, unlike the case of John the Baptizer, none of Jesus's disciples carries out his burial. Women, commonly the ones who performed the duty of anointing a corpse, unsuccessfully attempt to anoint Jesus's body after its burial (16:1–8).

Joseph is not a spectator of Jesus's burial, unlike Mary Magdalene and Mary the mother of Joses, who are labeled as onlookers (15:47). He is depicted as directly handling the cadaver. We are given details concerning Joseph's preparation of and the materiality of Jesus's burial (15:46). He buys a linen cloth and then takes down the body from the cross. He wraps the body in linen cloth. The wrapped corpse is then laid in the tomb and a stone rolled against the door. Joseph's actions depict touch, the bodily interaction between his body and the corpse of Jesus, as well as the interaction of Joseph's body with the materiality of the burial.

---

31. John the Baptizer's beheaded corpse is also depicted as receiving funerary rites at the hands of his disciples (6:29). The description lacks the detail of Jesus's burial: they take his corpse (πτῶμα) and lay it in a tomb (6:29). Nonetheless, his loss is thus mourned and his life and violent death are commemorated in the narrative.

32. Emma Jayne Graham, "Memory and Materiality: Re-Embodying the Roman Funeral," in *Memory and Mourning: Studies on Roman Death*, ed. Valerie M. Hope and Janet Huskinson (Oxford: Oxbow, 2011), 30.

Another element to this account of a violent death is the notion of a continuing bodily existence after burial. Earlier, in 6:14, 16, "some" and Herod are depicted as thinking that Jesus embodies a resurrected form of John the Baptizer, denoted in the use of the verb ἐγείρω. Here we catch possible glimpses of an understanding that the resurrection of an individual in a different bodily form was possible. Although, it is evident in 12:18–27 that debate also existed around this understanding.[33] In the postburial narrative, there is ambiguity concerning the existence of Jesus. Representations of Jesus's corporeality appear obscure. While the burial rites for Jesus's cadaver are narrated in the language of realism, the language of the postburial account is opaque. As Mary Magdalene, Mary the mother of James, and Salome prepare to anoint the corpse, the language of materiality is used: They buy from the market (ἀγοράζω) spices (ἄρωμα) to anoint the body (16:1). The term ἄρωμα evokes fragrance and the sense of smell, connoting the perfume and herbs of the aromatic oil or salve for embalming the dead.[34] It also suggests corporeal touch in the act of anointing.

The language shifts, however, to a stylized form from 16:5. As they enter the tomb to anoint Jesus's body they encounter a youth dressed in a white shining garment (16:5). While taking human bodily form, the description of the figure possibly connotes an angel or heavenly being (e.g., two men in white robes, Acts 1:10; a youth as an angel, Josephus *A.J.* 5.277).[35] The youth is seated at the right hand suggesting power and triumph (Mark 12:36; 14:62).[36] The first to speak of Jesus being raised from the dead, this resplendent young male figure (νεανίσκος)—whose very youthfulness may suggest the beginning of a new time—redirects the women to Galilee.[37] The dead body of Jesus is now absent, with a suggestion that he is relocated

---

33. For a discussion of the notion of the body in 12:18–27, see Caroline Vander Stichele, "Like Angels in Heaven: Corporeality, Resurrection, and Gender in Mark 12:18–27," in *Begin with the Body: Corporeality, Religion and Gender*, ed. Jonneke Bekkenkamp and Maaike de Haardt (Leuven: Peeters, 1998), 215–32.

34. Johannes P. Louw and Eugene A. Nida, *Greek English Lexicon of the New Testament: Based on Semantic Domains*, 2nd ed. (New York: United Bible Societies, 1989); Timothy Friberg, Barbara Friberg, and Neva F. Miller, *Analytical Lexicon of the Greek New Testament* (Grand Rapids: Baker, 2000).

35. Also 2 Macc 3:26, 33; Mark 9:3; Acts 10:30; Rev 6:11, 7:9. Cited in Moloney, *Mark*, 345. See also Yarbro Collins, *Mark*, 795–96.

36. Joel Marcus, *Mark 8–16: A New Translation with Introduction and Commentary*, AB 27B (New Haven: Yale University Press, 2009), 1085.

37. Marcus, *Mark 8–16*, 1085.

to Galilee in a resurrected state that the author does not expound further, although the figure does indicate that the women will be able to "see" Jesus (ὁράω, 16:7). He will be perceptible. As the talk turns to notions of resurrection, the language describing the youth possibly evokes a sense of the supernatural, while the depictions of Jesus's corporeality are vague.[38]

The women's response is visceral. Upon seeing the youth dressed in a white robe, the women are described as becoming alarmed, or "amazed out of themselves" (ἐκθαμβέομαι, 16:5).[39] This state is described in physical terms: their bodies tremble with fear (τρόμος, 16:8). They move into a trance or are astonished (ἔκστασις, 16:8). Their bodies hold and convey the emotions of the episode. Instead of telling others of the raised body, they tell no one. The three women flee the tomb (φεύγω) driven by fear (φοβέω, 16:8). While the descriptions of the women remain in the realm of the concretely corporeal, the portrait of Jesus has shifted to that of a physically absent figure that leaves the women fearful.

Beyond the treatment of Jesus, other figures in the gospel are represented as affected by violence also—either as perpetrators or as victims. The author takes up images of corporal violence in the teachings and speech acts of Jesus. In some instances, bodies are depicted as mutilated, violated, and even killed with no sign of being saved. In 9:42–50, for instance, the notion of the body as a source and site of sin is explored. Initially, the image of suicide through drowning is offered as a reasonable consequence for having put a stumbling block (σκανδαλίζω, 9:42) before little ones (τῶν μικρῶν τούτων, 9:42). There is no saving of such a person, conveyed in the image of having a "great millstone hung around their neck" before they are thrown into the sea (9:42). From 9:43–47, the body itself becomes a site of sin. Three body parts, all of which come in pairs, are causes of sin and are thus mutilated: the hands, feet, and eyes. If the hand causes a person to stumble (σκανδαλίζω), it ought to be severed (9:43).[40] Mark considers being maimed a better option than having two hands and going to hell (9:43). Similar patterns are set up for the foot and eye. The foot is also to be severed (9:45) and the eye torn out (9:47). The disfigured, disabled body, brought about by a grisly mutilation, is preferable to being a sinner or causing others, particularly little ones, to sin. In none of these images is the dismembered body restored.

---

38. Marcus, *Mark 8–16*, 1085.
39. Moloney, *Mark*, 344.
40. The verb σκανδαλίζω can also refer to sin or to being led into sin; giving offense, anger, or shock.

Similarly, pictures of violence and murder are adopted in the parable of 12:1–12. Slaves of a vineyard owner are subjected to brutality at the hands of tenants. The force of the violence increases incrementally as each slave enters the scene: the first is seized, beaten, and sent away empty-handed (12:3); the second beaten over the head and degraded (12:4); the third killed (12:5); others are subsequently beaten and killed (12:5). As the violence intensifies, there are no signs of restoration. In 12:7 similar treatment is meted out to the tenants' ultimate victim: the beloved son of the vineyard owner. That this son is cherished is evident in the familial affection that is signaled in the use of the descriptor ἀγαπητός. In an additional detail, the tenants are described as throwing him—the corpse of the beloved son—out (12:8). His body is discarded, with no further detail of being found or saved. In a final retributive gesture, the owner subsequently destroys the tenants (12:9).[41]

Some final observations are in order concerning the specific portrayals of women in relation to illness, suffering, violation, and death. When we read the narrative with a focus on the body, we notice that adult females are commonly depicted in relation to sickness or to suffering in one form or another, either through disease or through violence.[42] In most instances, the associations are clear. The bleeding woman is a unique figure as she is the only character whose body is described as suffering with the same language used for Jesus in his suffering (πάσχω, 5:26; 8:31; 9:12).[43] Other adult female characters include Simon's mother-in-law (1:29–32), Herodias and her daughter (6:14–29), and the Syrophoenician mother (7:24–31). To signify the end times in chapter 13, the author takes up an image of the suffering to be experienced by pregnant (γαστήρ refers to the belly or womb, i.e., to be pregnant) and nursing women (13:17–19).[44]

---

41. Despite the dominant imagery of destruction, the author introduces a notion of transformation in 12:10. The image of the discarded beloved son is symbolically associated with a context of construction, signified in the image of the cornerstone. Killed and abandoned, the body of the beloved son is correlated to the image of the strongest structure of a building. Through this imagery, the author possibly communicated a notion that fatal violence could become a means through which construction was possible. Put simply, the abject body could mediate hope.

42. Females that are not depicted in relation to bodily sickness and suffering are Jesus's mother (3:31), the poor widow (12:41–44), and the servant girl (14:66–72).

43. Wainwright, *Women Healing/Healing Women*, 119–20.

44. Also 12:18–22. Other teachings that take up images of females but not in relation to bodily sickness, suffering, or death are 10:1–12; 12:40.

There are instances in which the association is less direct. In the case of Mary Magdalene, Mary the mother of James, and Salome, who go to the tomb, they are indirectly associated with suffering and death. They unsuccessfully seek to anoint the body of Jesus whose death and burial they have seen (15:40, 42–47). The woman who anoints Jesus in 14:3 is also indirectly associated with death, anointing Jesus's living body for its eventual burial (14:8). Moreover, she anoints Jesus in a house that is identified with Simon, a man physically sick with leprosy (14:3). Women are largely, although not exclusively, aligned with the vulnerable. This does not preclude them from being depicted as perpetrators, counted among those whose influence is a dangerous tool in the death of the innocent (6:24–28).

2.3. The Body and Emotion

I now turn to another observation concerning the depiction of bodies: expressions of emotion have a corporeal dimension. We have noted this already in the description of Mary Magdalene, Mary the mother of James, and Salome when confronted by the tomb in which Jesus's body was absent. Seized with fear (φοβέω), their bodies trembled (τρόμος), they fled the tomb (φεύγω) and said nothing (16:8). Throughout the narrative, fear is a dominant emotion among adult males and females, with the experience of fear taking on bodily expression, or being associated with physical acts.[45] In 5:33, in response to Jesus's question about who had touched him, the woman is described as coming in "fear [φοβέω] and trembling [τρέμω]."[46] The description of her trembling body communicates her fear. In 6:45–52, the response of the disciples who encounter the φάντασμα is conveyed in their vocalization of fear. Mark notes that they cry out (ἀνακράζω, 6:49) when they see the figure, as they are terrified (ταράσσω, 6:50). The term ἀνακράζω suggests acts of human sound and volume to connote fear. Fear inhibits some characters from killing others (6:14–29; 12:12), and is explained as the basis of the chief priests' desire for Jesus to be killed (11:18). The perception that they are perishing at sea generates a cowardly fear (δειλός) in the disciples, which Jesus further associates with a lack of faith (4:40).

---

45. Amazement is a common reaction also.
46. The term φοβέω is also taken up Mark 5:14 but with no bodily explanation. In 9:32 the disciples are too afraid (φοβέω) to clarify the meaning of Jesus's Son of Man saying in 9:32, which has references to violence, death, and rising.

In a similar way, courage is embodied. In 10:49, Bartimaeus is urged to take courage (θαρσέω). To signify this disposition, he throws off his cloak and responds to Jesus's call. Joseph of Arimathea is described as having courage (τολμάω) that enables him to ask Pilate for the body of Jesus, implying the task was risky (15:43). Suggestions of fear and courage are mediated through bodily sensations and physical acts.

Allusions to or narratives of violence are accompanied by descriptions of the emotions they trigger in particular characters. Herodias's daughter's request for the head of John the Baptizer on a platter stirs sadness in Herod (περίλυπος, 6:26). The disciples are depicted as becoming sad when Jesus suggests that one of those eating with him will betray him (λυπέω, 14:19).[47] As Jesus's death becomes imminent, the language of emotion is evident in the descriptions of Jesus. References to his emotional state occupy three verses of the scene in Gethsemane with Peter, James, and John: two terms are taken up to convey his distress, ἐκθαμβέω and ἀδημονέω (14:33). In 14:34, we encounter references to grief: "And he said to them, 'I am deeply grieved [περίλυπος], even to death; remain here, and keep awake.'" In 14:35, his emotional state is intensified as he throws himself down to pray. According to F. Wilbur Gingrich, the term πίπτω may denote "to collapse," as in a passive form of the idea expressed in βάλλω.[48] The term may also indicate, as is generally the case, to pray or to fall down in an act of devotion. Either way or even taken together, the term may have conveyed an embodiment of the distress and grief of 14:33 and 34.

The experiences of suffering and grief woven throughout the narrative are commonly communicated through the depictions of voice and sound. In 15:34, Jesus's last words are words of abandonment. Uttered in Aramaic in the story, they are then translated into Greek. What is also possibly translated is the bleakness that accompanies the scene of rejection and death. The term used to convey Jesus's final speech act is βοάω, "to cry aloud or shout" (15:34). A loud volume is suggested in the term. The act is given a further acoustic qualifier in the addition of the descriptor: with a loud voice (φωνῇ μεγάλῃ, 15:34). The desolation of the scene is potentially conveyed in the words put on Jesus's lips and intensified in the description of how those words were physically articulated. Likewise, in 14:72, Peter's

---

47. The term λυπέω is used in 10:22 to describe the response of the man to Jesus's suggestion that he sell what he has and give it to the poor and follow Jesus.

48. F. Wilbur Gingrich, *Shorter Lexicon of the Greek New Testament*, rev. Frederick W. Danker, 2nd ed. (Chicago: University of Chicago Press, 1983), s.v. "πίπτω."

grief at his denial of Jesus is physical, expressed in movement and sound. He is described as breaking down or throwing himself down (ἐπιβάλλω) and weeping (κλαίω). The term κλαίω refers to crying or weeping but also implies a lament or wailing. Like the suffering and abandonment that was vocalized through bodily sound and volume in 15:34, grief, too, could be embodied in sound and movement.

Jesus's responses to the person with leprosy in 1:41 and to the crowds in 6:34 and 8:2 are further examples of how bodies are sites of emotion. In each case, it is possible that the terminology that is used links emotions to parts of the body. The term σπλαγχνίζομαι is employed in all three episodes to describe Jesus's reactions. In 1:41, the term explains his response to the person with leprosy who kneels before him begging, asking to be made clean/healed: Jesus is moved with compassion, καὶ σπλαγχνισθεὶς ἐκτείνας τὴν χεῖρα αὐτοῦ ἥψατο καὶ λέγει αὐτῷ·θέλω, καθαρίσθητι· (1:41). In 6:34, the term is used to describe his reaction to the crowd who appear to Jesus "like sheep without a shepherd" (6:34). The term is again employed in chapter 8 to explain Jesus's response to the crowd who had been with him for three days but had nothing to eat (8:2).

Francoise Mirguet's work on the evolution of this term in Judeo-Hellenistic literature illuminates possible seams of meaning in the narrative of Mark.[49] She contends that words with the root σπλαγχν are derived from the noun σπλάγχνα, which referred to any part of the innards, for example, stomach, kidney, heart, lungs, womb.[50] Around the second century BCE, the term was invested with meanings associated with the emotions, particularly feelings of compassion. In Jewish literature, σπλάγχνα could suggest a seat of emotion; in some cases the emotions could be so intense that they moved the body, or even damaged organs (Josephus, *B.J.* 1.81). It also connoted parental affection (both maternal and paternal) in response to the suffering or vulnerability of a child (e.g., 4 Macc 15:23). She observes that

---

49. Francoise Mirguet, "Emotional Responses to the Suffering of Others: Explorations in Judeo-Hellenistic Literature" (paper presented at the Research Symposium Harvard Center for Hellenic Studies, Washington, DC, 26 April 2013). Here I follow NA[28], which goes with the majority reading, but note that the SBLGNT adopts the reading in D: ὀργισθείς ("to anger").

50. E.g., Philo, *Opif.* 118. For another example whereby a body is associated with emotion in Mark, see the reference to the people being "hard of heart" in 3:5. This state, visible to Jesus, provokes anger and grief (3:5). Another example of Jesus's anger is 10:14.

this usage was also taken up metaphorically to represent responses to the suffering and vulnerability of others beyond children. In these situations, the term connoted a deeply felt emotion akin to that of a parent. She notes, "Feeling in one's σπλάγχνα the suffering of others evokes the immediacy and intensity of a mother's or father's affection for a child."[51] Terms that were constructed from σπλαγχν, therefore, conveyed, "a sensation, felt in the body," an embodied compassion.[52]

When we read the story of the person with leprosy (1:41) and the feeding of the crowds (6:3; 8:2) in light of these connotations, an additional layer in their representations becomes visible. Their circumstances rendered them vulnerable in such a way that they evoked a visceral response of compassion in Jesus that may have been likened to that of a parent for a child who suffered or was in danger. The use of σπλαγχνίζομαι therefore possibly conveyed a pathos concerning those who were diseased, lost without a leader, and hungry as a result of following Jesus. Concomitantly, the application of the term revealed an image of Jesus who was physically affected by such vulnerability.

In my view, the narrative draws a person into the realm of emotions. The body and the world of emotions appear inseparable; the physical and the emotional are interrelated. Expressions of fear, sadness, and grief are prominent, bringing the pathos of abandonment, violence, and death up close to anyone who engaged with the narrative. The descriptions of emotion reveal an interpretation of the actions committed by and upon the body in the unfolding narrative. In this way, experiences of betrayal, suffering, and death are interpreted through expressions of fear and grief. Those lost without a shepherd, those who identified with the figure of Jesus but were now without food, and those who continued to be ill, encountered images of deeply felt compassion in the narrative. For others removed from such experiences, they were confronted with a narrative world in which distress, fear, and grief defined experiences of rejection, suffering, and death in relation to Jesus, and in which the abandoned and those who suffered elicited compassion. Courage in such circumstances was translated through actions.

---

51. Mirguet, "Emotional Responses to the Suffering of Others," 20.
52. Mirguet, "Emotional Responses to the Suffering of Others," 48.

2.4. Sensory Functions

We now consider my final observation: throughout the narrative, the body is depicted in terms of its sensory functions.[53] Many of the characters we encounter are painted as sentient beings. References to the voice and speech, to ears and hearing, eyes and seeing, to touch, taste, movement, and possibly smell populate the narrative from the beginning to end.[54] Of these functions, bodily activity related to the voice, particularly speech, is the dominant sensory act.[55] Numerous characters throughout the gospel are depicted in terms of orality, that is, in terms of what they express aloud in words and sound. I will concentrate on four dominant forms: commands, questions, notions of the voice, and requests.

2.4.1. Orality

2.4.1.1. Commands

The most prevalent representation of speech takes the form of commands. One of the main ways in which Jesus relates to the disciples is through sets of commands and instructions. From the first chapter, Jesus is depicted as calling for specific men to follow him, and they immediately respond (1:17, 20; 2:14; 3:13–14). Later in the narrative, Jesus calls for them again,

---

53. By the terms *senses* and *sensory function*, I mean "bodily ways of acting and knowing." See Louise Lawrence, "Exploring the Sense-Scape of the Gospel of Mark," *JSNT* 33 (2011): 391.

54. The use of the term ἄρωμα, which refers to the sweet perfume or herbs to be used for anointing Jesus's body, may have evoked a sense of smell (16:1). Likewise, the reference to μέρον, a perfume considered to be a luxury item that was used for religious festivals, burial practices, and "personal indulgence," may have brought to mind a sense of smell when the woman anointed Jesus in 14:1–11. See Raoul McLaughlin, *The Roman Empire and the Indian Ocean: Rome's Dealings with the Ancient Kingdoms of India, Africa and Arabia* (London: Pen & Sword, 2014), 38–39. Taste is referenced in 9:1, "Truly I tell you, there are some standing here who will not taste death until they see that the kingdom of God has come with power." Lawrence comments on the rare occurrences of taste and smell in Mark's Gospel ("Exploring the Sense-Scape," 389).

55. Speaking is a sensory faculty—a "bodily way of acting and knowing"—in Mark. Lawrence argues that the act of speaking is the most important faculty for Mark. Jesus's identity is expressed through speech or proclamation. Concomitantly, revelation is understood by hearing, which, statistically, is the most featured sense in the gospel (Lawrence, "Exploring the Sense-Scape," 391–92).

sends them out, instructs them what to wear and tells them what to do when they encounter hostility (6:7–11). In 6:8 the author uses the term παραγγέλλω to paint Jesus as ordering the disciples to be frugal as they set out on the way, with instructions that they "take nothing for their journey except a staff; no bread, no bag, no money in their belts; but to wear sandals and not to put on two tunics" (6:8–9).[56] Later in chapter 6, Jesus directs the disciples to attend to the hungry crowd. When the disciples wish to send the crowd away to purchase food, Jesus directs them instead to feed the crowd, conveyed through the use of the imperative of δίδωμι, "You give them something to eat" (6:37). This directive comes on the back of the instruction to give something to eat to Jairus's restored daughter in 5:43. In this case, Jesus tells the three hand-picked disciples—Peter, James, and John—as well as the girl's parents to feed the child. By chapter 6, Jesus's directive to feed others has broadened to incorporate the twelve disciples. The population they must feed numbers at least five thousand men (5:44).[57]

Jesus intervenes in times of extremity through the use of spoken commands. Confronted by a ghost-like figure that terrifies the disciples, Jesus instructs them to "Take heart, it is I; do not be afraid" (6:50). As Jairus encounters the news that his daughter has died, Jesus tells him, "Do not fear, only believe" (5:36). In each case, the imperative mood is used to construct Jesus's commanding speech acts. When the disciples are confronted with a turbulent sea and wind that fuels their fears of perishing, Jesus rebukes the wind (ἐπιτιμάω) and commands the sea, "Peace! Be still!" (4:39). Both verbs, σιωπάω and φιμόω, are used in the imperative. The wind and sea subsequently obey Jesus's commands. Early in the narrative, Jesus is recognized for his capacity to voice commands (ἐπιτάσσω) that unclean spirits subsequently obey (1:27). This authority over unclean spirits that is embodied in his commands is illustrated throughout the narrative (3:12; 5:8; and 9:25). In extreme times, Jesus's commands engender faith, calm, and restoration.

Jesus voices commands to those who possess extreme bodily conditions. The man who was unable to move (2:11), the man with a withered hand (3:5), the man described as deaf and having a speech impedi-

---

56. Jesus instructs the man in 10:21 likewise to live frugally—in addition to enacting the commandments—in order to gain eternal life.

57. Despite the directive to feed the crowd, Jesus takes over the activity of the scene in directing the crowd to sit down and taking, blessing, and giving the loaves and fish to the disciples for distribution, 6:39–41. Likewise 8:6.

ment (7:34), and the dead daughter of Jairus (5:41) are each in a state in which their bodies are understood to have limitations. Clearly, Jairus's deceased daughter is the most extreme case of these. In each instance, Jesus's command is concerned with causing an alteration to the state of the character's body. In the case of the deaf and voiceless man and the deceased daughter of Jairus, the author articulates these commands first in Aramaic and then in Greek.[58] In all cases, Jesus voices a command that leads to physical restoration.

In two of these stories, once the character has been restored Jesus delivers further orders. In the restorations of the deaf, voiceless man and the dead child of Jairus, Jesus is depicted as expressly telling no one to communicate what has occurred (διαστέλλομαι, 5:43; 7:36). In the latter case, the command goes unheeded as they proclaim what has happened throughout the Decapolis. In the former case, there is no further detail (also 9:9).

In contrast, there are instances in which Jesus directs those who have been restored from sickness to health not to desist from living the benefits of restoration openly. The Gerasene demoniac is told to "go" (ὑπάγω) to his family and tell them of the mercy he has been shown. He does this, extending his proclaiming throughout the Decapolis (5:20). The bleeding woman is told to "go [ὑπάγω] in peace, and be healed of your disease" (5:34). Bartimaeus, having regained sight, is told by Jesus to "go" (ὑπάγω), and he subsequently follows Jesus on the way (10:52).[59]

Speech has power in the narrative. It is a physical act that affects bodies. The commands voiced by Jesus function to convey his power over the destructive forces of nature, of unclean spirits, of illness, and over death itself.[60] On the one hand, this capacity is proclaimed widely, demonstrated in the response to the transformation of the Gerasene demoniac. On the other hand, there is also a need to conceal Jesus's power over the forces of physical impairment and death.[61]

---

58. Mark 5:41: "ταλιθα κουμ … σοὶ λέγω, ἔγειρε." ("Talitha cum," which means, "Little girl, get up!"); 7:34: "εφφαθα, ὅ ἐστιν διανοίχθητι." ("Ephphatha," that is, "Be opened,"). The Markan Jesus again utters words in Aramaic when his own body is an extreme state in the crucifixion in 15:34. In this instance, he voices words of rejection, not commands.

59. The case appears ambiguous in 8:26.

60. Lawrence, "Exploring the Sense-Scape," 391.

61. For observations about this concealment of Jesus's power in relation to the

While most of the commands that are voiced in the gospel are placed on the lips of Jesus, he is not the only character who issues instructions. In order to observe the oath that he has made to the young Herodias at a birthday banquet in the presence of his elite guests, Herod (albeit reluctantly) orders (ἐπιτάσσω) a soldier to bring to him the head of John the Baptizer (6:27). The Baptizer is subsequently beheaded and his head brought to the girl on a platter (6:28). This is no story of restoration but an account of grisly violence. Likewise leading into an act of violence, the crowd is depicted as giving directives during the passion narrative. In 15:13–14, they cry out to Pilate to have Jesus killed. Depicted as being incited by the chief priests, the crowd demands that Jesus is to be crucified, a demand to which Pilate acquiesces (15:13–15). In both 6:27 and 15:13–14, spoken directives convey the power of the speakers over the life and death of others. In contrast to the commands of Jesus, however, the speech acts of Herod and the crowd lead only to death. Their instructions provoke extreme situations rather than intervening in experiences of liminality; they are depicted as possessing no capacity to restore life or to enable peace and faith. Unlike the orders voiced by Jesus, in the cases of Herod and the crowd their directives lead to death.

2.4.1.2. Questions

The voicing of questions is another common feature of the narrative. Individuals and groups, invariably comprising Pharisees and in some instances Sadducees and scribes, are routinely depicted as posing questions in scenes of debate. Some questions reveal various views concerning how the law was to be observed, for example, fasting (2:18) and levirate marriages in relation to notions of resurrection (12:18–22). On other occasions, the questions are concerned with Jesus's authority (6:2–3; 11:27–33). In some instances, Jesus's answers are monological, thus moving away from a debate of views to a medium for communicating Jesus's stance (2:16–17, 24–28; 7:5–13).

Other questions are explicitly presented as a means of trapping Jesus. The Pharisees (10:2) and the Pharisees and Herodians (12:13–15) feature in scenes of debate over questions of Jewish practice, that is, approaches to

---

secrecy motif in Mark's Gospel, see Moloney, *Gospel of Mark*, 111 n. 207, and 150 n. 70.

2. The Body in the Gospel of Mark

divorce (10:1–2) and to paying taxes to the emperor (12:14). The motivation behind their questions is presented pejoratively. The term πειράζω ("to test or tempt") is used to describe the motivation of the Pharisees (10:2).[62] In 12:13, the Pharisees and Herodians are sent to trap Jesus (ἀγρεύω). The questions then become a vehicle for depicting hostility between the groups and Jesus, portraying the groups as a menacing presence in the narrative. This hostility and the negative imaging of the high priest, chief priests, elders, and scribes reaches its peak in the questions posed to Jesus in the passion narrative. The high priest's question: "Are you the Messiah, the Son of the Blessed One?" (14:61) is voiced within a context in which the chief priests and whole council have previously been depicted as desiring the death of Jesus (14:55). Pilate's subsequent question also concerns Jesus's identity, "Are you the king of the Jews?" (15:2). On both occasions, the questions function to allow Jesus to assert his identity, which in turn further fuels the hostility of the chief priests.

Other forms of questions are concerned with seeking understanding. The man with many possessions, for example, asks Jesus about attaining eternal life (10:17). The wise scribe asks which commandment is the first (12:28). The disciples ask why they could not cast the unclean spirit from the boy (9:28).[63] Each question functions to provide opportunities for Jesus to articulate a teaching.

In 14:4–5, questions convey a lack of understanding. The disciples' angry question about why a woman should waste money on expensive ointment to anoint Jesus's head is countered by Jesus's explanation that she has anointed his body for its burial. In addition, he affirms her action: "wherever the good news is proclaimed in the whole world, what she has done will be told in remembrance of her" (14:9). Jesus's response suggests that the question posed by the disciples is misguided. The depiction of the disciples as misguided is a common theme in the narrative. The questions articulated by the disciples sometimes contribute to their portrayal as figures who fail to understand Jesus. In 6:37, they question how they can feed the hungry crowd whom Jesus has previously directed them to feed. In 9:10, Peter, James, and John struggle to comprehend Jesus's statements about rising from the dead. They are described as asking what this could mean, although the questions are not posed to Jesus in this

---

62. The verb πειράζω is used to describe the motivation of Satan in 1:13. For other applications to the motivation behind the Pharisee's questions, see 8:11 and 12:15.
63. Also 4:10; 9:11; 10:26; and 13:4.

case but kept to themselves, possibly suggesting a discomfort in being uncertain.[64] Not the reserve of the disciples, in 6:6 the questions of those in the synagogue communicate that Jesus's own kin do not understand fully who he is.

2.4.1.3. The Voice

While some characters articulate questions that reveal a lack of understanding of who Jesus is or what he is on about, in some instances the spoken word is used explicitly to identify Jesus. The narrative begins with a voice that is associated with God. Moloney explains it as the "voice of the narrator open[ing] the story, but what he announces reflects an omniscience [associated with] the design of God."[65] Together, the narrator and God can be understood as verbally announcing that the story to follow is the good news of Jesus Christ (Χριστός), the Son of God (1:1).[66] In 1:2–3, God speaks through the words of the prophet Isaiah to state that a "voice [φωνή] in the wilderness"—John the Baptizer—will precede the coming of "the Lord [Κύριος]."[67] The role of the Baptizer will be *to voice* the coming of the Lord.[68] In these instances, references to the voice conjure up the realm of the divine. They are used as a vehicle for asserting who Jesus is: the Anointed One, the Son of God, the Lord.[69]

Through the divine voice in 1:11, another elaboration of the identity of Jesus is evident. A heavenly voice (φωνή) speaks, identifying Jesus as

---

64. They also keep their questions to themselves in 9:10.
65. Moloney, *Gospel of Mark*, 29.
66. I note the phrase "Son of God" does not appear in some manuscripts, notably Codex Sinaiticus. I follow Moloney, who argues that whether the title is authentic in 1:1 is not crucial; the title "Son of God" for Jesus in Mark's Gospel is appropriate (Moloney, *Gospel of Mark*, 29 n. 11).
67. On Mark's use of Isaiah, see Moloney, *Gospel of Mark*, 29.
68. The spoken activity of proclaiming is described of John the Baptizer (1:4, 7), Jesus (1:14–15, 39), the disciples (6:12), and the Gerasene demoniac (5:20).
69. The speech act of the centurion, indicated by the verb λέγω, also identifies Jesus as God's Son in 15:39. The centurion's words are a result of what he "sees" (ὁράω) while facing Jesus as he breathes his last (15:39). Unclean spirits identify Jesus as the Son of God through acts of speech: 3:11; 5:7. In 1:24, the unclean spirit identifies Jesus as "Jesus of Nazareth" and the "Holy One of God." Note that in 1:34 and 3:12, Mark describes Jesus as not permitting the unclean spirits to speak because they know him. Bartimaeus identifies Jesus as "son of David" as he cries out to him (10:47, 48).

"my Son, the Beloved." The reference to the voice ascribes to God a human bodily feature. The words uttered by God to describe the relationship between God and Jesus are affectionate, "the beloved" (ὁ ἀγαπητός, 1:11) and are derived from the realm of language associated with family, "my son" (ὁ υἱός μου, 1:11; also 9:7). Through a divine voice, the author presents Jesus as a deeply loved son and God as a loving parent.

2.4.1.4. Requests

Other utterances that disclose an understanding of Jesus's identity are expressed in the form of requests. On several occasions, characters request the intervention of Jesus. Many beg (παρακαλέω) Jesus: the person with leprosy begs to be made clean (1:40); Legion begs not to be sent to the country (5:10); Jairus begs that Jesus lay his hands on his daughter so that she may be made well and live (5:23).[70] The Syrophoenician woman asks (ἐρωτάω) Jesus to cast the demon from her daughter (7:26). Blind Bartimaeus cries out to Jesus (κράζω) for mercy (10:47). In these utterances, each character is depicted as voicing a belief that Jesus has the capacity to intervene in what are extreme physical states; the utterances are not described as polite requests but connote the speech acts of desperate figures who seek to attract Jesus's attention in the hope of gaining a form of transformation. In other words, the distress that might have been conveyed through the use of terms such as παρακαλέω and κράζω functions to underscore the portrait of Jesus's successful capacity to alter the trajectory of extreme illness and suffering.[71]

Not all requests point to the identity of Jesus and to aspirations for transformation. Some requests to Jesus highlight the disciples' misguided notions of who Jesus is and the implications of identifying with him (10:35, 38). In two instances, requests lead to violent deaths. The crowd approaches Pilate to ask (αἰτέω) for the release of a prisoner, which contributes to the dynamic of the narrative whereby the crowd, depicted as being prompted by chief priests (15:11), move to demand the crucifixion of Jesus (15:8). In 6:25, having been asked by Herod to request (αἰτέω) whatever she wishes, the young Herodias requests John the Baptizer's head on a platter. The girl's request—the only speech act uttered by a child in

---

70. Also 5:12, 17, 18; 6:56; 7:32; 8:22.
71. Elaine Scarry, *The Body in Pain: The Making and Unmaking of the World* (Oxford: Oxford University Press, 1985), 6.

the narrative—suggests her obedience to her mother's words.[72] The girl voices the desire of her mother, Herodias, who is represented as wanting the baptizer dead (6:19, 24). She repeats her mother's request, embellished with the descriptor, "on a platter" (6:25), the words of which, when voiced by the young girl, possibly reinforce the corruption of the scene.[73] The fulfillment of the request is represented with the grisly image of John's decapitated head being brought into the imperial banquet scene on a platter usually associated with serving food (πίναξ) and given to the girl who gives it to her mother (6:28). There is no reference to the thinking or emotions of either the crowd nor the girl, which is perhaps striking given the outcomes of their requests and the fact that on occasions throughout the narrative the thoughts and feelings of characters are identified. Instead, their requests may be viewed as vehicles for articulating the iniquitous desires of the chief priests, Herodias, and Herod.

2.4.2. Aurality and the Visual

Given the importance of speech and voice in the narrative, it stands to reason that the faculty of hearing is also significant. This is apparent in 9:7, during the transfiguration, when a voice (φωνή) from the cloud identifies Jesus as its beloved son and directs those present to "listen" (ἀκούω) to him. It is also evident in 4:9 when, after having taught the crowd through the parables of the sower and the seed (4:3–20) and the lamp (4:21–22), Jesus directly commands those with ears (οὖς) to hear (ἀκούω; also 4:23). The sense of hearing, as Louise Lawrence puts it, "had an important part to play in 'making sense of' the good news among Mark's hearers."[74]

Alongside the faculty of hearing, another sense that is prominent in the narrative is that of sight. That the possession of sight is important

---

72. I refer to the girl as a "child" on the basis that she is depicted as a daughter in a familial context. She is labeled as θυγάτηρ and κοράσιον, as is Jairus's daughter (5:35, 42) and the daughter of the Syrophoenician woman (7:25, 27, 29), both of whom are explained in relation to parental figures and are regarded as children. Moreover, there is no reference to her marital status. See Betsworth, *Children in Early Christian Narratives*, 59.

73. Betsworth observes that Herodias junior is the only child in the gospel who is not brought to Jesus for healing or a blessing touch. Instead, the girl obeys the requests of her mother and is thus brought into "corrupt human ways" (*Children in Early Christian Narratives*, 62).

74. Lawrence, "Exploring the Sense-Scape," 389.

in the narrative is clear in 10:51–52.[75] Bartimaeus is described as blind (τυφλός, 10:46), a state that he wishes to overcome, signified in his speech to Jesus (10:47, 48, 51). His desire for sight is intensified with the application of κράζω; he cries out loudly so that his requests may be heard (10:47, 48).[76] His sight is subsequently restored (ἀναβλέπω) by Jesus, a state that is affirmed by the description that Bartimaeus then follows Jesus on the way (10:52). Seeing and hearing are distinct sensory functions in the narrative, and are treated separately, but they are also paired in the gospel. When combined, they function to mediate ideas about understanding and misunderstanding.

The faculty of hearing is primarily concerned with the process of perception in the narrative, rather than the capacity of a person to take in sounds through their ears. Aural perception is constructed in such a way so as to depict those who correctly understand the words of Jesus and, in contrast, to portray figures who perceive his words and take offense. The bleeding woman, falling into the former category, approaches Jesus in the hope of being made well on the basis of what she has heard (ἀκούω) of Jesus (5:27). The implication is that the woman has done more than take in the sounds of the spoken testimonies to Jesus's cures. Her hearing of such words has involved an understanding that they attest to a particular occurrence associated with healing. Likewise, the Syrophoenician mother approaches Jesus to cast demons from her daughter on the basis of what she too has heard of him (ἀκούω, 7:25). Hearing in both instances involves understanding, and is associated with the perception of Jesus's capacity to restore the ill (also 7:14). In the case of the chief priests and scribes, their hearing of what Jesus says about the temple serving as a "den of robbers" (11:17) involves perception but their understanding is depicted as leading to fear and a desire for Jesus's death (11:18).

Sight is also associated with perception. Jesus "sees" disciples and then tells them to follow him (ὁράω, 1:16, 19; 2:14). He "sees" the disciples speak

---

75. I concur with Lawrence, although, that, in the case of Bartimaeus, blindness does not correlate with having an "obtuse faith" or being "unperceptive." Blind, Bartimaeus nonetheless identifies Jesus as "Son of David" and "my teacher," which may signal his perception of Jesus's messianic role (Lawrence, "Exploring the Sense-Scape," 391).

76. Lawrence notes that the human cry can be the act of rising above one's situation, or acting against it ("Exploring the Sense-Scape," 392). She cites Scarry, *Body in Pain*, 51.

sternly to children and those who bring them, and becomes indignant (ὁράω, 10:14). In 2:5, the term ὁράω is used to note that the faith of those who bring in the paralytic is able to be seen by Jesus. Faith is perceptible through sight. In 10:21, Jesus is described as fixing his gaze on the man (ἐμβλέπω) who asks him about eternal life, and subsequently loving him, presumably on the basis of what he perceives. Each instance demonstrates that perceptions are formed through acts of seeing, which then prompt action or emotion (also 14:67).

Sight and its association with perception are a means of recognizing Jesus. In a similar vein to those who had *heard* of Jesus's reputation to heal, other figures *see* Jesus and then approach him. The Gerasene demoniac and Jairus both "see" (ὁράω) Jesus and fall before him (5:6, 22; also 9:20). The demoniac falls at Jesus's feet in a posture associated with worship, προσκυνέω (5:6). Jairus throws himself at the feet of Jesus, πιπτώ, also in a gesture possibly associated with devotion (5:2). Their seeing and subsequent actions suggest an acknowledgement of Jesus's identity as one worthy of being exalted, if not worshiped. What the Roman centurion sees and perceives in 15:39 is particularly instructive. "Facing" (ἐναντίος, 15:39) Jesus, the centurion sees Jesus die (ὁράω, 15:39). Jesus's death is depicted in terms of a loud scream and a last breath, accompanied by the tearing of the temple curtain (15:38). The combination of these events leads the centurion to identify Jesus as the Son of God (15:39). In this instance, the author presents sight and perception in relation to Jesus's death as constitutive of an understanding of who Jesus is as a son of God.[77]

Given that both sight and hearing are taken up in relation to possessing understanding, it is not surprising that they are also paired up in the discussions of who understands and who misunderstands Jesus. In the conversation between Jesus and the disciples concerning the parables, Jesus points out that those on the "outside," or out of doors (ἔξω), are unable to understand despite being able to see and hear: "they may indeed look [ὁράω], but not perceive, and may indeed listen [ἀκούω], but not understand; so that they may not turn again and be forgiven" (4:12). In other words, those on the *inside* are able to make sense of the mystery

---

77. Mark also takes up references to sight to describe variants in understanding. The disciples see the pressing crowd in 5:31, for instance, and cannot understand why Jesus would ask who has touched him. Jesus, on the other hand, continues to look around (περιβλέπομαι) to identify the guilty party amid the throng. See also the gradual restoration of sight in 8:23, 24, 25.

of God's reign through what they see and hear, and thus understand. For those on the outside, their perception is partial.[78]

If Jesus's words in 4:12 suggest the disciples possess the capacity to understand Jesus, then his words of 8:18 indicate otherwise. Pictured as thinking they have no bread—despite the abundance of 8:8—Jesus questions the disciples' ability to understand him (8:17). Their lack of perception is described in terms of having eyes but failing to see, and ears but failing to hear (8:18). This state is correlated further with another corporeal image, "hardened hearts" (8:17). The lack of understanding of Jesus's actions—the inability to see and hear—is related to a petrification (πωρόω, 8:17) of the disciples' own being (καρδία, 8:17).[79] Using the term καρδία, this hardening is not merely related to the realm of a person's disposition but also appears embodied. The disciples' incapacity to make sense of Jesus has a bodily dimension.

2.4.3. Touch

We have been concentrating on how the faculties of speech, hearing, and sight—the dominant sensory functions in the narrative—convey ideas. A number of episodes, however, feature gestures involving physical touch. As we have already observed, touch is an element in many accounts in which ill and disfigured bodies are altered. In particular, the interaction of Jesus's body, often his hands, with the body of another person is the locus of transformation. These instances of touch, however, do not encapsulate the full picture of this sensory action. In addition to healing people, in his teachings concerning the reign of God Jesus touches children who appear neither ill nor disfigured. [80]

---

78. From 4:14–20, Jesus uses the metaphor of hearing the word (λόγος) in the parable of the sower. Each act of hearing the word (λόγος) faces a threat: Satan immediately takes the word away (4:15); when trouble or persecution arise some immediately fall away despite initially receiving the word with joy (4:16–17); the lure of wealth and desire for things to come choke the word and it yields nothing (4:19). In contrast, those who "hear the word and accept it bear fruit" (4:20).

79. Danker explains καρδία as an expression of a person's physical being and need; the center of their personhood. Frederick William Danker, *The Concise Greek-English Lexicon of the New Testament* (Chicago: University of Chicago Press, 2009), s.v. "καρδία."

80. Two other instances in which gestures of touch are unrelated to healing are 4:44–45; 14:3–9.

In both 9:33–50 and 10:13–16, Jesus is depicted as touching children. In 9:36, he takes a little child and puts it among the disciples. He then takes the child in his arms (ἐναγκαλίζομαι, 9:36) as he launches into his teaching on hospitality (9:37). In 10:13, "people" bring children to Jesus in order that he might touch them (ἅπτω). His response, despite the protestations of the disciples, is threefold with the first two actions explicitly involving touch (10:16). First, he takes them in his arms, again signaled by the use of the term ἐναγκαλίζομαι. Then, he lays his hands on them. Finally, he blesses them (κατευλογέω). While each episode occurs in a house, the children are separated by Jesus from the other adults and positioned in close proximity to him and, particularly in the case of 9:36, amidst the disciples.

In whatever way these gestures may have been understood by a hearer in the first century CE, one possible interpretation is that they conjured up ideas about the bonds that existed between children and adults among those who identified with Jesus. Images of physical contact between children and their family members were commonplace in the first century CE, and could connote the ties that bound families.[81] The tactile gestures ascribed to Jesus, in tandem with teachings about hospitality (9:37) and to whom the reign of God belongs (10:14), and who may enter it (10:15), possibly identified children within the fold of those associated with Jesus.[82]

---

81. The discussion of the use of physical contact to depict familial bonds between children and adults/parents appears in ch. 4. Larsson Loven observes that by the first century CE, more interaction and physical contact between family members, such as placing arms around each other, is evident in Roman commemorative art. For her discussion of how bonds are created through depictions of physical contact, see Lena Larsson Loven, "Children and Childhood in Roman Commemorative Art," in Bell, Grubbs, and Parkin, *Oxford Handbook of Childhood*, 306–7.

82. Betsworth raises the question as to whether "such as these" (10:14) implies that the reign of God belongs to children, or alternatively that children are included in the reign of God. She appears to consider either option as plausible as both allow for a reversal of what she considers as the marginalized status of children in the first century CE. In light of the reading that I have offered that considers the physical dimensions of the story, the second option that discusses inclusion is reinforced (Betsworth, *Children in Early Christian Narratives*, 68–69). Likewise, Murphy argues that the better reading is the one concerned with inclusion. He discusses a problem with the notion of children "possessing" the kingdom: "A gift to a child from his father is one thing, but a gift from a stranger would likely be subject to the approval of the *pater*." Reading with the place of the body in mind, the children are set apart and brought into physical relationship with Jesus and into physical proximity to the disciples, suggesting that the connection to family is of lesser significance than the connection to Jesus and the

While the activities are located in a house, and therefore possibly implied familial life, Jesus's gestures position the children somewhat apart from their family members and place them within a context of discipleship, thus painting a picture in which children share ties with him and his disciples, possibly one step removed from their own families.

2.4.4. Movement

The narrative of Mark is characterized by movement. Jesus is depicted as a man who "never rests," who is "endlessly on the move."[83] Not limited to Jesus, the disciples and those men and women associated with him beyond the Twelve are also often characterized by movement. Characters who identify with Jesus routinely "follow" him (1:17–18, 20; 2:14; 3:7; 5:37; 6:1; 9:38; 10:32; 14:51, 54; 15:41), accompanying him "on the way" (9:33; 10:32, 52). Despite the prevalence of these images, there is also another form of physical movement, however, which is entirely distinct from that of traversing territories and domestic and public spaces with Jesus, often in seeming haste. The daughter of Herodias stands out as the only figure in the narrative described in terms of dance (6:22).

Herodias's daughter is uniquely described as dancing. The physicality of no other character throughout the narrative—male or female, child or adult—is depicted this way. There are no indications in the story that she is married. Nor does the author suggest that her identity is primarily that of an unmarried or soon to be married female. In first-century CE literature, this latter state was commonly signaled by the use of the label παρθένος, but the term does not appear in the episode.[84] It is thus conceivable that she is still a child, or at least not an adult, and her identity is primarily defined by the familial and imperial contexts. From this perspective, the girl can be understood as a female child of an elite family dancing at a banquet for prominent members of the court.

There are no descriptions concerning the type of dance performed by the girl, nor how she performs the dance. The recent insights of Betsworth prove helpful in understanding the possible dynamics in the scene that Mark paints. She observes that, while women were gradually

---

disciples. This reading supports Murphy's interpretation of inclusion rather than possession (*Kids and Kingdom*, 84–85).

83. Moloney, *Gospel of Mark*, 51.

84. For comments on the term παρθένος, see chs. 4 and 5.

being permitted into public banquets, women who performed at such banquets would have been considered prostitutes. The image of a child of an elite family dancing at such a banquet, therefore, would have been deemed "shocking" and indicative of "debauchery."[85] As a result, such a scene with the female child at the center possibly carried suggestions of corruption.

The emphasis of the dance is the effect it has on Herod and his guests: she pleases them (ἀρέσκω, 6:22). This results in the king promising the girl anything she desires, including half his kingdom (6:23). The largesse of the promise suggests that the appeal of the dance is powerful. It is through the child's body that she exercises power—knowingly or unknowingly, as there are no markers to reveal her thinking. Instead, it is the thinking of Herod that is made known (6:26). While the girl's dance is provocative, it is plausible that her depiction functions to underscore the status and disposition of Herod, rather than to say anything about her. Put differently, the image of the dancing female child-daughter can be seen to reinforce a portrait of Herod (and his wife Herodias) as corrupt.

2.5. Summary

My assessment of the many depictions of the body indicate a narrative in which illness, disfigurement, suffering, violence, and death were fundamental themes. Not the preferred state of being, often these extreme situations provoked emotions of fear, sadness, distress, and grief, relieved with the occasional expressions of compassion and courage—emotions all associated with the body. These extreme experiences were not absolute, however. Instead, through interaction with Jesus's own body illness and suffering could be transformed. Engagement with Jesus's body is depicted as the medium by which people were restored to health, peace, and life.

Ideas are also mediated throughout the narrative through the ways in which the senses are constructed. The voice is a vehicle by which notions concerning Jesus's identity are made audible. The speech acts of Jesus reveal a man who had power over the forces of destruction to restore peace and life, while the speech acts of other powerful figures lead only to death. Hearing and seeing are associated with the process of perception, and come to communicate ideas about understanding and misunderstanding

---

85. Betsworth, *Children in Early Christian Narratives*, 60.

Jesus. Gestures of touch, powerful sources of healing for the ill and disfigured, are also used with children to convey ideas about who is included in the reign of God. At the same time, the provocative dancing body of the child—Herodias's young daughter—underscores the darkness of Herod's and Herodias's world.

Conspicuous by their absence in a narrative that promotes the power of speech, children are the only figures who do not speak, with the exception of Herodias's daughter, who arguably speaks for her mother. Likewise, in a narrative that explores ideas about hearing and understanding, it is striking that Jesus never speaks to children, with the exception of Jairus's daughter in 5:41, which we will discuss in chapter 7. Even in 9:37 and 10:14, 15, where children are hugged by Jesus, he speaks to the disciples only, not to the children.

While these insights are apparent to this twenty-first century reader, they raise the question as to what extent a person in the first century CE would have also noticed them. Furthermore, if they did observe the usage of bodily imagery, what bearing might it have had on their understanding of the story of Jairus's daughter? In order to explore these questions, it is necessary first to address some rudimentary questions: What do we know about those who may have engaged with Mark's narrative? What do we know about how they thought about the body, particularly the bodies of women and female children? We now turn out attention to these questions.

3
The Landscape of the Hearer in the First Century CE

> Let anyone with ears to hear listen!
> —Mark 4:23

We have observed that depictions of the body can be understood to function as a vehicle for mediating ideas in Mark's Gospel. We will now consider how a person living in the first century CE may have heard the story of Jairus's daughter, a story that has the image of a dying and deceased daughter as its focus. The world of the first century CE was populated with images of the body, including representations of women and female children. These images were part of the world in which people encountered the story of Jairus's daughter. Before we embark on the investigation of those representations that were part of shaping a hearer's thinking, it is necessary first to identify the sources that will form the basis of our examination and to discuss how these sources will be used.

3.1. The World of a Hearer

3.1.1. Markan Provenance

Our discussion of sources starts with the issue of identifying the context of the hearer of Mark's Gospel. To begin with, it is necessary first to comment briefly on my use of the term *hearer*. As we have already noted in chapter 2, the faculty of hearing is prized in Mark. As Mark 4:23 suggests, it is not merely the ability to take in sound but also the capacity to perceive what is being said (especially by Jesus) that is valued. My use of the term hearer in this investigation also indicates a focus on perception. I am interested in some of the factors that may have influenced the perceptions of people in the first century CE when they encountered the story of Jairus's daughter.

On a pragmatic level, it is likely that the majority of people in the ancient world were unable to read complex written texts, certainly with any ease.[1] We may assume, therefore, that one of the main ways people readily accessed information and ideas was as a hearer. They engaged aurally with a variety of texts that were delivered orally. Indeed, it is likely that Mark's narrative was predominantly heard rather than read.[2] Visual media also communicated ideas throughout the world of the first century CE. While some of these media incorporated written texts, they also featured pictorial images to convey ideas, and people therefore accessed information and attitudes as viewers or observers. As our investigation will reveal, there was a complex network of text (oral and written) and image that came to bear on a person's consciousness, as they inhabited the world of the first century CE. Bearing this complexity in mind, my use of hearer generally denotes a person who may have encountered the narrative.

One possible starting point for attempting to situate the Markan hearer is along the lines of one of the current hypotheses regarding the provenance of Mark. The issue of specifically where and for whom Mark's Gospel was written remains a vexed one. Theories currently occupying the debate propose one of three possible locations: Galilee, Rome, and Syria.[3]

The roots of the tradition that locates the provenance of Mark's Gospel in Rome reach back to the writings of Papias, the bishop of Herapolis (130 CE), which appear in Eusebius's work, *Ecclesiastical History* (3.39.14–15), ca. 303 CE. In this work, Mark is identified as the interpreter of the apostle Peter. Later in the same work (6.14.6), Eusebius notes that Clement of Alexandria (ca. 150–215 CE) reiterated an association between Mark and Peter, and went on to locate the pair in Rome.[4] Any further external

---

1. Larry W. Hurtado, "Oral Fixation and New Testament Studies? 'Orality,' 'Performance' and Reading Texts in Early Christianity," *NTS* 60 (2014): 330. The article as a whole comments on the oversimplification of claims of illiteracy and the complexity of approaching literacy in the Roman Empire in New Testament studies.

2. Rhoads, Dewey, and Michie, *Mark*, 10–11. I accept that there were readers, but, given the limited rate of literacy and limited number of copies, most people accessed the story in an aural setting.

3. Cilliers Breytenbach, "Current Research on the Gospel according to Mark: A Report on Monographs Published from 2000–2009," in *Mark and Matthew I: Comparative Readings; Understanding the Earliest Gospels in Their First-Century Settings*, ed. Eve-Marie Becker and Anders Runesson, WUNT 261 (Tübingen: Mohr Siebeck, 2011), 13–32.

4. Moloney, *Gospel of Mark*, 11.

evidence for Roman provenance, however, is unclear. While other early Christian writers also supported the association between Mark and Peter (e.g., Tertullian and John Chrysostom), they did not explicitly mention a connection to Rome. Moreover, Mark is never mentioned in relation to Rome without the Petrine association.[5] Some Eastern writers departed entirely from a location in Rome, such as the fourth century writer John Chrysostom who situated the Markan author in Egypt.

The historical value of the Peter-Mark-Rome triad is considered questionable in modern scholarship and the results of assessments are well-documented. Commentaries on Mark, as well as works dealing specifically with issues of Markan provenance, commonly provide appraisals of the external evidence for locating Mark in the city of Rome.[6] With a general consensus indicating that the early tradition is dubious as the sole basis for positing Rome as the location for the composition of Mark, scholars frequently move to examining the narrative itself for the indicators of provenance.

Among modern proponents of a Roman origin, the persecution of Christians in Rome is understood to be the central context of Mark. The gospel's emphasis on trauma and suffering, the references to the fears of arrest and execution and to crucifixion, and descriptions of betrayal and failure are understood to correlate with the experiences of those in Rome who had lived under the threat of execution during or since the Neronian persecutions of 64 CE.[7] Adam Winn notes, for example, that the Markan motif of a suffering discipleship links with the city of Rome in which the "most horrific suffering of the first century took place."[8] Allusions are identified between episodes in the Markan narrative and the events surrounding the destruction of the temple in Jerusalem in 70 CE and the

---

5. Beavis, *Mark*, 8–9. The association between Mark and Peter also has roots in 1 Pet 5:13. Scholars today do not attribute this work to the apostle Peter, but to a writer at the turn of the second century CE. See Beavis, *Mark*, 9.

6. For some examples, see Beavis, *Mark*, 6–9; Yarbro Collins, *Mark*, 7; Donahue and Harrington, *Mark*, 40–41; France, *Gospel of Mark*, 35–41; Hooker, *Saint Mark*, 5–8; Marcus, *Mark 1–8*, 21–24, 30; Moloney, *Gospel of Mark*, 11–13.

7. Donahue and Harrington, *Mark*; Brian J. Incigneri, *The Gospel to the Romans: The Setting and Rhetoric of the Mark's Gospel*, BibInt 65 (Leiden: Brill, 2003); Adam Winn, *The Purpose of Mark's Gospel: An Early Christian Response to Roman Imperial Propaganda*, WUNT 2/245 (Tübingen: Mohr Siebeck, 2008).

8. Winn, *Purpose of Mark's Gospel*, 83.

triumphant return of Titus to Rome under Vespasian in 71 CE.[9] Mark's usage of Latinisms is cited as further evidence of a Rome location.[10]

Although the arguments for Roman provenance are plausible and the exegetical work undertaken from this vantage point makes sense, scholars continue to identify the shortcomings in the case for Rome. While there is general agreement that Mark writes for or within a context of persecution, there is debate as to whether Rome may necessarily be the only location from which an author may have referred to Christian suffering in the first century CE. Given the amount of travel that Christians undertook in the first century, Yarbro Collins, for example, speculates whether accounts of Christian persecution would have been known further afield in the East. She also raises the possibility of sporadic persecutions of Christians in the East that may have provided a context for Mark, in addition to the persecution of Jews by gentiles in Antioch and Alexandria.[11] Against the assertion that references to crucifixion strengthen the case for Rome, Yarbro Collins notes that this form of execution was known in the East also, if indeed Mark was making purely literal allusions to how Christians in his context were being executed given other forms of execution that may have existed.[12] Finally, the use of Latinisms is contested as an indicator that Mark may have been composed only in Rome. During the empire, these items of speech had been taken up in the common speech of Jews beyond Rome, becoming loanwords wherever Greek was spoken in the empire.[13]

A second option for the location of Mark is Syria. Numerous observations come into play to make this case. Many of these observations relate to the significance of geography in Mark's narrative. The proximity of Syria to Judea opens up the possibility for a close connection with the Jesus traditions, the memory of Jesus's crucifixion and the Jerusalem church.[14] The

---

9. See, e.g., Incigneri's discussion on the use of the imagery of the veil of the temple in Mark 15:38 and its relationship to the veil and other sacred objects of the destroyed temple in the triumphant procession in Rome in the summer of 71 CE (*Gospel to the Romans*, 204–7).

10. Incigneri, *Gospel to the Romans*, 100–103; Winn, *Purpose of Mark's Gospel*, 82.

11. Yarbro Collins, *Mark*, 12.

12. Yarbro Collins, *Mark*, 99.

13. Hendrika N. Roskam, *The Purpose of the Gospel of Mark in Its Historical and Social Context*, NovTSup 114 (Leiden: Brill, 2004), 94–95; Yarbro Collins, *Mark*, 100.

14. Timothy Wardle, "Mark, the Jerusalem Temple and Jewish Sectarianism: Why Geographical Proximity Matters in Determining the Provenance of Mark," *NTS* 62 (2016): 60–78. In his comments on the Jesus tradition, Theissen also includes a discus-

content of Mark 13, in particular, suggests that Mark was composed in close proximity to the time and location of the Jewish War.[15] The author's ongoing references to Jewish sects as well as the presence of a general anti-temple rhetoric also make it possible that the narrative was constructed in geographical proximity to the Jerusalem sanctuary.[16] The attention to non-Jews in the narrative, however, implies that mainly Jewish regions such as Judea and Galilee are unlikely sites of origin, with Syria being the better candidate. Syria was known to be predominantly gentile, a fact that may explain why Mark clarifies Jewish terms and customs, including the use of Aramaisms.[17] Gerd Theissen, a well-known champion of the case for Syria, detects an emphasis on rural settings rather than cities, suggesting that the author's primary audience would not have been located in a metropolis like Rome but in a less urban environment such as Syria.[18]

Other observations concern the influence of Paul on the Markan narrative. Themes in the gospel that consider relationships with non-Jews and freedom from observing the law are understood to suggest that the author was in contact with pre-Pauline and Pauline traditions with roots in Syria, and point to a Syrian Christian influence on Mark.[19]

The case for Syria is not without its complications. Working against the argument for Syrian provenance is the lack of direct evidence of Christian persecutions either during the Jewish War or in Syria after the war, an observation that is problematic given the themes of persecution and suffering that permeate the narrative. Along with Theissen, Marcus—another

---

sion of Jesus's associations with John the Baptizer. See Gerd Theissen, *The Gospels in Context: Social and Political History in the Synoptic Tradition*, trans. Linda M. Maloney (Minneapolis: Fortress, 1991), 240.

15. Marcus, *Mark 1–8*, 33.

16. Wardle, "Mark," 70–76.

17. Marcus, *Mark 1–8*, 36; Theissen, *Gospels in Context*, 238; Wardle, "Mark," 64–65. Marcus also notes that the description of fleeing to the hills in 13:14–15 may refer to the Judean church that fled to Pella before the war or after the siege of Jerusalem (*Mark 1–8*, 36).

18. Theissen, *Gospels in Context*, 239. Cadwallader, while not specifying Syria, has argued for an Eastern provenance on the basis of Mark's use of the term κωμόπολις. See Alan H. Cadwallader, "Sometimes One Word Makes a World of Difference: Rethinking the Origins of Mark's Gospel (Mk 1:38)" (paper presented at the research seminar for the Centre for Biblical and Early Christian Studies at Australian Catholic University, 4 May 2017), 1–24.

19. Marcus, *Mark 1–8*, 26; Theissen, *Gospels in Context*, 239.

proponent of a Syrian location—proffers ways to address this dilemma. In Marcus's view, the fact Christians came under attack during the Bar Kokhba Revolt (132–135 CE), a crisis driven by messianic hopes, could suggest that they were also included among the targets of the earlier revolt which also was fueled by messianic fervor.[20] Or, as Theissen explains, it is conceivable that Christians in Syria were understood to be a group that was broadly associated with Jews and therefore were subjected to the violence that Jews experienced.[21] Even if these explanations hold (which is arguable), a further complication remains in the area of language. Mark's use of Aramaisms ensures that the question of a Syrian location remains open. The author's occasional explanations of Aramaic appear confusing in an eastern location where Aramaic was known, and raise questions as to the extent a non-Jew in Syria may have been familiar with the language.

A third option for locating Mark is in Galilee. Hendrika Roskam identifies several indicators within the narrative that form the basis of a case for Galilean provenance. First, the narrative contains references that assume the readers' knowledge of people and places associated with Galilee, for example, Simon of Cyrene, the father of Alexander and Rufus (15:21); Magdala (15:40, 47; 16:1, 9); and Dalmanutha (8:10). Mark cites these names and locations without needing to explain who or where they are.[22] Second, Mark appears to pay particular attention to Galilee. The witnesses to the empty tomb, for instance, are Galilean women who are named: Mary Magdalene, Mary the mother of James, and Salome (15:40–41; 16:1–8). After Jesus's burial, Galilee is singled out as the place where Peter, the disciples, and the Galilean women are told they will find Jesus, not the empty tomb in Jerusalem (14:28; 16:7).[23] Moreover, the geographical information concerning the geography of Galilee is "adequate," in Roskam's view, if not "faultless" in chapters 1–4, suggesting Mark's knowledge of the area.[24]

The threat of persecution for those in Mark's context is a further key to understanding the case for Galilean provenance. In order to maintain peace and security in Galilee after the Jewish War, leading Jews in the region sought to appease Roman leadership by ensuring public order. So as to avoid conflict (and therefore escape persecution) with either

---

20. Marcus, *Mark 1–8*, 34.
21. Theissen, *Gospels in Context*, 268.
22. Roskam, *Purpose of the Gospel of Mark*, 14–15.
23. Roskam, *Purpose of the Gospel of Mark*, 103.
24. Roskam, *Purpose of the Gospel of Mark*, 104–9.

Jews or Romans, Mark sought to counteract any notion that those who identified with Jesus constituted a subversive Jewish movement that rejected Roman rule. In Roskam's view, Mark sought to present Jesus as "God's envoy," not as a political figure or messianic pretender whose followers posed a threat to the social order.[25] Despite Jesus's execution as an insurrectionist, Mark assuaged possible tensions inherent in this label for those living in Galilee by characterizing Jesus as "a righteous man who accepts suffering and even death as a consequence of his faithfulness to God."[26] Mark's descriptions of Jesus's commands to silence exemplified the author's desire to present a Jewish figure that did not harbor political aspirations.[27]

There are at least three stumbling blocks in the case that Roskam makes for Galilee. First, there is no further evidence for a major Christian community in Galilee in the earliest period. It is difficult, therefore, to see how the resources necessary for generating the gospel may have been readily available.[28] Second, Roskam's argument that Mark sought to resolve tensions with the Jewish leaders who may have viewed Christians as jeopardizing their safety and well-being rests on an assumption that Galilee was an exclusively Jewish region. Yarbro Collins questions that this was in fact the case. Mark's occasional explanations of Jewish traditions and Aramaisms may indicate that there were also gentiles residing in Galilee or, indeed, that the narrative was composed beyond Galilee where gentiles certainly did live.[29] Third, while Roskam is assured that Mark's information about Galilean geography is adequate enough to attest to a personal knowledge of the region, other scholars are not so convinced. Inaccuracies concerning the author's location of the Gerasenes area next to the Sea of Galilee (5:1) and the perplexing account of Jesus's travels through Sidon and the Decapolis as he treks from Tyre to the Sea of Galilee (7:31) undermine any certainty.[30]

---

25. Roskam, *Purpose of the Gospel of Mark*, 137, 169.
26. Roskam, *Purpose of the Gospel of Mark*, 207.
27. Roskam, *Purpose of the Gospel of Mark*, 176.
28. Yarbro Collins, *Mark*, 100.
29. Yarbro Collins, *Mark*, 111.
30. Beavis, *Mark*, 10; Yarbro Collins, *Mark*, 107; Incigneri, *Gospel to the Romans*, 97–98. I note Roskam's counterargument that 7:1 merely indicates that Mark did not know the location of Sidon in relation to Tyre and the Sea of Galilee. It does not automatically signal a general ignorance of the whole Galilean region (Roskam, *Purpose of the Gospel of Mark*, 107).

None of the three cases for assigning provenance offers certainty. While the current scholarship agrees that Mark was composed in a context of persecution, there is neither a consensus nor conclusive evidence for one specific location. Even Marcus, a prominent proponent for Syria, points out the ambiguity in his observation that while Syrian provenance seems to be the strongest available case, it is "not a mathematical certainty.... Most of the exegesis would work just as well if the setting were Rome or some other places where Christians were under pressure."[31] Beavis sums up the current impasse:

> While the weight of the evidence tips the balance in favor of Roman (or at least Western provenance), it is not compelling enough to assign Mark to Rome or any other location, although the fact that most early Christian communities were founded in cities makes an urban setting likely.[32]

Identifying the context of a hearer of Mark's narrative on the basis of a specific geographical location for the purposes of reading the account of Jairus's daughter is therefore problematic.

One way of addressing this dilemma is to take up one of the three current options and to read the story of Jairus's daughter from that vantage point. Despite the acknowledged uncertainty of its location, it is not unusual for commentators on Mark's Gospel to weigh up the evidence and make an on-balance assessment as to which location is the most plausible from their own point of view, and to subsequently interpret the narrative from that geographical frame of reference. In this approach, the exegesis of Mark is anchored to a particular albeit conditional place, people, and set of contextual issues.

While most certainly a legitimate approach, it is not without its hazards. Proponents of this approach run the risk of what Keith Jenkins observes as "'knowing in advance what things 'look like,' the emergent forced to fit in with and conform to the already-existing weight of already known sign-systems.'"[33] In other words, an interpreter of Mark's Gospel

---

31. Marcus, *Mark 1–8*, 136.
32. Beavis, *Mark*, 12.
33. Keith Jenkins, "Sande Cohen: On the Verge of Newness," in *At the Limits of History: Essays on Theory and Practice* (London: Routledge, 2009), 288. Jenkins quotes Sande Cohen, *Academia and the Luster of Capital* (Minneapolis: University of Minnesota Press, 1993), 120–21.

can find themselves correlating their exegesis to a predetermined theology, Christology, and set of issues that limit or control their analysis on the basis of a specific geographic location which, in the case of Mark, is conditional from the beginning. The possibilities for new insights are therefore potentially curtailed.

3.1.2. Temporal Context

An alternative approach for situating the Markan hearer is to take what we *do know* about the narrative of Mark, and to use this as a basis for describing the context of the hearer. While there is uncertainty about the provenance of Mark's Gospel, there are three aspects of the work that are known. First, the narrative was constructed in the first century CE. Scholars generally date the gospel to between the late 60s and early 70s, identifying the Jewish rebellion and the destruction of the temple in Jerusalem as key contextual factors for dating. Work by James Crossley suggests, however, that the gospel was composed between the mid-30s to mid-40s, an argument that would see the possible dates of composition falling within a span that ranges from the mid-30s to the early 70s C E.[34] Notwithstanding these variations, we can say that the narrative is a composition of the first century CE. Second, the narrative has a Jewish context. It tells a story set in the Jewish homeland in the first century CE. It includes references to the Old Testament, to Jewish sects, sites, and practices, and incorporates Aramaisms. Third, the narrative reaches beyond Judaism to a Greco-Roman context. It is written in Koine Greek with some Latinisms, and it includes references to gentiles, Romans, and to gentile territories.

Rather than work from an uncertain specific geographical context, the starting point of this study is based on what is known about the context of a Markan hearer. While a specific Markan author, location, and audience is not clear, knowing the narrative was constructed in the first century CE and that it bears Jewish and Greco-Roman imprints creates an opportunity to examine the depictions and thinking that were operative in Judaism and Greco-Roman society during that period.[35] This study,

---

34. James Crossley, *The Date of Mark's Gospel: Insight from the Law in Earliest Christianity*, JSNTSup 266 (London: T&T Clark, 2004).

35. I am aware that there is Pauline material concerning the imagery of the body. I am choosing not to go into this material, however. Unlike the traces of Jewish and Greco-Roman contexts that we find in Mark's narrative, there is nothing in the

therefore, is a historical investigation into the temporal reality of a hearer. It takes seriously the Jewish and Greco-Roman sources about children and females in the first century CE that are available, paying attention to the variety of voices across the landscape of the period that provide glimpses of how some in society talked about themselves, and the place of females and children in their world.

It is important to clarify further what I mean by the hearer. When I use this term, I do not refer to a hybrid person who may have been conversant with all of the sources outlined below. Instead, in using the term I recognize that there were various hearers of the Markan narrative, from various circumstances and locations. It is plausible that some who encountered the story of Jairus's daughter may have had connections to Judaism, while others were gentiles who would have been associated with elements within Greco-Roman society and culture. Notwithstanding this diversity, people in the early Roman Empire had some connection to a Greco-Roman setting, albeit with variations. Those inhabiting a city in the Roman Empire, for instance, were more likely to have had greater exposure than those living in a rural area in a minor province. Those who lived within the sphere of the Roman Empire—Jew and gentile, man, woman, and child—were engaged to varying degrees in the Greco-Roman world. Even those who did not subscribe to all of its tenets, practices, and institutions were, by their very resistance, responding to the shaping influence of Greco-Roman culture. In this way, we can say that all hearers of the Markan narrative, both Jews and gentiles, were hellenized in some form.[36]

---

narrative to suggest definitively a Pauline setting. To guarantee that a hearer of Mark in the first century CE may have particularly engaged with the Pauline tradition requires the establishment of direct lines of influence between Mark, Paul, and a hearer. This task goes beyond the scope of what I am doing in this study. For recent discussion on the relationship between Mark, Paul, and audience/hearers, see Oda Wischmeyer, David C. Sim, and Ian J. Elmer, eds., *Paul and Mark: Comparative Essays, Part I; Two Authors at the Beginnings of Christianity*, BZNW 198 (Berlin: de Gruyter, 2014); Eve-Marie Becker, Troels Engberg-Pedersen, and Mogens Müller, eds., *Mark and Paul: Comparative Essays, Part II; For and against Pauline Influence on Mark*, BZNW 199 (Berlin: de Gruyter, 2014).

36. Hellenization, a modern term, refers to the complex processes of appropriating and adapting Greek languages, literature, ideas, motifs, and forms of expression by non-Greeks. Jörg Gerber and Vera Binder, "Hellenization," *BNP*, https://doi.org/10.1163/1574-9347_bnp_e506840; Emma Dench, "Beyond Greeks and Barbarians: Italy and Sicily in the Hellenistic Age," in *A Companion to the Hellenistic World*,

3. The Landscape of the Hearer in the First Century CE

Some further explanation of what I mean by temporal reality or temporal context is also necessary. The study is based on the assumption that there is an interaction or interconnectedness between the Markan narrative and the broader first-century world out of which it emerged. This world comprised texts—written, visual, and oral—that today suggest a temporal reality of Mark's author and hearers. This contemporality of Mark is not *background* to the story, but is the *context* in which the narrative was both composed and heard. The notion of a temporal context therefore recognizes that the narrative of Mark's Gospel is part of a broader landscape of texts, indeed "a larger framework of texts, customs, practices and institutions," that potentially influenced how the narrative was both written and heard.[37]

The legitimacy of approaching Mark's context in this way is supported in the recent studies of Teresa Morgan.[38] Her approach to New Testament studies is particularly instructive in drawing out what I mean by the context of Mark. She observes that the early Roman Empire encompassed numerous "micro-societies and subcultures" that each possessed "their own language or dialect," customs, practices, histories, and structures. Together, these diverse groupings formed "a single, vast, multicultural complex," characterized by the "interaction and interpenetration" of Roman, Latin, and Greek culture and ideas, as well as Aramaic, Syrian, and North African among many others.[39]

None of the works we examine in this study is immune to some form of interaction with the subcultures and ideas that were operative in the

---

ed. Andrew Erskine, BCAW (Malden, MA: Blackwell, 2005), 297. Romanization refers to the "diffusion of Roman-Italic civilization, language, and culture within the Roman Empire and beyond." Greg Woolf, "Romanization," *BNP*, http://dx.doi.org/10.1163/1574-9347_bnp_e1024530. The process of hellenization occurred to varying degrees among Jews, e.g., the influence on religious belief was different from that on social mores and from that on material culture. It also varied from region to region, and class to class, and from urban to nonurban settings. Levine observes that by the first century CE, even in Jerusalem, the Jewish city par excellence, there was evidence of hellenization in terms of its "population, languages, institution and general cultural ambience." See Lee I. Levine, *Judaism and Hellenism in Antiquity: Conflict or Confluence?* (Seattle: University of Washington Press, 1998), 33–95, esp. 22, 37, 95.

37. Gina Hens-Piazza, *The New Historicism*, GBS (Minneapolis: Fortress, 2002), 11.

38. Teresa Morgan, *Roman Faith and Christian Faith: Pistis and Fides in the Early Roman Empire and Early Churches* (Oxford: Oxford University Press, 2015).

39. Morgan, *Roman Faith*, 28.

early empire. Each bears witness to a level of engagement with people, practices, and ideas that were beyond their own immediate or original affiliations. The works of the New Testament are clear examples of Morgan's notion of interpenetration, not least Mark's Gospel with its obvious traces of Greek, Roman, Jewish, and Aramaic influence. Morgan notes, "The mindset of the writers of the New Testament, like that of subjects throughout the Roman empire, includes concepts, structures, and relationships which operate right across the empire in both Greek and Latin, to say nothing of other languages."[40] Each of these cultural traces is part of the "experience and thought world" of the Markan author, in addition to the people of which Mark writes, to those for whom Mark writes, and those who may have encountered the narrative that was composed.[41] Understanding the hearer of Mark's Gospel to be embedded in a context where myriad cultures and ideas intersected with Mark's own and those who encountered the narrative, I pay attention to the (dis)connections between the narrative of the gospel and other texts of the first century CE: visual, written, and oral. I am not concerned with investigating relationships of dependence or establishing direct lines between texts. Instead, I read the story of Jairus's daughter *in dialogue* with voices of the first century CE, observing instances of overlapping, of resonance and divergence.[42]

It is important to note that this study is not intended to provide a better or more accurate interpretation of the story of Jairus's daughter based on the examination of a new set of written and visual sources from the first century CE. Similarly, I am not contending that the sources we examine are authoritative for Mark's Gospel. Instead, the focus on the temporal reality of Mark's narrative provides a new and different entry point into the analysis of the story in such a way that it "opens the possibility for creating a larger explanatory palette" than if we were to limit the Markan context according to the theories of a specific geographic location.[43] In

---

40. Morgan, *Roman Faith*, 28.
41. Morgan, *Roman Faith*, 28.
42. Miri Rubin, "What Is Cultural History Now?," in *What Is History Now?*, ed. David Cannadine (Basingstoke: Palgrave MacMillan, 2002), 80–94.
43. Alice Kessler-Harris, "What Is Gender History Now?," in Canadine, *What Is History Now?*, 95–112. Nor am I arguing that understanding the particularity of a geographical location is irrelevant, an absurd position to take in historical studies. My approach is one in which, given we do not know for certain where Mark was

other words, the analysis of the temporal context of Mark can expand (not replace) our vision of the account of Jairus's daughter, and contribute further to how the gospel may be processed.[44]

In tracing the depictions of children and females in the first century CE and the trails of possible meaning attached to their various representations, this study intends to widen the scope for understanding the influences on a person who heard the story of Jairus's daughter. I base this intention on an assumption that the hearer of a story, like the composer of a story, is shaped by the world in which they interact. To expound my approach to the hearer, it is necessary to comment on how I think about the written and visual data for analysis. I assume that one way in which a person was shaped was through the ideas, values, and attitudes that were mediated through the concrete objects that were part of the world that a person inhabited, that is, through the words and images proffered by some to others. In the first century CE, these concrete materials included written (and spoken) works such as inscriptions, letters, speeches, biographies, and histories, as well as visual images that featured on coins, statues, reliefs, and monuments.[45] Beliefs and attitudes were communicated through these media.[46]

The meaning attached to language and imagery does not rest with the creator alone. The person who hears or views the text or image also constructs it. Meaning is generated both in the creation of word and image and in the encounter of others with the object. It is therefore a dynamic process, as Stephen Greenblatt explains:

> A work of art is the product of a negotiation between a creator or a class of creators, equipped with a complex, communally shared repertoire of conventions, and the institutions and practices of society. In order to achieve the negotiation, artists need to create a currency (money, prestige) that is valid for a meaningful, mutually profitable exchange.[47]

---

composed and where an audience was located, another starting point to examine the context of a hearer, namely, the temporal context, is appropriate and legitimate.

44. Kessler-Harris, "Gender History," 98.

45. I note that some objects contain both written and visual elements, e.g., coins and some inscriptions.

46. Written and visual media were not the sum ways of communicating beliefs and attitudes. These could also be expressed through customs and practices.

47. Stephen Greenblatt, "Towards a Poetics of Culture," in *The New Historicism*, ed. H. Aram Veeser (New York: Routledge, 1989), 12.

Greenblatt notes the dialogue that occurs between a creator of an object and the world in which they create. He also observes that creators take up language and images that already have traction with the intended viewer and hearer in such a way that there is an exchange between the language or images and the viewer/hearer. This notion of an exchange suggests that meaning-making is not static. While specific language and imagery—and the ideas and attitudes that they are intended to convey—may be familiar, they undergo further interpretation as those who encounter them bring their own experience and thinking to the encounter.[48]

This understanding of how text and context are in mutual dialogue has implications for how I approach the hearer of Mark's narrative. The shaping influence that the cultural environment has on a hearer of Mark's narrative in the first century CE contributes to how they interact with this work. They bring awareness to their hearing that is affected by the images, language, and ideas of the time in which they live. The hearing of the narrative however is not unidirectional. Akin to Greenblatt's line, I assume that there was a dynamic interaction between the hearer of Mark, the broad culture and society in which they participated, and the narrative that is set out.

A caveat is required at this stage. While I examine the language and images that were part of the world of a first-century hearer of Mark, I cannot say with certainty how they were interpreted or what they really meant to those who encountered them (any more than any other commentator on Mark can, including those who subscribe to a particular provenance). What is not known is how Greco-Roman and/or Jewish representations of children and females acted on a person who heard the story of Jairus's daughter. All the same, even if hearers did not subscribe fully or even in part to the ideas being communicated in some of the Greco-Roman and Jewish sources, the representations were part of the cultural landscape and would have evoked some form of reaction. How various children and adults may have related to any of the sources remains speculative, but given the overt public presence of images and language related to children and females, they could not have ignored them. Put differently, the meanings attached to the representations of children's and females' bodies in the first century CE would have exceeded the stories

---

48. As Hens-Piazza, reflecting the sentiments of Mikhail Bakhtin and Julia Kristeva, observes, "Every communicative act is in dialogue with its context and all its prior enactments" (*New Historicism*, 51).

they were initially intended to tell by their creators. Further stories or associations, unknown to us today, may have been told by those who encountered the depictions.[49]

3.2. Voices That Sound in the Landscape of the First Century CE

There is an abundance of written and visual source material to assist us in describing the temporal reality of a hearer of Mark's Gospel in the first century CE. Depictions of children and females, including representations of dying and deceased figures, populated the worlds of Jews and Greco-Romans alike in the periods of Second Temple Judaism and the early empire respectively. Given the plethora of written source material, it is necessary to limit the sources that will form the basis of our investigation. Mark's Gospel may be considered a form of narrative.[50] Therefore, the literary sources that we will concentrate on will be those that generally contain elements of narrative writing. Here I provide an outline of the voices that will provide points of reference in the study with brief comments about the context in which each composer lived and from which their writings emerged. I concentrate on any contextual factors that may have a bearing on how we understand the content of those sources.

3.2.1. Literary Sources

3.2.1.1. Voices in Late Second Temple Judaism

Four voices are explored in the examination of written sources from the period of Second Temple Judaism: the works of Philo, Josephus, Pseudo-Philo/Biblical Antiquities/ Liber Antiquitatum Biblicarum (LAB), and the book of Jubilees. The first two authors composed historical works in Greek

---

49. Jennifer A. Glancy, *Corporal Knowledge: Early Christian Bodies* (New York: Oxford University Press, 2010), 17, 19.

50. The written text of Mark's Gospel broadly takes the form of a story. In approaching Mark as a narrative, I mean that it can be approached as a story that features the general characteristics of a narrative: a narrator, setting, plot, characters, and rhetoric (Rhoads, Dewey, and Michie, *Mark*, 17-18). In so doing, I acknowledge the scholarly debate concerning the particular genre of Mark, including biography, Greek tragedy, eschatological historical monograph, and Jewish apocalypse. Whatever the author's original intention, I take the approach that a narrative was composed (Rhoads, Dewey, and Michie, *Mark*, 14; Yarbro Collins, *Mark*, 15-43).

in the first century CE. The latter two works are examples of rewritten scripture.[51] Liber Antiquitatum Biblicarum was composed in the first century CE, while Jubilees was composed earlier, with a possible dating circa 160–150 BCE. Each voice, while writing within a particular Jewish religious affiliation, was composed within a Greco-Roman world and ought not to be viewed as separate from that context. Each is occupied with specific audiences and intentions, thus requiring further comment.

Philo the Alexandrian lived between 20 BCE–50 CE. A member of the Jewish elite, he had associations with Agrippa I and the imperial family.[52] It is possible that Philo was a Roman citizen as well as an Alexandrian citizen and a member of the Jewish community. Consequently, he was aware of both Jewish thought and Greco-Roman culture and his works are understood to reflect his engagement with both worlds.[53] An education in the gymnasium, for instance, is likely. At the same time, the Alexandrian synagogue is understood to have used the Septuagint for instruction, which may have had a bearing on Philo's use of the Pentateuch in his own writings in preference to other Jewish works.[54] His historical writings in particular are understood to be contextualized within the tensions of the 30s, especially the anti-Jewish violence of 38 CE.[55]

While Josephus was also familiar with Jewish and Greco-Roman culture, he wrote later than Philo and from a different geographic location. Born into a wealthy, priestly family, Josephus was born and bred in Jerusalem while it was under Roman occupation. He was a participant in and witness to the Jewish revolt in Jerusalem before relocating to Rome with

---

51. Susan E. Docherty, *The Jewish Pseudepigrapha: An Introduction to the Literature of the Second Temple Period* (Minneapolis: Fortress, 2015), 12.

52. William R. G. Loader, *Philo, Josephus, and the Testaments on Sexuality: Attitudes towards Sexuality in the Writings of Philo and Josephus and in the Testaments of the Twelve Patriarchs* (Grand Rapids: Eerdmans, 2011), 2. In this study, the term *elite* refers to those men and women who were wealthy, educated, powerful figures who exercised political, economic, and cultural influence in society. Elite women were further characterized by lives of luxury and leisure. See Jerry P. Toner, *Popular Culture in Ancient Rome* (Cambridge: Polity, 2013), 5–10.

53. Kenneth Schenck, *A Brief Guide to Philo* (Louisville: Westminster John Knox, 2005), 10.

54. Schenck, *Philo*, 10–11.

55. Daniel Schwartz, "Philo, His Family, and His Times," in *The Cambridge Companion to Philo*, ed. Adam Kamesar (Cambridge: Cambridge University Press, 2009), 15.

the support of the Flavians.⁵⁶ He composed his works there in the late first century CE for elite non-Jews as well as for fellow Jews.⁵⁷

In this study, we look at all of Josephus's works. *Jewish War*, composed sometime from the late 70s CE, is the author's narration of the Judean War. Despite Josephus's claims to writing an accurate account of the war and the events leading up to it, the work is understood to reflect his own personal concerns. Central among these is his intention to explain the revolt both in Jewish and Roman terms. On the one hand, Josephus is concerned with honoring the Romans under whose patronage he existed in Rome. On the other hand, he presents most of the Jews in Jerusalem as innocent in the face of Roman aggression in his negative portrayal of the Jewish rebels.⁵⁸ *Jewish Antiquities*, written in 93 CE, is a history of the Jewish people narrated through the retelling of biblical stories and events preceding 70 CE. It was intended for gentile readers, or "interested outsiders," sympathetic to Jewish culture.⁵⁹ *Life*, written around 93–94 CE, is a supplement to *Jewish Antiquities*. The work is autobiographical, and aimed to present Jewish culture and tradition to interested Greeks in Rome through the lens of Josephus's own life.⁶⁰ The fourth work we pay attention to is *Against Apion*, a work dating sometime between 94 and 105 CE. It is a defense that takes up either real or fictional accusations leveled at Jews. Its dual purpose was to: (1) bolster support for Jews among the non-Jews in whose circles Josephus moved; (2) support Jews residing in Rome to counter the experiences of vilification to which Josephus purports they were exposed and therefore to find ways of accommodating a life amidst Romans.⁶¹ In each of these works we are treated to Josephus's own perceptions of Judaism and of the Greco-Roman context with which he was engaged.

The book of Jubilees provides another snapshot of how Jewish culture responded to the influence of non-Jewish thought. The author of the work

---

56. Caryn A. Reeder, *The Enemy in the Household: Family Violence in Deuteronomy and Beyond* (Grand Rapids: Baker Academic, 2012), 110.

57. Steve Mason, *Josephus, Judea, and Christian Origins: Methods and Categories* (Peabody, MA: Hendrickson, 2009), 47.

58. James S. McLaren, *Power and Politics in Palestine: The Jews and the Governing of Their Land, 100 BC–AD 70*, JSNTSup 63 (Sheffield: JSOT Press, 1991), 37–38; Reeder, *Enemy in the Household*, 110.

59. Louis H. Feldman, *Judean Antiquities 1–4*, FJTC 3 (Leiden: Brill, 2000), xix–xx.

60. Steve Mason, *Life of Josephus*, FJTC 9 (Leiden: Brill, 2001), xiii–xlix.

61. John M. G. Barclay, *Against Apion*, FJTC 10 (Leiden: Brill, 2007), xvii–li.

is unknown although it was most probably a priest and possibly a member of the Essenes or a group associated with the tradition that evolved into the Essenes.[62] Seemingly composed in an environment in which some Jews were influenced by Hellenistic culture and/or in which gentiles sought to convert to Judaism, the book of Jubilees takes a stance against any such assimilation. Through a rewrite of the book of Genesis and the opening chapters of Exodus, the book's author emerges as a strong advocate for observing the covenant and for maintaining separation from non-Jews.[63]

The final remaining Jewish literary work that we examine is Pseudo-Philo/Liber Antiquitatum Biblicarum/Biblical Antiquities. The work dates to the first century CE with provenance in Palestine, possibly Galilee.[64] It is concerned with supporting Jews in Palestine to deal with adversity, particularly the difficulties associated with the destruction of Jerusalem and its temple in 70 CE. Liber Antiquitatum Biblicarum argues that the people's suffering was part of God's design for their salvation.[65] The narrative builds on the Old Testament, rewriting the stories of Adam through David and continuing on to the demise of Saul. While it has its basis in Jewish thought, Liber Antiquitatum Biblicarum also shows signs of engagement with Greek and Canaanite culture. The reworking of the death of Jephthah's daughter, for instance—particularly Seila's lament—suggests awareness of the Greek laments over the deaths of young girls as well as the use of lament in Canaanite ritual.[66]

Each of these sources is taken up to examine the images and language that existed in the late Second Temple environment. Together they

---

62. James C. VanderKam, *The Book of Jubilees* (Sheffield: Sheffield Academic, 2001), 143.

63. VanderKam, *Jubilees*, 14. Also James L. Kugel, *A Walk through Jubilees: Studies in the Book of Jubilees and the World of Its Creation*, JSJSup 156 (Leiden: Brill, 2012), 1-4. For a view that disputes that Jubilees reflects opposition to hellenizing influences, see Michael Segal, *The Book of Jubilees: Rewritten Bible, Redaction, Ideology and Theology*, JSJSup 117 (Leiden: Brill, 2007), 321-22.

64. Howard Jacobson, *A Commentary on Pseudo-Philo's Liber Antiquitatum Biblicarum with Latin Text and English Translation*, 2 vols., AGJU 31 (Leiden: Brill, 1996), 1:210-11.

65. Jacobson, *Pseudo-Philo's Liber Antiquitatum Biblicarum*, 1:253. Although, for a dating of Liber Antiquitatum Biblicarum that precedes the destruction of the Jerusalem temple, see Frederick J. Murphy, *Pseudo-Philo: Rewriting the Bible* (Oxford: Oxford University Press, 1993), 6.

66. Jacobson, *Pseudo-Philo's Liber Antiquitatum Biblicarum*, 1:204.

represent a sample of the multiplicity of voices that were present in the world in which a hearer of Mark's Gospel lived. In the case of Jubilees, while composed before the first century CE, the opportunity to examine its depictions of children and females allows us to consider a course of thought that fed into one seam of Jewish thinking in the first century CE. The other three voices are clearly located in closer temporal proximity to the period of the gospel's composition. The provenance of Liber Antiquitatum Biblicarum broadens the discussion of Jewish depictions in Josephus's and Philo's works, associated with Rome and Alexandria respectively, to include representations that emerged in the Jewish homeland. While each source reveals how specific Jews depicted children and females, each also bears its unique imprint of an engagement with the Greco-Roman world in which it resided. It is important to make a final note. While the Septuagint was influential among first-century Christians, given my focus in this present study is attuned to sources composed in, or on the cusp of, the first century CE, I will not be examining the related biblical accounts in the Septuagint. To be sure, attention to these accounts is a significant line of investigation but it is beyond the scope of the current study.

3.2.1.2. Greco-Roman Voices

The abundance of written material from the first-century CE provides us with a substantial source from which to mine depictions of females and children. The dating of the texts we take up spans the late republic into the period of the early empire through to the cusp of the second century CE. A focus on this duration enables us to hear the diversity of voices that both shaped and were shaped by the environment in which a person in the first century CE interacted. It also assists us to take note of the possible overlaps and divergences in representations throughout the first century. Here I provide an overview of the authors I explore, noting any contextual factors that require us to take care when using these sources, or that particularly lend themselves to a study of children and females in the first century CE.[67]

---

67. Each of these authors has a connection to Rome, either having been raised there or having come to Rome later in life. I am not concentrating on these authors because of a connection to Rome, however. To reiterate, I am not assuming Roman provenance of Mark. Rather, my focus is on the hearer in the temporal context of Mark's composition. I have selected these authors because they composed works in a period contemporaneous with Mark and Mark's narrative, their works are extant and

The earliest writer we consider is Cicero (106–43 BCE), a well-known member of the ruling elite of Rome who was active during the period that led into the formation of the Roman Empire.[68] Cicero's letters are considered in this study. Often composed during traumatic periods of his life, they include references to females and to his family, including his cherished daughter Tullia and his wives.[69] Quintilian was another member of the Roman elite. Born in 35 CE in Spain, he was active during the early empire. Quintilian was recognized as a successful teacher and rhetorician, and references to the deaths of his wife and two young sons (who died most likely in 88 CE and 92 CE) form the preface to book 6 of *The Orator's Education*.[70] Plutarch (45–125 CE) was born and raised in Greece during the period in which it had been subsumed into the Roman Empire. While steeped in Greek culture and intellectual tradition, as a Roman citizen of a wealthy elite family, he was familiar with Roman ways of thinking.[71] His works contain portraits of females as wives, unmarried girls, and children, and contain references to the deaths of wives and daughters. We consider *Moralia*, *Lives*, and *Letter to Apollonius* in this study. Tacitus (56/57 CE) was especially critical of what he perceived as the role of the imperial household and family in the development of the early empire, particularly as it pertained to the function and power of the imperial women.[72] He was a contemporary of Josephus and a youth during the civil war in Rome (69 CE) and at the time of Nero's death

---

their compositions are narratives that reveal information about women and female children.

68. Catherine Steel, "Introduction," in *The Cambridge Companion to Cicero*, ed. Catherine Steel (Cambridge: Cambridge University Press, 2012), 1.

69. Gesine Manuwald, *Cicero* (London: Tauris, 2015), 159. Ruth Morello, "Writer and Addressee in Cicero's Letters," in Steel, *Cambridge Companion to Cicero*, 196–214.

70. Christopher P. Craig, "Quintilian," in *The Oxford Encyclopedia of Ancient Greece and Rome*, ed. Michael Gagarin (Oxford: Oxford University Press, 2010), https://tinyurl.com/SBLPress4534a2; Jorge Fernández López, "Quintilian as Rhetorician and Teacher," in *A Companion to Roman Rhetoric*, ed. William Dominik and Jon Hall, BCAW (Malden, MA: Wiley-Blackwell, 2007), 307–22; Matthew Leigh, "Quintilian on the Emotions (*Institutio Oratoria* 6 Preface and 1-2)," *JRS* 94 (2004): 122–40.

71. Philip A. Stadter, "Plutarch and Rome," in *A Companion to Plutarch*, ed. Mark Beck, BCAW (Malden, MA: Wiley-Blackwell, 2014), 2, 14. See also Robert Lamberton, *Plutarch*, Hermes Books (New Haven: Yale University Press, 2001).

72. Kristina Milnor, "Women and Domesticity," in *A Companion to Tacitus*, ed. Victoria E. Pagán, BCAW (Oxford: Wiley-Blackwell, 2012), 458–75.

(68 CE). We examine his representations of wives and children—including their deaths—that emerge in his narratives of the people, places, and events of this period. Among these are *Agricola*, the biography of his father-in-law and the governor of Britain; *Germania*, the treatise on Germany; *Histories*, which narrates the events of 69–70 CE; and *Annals*, an overview of the Julio-Claudian period. Juvenal composed *Satires* at a similar time to Tacitus's *Annals*. The five books of satires were probably composed for an elite Roman male audience. In *Sat.* 6, we encounter an angry tirade against Roman wives in an attempt to deter Juvenal's addressee from getting married.[73]

The study considers one example of a Greek novel. The possible dating of Chariton's romantic novel, *Chaereas and Callirhoe* spans from as early as the first century BCE to no later than the second century CE. One of the main protagonists of the novel is the female figure and heroine of the story, Callirhoe. While composed in the period of the late republic or early empire, the images and language provide one snapshot of attitudes to females in the literature of the Greek East, particularly in relation to the relationship between elite fathers and daughters.[74]

Of those Greco-Roman writers born during the second half of the first century, we look at Suetonius and Pliny the Younger. Born in Hippo Reggius in North Africa, Suetonius (61/62 CE or 70 CE) received some of his education in Rome and appears to have come under the patronage of Pliny.[75] While he enjoyed access to the emperor and wrote about the life of the emperor, the historical accuracy of his writings is questionable. His works paint a picture of how the emperor wanted himself to be described. "No such thing as a private life" was the flavor of the day in the early empire. The details of the emperor's domestic life were a concern to the public, as they were understood to reveal his character. It is in this context that Suetonius depicts the imperial women and children. On the one hand,

---

73. According to Morton Braund, little is known about Juvenal. Susanna Morton Braund, "Juvenal," in *Oxford Companion to Classical Civilization*, ed. Simon Hornblower, Antony Spawforth, and Esther Eidinow, 2nd ed. (Oxford: Oxford University Press, 2014), https://tinyurl.com/SBLPress4534a3.

74. Katharine Haynes, *Fashioning the Feminine in the Greek Novel* (London: Routledge, 2003).

75. For dating to 61/62 CE, see Barry Baldwin, *Suetonius* (Amsterdam: Hakkert, 1983), 28. For dating to 70 CE, see Catharine Edwards, *Suetonius: Lives of the Caesars; A New Translation* (New York: Oxford University Press, 2000), vii.

these representations provide insights into what Suetonius perceived to be the ideal imperial family. On the other, the depictions essentially functioned as a commentary on the role of the emperor. We pay attention to the images and language that appears in Suetonius's biographical writing on Augustus, Tiberius, and Gaius Caligula.

The final voice that completes the sample of Greco-Roman voices is Pliny the Younger (61/62 CE). A contemporary of Suetonius and Tacitus, Pliny was educated in Rome under the tutelage of Quintilian. An ambitious man, he rose to great Roman heights and was eventually appointed as a consul. We examine a sample of his letters in the collection that was penned between 97 and 113 CE.[76] Pliny wrote letters mainly to men in his own social circle, although some of the addressees were women. His letters were compiled into a book by Pliny himself so the deposit from which we take our sample represents only Pliny's writings (i.e., he did not include any correspondence from his friends), and reflects his own interests as he wished them to be known. Along with letters scribed to women recipients, some of Pliny's letters make references to his own wife and family, and to the deaths of the wives and daughters of some of his friends.[77]

3.2.2. Material Sources

Material sources are another important contributor to our understanding of how children and females were depicted in the first century CE, including their representations as dying and deceased figures. Throughout this period, people who inhabited Jewish and Greco-Roman worlds were immersed in physical environments that were rich in visual imagery and text. As many people across the social spectrum went about their daily lives, they regularly encountered artwork, monuments, tombs, altars, and coins that communicated the attitudes and beliefs that those who created them wished to convey in the public arena. The interactions between these material objects and their creators, and those who engaged with the objects, meant that the physical environments of the first century CE functioned as social spaces, influencing people's consciousness of what was to be valued. A study of children and females in the first century CE needs, therefore,

---

76. Pliny the Younger was governor of Bithynia-Pontus, northern Turkey, from ca. 109–111 CE onward.

77. Joanne Shelton, *Pliny the Younger: Selected Letters* (Mundelein, IL: Bolchazzy-Carducci, 2016), xix.

to pay attention not only to the ways in which such figures were depicted in the concrete realia of Mark's time but also to the possible meanings that these objects were intended to convey.

3.2.2.1. Material Culture of Late Second Temple Judaism

Death was an everyday experience in the first century CE. The deaths of children were especially common. The ways in which children were depicted in death provide insights, therefore, not only into the funerary practices for children but also provide glimpses of some of the mindsets and ideas concerning children. Family tombs and funerary inscriptions are the main material sources that enable us to observe how children were depicted in concrete realia at the turn of the era. In this study we pay attention to the sites in Jerusalem and Jericho where many of the tombs and inscriptions concerning children and females have been unearthed.[78] The inscriptions provide information about the names of the deceased and their ages, and how they are identified in relation to others, particularly members of their families. The placement of skeletal remains and the locations of their burial can suggest possible causes of death, as these are often not recorded in the inscriptions. They can also reveal some of the attitudes to children and older females within a familial or social network.[79]

While the family tombs offer insight, they do not proffer a comprehensive overview of Jewish life in the Jewish homeland in the late Second Temple period. Most likely the possession of wealthier families who could afford their construction and maintenance, they provide a snapshot of life for some families. They do not, for instance, reveal the burial rites of less wealthy people. Caution is necessary therefore to avoid drawing generalized conclusions about family life from these data.

3.2.2.2. Greco-Roman Material Culture

Representations of children were prominent during the early empire. Indeed, the first visual depictions of children in Roman art began to appear

---

78. I do not examine funerary evidence from the diaspora, as, according to Rutgers, most of it postdates the first century CE. Leonard V. Rutgers, *The Hidden Heritage of Diaspora Judaism*, 2nd ed., BETL 20 (Leuven: Peeters, 1998), 69–71.

79. Rachel Hachlili, *Jewish Funerary Customs, Practices and Rites in the Second Temple Period*, JSJSup 94 (Leiden: Brill, 2005).

in the Augustan period on private tombs and reliefs as well as on imperial monuments. They even became commonplace in the public domain after the Augustan legislation that promoted the place of the family within the structuring of the Roman Empire.[80] We examine a range of material data in order to understand how representations of children and females functioned during this period in the Greco-Roman world. The sample comprises the imagery and text found on imperial coins and monuments, as well as funerary reliefs, inscriptions, and altars. These are drawn predominantly from Rome itself due to the sheer abundance of concrete realia that are now generally available from sites in that region.

It is necessary to comment briefly on some of the factors that have a bearing on how we approach these material sources, as well as to note the specific benefit they provide to the study. The imperial coins and monuments are illustrations of how the imperial family sought to identify itself and how the figures of women and children were co-opted for that task. In the early empire, any person who traversed the metropolis of Rome would have interacted with monumental art and sculpture. Imperial monuments such as the Ara Pacis could communicate ideas in the public arena about the empire and the role of the imperial family to those who interacted with these great structures. Naturally, there were some limitations on the communicative reach of these monuments given they were static installations in a single location. Coins, on the other hand, were a means of promulgating imperial ideology further afield. Whether they featured images of imperial women and children, or images of a subjugated Jewish woman, the images on coins conveyed to the general population who the emperor was and the values that were deemed important in the progression of the empire. Unlike monuments that were fixed to a specific geographical location, coins could be distributed throughout the empire and individuals from different levels of the social strata could interact with them—and the images, texts, and ideologies they bore—directly, with their own hands, on a daily basis.[81]

Members of the imperial family were not alone in depicting themselves in text and stone. Others took to memorializing themselves and members of their households in the reliefs and inscriptions on funer-

---

80. Beryl Rawson, *Children and Childhood in Roman Italy* (Oxford: Oxford University Press, 2003), 6.

81. Fleur Kemmers and Nanouschka Myrberg, "Rethinking Numismatics: The Archaeology of Coins," *Archaeological Dialogues* 18 (2011): 87–108.

ary altars and tombs that populated the physical environment of Rome in the early empire. Altars were installed in public spaces on roads and often featured depictions of groups of people—including women and children—who were associated with the deceased to whom the altar was erected.[82] Tombs with reliefs and inscriptions were often set in private or domestic settings. They depicted the deaths of individuals, including boys and girls.[83]

To ensure my use of the terms *private* and *domestic* is not misleading, I apply them to distinguish between public spaces that most people could access and private spaces to which access was regulated by a person of authority. In the case of domestic or private spaces, while access to these may have been controlled, these spaces were not necessarily isolated from the outside world. Indeed, domestic spaces were often sites of an entanglement of the public and household domains of life. The houses of wealthy families functioned as sites of business with guests from various walks of life frequenting the atrium to undertake business. Slightly further afield than Rome, the architecture of Roman mansions in Pompeii and Herculaneum suggests multiroom dwellings that housed servants, tenants, clients, and relatives. There were no separate sleeping quarters for women and children. Children could sleep with their wet nurse, their teachers, or the children of the household's slaves.[84] The houses of poorer families in Rome, usually one-room dwellings, were generally small and overcrowded. Spaces for daily activities such as cooking, cleaning, and working could be shared among families, with the courtyard functioning as a place of interaction between people. Public and private spaces intermingled as did the people in them.[85] Whether in domestic or public settings, as part of the physical and social landscape the material objects of commemoration visibly communicated to people across the social strata some of the attitudes and beliefs about children and the networks of which they were a part.

---

82. Larsson Loven, "Children and Childhood," 309–12.

83. Janet Huskinson, "Constructing Childhood on Roman Funerary Memorials," in *Constructions of Childhood in Ancient Greece and Italy*, ed. Ada Cohen and Jeremy B. Rutter, Hesperia Supplements 41 (Princeton: American School of Classical Studies at Athens, 2007), 334, 337.

84. Christian Laes, *Children in the Roman Empire: Outsiders Within* (Cambridge: Cambridge University Press, 2011), 36–37. The absence of separate quarters for women and children contrasts with the structure of Greek houses.

85. Rawson, *Children and Childhood*, 3, 211.

While there is a plethora of material data for our study, care is necessary when using these sources for two reasons. First, the portraiture of imperial women and children that appears on coins and monuments in the Julio-Claudian period is highly stylized. By that, I mean that the images were constructed with the intention of presenting these members of the household in a favorable light and a particular manner in order to transmit the values espoused by the emperor.[86] Women and children alike would have had little opportunity to influence how they were depicted. Any control a woman might have exerted over her representation would have depended on how closely her thinking aligned with the intentions of the emperor and other men in the family. Moreover, while the imperial women and children were represented in such a way so as to embody Roman values, the lives of those who regularly engaged with their images were a far cry from those in the emperor's fold, even women and children of the wealthy elite.[87]

Second, the images and texts in the material data provide us with traces of ideas about children and women but they do not offer a comprehensive entry point into their lives. The sources we use, while present in the general public arena, originate generally from within the folds of elite men. The sources do not voice the perceptions that women (for the most part) and children had of their own lives, nor do they express the reality of their lives. Children did not create, commission, or construct what we now identify as source material. It is important to remember what the sources do contribute to the study: some of the ideas and mindsets about women and children that were mediated through the language and images of mostly wealthy, educated, powerful men as they interacted within their own sociocultural settings.

3.3. Working with the Voices of the First Century CE

In the chapters that follow, I describe the role and function of representations of children's and females' bodies in the first century CE as they might be understood in the literary and material samples I have outlined. The discussion is guided by the question: What were the depictions of the bodies of females and children, particularly dying and dead bodies? In

---

86. Susan E. Wood, *Imperial Women: A Study in Public Images, 40 BC–AD 68*, Mnemosyne Supplements 194 (Leiden: Brill, 2000), 4–5.

87. Wood, *Imperial Women*, 22.

asking this question, I pay attention to three interrelated elements: gender, age, and ethnicity. By gender, I mean how the perception of sexual differences affected how a person's role, function, and possibilities were constructed.[88] The focus on age is concerned with how a period in an individual's life span, particularly as it is marked out in years, affected how a person's role and function was constructed. By ethnicity, I mean how the people, nation, or ancestry of a person, together with the cultural differences ascribed to such descent, affected how a person's role and function was constructed.[89]

Each of these elements relates to markers in the story of Jairus's daughter. A hearer of this account encountered a story that dealt with a female who was designated as a daughter, θυγάτηρ, a label that relates to her sex and specifically her positioning as a female in a family. By examining the representations of females in the first century CE through the lens of gender, we can observe how these depictions may have functioned and what they possibly symbolized. Likewise, the story refers to a female of a specific age—twelve years old—so the study pays attention to what significance might have been attached to labeling a person with a specific age or period in life, especially in relation to dying and death. Finally, the Jewish identity of the little daughter is evoked in the designation of her father as a synagogue leader. This marker lends itself to scrutinizing how representations of females functioned according to the ethnicity with which they were associated.

While I have delineated each interpretive optic for the sake of elucidating the approach of the study, they are not applied as singular and fixed entities in the examinations that occupy the following chapters. Nor do I approach them in isolation from each other. Rather, I recognize that notions of gender, age, and ethnicity can function in an interrelated dynamic, and are contingent on other sociocultural, political, and temporal factors at play in specific settings.[90]

Some clarification is needed as to what I mean by the term *body*. While studies of the subject of the body can refer to investigations into corporeal matter, for example, the scientific analysis of body parts such as extant bones, teeth, and hair, this is not the focus of our examination. Instead,

---

88. Caroline Bynum Walker, *Fragmentation and Redemption: Essays on Gender and the Human Body in Medieval Religion* (New York: Zone, 1992), 17.
89. Steve Fenton, *Ethnicity*, 2nd ed. (Cambridge: Polity, 2010), 3.
90. Wainwright, *Women Healing/Healing Women*, 13–14.

I am interested in how the physicality or corporeality of people is represented in the language and visual imagery employed by creators of the written and material sources we consider. By the physicality of a person, I mean their physical characteristics, the activities they undertake physically, and the perceptions that are associated with bodily senses. Jennifer Glancy refers to depictions of the body in antiquity as "cultural artifacts." For her, these representations are products of the dynamic interaction between those who generated them and the context in and for which they were constructed. They are objects that have been "shaped and experienced and interpreted" by both their creators and those who encountered them.[91] In this way, representations of bodies can be understood as objects that function as interesting entry points into understanding some of the attitudes and ideas that existed for those who beheld their works. In this study, they are windows into the cultural landscape in which a person of the first century CE participated.

I specifically examine this landscape by analyzing how corporal markers function in written and visual sources.[92] One aspect of this task entails noting the kinds of bodies and parts of the body that are depicted and observing how their state or condition is portrayed. To undertake this task, I pay close attention to how bodies appeared, analyzing factors such as how a person's body was labeled, described, dressed, adorned, and altered; which bodies a person encountered in detail over against those they did not. In terms of the body, I consider the age, size, and sex, as well as its physical positioning and geographical location. I note how emotions and sensations were represented in corporeal terms. This includes considering the sounds expressed by bodies, including references to volume and pitch. I observe those bodies that are described using literal and graphic or symbolic language.

A second aspect of the analysis involves observing the activities of bodies. This task has two facets. One facet is concerned with noting what bodies are depicted as doing. I consider, for example, the gestures and actions ascribed to specific figures. The other aspect is concerned with noting the actions that are directed at or committed on a human body. This dimension takes account of the descriptions of the effects of one figure's actions on the body of another.

---

91. Glancy, *Corporal Knowledge*, 7.
92. I note Glancy's use of the term *corporal markers*. See Jennifer A. Glancy, "Jesus, the Syrophoenician Woman, and Other First Century Bodies," *BibInt* 18 (2010): 350.

The following chapters are not a study of the body in general. We concentrate primarily on how women's and female children's bodies are portrayed in the range of sources we examine. Given that the story of Jairus's daughter concerns a daughter who is initially described as dying and then declared dead, we consider how dying and death is especially depicted in relation to the portraits of females. While women and female children are our primary focus, we will observe the representations of other figures beyond these where the contrast or comparison enables us to clarify our observations.

Before concluding, it is necessary to make some comments on those shaping influences on my own authorship of this study. The historical investigation at hand is not based on any one particular methodology, nor does it apply a specific theory. It should be clear by this stage that my starting point is the narrative of Mark's Gospel and the texts and images that were part of the broad milieu with which a hearer of the narrative intersected. I bring to bear on the analysis of these sources a range of assumptions that I have now elucidated. My approach does, nonetheless, have resonances with two other approaches. First, my concentration on the body and on the particularity of the representations of females' bodies certainly resonates with some of the concerns of feminist ideology.[93] I also assume recognition of the patriarchy embedded in the sociocultural fabric of life in the first century CE. My approach presupposes that questions of gender pertain to the representations of children as they do to adults. This awareness does not, however, automatically signal that I take for granted from the outset that all children and females were necessarily oppressed and marginalized in the first century CE, much less in the same ways or in equal measures. I assume that the experiences of women and children, like those of men, were contingent on their social and cultural locations.

---

93. I note that studies of the body are not the sole domain of feminist thinkers. For examples of scholarship on the body that is identified as intertextual, disability studies, studies of religion and history, and studies of ecology and theology respectively, see Michael Trainor, *Body of Jesus and Sexual Abuse: How the Gospel Passion Narrative Informs a Pastoral Approach* (Northcote, Australia: Morning Star, 2014); Lawrence, *Sense and Stigma in the Gospels*; Caroline Walker Bynum, *Resurrection of the Body in Western Christianity, 200–1336* (New York: Columbia University Press, 2013); Sallie McFague, *The Body of God: An Ecological Theology* (Minneapolis: Augsburg Fortress, 1993).

At the same time, I recognize that, while female (and male) children are visible in the samples we consider, they are generally voiceless in the world that we focus on. There is a lack of data generated by children themselves.[94] Moreover, I undertake the investigation cognizant of the fact that the primary sources used, particularly the literary sources, are composed by men. While I bring the depictions of children's and females' bodies to critical attention, without the explicit voices of females and children sounding in the study, the analysis—and the resultant reading of the story of Jairus's daughter—still remains partial.

Second, this study has resonance with aspects of the new historicism. In my approach to sources, I share a view of new historicists that literary sources are "integrally tied to and identified with other material realities that make up a social context."[95] In the case of my approach to the narrative of Mark, I presuppose that the author and the first-century hearer were enmeshed in their sociocultural contexts and that both literary and nonliterary sources equally provide glimpses of these contexts. Gina Hens-Piazza, reflecting on new historicist readings of the Bible, describes the biblical traditions as "acts of engagement with a vast and diverse reality made up of different and even opposing beliefs, values, biases and investments. As interpretations of that reality, the [biblical] text both bears witness to, and is imprinted with, the complexity of these fashionings."[96] Along similar lines, my shift away from locating Mark in one specific geographic location and thus becoming identified with a predetermined person or group, to the temporal reality of the hearer of the Markan narrative enables us to explore the story of Jairus's daughter within a broader, more diverse set of voices and worldviews. It widens the vantage point from which the story can be viewed, and thus creates possibilities for different insights to surface than what may otherwise have come to light in the context of a specific geographic location.

My attentiveness to the representations of children has resonance with a new historicist interest in figures that seldom attract much scholarly attention. While the story of the bleeding woman often captures the attention of many scholars, due in part to the concerted efforts of some

---

94. Jeannine Diddle Uzzi, "The Representation of Children in the Official Art of the Roman Empire from Augustus to Constantine" (PhD diss., Duke University, 1998), 12.

95. Hens-Piazza, *New Historicism*, 6.

96. Hens-Piazza, *New Historicism*, 46.

feminist biblical scholars, we recall from chapter 1 that the story of Jairus's daughter is often regarded as peripheral. Her story is seldom analyzed in terms of the contribution it singularly makes to the broader Markan narrative. In modern scholarship, we can consider the figure of Jairus's daughter and the story in which she features to be marginal. Bringing the figure of Jairus's daughter and the representations of children's bodies to critical attention as objects of study has resonance with the desire of new historicists to concentrate on elements of stories and subjects that rarely receive treatment but may be uniquely illuminating.

4
Images of Female Bodies in the Greco-Roman Landscape

> The begetting of children, the prolongation of a name, the adoption of sons, the careful preparation of wills, the very burial monuments, the epitaphs—What meaning have they except that we are thinking of the future as well as the present?
>
> —Cicero, *Tusc.* 1.32

Having outlined what sources we will use and how we will go about our examination of those sources, we now begin the first part of our investigation of how women and female children were portrayed by some of the voices that were contemporaneous with Mark's Gospel. Our major concern in this chapter is the representations of female bodies in Greco-Roman culture of the early empire, with a particular focus on the depictions of those who were dying or had died. To gain an insight into how images of women's and female children's bodies functioned in this era, I will discuss their various representations in the works of several writers of the period as well as their appearance on coins, statues, reliefs, and monuments that populated the geographical landscape.

The quotation from Cicero that heads this chapter provides an insightful presage of what will be apparent as the chapter unfolds. In 45 BCE, Cicero's beloved daughter, Tullia, died a month after giving birth to her first child and Cicero's first grandchild. Her death was followed shortly after by the death of the infant.[1] Tullia's death sent Cicero into a period of deep grief, during which he wrote prolifically. One of the publications he generated during this period was *Tusculan Disputations*, composed in the very place where Tullia had died—in a house in Tusculum, near

---

1. Margaret Graver, *Cicero on the Emotions: Tusculan Disputations 3 and 4* (Chicago: University of Chicago Press, 2002), xiii.

Rome. The first book of this work is a treatise that deals with the fear of death. Pondering questions of what happens after death, Cicero draws on various motifs in a dialogue concerning how a person's life could be understood to continue after death. He discusses the significance of children, monuments, and epitaphs not only to signify the status of a father in the present, earthly life—in which they are "restricted to the narrow limits of their life"—but also a means of ensuring that the man's name and status endured, in the "good hope of immortality" (*Tusc.* 1.33).[2] Children, along with monuments and epitaphs that publicly attested to a person's station in life, were understood to furnish a future beyond death for a person who had died.

Cicero's reflection, composed earlier than most of the data we will examine, introduces us to images and ideas that were eventually to become part and parcel of the early imperial world. The broad context of *Tusculan Disputations*—the grieving of Tullia's death—resonates with one of the key images of daughters in the first century CE: the death of a beloved daughter. What will also be apparent in our study is the way in which images of children, including daughters, functioned as symbols of stability and hope for families and empire in visual, written, and oral media. The quotation from *Tusc.* 1.32, while mentioning the procreation of children ("quid procreatio liberorum") and the adoption of sons ("quid adoptationes filiorum"), makes no explicit reference to daughters. In some of the material we will examine, daughters may be assumed in the general category of children. As we shall observe, however, distinct images of women and female children also existed, which will contribute to our exploration.

A central representation of girls in the literary and material data of the early empire is that of a daughter. As such, she is clearly located within the structure of the family. To understand the construction of images of girls, it is necessary therefore to examine how families were represented in the

---

2. The senior male figure (and Roman citizen) of a family was the paterfamilias. He was granted *patria potesta,* the legal power over family members, slaves, and the property of the family. This legal authority did not extend, however, to the man's wife and her property. While a wife's father remained alive, she was considered part of his family and came under his legal authority. See Suzanne Dixon, "From Ceremonial to Sexualities: A Survey of Scholarship on Roman Marriage," in *A Companion to Families in the Greek and Roman Worlds,* ed. Beryl Rawson, BCAW (Chichester: Wiley-Blackwell, 2011), 250–51; Richard Saller, "The Roman Family as Productive Unit," in Rawson, *Companion to Families,* 119.

early empire and the roles understood to be constituent of familial structures. Integral to this task is the analysis of the imagery of adult females, whose representations have a direct bearing on how young females were characterized. Similarly, the portrayals of children also warrant our attention to appreciate the particular depictions of girls. Given these interrelated elements, the chapter will undertake an examination of the following areas to demonstrate how girls were conceptualized among some of the voices within the early empire:

1. The family as a central image in the early empire;
2. Images of adult females within the family;
3. Children in general within families as symbols of hope and status;
4. The young female in the context of the family;
5. Depictions of dying and deceased girls.

This analysis will reveal that representations of a daughter who had deceased were commonplace in the literary and material landscapes of the early Roman Empire. These images functioned as icons, publicly mediating the aspirations of families and the values of Roman society more broadly. At the same time, they enabled families to mourn the loss of those aspirations that their daughters had come to represent.

4.1. The Family as a Central Image in the Early Empire

Images of families were a common feature in the early empire.[3] Their depictions became visible in the public arena in inscriptions and reliefs on monuments, in public art and architecture, processions and rituals, and on coins. Their representations also appeared in the texts of various writers during the Julio-Claudian and Flavian dynasties. The family functioned

---

3. Terms associated with the family included the following: *domus* or household, which could include slaves; *oikos* or the house or household; *paterfamilias* or the senior male figure of the *familia*; *familia* could refer to the conjugal or nuclear family as well as slaves. The emperor was the *pater patriae* or father of the nation. See Stephen L. Dyson, "The Family and the Roman Country-Side," in Rawson *Companion to Families*, 431; Tim Parkin, "The Roman Life Course and the Family," in Rawson, *Companion to Families*, 283; Beryl Rawson, "Family and Society," in *The Oxford Handbook of Roman Studies*, ed. Alessandro Barchiesi and Walter Scheidel (Oxford: Oxford University Press, 2010), 611, 612, 615, 617, 621; Saller, "Roman Family," 217.

as an institution in the Roman Empire and, as such, both shaped and was shaped by the society of which it was a part.[4]

While a prominent feature of Roman life, the family was not, however a homogenous unit.[5] Family life took various forms and expressions. Membership of a family, for example, could change over the course of time due to factors such as divorce, war, death, and remarriage, with the size of a family, and the roles contained within it also shifting over time.[6] Furthermore, some Romans did not place equal value on all families. The families of enemies and foreigners, for instance, were routinely depicted as being fragmented, humiliated, and even murdered at the hands of their Roman conquerors.[7] Notwithstanding such diversity, the high visibility of the family in Roman culture suggests it was operative in the consciousness of Roman society and held a degree of import.

Large honorary monuments such as the Ara Pacis and the Germanicus Arch are potent examples of the prominence of familial images, as well as testimonies to the power of those images to express Roman values. Both monuments were erected in a public setting to preserve the memory of the imperial family. The Ara Pacis was inaugurated in 9 BCE to celebrate the return of Augustus from a successful campaign in Spain and Gaul. It was erected at Campus Martius, a location in the northern part of Rome. An urbanized area, Campus Martius had once been the site where the Roman army and cavalry had practiced maneuvers, and had since become the place where Roman youth carried out athletic activities. We can, therefore, assume it was a place that people frequented.[8]

The monument was also positioned in close proximity to the Horologium (a solar meridian) and the earlier constructed Mausoleum. Together these three structures publicly commemorated Augustus. Peter Heslin's observations of this triad are pertinent for our study:

> Each of the three is a family monument for the Julii: the Mausoleum for their burial; the altar, which was dedicated on Livia's birthday, depicting

---

[4]. The focus of this study is the period of the early empire. Prior to this period, the family was already relevant in republican Rome.

[5]. Rawson, "Family and Society," 611–13.

[6]. For observations about the variances in family life in the Roman Empire, see Laes, *Children in the Roman Empire*, 26–37, 45–47.

[7]. Rawson, "Family," 622.

[8]. Orietta Rossini, *Ara Pacis Guide* (Milan: Electa, 2007), 6, 12.

them in procession; and the meridian that celebrates the moment when finally, late in life, as an ostentatious token of his unsurpassed clemency and forbearance, Augustus took over the position of Pontifex Maximus that his father had occupied early in life, as a token of his unprecedented ambition.[9]

The triangulation of the monuments can be understood to have symbolized the importance of the imperial family, headed by Augustus, in the establishment of peace.

The Ara Pacis depicted the broad membership of the imperial family, encompassing female and male adults as well as representations of their actual children, both male and female.[10] The children in the southern and northern friezes of the monument were intermixed with the adults in a procession of the imperial family. Neither separated from nor concealed by the adults in either frieze, each child was individually depicted. Each appeared as integral to the collective identity of this triumphant family led by its adults, their prominence helping convey notions of the continuity, future stability, and ongoing power of the imperial family and thereby of the empire.

The Germanicus Arch in Rome, dedicated in 19 CE to commemorate the death of Germanicus, also promoted the family as central to the ongoing military might of the empire.[11] According to the decree of the senate, the monument was to include reliefs of conquered peoples as well as an inscription that detailed the military triumphs of Germanicus. The arch was also to feature images of Germanicus in a triumphal chariot with representations of his extensive family: Drusus, his father; Antonia, his mother; Agrippina, his wife; Livia, his sister; Tiberius, his brother and future emperor; and his three sons and two daughters.[12] Indeed, each of the twelve members of the family

---

9. Peter Heslin, "Augustus, Domitian and the So-Called Horologium Augusti," *JRS* 97 (2007): 16.

10. For observations on the identities of the children in the Ara Pacis, see Jeannine Diddle Uzzi, *Children in the Visual Arts of Imperial Rome* (New York: Cambridge University Press, 2005), 142–44. See also Rossini, *Ara Pacis*, 50–53.

11. Catalog listing 35. Charles Brian Rose, *Dynastic Commemoration and Imperial Portraiture in the Julio-Claudian Period* (Cambridge: Cambridge University Press, 1997). The Arch of Germanicus in Rome no longer exists. What is known now about the arch is derived from the Tabula Siarensis. According to Rawson, this is the most complete extant copy of the senatorial decree (*Children and Childhood*, 36 n. 33).

12. Cicero also takes up the images of children and descendants standing in close proximity to the statue of their father during a public spectacle in his argument for a public tomb to honor Servius Sulpicius (*Phil.* 9.16–17).

was to be represented with their own statue, to signify not only the size of the family's membership but also the importance of individual members of the family—including children—to the ongoing might of the empire.

The representation and location of the Germanicus Arch further underscored its symbolic import. Arches signified the imperial expansion and might of Rome.[13] The inclusion of members of the imperial family on this arch reinforced the idea that the entire family was fundamental to the potency of the empire. The site of the Germanicus Arch was the Circus Flaminius, an area already populated with monuments that celebrated former leaders of Rome and statues commemorating Augustus and his family.[14] Locating the arch of Germanicus in this place not only emphasized the social status of Germanicus as a member of the Augustan dynasty, it also conveyed the importance of the entire imperial family in the ongoing prosperity of the empire.[15]

Some one hundred years after the dedication of the Germanicus Arch, Tacitus took up the image of the triumphant Germanicus in *Ann.* 2.41. In this text, he described the spectacle that publicly honored Germanicus's victory over the Germans. Captives and the spoils of war were paraded to reinforce the triumph, as was the standard practice. At the same time, Tacitus identified the victor's five children sitting in the chariot with the commander, their father. In Tacitus's account, they are positioned in close proximity to their father, sharing in his victory. The scene is devoid, however, of the presence of Germanicus's parents, siblings, and wife, unlike that which we observed in the instructions for the Germanicus Arch. Perhaps the excision of these family members reflects Tacitus's concerns with what he saw as the unhelpful intermingling of the imperial household with the politics of the empire. In the *Annals*, the imperial wives in particular were cast as powerful figures that unduly influenced the civic and political domains of Roman life, which in Tacitus's view ought to have been the dominion of men.[16] Tacitus's emphasis in recounting Germanicus's

---

13. Gwynaeth McIntyre, *A Family of Gods: The Worship of the Imperial Family in the Latin West*, Societas (Ann Arbor: University of Michigan Press, 2016), 47.

14. Statues associated with *domus Augusta* (the Augustan house) and Divus Augustus were located in this area. See Marleen B. Flory, "Dynastic Ideology, the Domus Augusta, and Imperial Women: A Lost Statuary Group in the Circus Flaminius," *TAPA* 126 (1996): 289.

15. Flory, "Dynastic Ideology," 302–3.

16. E.g., Tacitus's depiction of Livia in *Ann.* 1.10.5 (Milnor, "Women," 467–73).

triumphant parade was on fatherhood and dynastic continuity. Indeed, Germanicus was characterized as the "epitome of the family man."[17] Juxtaposing images of victory with images of fatherhood, Tacitus upheld the family-line of Germanicus—specifically in the figures of the father and his children—as integral to the ongoing success of the empire.[18]

Early in the first century CE, these two public imperial monuments were erected, which promoted the importance of children and the willingness to have them seen as part of what constituted a family. The inclusion of children was still evident—perhaps even more so—one hundred years later in Tacitus's literary account of the procession celebrating the triumphant Germanicus. In both examples, the image of the family played a role in communicating values concerning the present and ongoing power of a triumphant empire. The children were held up to the viewers' eyes as important figures within the complex of the family. Their inclusion was not an embellishment of the monument or narrative. Instead, they were co-opted to convey notions of the family's continuing power.

4.2. Images of Adult Females within the Family

Images of females also feature in the literary and material domains of the early empire. They occur within the context of family, as wives, mothers, daughters, and sisters.[19] These latter two categories emerge in depictions of female adults and children. As we have observed, images of families with children were visible and sought to suggest specific ideas in the early empire. This remains the case in the specific depictions of young daughters and sisters. There is a correlation, however, in the way in which ideas about

---

17. Rawson, *Children and Childhood*, 314.

18. Representations of the father as head of the household were common in Roman culture, e.g. Plutarch, *Comp. Lyc. Num.* 3.1–7; 4.2–5. The image of the father is foundational in the imagery of *pietas* in Cicero, *Rep.* 6.14. Dixon, however, argues that many Romans would not have had a father living by the time they married; therefore, they would have acted independently of paternal authority (Dixon, "From Ceremonial to Sexualities"). Along similar lines, Laes calculates that by age ten, one quarter of Roman children had lost their fathers. By age fifteen, 62 percent of females had a living father and 71 percent had mothers. This, he argues, qualifies the idea of the *pater familias* (*Children in the Roman Empire*, 28–29).

19. An exception is the image of a non-Roman woman to represent the captured Judea, where the female is depicted as a captive, rather than a wife, mother, or daughter. E.g., *RIC* 2:58, nos. 1, 2, 3, 4.

women and female children were constructed. Put differently, the role that images of female children may have played is partly contingent on how female adults were valued. In order to appreciate the possible meanings that may have been attributed to female children, we need to examine the main ways by which adult females were represented.

4.2.1. Females as Wives

The representation of a woman in the period of the early empire was derived predominantly from her role in the family. One of the central ways in which this imagery found expression was in the importance attached to her role as a wife. This is evident is the literature and the material culture of Rome where we find examples of the qualities—both physical and dispositional—that are extolled in Roman wives. Women were noted positively for their domestic activities: staying at home, tending to children, and keeping the home in order (Plutarch, *Cons. ux.* 9b, c; 611c, d). In the mid-first-century stela of Menimani and Blussus, for example, we find a familial triad of mother, father, and son. The wife, Menimani, is seated next to her husband, Blussus, with the son standing behind both parents. Blussus, a sailor, holds money while Menimani has a wool-basket to symbolize domestic productivity and virtue (*CIL* 13.7067B).[20] In other examples, wives commonly noted for their beauty, are also commended for their physical modesty. This reveals itself in comments about chastity and the simplicity of dress and appearance (*CIL* 6.11602, 1527, and 31670). It is also evident in remarks such as those of Plutarch, who praised women who practiced sobriety and silence (*Comp. Lyc. Num.* 77). These examples illustrate values that some Romans associated with an ideal wife. Her natural habitat was the home. She was productive, modest, and chaste, practicing self-control and, in Plutarch's case, silence.[21]

The model Roman wife was also devoted to her husband. A dramatic physical expression of this devotion was a wife's suicide following the death of her husband. Tacitus reveals this gesture in his narrative of the

---

20. Other examples of wives being extolled for working with wool include *CIL* 6.11602, 1527, and 31670. See also Suzanne Dixon, *Reading Roman Women: Sources, Genres, and Real Life* (London: Duckworth, 2001), 154.

21. Juvenal notes that women do exercise voice—and in public—but he describes this activity most unfavorably (*Sat.* 6.415, 435–477). In contrast, Cicero refers to both parents using speech as part of raising children (*Brut.* 211).

fate of Seneca. Faced with the impending death of her husband, Paulina is directed to moderate her grief (*Ann.* 15.63). This coheres with the social virtues of moderation and self-control. As a sign of affection for her husband, however, she contemplates suicide. As such, her suicide is regarded by Tacitus as a "glorious death" (*Ann.* 15.63). It is worthy of praise. Along similar lines, Pliny recounts the suicidal aspirations of a "heroic" Arria, the wife of the captured Aulus Caecina Paetus. With dramatic detail, Pliny describes Arria's suicide attempt in which she plunges a dagger into her breast. After pulling the dagger out and handing it to her husband, she dashes her head against a wall so that she falls senseless (*Ep.* 3.16). As in the case of Paulina, Arria's desire to suicide is also labeled in terms of a "glorious" death (*Ep.* 3.16).

Both of these suicides are presented by Pliny and Tacitus as good deaths. Each wife has agency, acting out of her own initiative and her love for her husband; she meets her death with purpose. Yet these deaths are as equally concerned with politics as they are with love.[22] While the prospect of life without a husband may have felt unbearable for each wife, the prospect of living with the indignity that resulted from a husband's death or captivity, as in the respective cases of Paulina and Arria, may have been just as unbearable. Indeed, Tacitus reveals this element to a wife's suicide. Paulina's suicide is a means of averting "exposure to outrage" that is a consequence of her marriage to Seneca, who has been sentenced to death (*Ann.* 15.63). It is a way of Paulina achieving fame from what is understood to be a state of disgrace. In this way, a wife's suicide may have been a means of reclaiming her honor in the face of civic humiliation (*Ann.* 15.63). The actions of a husband had ramifications for the status of his wife. While the role of wife was presented as generally worthy and granted women respect, it also potentially rendered women vulnerable.

In addition to their physical qualities, wives were also extolled for their disposition. An epitaph on a public funerary monument in the late first century BCE praises a wife for her obedience, loyalty, and affability, her good nature, and her adherence to religion (*CIL* 6.1527, 31670). The dedicator, her husband, commends his wife for maintaining domestic harmony. He notes her devotion to her family, particularly her in-laws, indicating the care she took for her mother-in-law, which ensured a peace-

---

22. Hope and Huskinson, *Memory and Mourning*, 39. They note that men suicided too, but this is commonly located in contexts of warfare not as a sign of marital devotion at the death of one's wife.

ful life for the extended family. This complements the opening line of the inscription in which the husband indicates their marriage had been atypically long, having evaded divorce. For this dedicator, an ideal woman was one who was equally compliant and committed to husband and family, features that can be seen to have some resonance with the physical traits and activities of women that we noted in the earlier examples.

4.2.2. Females as Mothers

Another way in which a woman's position in the family found expression was in the significance afforded to her as a mother. The value of motherhood in the early empire could be seen on honorary and funerary monuments, on coins, and in the literary sources. People were immersed in an environment that highlighted the perceived importance of being a mother.

Mothers associated with the imperial family were highly visible on coins that bore their images. Women first appeared on Roman coins during the Julio-Claudian dynasty with the appearance of Julia and Octavia. Both were depicted in terms of their role as wives and mothers.[23] In 13 BCE, two coins were struck that featured portraits of Lucius and Gaius, the grandsons and adopted sons of Augustus, with their mother, Julia (*RIC* 1:72, nos. 404, 405). Julia's head is adorned with a wreath and she sits in between both boys. During the reign of Nero, Agrippina II appeared on coins that labeled her as the mother of Augustus (*RIC* 1:185, nos. 607, 608, 609, 610). Later, in the Flavian era, the figure of Domitia appeared on coins, labeled as the mother of Caesar (*RIC* 2, nos. 132–135). In each image, the woman sat on a seat, with her hand extended to a child. It is clear that the role of mother was being extolled.

In Beryl Rawson's view, the inclusion of children on coins symbolized imperial succession.[24] Their images conveyed to those who handled the coins in the empire that there was progeny who would continue the family line. While the focus of the coin was the child, we might consider that the image of the woman as mother reinforced this notion of succession. If Rawson's interpretation is correct, it is possible that the inclusion of images of mothers suggested that motherhood was also perceived to be

---

23. Beryl Rawson, "The Iconography of Roman Childhood," in *The Roman Family in Italy: Status, Sentiment, Space*, ed. Beryl Rawson and Paul Weaver (Oxford: Oxford University Press, 1997), 205–32.

24. Rawson, "Iconography," 215.

4. Images of Female Bodies in the Greco-Roman Landscape

integral to the continuity of the imperial dynasty. It was publicly promoted as an important ingredient to the empire's future and success.

Given the representations of mothers and sons in the imagery of dynastic succession, it is not surprising that another way in which the value for motherhood found public expression was in relation to images of fertility and childbearing. This is apparent in the early empire in the panel of Tellus on the Ara Pacis.[25] The panel features an adult female with drapery slipping off her shoulders, revealing the silhouette of her breasts, abdomen, and legs. Her hair is adorned with signs of natural fruitfulness: poppies and grain. On her lap, we see further such signs: grapes, pomegranates, corn, and poppies. The scene behind her conveys a lushness: plants, sheep, and grazing oxen.[26] She holds a baby in either arm, both of whom reach for her breast.

Paul Zanker speculates whether the scene separately connotes the goddesses Venus or Ceres or the earth goddess, Tellus, or if it simultaneously evokes all three deities who were associated with fertility. Either way, in Zanker's view the figure connotes notions of fecundity, divinity, and growth.[27] The veiled head that signifies a married woman and the gesture of babies who reach to be breastfed reinforces the image of the breastfeeding mother being conflated with the gods and the ideal of fertility. These ideas of motherhood, fecundity, and divinity are further associated with the empire given the placement of the Tellus panel on the Ara Pacis. As we have already noted, images of the imperial family on the Ara Pacis conjured a sense of imperial continuity. We see in the Tellus panel that a woman's capacity for childbearing and suckling babies was keenly promoted as a central dynamic in realizing the future of the empire.[28]

While the wives and mothers of the imperial households were highly visible, the promotion of motherhood in general as integral to a

---

25. Rossini, *Ara Pacis*, 36–45.

26. Paul Zanker, *The Power of Images in the Age of Augustus*, trans. Alan Shapiro, Jerome Lectures (Ann Arbor: University of Michigan Press, 1988), 172.

27. Zanker, *Power of Images*, 174.

28. The images of a woman's breast and of breastfeeding were commonly taken up in relation to motherhood. While women practiced breastfeeding, however, it was not necessarily the biological mother who took up this role. In wealthy families, wet nurses could be employed to suckle an infant. At the same time, slave women who were charged with household duties also used wet nurses to breastfeed their babies (*CIL* 6.19128; Rawson, *Children and Childhood*, 124). Women who opted for wet nurses in preference to breastfeeding their own offspring are criticized by Tacitus (*Germ.* 20.1).

flourishing empire also found expression in the public arena. One illustration of this takes place in the role of mothers in the secular games of 17 BCE (*CIL* 6.323232-6). Along with children, mothers had a prominent place in the ritual. Two elements are pertinent here. First, Augustus is described as making sacrifices to Ilythia, the Greek goddess of childbirth (*CIL* 6.323232-6, lines 115–118). Second, 110 Roman mistresses of households are identified as offering a prayer (dictated by Marcus Agrippa) to Juno. Commanded to assemble on the Capitoline, the women pray to, "[Increase the power] and majesty of the Roman people … [Grant … safety], victory, [and health to the Roman people], [keep safe and make greater] the state [of the Roman people]" (*CIL* 6.323232-6, lines 123–132).[29] The motherhood of Roman citizens is presented as a fundamental element of society in these games. The emperor himself recognizes the importance of childbearing among citizens as well as the imperial family in his gesture to Ilythia. The words put on the lips of the Roman wives further contextualize the significance of childbearing: Its function was to support the ongoing strength and security of the empire. For those immersed in this spectacle, the message being communicated to them was clear: the ideal Roman woman was a mother who bore children to ensure the vitality of the empire.[30]

In so much as the adult female body was valued for its capacity to bear children, it was equally scorned, however, for its expressions of sexuality. Women perceived not to conform to the ideals of the Roman wife and mother were sexualized and described pejoratively in terms of their sexual status. This is evident in some of the writings of the early empire. Tacitus's depiction of Messalina, the wife of the emperor Claudius, is a case in point. She is described as having a sexual relationship with Silius that results in a secret marriage to him. This activity is labeled as debauchery (*Ann.* 11.34).[31] What is identified as her sexual appetite is associated with corruption (*Ann.* 11. 38). Characterized this way, Messalina is rendered

---

29. Mary Beard, John North, and Simon Price, *Religions of Rome*, 2 vols. (Cambridge: Cambridge University Press, 1998), 142.

30. For a representation of a woman in the early empire (late Flavian period) who is not necessarily commemorated in terms of childbearing, see the relief on the Haterii monument in J. M. C. Toynbee, *Death and Burial in the Roman World* (Ithaca, NY: Cornell University Press, 1971), 44, pl. 9. The figure of an adult female lying in state is surrounded by images of fertility but there is no clear reference to her marital status.

31. Also Juvenal, *Sat.* 6.114–140.

a dishonorable woman. Any attempt on her behalf to secure decency in death through suicide is thwarted when, instead, she is murdered by a tribune, a fitting death in Tacitus's view (*Ann.* 11.38). The treatment of her corpse further reflects Tacitus's appraisal of her activity. She is handed over to her mother, but there is no description of funerary rites. Her violent death elicits no emotion from her husband, in terms of either joy or sadness. Her loss is not mourned in Tacitus's narrative.

Likewise, women who were understood to be controlling their fertility could be regarded unfavorably by some. Tacitus labels Roman women whom he perceives to be limiting the number of children they had as "abominable" (*Germ.* 19). The resistance to bear children was imputed to women.[32] In a society that sought to promote the family, female fertility was a prized asset and a women's ability to control it could be perceived by some to pose a threat. In Tacitus's view, the desire to restrict childbearing was indicative of a broader corruption among Roman women, to whom he also attributed the infelicitous behavior of adultery and desisting from breastfeeding their own children.

Further representations of women who did not conform to the Roman ideals of wife and mother are evident in the depictions of women who take on stereotypically male-oriented activities. Again, these images emerge among the literary voices. An expression of this is found in Juvenal. He identifies literate women who participate in dinner parties of mixed company but labels their spoken word disparagingly as "verbiage" and noise (*Sat.* 6.435–477).[33] Those wives whose movements take them beyond the domain of the household are commonly pictured as licentious (*Sat.* 6.220–229). Women mete out violence on others, appearing as cruel and indifferent to the suffering they inflict (*Sat.* 6.500–510). The judgment against those wives who enact violence on innocent neighbors is embodied in their faces, which become "hideous," contra the cultural normativity that valued women's physical beauty (*Sat.* 6.410–415).[34] Those women who take to the wrestling floor as gladiators, wearing the

---

32. Also, Juvenal, *Sat.* 6.590–600. According to Dixon, Roman women were sometimes presented as symbols of decadence in the criticism of the declining morality of the upper classes. This manifests itself in women being accused of adultery, debauchery, and abortion (*Reading Roman Women*, 56–63).

33. Rawson, *Children and Childhood*, 203–4.

34. Juvenal, however, also problematizes the physical beauty of wives (*Sat.* 6.140–150).

purple garb and helmet and taking up the sword and shield, are presented as having run away from their gender (*Sat.* 6.245–265). In other words, those women who exercise voice and bodily agency, and engage in domains beyond those of the household, act against the norms of their gender in the view of Juvenal.[35] In these instances, women function as symbols of corruption.

4.2.3. Female Bodies and Expressions of Grief

A third representation of women that was commonplace in the early empire was that of grieving women. High rates of infant and childhood mortality, maternal deaths in childbirth, in addition to the prevalence of disease, violence, and fatal accidents all meant that death was ubiquitous. In this context, women became symbols for communities who mourned, voicing their loss and embodying their grief. Such images were highly visible, evident in both material and literary sources.

Mourning the loss of a deceased person had a corporeal dimension. Scenes on funerary reliefs incorporated images of particular bodily gestures and states that were associated with the rites of mourning. This is exemplified in the Haterii monument.[36] Two female mourners with disheveled hair and hands raised to beat their breasts are positioned to the left of a woman lying in state. In front of the curtain below the corpse, both men and women—two apiece—are similarly represented as beating their breasts. The women have hair that hangs by their shoulders. At the head of the couch, three women, also with disheveled hair, clasp a knee in a gesture of grief. The beating of the breast and the appearance of unkempt hair signal the scene of grief for the deceased woman.

The gesture of the beating of the breast is likewise taken up by Plutarch in *Consolation to His Wife*, although he also incorporates descriptions of human sound to the picture of grief. His references to weeping and wailing vocalize the sense of loss (*Cons. ux.* 4). Plutarch takes up this image, however, not to commend women who grieve in such a manner but on the contrary, to critique such an expression of grief. The physical outpouring of grief shown by a mother at the loss of a child is excessive and

---

35. In contrast, Cicero, writing earlier than Juvenal, extols the exercising of voice in the rearing of female children by both male and female parents and grandparents (*Brut.* 211).

36. Toynbee, *Death and Burial*, 44, pl. 9.

therefore shameful in Plutarch's view. In this case, it is the death of his own beloved two-year-old daughter about which he writes. He extols the virtues of his wife who does not lament her loss in such an extreme way. She does not beat her breast, or wail and weep. Neither does she crop her head in mourning, dye her clothes black, sit in an uncomely posture or lie in discomfort—gestures that Plutarch associates with the excessive displays of women's mourning (*Cons. ux.* 4). Instead, Plutarch notes that in the reports received regarding his daughter's funeral, his wife had conducted herself with "decorum and in silence, in the company of our nearest kin" (*Cons. ux.* 4).

Similarly, Pliny takes up the image of the weeping mother in his account of Arria's response to the death of her son. Likewise, it is her ability to conceal her physical signs of grief, signified by dry eyes and a composed face, that renders her brave in the author's account (*Ep.* 3.16). Along similar lines, in his narration of the funeral rites for Germanicus, Tacitus does not represent the wife Agrippina in terms of physical expressions of grief, nor the children (*Ann.* 3.1–3). Agrippina appropriately maintains her composure. Instead, it is the crowd to whom the sounds of mourning are ascribed: a groan and wailing (*Ann.* 3.1–2). Tacitus communicates the sense of loss at the death of Germanicus through the voice of the crowd, while concomitantly preserving the dignified status of Agrippina and the children. Tacitus uses both images—the poignant grief of the crowd and the self-composure of the family—to reinforce the esteem he associated with Germanicus's life.

While both men and women are represented as giving expression to grief, in the literary sources it is women who are described as grieving excessively and who therefore attract criticism. Darja Šterbenc Erker observes that excessive forms of grief indicated that a person was out of control, a state that was incompatible with the Roman ideal of self-control.[37] Thus, while on the one hand, outpourings of emotion in the literature mediated the grief of a community, on the other hand the criticism of such outpourings conformed to the Roman value for moderation. Scenes of grief took on a meaning not merely concerned with the loss of the individual. They also communicated broader values about what it meant to be a good citizen.

---

37. Šterbenc Erker, "Gender and Roman Funeral Ritual," in Hope and Huskinson, *Memory and Mourning*, 49.

4.3. Images of Children within the Family

As we have now observed, any person who walked the pavements of Rome in the early period of the empire was likely to encounter images of families. Likewise, those who engaged with various literary voices of the time also came across depictions of families. The family, albeit manifesting itself in various forms, was a valued social unit. Literary and material representations of mothers and fathers conveyed notions about who and what constituted ideal parents and citizens. Similarly, children were also discernible in the social landscape of the early empire. Their depictions on honorary and funerary monuments, in processions, on coins, and in texts gave them a visible presence in the public arena. Like those of adults, images of children communicated ideas that were less about the individual child and more about the broader issues and principles of the time. It is to these images that we now turn.

4.3.1. Children as Symbols of the Future

The value of children was located primarily in the context of the family. Images of children were generated in families as a testimony to the aspirations of their families. An expression of this is apparent in the way in which the imperial family used images of their own children. As we have previously noted, coins that were struck during the Julio-Claudian era, for example, featured the adopted sons of the emperor Augustus, Lucius and Gaius (*RIC* 1:72, nos. 404, 405). This kind of imagery reinforced public awareness that there were sons who would continue the imperial family's line. The pictures of the two boys on the coins feature only their busts; they are not depicted in terms of any action. What was of greatest import in representing the sons was their obvious familial identity and status, not anything the boys had said or done, or even what potentially they might do. The images sought to convey a belief in the value of dynastic continuity.

The association of children with beliefs about a family's stability and ongoing survival permeated early imperial society. We have already noted the presence of children on the northern and southern friezes of the Ara Pacis as symbols of continuity. A closer examination of how the children are depicted, however, demonstrates how gestures of touch could specifically embody a connection between the present and the future. While the exact identities of the children are arguably not clear, the fact that they are children is readily apparent.[38] A feature of the children is that they generally physically interact with the adults throughout the familial procession. A male adult, for example, places his hand on Julia Minor in the northern frieze. Other children—with the exception of Domitia in the southern frieze—hold the hands of adults or grasp their togas.[39] These ordinary yet intimate physical gestures further underscore the ongoing successful trajectory of the imperial family that is being communicated.[40] Through the depiction of touch, the children in this monument embody both the thriving reality of the imperial family in the present and its potentially flourishing future.

Portraits of the interconnectedness between generations, however, were not the reserve of the imperial family. The material landscape contained monuments of other families that similarly conjured up images of family continuity through the depiction of children in close proximity to their parents. Indeed, the late first century BCE saw a shift in the visual representations of families to one where children physically interacted with parents. In the earliest of these (13 BCE–5 CE), a young female child interacts with her mother and father.[41] She is positioned in between her parents, reinforcing the familial context of the piece. Her parents hold hands, signifying they are married, while the girl grasps her mother's dress and right thigh.[42] These physical gestures paint a picture of closeness among the triad.[43] Her father wears the toga, demonstrating his status as a Roman citizen. The child, therefore, is not only clearly

---

38. On public monuments, the figures of children are often smaller than adults. While their dress may not always necessarily distinguish them from the adults, their physical size does. See, e.g., Valentin Kockel, *Porträtreliefs stadtrömischer Grabbauten: Ein Beitrag zur Geschichte und zum Verständnis des spätrepublikanisch-frühkaiserzeitlichen Privatporträts* (Mainz: von Zabern, 1993), 145–46, fig. 9.5, pl. 56a; Rawson, "Iconography," 217.

39. Rossini, *Ara Pacis*, 50–53.

40. Uzzi, *Children*, 144.

41. Rawson, "Iconography," 217, fig. 9.5.

42. For an example of how the marital relationship is accentuated when parents join right hands, see Kockel, *Porträtreliefs stadtrömischer Grabbauten*, 532, nos. C3, F11, F12, and L20. See also, Sabine Müller, "Dextrarum Iunctio," in *The Encyclopedia of Ancient History* (New York: Wiley & Sons, 2013), https://doi.org/10.1002/9781444338386.wbeah22079.

43. Janet Huskinson, "Picturing the Roman Family," in Rawson, *Companion to Families*, 532.

recognizable as part of the family core, she is also unmistakably part of a Roman family. The physical interconnectedness between the girl and her parents embodies the continuation of the family as Roman citizens through their daughter.

Representations of physical touch and the holding of hands among family members are also evident in the mid-first century CE. The Sertorii relief (50 CE), for example, features a boy and a girl interspersed between three adults.[44] The adult male is in the center and two female adults are located at either end of the horizontal relief. The adults and children are physically interconnected through the linking of hands, a gesture possibly denoting the family ties that unified the group.[45] It is probable that these instances of physical contact through the linking or holding of hands functioned to symbolize the bonds that existed within a family unit.

Along with representing the bonds that united families, images of children embodied the expectations of hope held by the adults around them. This is exemplified in the role children played in the secular games of 17 BCE. We have briefly observed the role of mothers in the rituals of the games. Children, too, had a key role in this facet of the event. Equally represented, twenty-seven boys and the same number of girls exercised a prominent role in the singing of the hymn. The inscription reveals that the children were the offspring of living mothers and fathers, a detail that reveals that the primacy of the family was being promoted (*CIL* 6.323232-6). As we noted earlier, the games featured Augustus's prayer to the goddess of childbirth and the mothers' prayer for the ongoing power of the empire. When placed alongside these, the presence of children in the ritual conveyed a belief that the future of the empire was possible in them.

Indeed, we might even contemplate that the inclusion of children in the games was part of a strategy to ensure that they would eventually fulfill this aspiration. Their participation in the games (and possibly the role of children as observers of the games) may attest to the power of the spectacle to form children in the ideals of Roman society.[46] As children sang the hymn, or as other children watched them sing, they were potentially socialized into the beliefs and hopes of the emperor for the future of the empire.

---

44. Larsson Loven, "Children and Childhood," 308, fig. 15.4.

45. Larsson Loven, "Children and Childhood," 307.

46. Rawson suggests that children may have witnessed the secular games as either "direct participants or observers" (*Children and Childhood*, 317).

A similar picture emerges later in Tacitus's *Histories*. Boys and girls are part of the scene he paints to describe the ceremony inaugurating the restoration of the temple to Jupiter in 70 CE. They accompany the vestal virgins who sanctify the site by the sprinkling of water. Signs of life permeate the scene: "fillets and garlands," "soldiers [with] auspicious names ... carrying boughs of good omen," and "water from fountains and streams" (*Hist.* 4.53). The boys and girls who participate are identified as children of mothers and fathers who still live. Tacitus renders a scene of restoration that abounds with images of continuity and hope; elemental to this picture is the presence of children.

Conversely, the shaping influence of the image of the child as a symbol of continuity and hope is also conveyed in the dangers that they were perceived to pose. In practical terms, the high incidence of infant and child mortality created tensions around the ongoing viability of families. The death of a son, for instance, could elicit fears about the long-term sustainability of a family. One funerary inscription provides evidence of the anxiety generated in a family with the death of their two-year-old son (*CIL* 6.18086). The premature death of the boy is understood to spell the end of his grandmother's source of financial support. With the prospective family steward dead, the family (at least the elderly female) is left vulnerable. There is also evidence, albeit far less, that adult daughters cared for adult family members of the family. Valerius Maximus, for example, reflects this Roman notion of *pietas* or reciprocal affection and duty in his description of how a daughter succors her imprisoned mother (*Fact.* 5.4).[47] In a society in which families anticipated that children would eventually become adults who took care of aging family members, the deaths of children potentially exposed them to peril.[48] The loss of hope that accompanied a child's death could be pragmatically real.

As potent symbols of continuity and hope, children were also perceived to pose a threat to the political aspirations among some of the adults of the empire. Children who had become emblematic of the future stability and triumph of a family, such as those associated with the imperial families, were vulnerable. This is reflected in Suetonius's narration of the destruction of Germanicus's family in the wake of his death (*Cal.* 7). Suetonius recounts the mourning of the death of the popular Germanicus

---

47. See also sources from Roman Egypt: P.Mich. 321, 322a; and sources dated to ca. 287 CE: Codex Justinianus 8.46.5; 8.54.1.

48. Parkin, "Roman Life Course and the Family," 285–88.

in scenes that depict wide-spread destruction of all signs of hope (*Cal.* 5). He intensifies the sense of destruction further in the scenes that follow the mourning. Three of Germanicus's nine children are taken to be murdered at the behest of Tiberius. Two are infants and one is a little older, "just as he was reaching the age of boyhood" (*Cal.* 7). That Suetonius regards the children positively, considering them to be favored and to have had currency in the public life of Rome is clear when he speaks of the oldest boy who is killed. He says of him, "a charming child, whose statue, in the guise of Cupid, Livia dedicated in the temple of the Capitoline Venus, while Augustus had another placed in his bed chamber and used to kiss it fondly whenever he entered the room" (*Cal.* 7). Six of Germanicus's children survive: three girls and three boys although the senate, influenced by Tiberius, declares two of the boys public enemies, Nero and Drusus.

According to Suetonius, the three boys die prematurely, before they are able to fulfill the hopes vested in them by the adults around them. Their deaths signify a fragmentation of Germanicus's family and therefore the limiting of their father's ongoing influence.[49] For the same reason that images of children in the early empire projected the aspirations of the adults in their world, narratives of murdered offspring could also be taken up to convey the destruction of a family's continuing presence.

Up to this point, we have observed that families were highly visible in the early empire. Images of families in the material culture and literature of the time had symbolic weight and provided exemplars of how to live and be in Roman society. Children were prominent in these representations. Not hidden from public gaze, ensconced in some private domain of the household, boys and girls were represented in public life. Their presence in the civic landscape contributed to shaping ideas about what it meant to be a Roman. Whether in life or in death, images of children mediated key values of Roman culture. In death, in particular, children became icons for Roman society. It is to this point that we now focus our discussion.

4.3.2. Deceased Children

It is clear by now from previous discussions that the deaths of infants and children were a common experience in the period of the early empire.

---

49. Although note Suetonius's description of the progression of Gaius Caesar in the following sections (*Cal.* 8–10).

4. Images of Female Bodies in the Greco-Roman Landscape 129

While the ancient world was populated with lots of children, and could well be labeled a young person's world, many children never actually lived to become adults.[50] The causes of infant and childhood mortality were varied. It could be attributed to numerous interrelated factors, such as levels of urbanization; levels of sanitation and hygiene; medical care; nutrition; lack of quarantine sites; rearing practices; levels of poverty; exposure to infectious disease; seasonal or ecological changes such as drought.[51] Tim Parkin calculates an extremely high infant mortality rate: 450/1000, or nearly 50 percent of the infant population. If children survived to five years of age, they could be expected to mature to adulthood. Nonetheless, the average life-expectancy at birth was twenty-five years old with 200/1000 attaining this.[52] Christian Laes observes that approximately 50 percent of children reached the age of ten years old.[53] Deaths of children, therefore, were regular occurrences that affected people's lives and how they thought about their lives.

Children's deaths were mourned and, like their adult counterparts, the loss of some children was recognized through public funerary rites. The epitaph of Quintus Caecilius Optatus, who lived two years and six months, indicates that he had been cremated (*CIL* 9.3184). The child's ashes were buried in the earth, which is described as the child's new mother. The image of the boy that is preserved is that of a child. Even in death, the boy continues to need a mother, a role that is now taken up by the earth. While he had been cremated, the inscription evokes images of him in his former corporeal state: he now "lies" at the burial site. The dedicators of his epitaph are his parents, as was the usual practice, and they are labeled as "dutiful," along with his brother. According to the inscription, the infant is remembered as one "known to all for his devotion." The values of the parents are imputed to the infant. This is the site of an infant whose public memorial communicated that he was loved within the family and that it was his parents' duty to ensure his body received the appropriate funerary rites, which in this case included the cremation of his body, the burial of ashes, and the construction of an epitaph. The memorial also functioned

---

50. Parkin estimates that roughly one third of the population in the ancient world were children in comparison to 19 percent in today's context ("Demography of Infancy," 41–43).
51. Parkin, "Demography of Infancy," 46–48.
52. Parkin, "Demography of Infancy," 50.
53. Laes, *Children in the Roman Empire*, 26–28.

as a public testimony to the family's alignment with Roman values of familial duty and dedication.

Cicero describes similar burial rites being afforded to a child in *Pro Cluentio*. In the narrative, Oppianicus's son dies in suspicious circumstances and is then cremated and buried in the space of a few hours. The speed with which the events take place mean that the funerary rites occur before the child's mother hears of the news. Distraught at her child's sudden death and being prevented from taking her rightful public role in his funeral, another funeral takes place even though the child had already been buried (*Clu.* 27, 28). Cicero narrates this episode to reinforce the picture of Oppianicus as a negative character. Not only has he orchestrated the death of his own son, Oppianicus has also precluded the child's mother from fulfilling her public role in the funeral. The duty of both parents to cremate and bury their children is clear in the view of Cicero. The presentation of Oppianicus's action as a dishonorable deed, perhaps also indicates the importance that the funerary rites and mourning of children held in the public's consciousness.

The significance of mourning children's deaths also comes to the fore in book 6 of Quintilian's *Institutio oratoria*. His book on emotions is prefaced by a commentary on the deaths of his own two sons, a ten-year-old and a five-year-old. The death of both sons is especially poignant as Quintilian contextualizes them alongside the premature death of his wife and their mother, for whom he also grieves. The grief for the younger son is expressed physically in tears, and through the metaphor of light being taken away, "My younger son, just past his fifth year, went first, and took away one of the two lights of my life. I have no desire to flaunt my troubles or exaggerate the causes of my tears" (*Inst.* 6.7). The grief at the death of the older son is for what has been lost, "Bereavement struck me a second time; I lost the child of whom I had such expectations, and in whom I rested the sole hope of my old age" (*Inst.* 6.3). He describes this quashing of expectations and the loss of hope as a source of misery and torment (*Inst.* 6.12–13).

Quintilian spells out what has been lost in the older son's death. The substance of his grief is concerned with the qualities that he had discerned in his son (or at least those he wished to associate with his son). Of the boy's disposition, he recalls:

> a natural capacity for learning (and I never saw anything more outstanding in all my experience) and of application, which even at that age

needed no compulsion (as his teachers know), but also of honesty, piety, humanity, and generosity. (*Inst.* 6.10)

He also mourns the loss of the boy's physical capabilities, some of which were budding, others that were "ripe" or had already reached maturity:

> a clear and pleasant voice, a sweetness of speech, and an exact pronunciation of every letter in either of the two languages, as though it was the one he was born to. All this was still only promise: he had other qualities already ripe—constancy, dignity, strength to face pain and fear. (*Inst.* 6.11)

Taken together, these sets of qualities reflect values and ideals that were prized in Roman society. Prior to his death, the son (at least in his father's reminiscences) had shown signs of becoming an exemplary Roman citizen. In other ways, even at ten years old, the boy had already demonstrated dimensions of this status. Now, all hopes that his son would fully attain such stature had been dashed. Quintilian's words speak of mourning the loss of a future model citizen.

We observed earlier that public representations of children were associated with ideas about a family's continuity. It comes as no surprise therefore that the deaths of children, major disruptions to a family's stability, could be a source of grief within families and that children's deaths were ritualized by family members. Parents are depicted as mourning the loss of their child, bereaved of the hopes that had been projected onto the child's life. The examples of Quintus Caecilius Optatus's epitaph and Quintilian's commentary on the deaths of his two sons also offer glimpses of how children's deaths could be described in relation to Roman ideals. They demonstrate how the memorialization of children's deaths could communicate ideas about Roman values and a family's standing in Roman society.

4.3.3. Children as Symbols of Status

Inscriptions and visual depictions on funerary monuments suggest that representations of children were integral to communicating ideas about a family's identity in the public domain. How children were dressed and adorned in public reliefs, for instance, conveyed to passers-by information about a family's status in the civic life of Rome. The Sertorii relief of 50 CE is a case in point. As we have already noted, the relief comprises three adults and two children—a boy and a girl—in a horizontal setting. All five figures physically interact to denote their familial bonds.[54] The boy clearly wears a bulla, signifying his freeborn status. The girl does not wear a bulla but features an elaborate coiffure, which may have reflected the social and financial status of her family. Her decorative hairstyle contrasts with the less elaborate style of the female adult in the relief, possibly her mother. This feature of the girl may have connoted her unmarried status and possibly functioned as a sign to likely suitors, a detail also reinforced by the absence of any *pella* on the girl.[55]

Taken together, the dual images of freeborn son and the unmarried daughter suggest the aspirations of this family: the continuing elite Roman status of the family embodied in the freeborn son and the prospects for marriage and children implied in the image of the daughter. The depictions of children on these reliefs were frequently concerned with the social concerns of their parents and the adults of society.[56] Therefore, these same images when appearing on a funerary relief also conveyed what was lost in the deaths of children: prospects for the family's continuing status.

A further case in point is the Seruili relief (*CIL* 6. 26410a).[57] In this instance, we find a family depicted on a funerary monument in terms of the familial triad: father, mother, and son. The son is decorated with the bulla, distinguishing him from his parents who are a freed couple. His status as a freeborn male is clearly on show to those who pass by the monument revealing the social trajectory of the family that was embodied in the boy.[58]

It is necessary to make some comment on the depiction of small families on funerary monuments. At first sight, this may seem an anomaly given the Augustan laws that encouraged men and women to marry and

---

54. Larsson Loven, "Children and Childhood," 308, fig. 15.4.
55. The *pella* was worn in public by married women. Kelly Olson, "The Appearance of the Young Roman Girl," in *Roman Dress and the Fabrics of Roman Culture*, ed. Jonathan C. Edmondson and Alison Keith, Phoenix Supplement 46 (Toronto: University of Toronto Press, 2008), 146–47.
56. Huskinson, "Constructing Childhood," 327.
57. The Seruili relief has an earlier dating of 30–20 BCE but reflects the trajectory into the first century CE (Rawson, "Iconography," 205–30). The son in the familial triad in the mid-first-century stela of Menimani and Blussus wears the bulla (*CIL* 13.7067B).
58. See also the Vibii relief, 13 BCE–5 CE, which features a son clothed in princely attire with his mother and father (*CIL* 6.28774).

have several children.⁵⁹ It is apparent, however, that the monuments were not concerned with literally depicting the precise make-up of a family. Rather, the images on reliefs functioned to convey the civic aspirations of a family. The relief of C. Vettius C. f. Secundus, 13 BCE–5 CE is a case in point.⁶⁰ A young boy forms part of the familial scene, depicted in a horizontal relief, comprising an adult male and female respectively, and an older girl. The girl's youth is revealed in her unlined face and flowing hair but the boy's status is also prominent. He wears the toga and the bulla. It is the status of the family that is in focus. The status of the boy as freeborn coupled with the emphasis on the girl's youth suggests the upward mobility of the family.⁶¹ The funerary monument therefore is not first and foremost concerned with conveying the loss of a specific individual, or necessarily with painting a picture of the precise composition of the family. Instead, it functions to make a statement about the status of the family.

It is clear that adults and children who walked the streets of Rome in the early Roman Empire, or engaged with some of its literary voices, would have encountered images of children and families. While these images potentially had a shaping influence on people's thinking, how children made sense of their own lives and the deaths of children remains unknown. Their voices are silent. We do not know what children thought, said, or did as they engaged with these images. Nor do we have sources that tell us, from a child's perspective, how they perceived their lives more generally. Like those of women, the representations of children are constructs, symbols that mediated the values of some others around them. Nevertheless, having built up various pictures of how ideas about children and families occupied the public domain, in the final part of the chapter, we will examine the particular representations of young females within this landscape.

---

59. Judith P. Hallett, "Women in Augustan Rome," in *A Companion to Women in the Ancient World*, ed. Sharon L. James and Sheila Dillon, BCAW (Chichester: Wiley-Blackwell, 2012), 373–74; Huskinson, "Picturing the Roman Family," 532–33. Although the earlier comments concerning the high rates of infant and child mortality might also be a factor in the depiction of elite families with small membership (Parkin, "Demography of Infancy," 43–44).

60. Diana E. E. Kleiner, *Roman Group Portraiture: The Funerary Reliefs of the Late Republic and Early Empire* (New York: Garland, 1977), fig. 84.

61. Huskinson, "Picturing the Roman Family," 533.

4.4. The Young Female in the Context of the Family

In the early empire, images of young women were evident in public monumental sculpture, funerary commemorations, and in the narrative literature of the time. The dominant way by which young females were represented in these media was as a daughter, usually unmarried. Those who created these images typically located the unmarried daughter in the family. People frequenting the city or interacting with the literary voices of the time, would have routinely encountered a model of the young female as unmarried, a daughter, embedded in her familial network.

When we turn to the depictions of unmarried daughters, we notice that they are commonly portrayed as holding a cherished place in their families. The relationship between daughters and their parents was often highlighted, and was frequently characterized in terms of affection. At the turn of the millennium, in the Villa Doria Pamphili monument for example, we see a small female child standing between both parents, physically interacting with her mother.[62] The relationship is depicted as close and intimate. The first-century inscription for Julia Victorina (*CIL* 6.20727) suggests she, too, was regarded with affection in death. The inscription places the deceased ten-year-old girl in a familial triad of mother, father, and daughter. Her parents, C. Iulius Saturninus and Lucilia Procula, label her as *filiae dulcissimae*, "sweet daughter," in her death (*CIL* 6.12087). In another example, the inscription of a little girl by the name of Anullina talks of the child escaping the underworld associated with death (*CIL* 6.12087). The inscription suggests that her parents found the idea of their deceased daughter inhabiting the underworld abhorrent. The inclusion of this detail possibly signaled the affection by which they held, and continued to hold, their daughter, even in her death.[63]

Not confined to the world of material culture, illustrations of these affectionate relations also emerge in the literature. In the Greek novel, *Chaereas and Callirhoe* Chariton depicts Callirhoe as the cherished daughter of an elite father, Hemocrates. Upon hearing that his daughter who was thought to be dead is alive, Hermocrates leaps onto the warship carrying his daughter, embraces Callirhoe in joy, and identifies her with the term of affection, τέκνον, "my child" (*Chaer.* 8.6.8). Tacitus's narration of the

---

62. Rawson, "Iconography," 217, fig. 9.5.
63. Rawson, *Children and Childhood*, 361.

birth of Nero's daughter depicts a child who was cherished by her father and whose entry into the world was celebrated widely. Nero is described as responding to the birth with "more than human joy" (*Ann.* 15.23). Embedding the child firmly within the imperial family, he names his daughter (and also his wife) Augusta. Tacitus describes Augusta's birth as attracting public thanksgiving. A temple of Fertility is decreed, contextualizing her birth in terms of divinity and fecundity. Even as a newborn, the trajectory of the female child's life is symbolically marked by childbearing. Tacitus's account reveals how the portrait of the beloved, unmarried daughter was a constituent part of the narrative of the flourishing imperial family. The narration of the birth of this daughter encapsulated the hopes for dynastic continuity that were embodied in imperial children.[64]

Both Cicero and Pliny also speak of daughters as beloved figures. Unlike the daughters in the previous examples, the females in the cases of Cicero and Pliny are married. Nevertheless, they are described in terms of being highly valued daughters in their respective families. Cicero often makes reference to his daughter Tullia. Writing while in exile in Thessalonica, Cicero describes his offspring—a son and daughter—in terms of deep affection (*Quint. fratr.* 3.1). The regard he has for his son, "My charming, darling little boy, whom I, cruel brute that I am, put away from my arms," applies equally to that which he holds for his daughter, Tullia. Cicero writes that he misses his daughter while he dwells in exile: "And then at the same time I miss my daughter, the most loving, modest, and clever daughter a man ever had, the image of my face and speech and mind." His affection for his daughter is twofold. On the one hand, he lauds her for her mental acuity and her disposition. On the other hand, she is prized because she reflects the image of her own father. References to the girl's voice and discourse and to her physiognomy, and the resemblance to her father, reinforce the ties that bind the daughter to her father.

In a letter to Neratius Priscus, Pliny describes how he is affected by the illness of Fannia, the wife of Helvidius and the daughter of Thrasea. Her imminent death represents the passing of a role model for both Roman men and women, which triggers grief in Pliny. She is a woman of "purity and integrity,… nobility and loyal heart.… Friendliness and charm,… being able to inspire affection as well as respect. Will there be anyone now whom we can hold up as a model to our wives, from whose courage even

---

64. Rawson, "Iconography," 219–21.

our own sex can take example?" (*Ep.* 7.19). He appears to perceive the significance of her death to be so great that it potentially embodies the end of her family line; her descendants are not sufficiently able to carry out deeds to the same degree of greatness that she is able to do.

At a personal level, the author explains how Fannia's death reignited the grief he experienced when Fannia's mother died, a woman whom Pliny had clearly admired. For Pliny, Fannia's mother had been made present in her daughter: "The mother was restored to us in her daughter, but soon will be taken away with her, leaving me the pain of a reopened wound to bear as well as this fresh blow." Fannia's death, therefore, was not only to be mourned because of what was lost in her, but also because her death was like a second passing of her mother.

Pliny paints a picture of a mother and daughter playing significant roles to convey the values of the empire. While we have previously observed that the portraits of mothers were often constructed to transmit imperial ideology, we now see that some daughters followed in their mother's footsteps. Representations of daughters could also be specifically used to mediate the ideals of Roman society. In the case of Fannia, Pliny particularly emphasizes the interconnectedness between the daughter and her lauded mother. Fannia had continued the family line not solely in terms of the physical descendants she had produced, but in terms of the qualities that she had come to personify: purity, integrity, nobility, charm, and courage (*Ep.* 7.19). Values could be transmitted through generations and in this case through the relationship between a mother and daughter. Continuing to exemplify these ideals, Fannia was cherished as her mother's daughter.

Other links between mothers and daughters were also constructed by writers. The dominant imagery found in both literary and material sources by which adult females were generally wives, mothers, and childbearers, extended to unmarried daughters. These figures were commonly portrayed in relation to marriage and childbearing. As an extension of this preoccupation, the sexual status of the body of the unmarried female also attracted comment by writers in the early empire.

The sexuality of unmarried females was a focus among authors. This is exemplified in the writing of Plutarch in *Lives: Comparison of Lycurgus and Numa*. In a broader comparison of Spartan and Roman marriages and parentage, Plutarch distinguished between his perceptions of the Spartan and Roman παρθένος, or maiden. Those unmarried females who were associated with Numa are favorably described in terms of "feminine decorum" (*Comp. Lyc. Num.* 3). Contrary to this picture, Plutarch disapproves of those females aligned with Lycurgus, on the basis of his appraisal of what they do with their bodies. He describes them as "being entirely unconfined and unfeminine." By this he means "bare-thighed," "mad after men," "their thighs are naked, flying free their robes." Clothing that reveals their upper legs particularly provokes Plutarch's scorn:

> For in fact the flaps of the tunic worn by their maidens were not sewn together below the waist, but would fly back and lay bare the whole thigh as they walked. Sophocles pictures the thing very clearly in these words: "And that young maid, whose tunic, still unsewn, Lays bare her gleaming thigh between its folds, Hermione." (*Comp. Lyc. Num.* 3)

Unmarried women who expose their bodies by wearing revealing clothing are the antithesis of feminine decorum, a state highly valued in Plutarch's view, and they were therefore deemed undignified. Plutarch's zeal for bodily modesty among unmarried females coheres with the picture he paints of married women in the same section. Wives are also extolled for their restraint, incarnated in modesty, sobriety, silence, gentleness, and compliance (*Comp. Lyc. Num.* 3).[65] Unmarried females in Plutarch's presentation become further expressions of the literary trope in which females who are considered bad are sexualized.[66]

On the other hand, Plutarch offers a much more favorable impression of the sexuality of unmarried females when he considers them in relation to marriage and childbearing. The signs that a girl is ready for marriage—a union Plutarch approves—are physical. Reading Lycurgus's view through his own lens, Plutarch describes the girl's body as "fully ripe" and "vigorous enough to endure the strain of conception and childbirth" (*Comp. Lyc. Num.* 4). She has reached a stage in which she has the capacity to naturally crave sexual intercourse with a prospective husband rather than being coerced when there are no natural feelings of physical desire. Procreation is the goal of sex and marriage in Plutarch's view. It is not surprising, therefore, that he represents the sexuality of young females in such a way that affirms their capacity to fulfill this fundamental role.

---

65. Note also the contrast with the positive depictions of young males in relation to public speech in Suetonius, *Cal.* 10.

66. Dixon, *Reading Roman Women*, 43. See Plutarch's descriptions of the vestal virgins as chaste, undefiled, barren, and unfruitful as further examples of how the ideal woman is not sexualized pejoratively (*Num.* 9). For an extensive diatribe on female sexuality, see Juvenal, *Sat.* 6.

The Roman view of a girl's readiness to marry is different from that of Lycurgus's, in Plutarch's reading of it. A young girl approaches marriageable age at precisely twelve years of age or younger. The reason given for this is not related to notions of a girl's fertility or capacity for sexual desire and childbirth, but is on account of her body and character not having been corrupted (*Comp. Lyc. Num.* 4). At the age of twelve, she is considered to be chaste and pure. Plutarch employs the term ἄθικτον to denote a girl of marriageable age who is untouched, never having engaged in sexual activity. He also takes up the label καθαρόν to convey that she ought to be pure or undefiled. In his rendering of the Roman view, a young girl's sexuality is irrelevant; instead it is her character and the chaste state of her body that determine her fitness for marriage.

Another dimension to Plutarch's representation of young, unmarried females is the role of the girl in securing a marriage. Plutarch talks of young maidens being *given* in marriage (*Comp. Lyc. Num.* 4, emphasis added). There is no suggestion that females have a voice or agency in determining their spouse. Someone else is the subject of the action of handing them to a husband, who then takes control of them. In *Pompeius,* for instance, Julia has neither voice nor agency in the choice of Pompey for a husband (*Pomp.* 48). She is passive in the negotiations concerning her marriage, first promised to one man and then to another. She is portrayed as the object of the political machinations of the males in her context, her marriage serving the political interests of the men around her.

A slightly different approach to the agency of unmarried females transpires in Chariton's portrait of Callirhoe. In book 1, the chief protagonist of the story, Callirhoe, falls in love with Chareas. The passion of each for the other is mutual, with the author permitting both Chareas and Callirhoe to express their desires. Locating Callirhoe in a setting that conjures notions of love, sensuality, and procreation, the female character voices her feelings, "As for the girl, she fell at the feet of Aphrodite and, kissing them, said, 'Lady, give me as my husband this man you have shown me'" (*Chaer.* 1.1.7–8). The reader/hearer of the story is made aware of the aspirations of the girl—Chareas is the person whom she wishes to marry. The basis for her preference is passion, as it is for Chareas, rather than the political aspirations of their families.

Chariton does reveal a tension, however, in the idea of the female articulating this desire, adding the explanation that she could not publicly disclose her feelings, "she had to keep silent for shame of being exposed" (*Chaer.* 1.1.7–8). This perhaps implies that while female desire

4. Images of Female Bodies in the Greco-Roman Landscape

in unmarried females may have been acknowledged more broadly, it was not necessarily or wholly accepted.[67] Moreover, as the story progresses, the author presents Callirhoe as having no voice in the choice of husband in her impending marriage (*Chaer.* 1.1.7–8). It is her father who gives consent to the marriage taking place, at the petitioning of the people. Callirhoe is not even present at the public spectacle when Hemocrates agrees for the marriage to take place. While the representation of the unmarried Callirhoe does not conform to the trope of sexualized, bad females, it does reinforce a stereotype of elite females whose lives were determined by others, particularly their fathers.

4.5. Depictions of Dying and Deceased Girls

One of the most publicly visible depictions of unmarried females in the early empire occurred in relation to their death. Images and stories of young daughters dying prematurely—that is, before they had married and bore children—appear in funerary monuments and in the literature of the early empire. Valerie Hope discusses the approach to death in Roman culture whereby the dead could be understood not only in terms of being corpses but also in their capacity to mediate meaning as "powerful symbols in the negotiation of power and identity."[68] On the one hand, the memorializing of the dead in a monument or text could be an exercise in catharsis, enabling family members (or commemorators) to grieve publicly.[69] On the other hand, how a person was portrayed in death could communicate ideas about the identity and aspirations of the commemorator.[70] Serving dual purposes, memorials therefore often reflected how people felt and thought about the death of the individual as well as conveying ideas about what the broader Roman society deemed culturally significant. We have observed evidence of this phenomenon in the examinations undertaken

---

67. Dixon, *Reading Roman Women*, 39–40.

68. Valerie Hope, "Contempt and Respect: The Treatment of the Corpse in Ancient Rome," in *Death and Disease in the Ancient City*, ed. Valerie M. Hope and Eireann Marshall (London: Routledge, 2000), 126.

69. Hope and Huskinson, *Memory and Mourning*, xv.

70. Graham argues that the cadaver was not a passive object to be exploited by the living in memorials. Instead, physical interaction with a cadaver in the preparation for funerals could also have a bearing on Roman remembrance and identity ("Memory and Materiality," 22–39).

so far regarding the data concerning families and children. When we turn to the representations of girls who had died, Hope's observation continues to be helpful.

In death, a person became powerless to influence how they were represented and remembered. Those constructing memorials or retelling the stories of the dead could construct the person in line with the worldview or broader narrative they were seeking to construct. They possessed great power, choosing who would be remembered and how. Ironically, as Hope explains, in death a deceased person also remained powerful in Roman culture. Their abiding presence was audible and visible in text and monument, simultaneously mediating and shaping fundamental ideas about the past, present, and future of society and empire.[71] Some unmarried daughters who had died played a part in this shaping process. Through their images and stories, seen and heard in the public domain, they remained present to their families and the larger community. At the same time, they contributed to a broader narrative that some in Roman society told of themselves.

While we have identified that daughters were commonly represented as being cherished by their parents, notably by their fathers, the age at which many of these beloved daughters died was also worthy of note. Julia Victorina, for example, was recorded as being ten years old when she died (*CIL* 6.20727); Iunia Procula was eight years old (*CIL* 6.20905); Minicia Marcellae, Fundanus's daughter, was twelve years old (*CIL* 6.16631);[72] the freeborn Ummidia Agathe and Publius Ummidius Primigenius, the slave, were both aged thirteen (*CIL* 6.29436). In the literary data, Plutarch's much-loved daughter was identified as being two years old when she died (*Cons. ux.* 8). Julia, the daughter of Caesar and the wife of Pompey, was identified as being sixteen years old when she died in childbirth (*Pomp.* 53).[73] The ages, as well as the girls' small stature and sometimes fashionable appearance in the case of reliefs, generally reinforced their status as unmarried and having not yet reached womanhood.

Julia, the daughter of Caesar, is clearly an exception in *Pomp.* 53. While her age is noted, the detail of her marriage and childbearing identifies her as a woman. After Callirhoe gives birth, Chariton states, "She soon

---

71. Hope and Huskinson, *Memory and Mourning*, xv.

72. In *Ep.* 5.16, Pliny describes Fundanus's daughter as being not yet fourteen.

73. See also Laes, *Children in the Roman Empire*, 254. Nero's daughter Augusta is not given a precise age, but Tacitus clearly denotes her as an infant (*Ann.* 15.23).

recovered from the birth and became stronger and bigger, no longer a girl but a mature woman" (*Chaer.* 3.8.3). If Chariton reflects anything of the worldview of the first century CE, his detail that childbirth and physical size could delineate adult females from female children suggests that Julia may have been considered an adult daughter, in addition to her status as a wife.

The deaths of treasured daughters triggered grief. Hope explains that while grief in Roman culture was understood to be a private act and mourning the loss of a person in the construction of funerary monuments was public, in fact both domains overlapped.[74] If we apply Hope's observation to the death of daughters, memorials were a vehicle by which families expressed their grief at the loss of their female child. We see an explicit intersection of these domains in the inscription for Iunia Procula: "She left her wretched father and mother in grief" (*CIL* 6.20905).[75] These words, featured on a funerary altar in the second half of the first century CE, publicly voiced the grief of the girl's parents.

In contrast, the epitaph for Minicia Marcellae, Fundanus's daughter, does not provide such explicit detail. It merely identifies the deceased girl by name and notes her age (*CIL* 6.16631). This brevity stands in contrast to the detail that Pliny takes to describe his grief at the girl's death. In Pliny's account, the girl's death prompted great sorrow. Pliny and others "lament [their] loss" while her father is in a state of "natural sorrow" (*Ep.* 5.16). If Pliny's description in any way reflects Fundanus's actual response to his daughter's death, it is plausible that the inscription acknowledging her death communicated publicly that her loss was recognized and felt, even if an allusion to her parents' grief was absent in the inscription. Rawson notes that the sparseness of the inscription may reflect a move within some of the wealthy to simplify their inscriptions in light of the popularity that was growing around memorializing family members. It could also have reflected a resistance among some to remember deceased daughters publicly given females were not permitted to take up roles in the political and military domains of civic life.[76] Both possibilities could explain the differences in the way the inscription and Pliny's letter represented the girl's death. Alternatively, it may also suggest how the noting of a daughter's

---

74. Hope and Huskinson, *Memory and Mourning*, xv–xvii.
75. The translation is from Rawson, *Children and Childhood*, 48.
76. Rawson, "Iconography," 224.

death along with her age was becoming a common practice by the end of the first century CE.

Tullia, the daughter of Cicero, was not a child when she died. Nevertheless, her death triggered intense sorrow in her father according to his letters to male friends: "But sometimes I am overwhelmed, and scarcely offer any resistance to grief" (*Fam.* 249). He describes his grief as an affliction, taking up the metaphor of a reopened wound to convey his pain. While he writes openly to his friend Servius Sulpicius Rufus about his grief, Cicero also indicates in his letter that he understood such sorrow to be excessive and therefore counter to what was considered socially acceptable. As we have noted earlier in the chapter, so-called excessive mourning was understood to be the domain of females. Even so, Cicero's letter gives voice to an overwhelming grief associated with the death of a daughter, albeit in the private domain of letter writing.

The observation that images of unmarried daughters were often associated with their sexuality, and their prospects for marriage and childbearing, provides a key for understanding the significance of their representations in death and the expressions of grief when they died. The altar of an eight-year-old Iunia Procula, dated to the Flavian period, illuminates our discussion further. The bust of Iunia Procula sits at the center of her funerary altar (*CIL* 6.20905).[77] Under the bust are representations of vines, apples, cornucopia, and a wolf—symbols of abundance, fertility, and fruitfulness. On the left and right is a god with horns, possibly Jupiter that perhaps connotes a connection to the well-being of Roman society. The inscription, as we know, states that her parents are grief-stricken by her death. The imagery beneath her bust possibly suggests that, in addition to the loss of a cherished daughter, hopes for fertility and children, and the continuity and prosperity they promised, have been lost in their daughter's death. Moreover, the girl is freeborn and enjoys a better status than her mother. Iunia Procula's mother had been freed by the girl's father (i.e., the mother's husband).[78] Thus the new status of the family is embodied in the daughter and recognized publicly while, at the same time, expressing the lost opportunity to realize this status in adulthood. In short, the detail of Iunia Procula's altar possibly conveyed to a first-century viewer the traditional expectations for a young female in Roman culture while

---

77. Rawson, *Children and Childhood*, 49, fig. 1.11.
78. Rawson, *Children and Childhood*, 48.

simultaneously allowing her parents to mourn the loss of these unfulfilled expectations publicly.

Similar ideas emerge in the literature of the early empire. Plutarch wrote to his wife concerning the death of their two-year-old daughter, Timoxena: "If you pity her for departing *unmarried* and *childless*, you can find comfort for yourself in another consideration, that you have lacked fulfillment of and participation in neither of these satisfactions" (*Cons. ux.* 9, emphasis added). Even a female infant's body could carry the expectations of marriage and childbearing in her society. Not to have fulfilled these expectations—even in the case of an infant death—provoked the pity of her parents in the case of Timoxena.

Likewise, Pliny associates the loss of Fundanus's daughter with her failure to have married. In recounting her final days, the author does not describe the illness from which the girl suffered. Instead, Pliny describes the qualities that the girl exhibited. It is not her illness that warrants his attention, it is her disposition in the face of death. Although she was not yet fourteen, Minicia displayed the qualities of an adult female:

> The *wisdom* of age and *dignity* of womanhood with the *sweetness and modesty* of youth and *innocence* ... *modest* affection ... she applied herself intelligently to her books and was *moderate and restrained* in her play. She bore her last illness with *patient resignation* and, indeed, with *courage*. (*Ep.* 5.16, emphasis added)

The image that Pliny provides gives voice to what he asserts are some of the characteristics of the ideal woman: wisdom, innocence, modesty, restraint, courage. In her death, Pliny represents Fundanus's daughter as an exemplary Roman woman, even though she had not completely crossed the threshold to adulthood.[79] This incompleteness is clear in the other distinguishing feature of Pliny's narration of her death: his focus on her nonmarried status. Pliny explains that Minicia's wedding day was imminent—the invitations had been sent (*Ep.* 5.16). Reinforcing the great hopes of status that were to be realized in the marriage, he notes that she was to marry a distinguished man. Instead, objects that adorned the female body at weddings, such as clothing, pearls, and jewels, had been replaced with substances that prepared the body for funerary rites: incense, ointment,

---

79. Janette McWilliam, "The Socialization of Roman Children," in Grubbs, Parkin, and Bell, *Oxford Handbook of Childhood*, 264–85.

and spices. The juxtaposition of these sets of acts and materials signifies how the tragedy of the daughter's loss was conveyed by Pliny: the dream for her from the perspective of her parents and/or Pliny was for her marriage. This dream was now cut short in her death. Her death was premature in the sense that it occurred prior to her marriage. Pliny and Fundanus lament the loss of this potentially quintessential Roman woman.

Another expression of this theme emerges in Tacitus's narration of the death of Nero's beloved daughter, Augusta (*Ann.* 15.23). The author describes how the baby's birth is associated with fecundity and divinity, signifying aspirations for the continuity and prosperity of the imperial family. It is not surprising then that Tacitus depicts the baby's death at less than four months old as a source of sorrow for the emperor. Notwithstanding this grief, the author describes how the infant is bestowed with deification in her death, "and she was voted the honor of deification, a place in the pulvinar, a temple, and a priest" (*Ann.* 15.23). In this way, the female child who was a symbol of civic importance, mediating ideas about fertility and familial posterity and honor, remains publicly present, engendering hope even in her death through the material structures erected to her.

The association between the death of a daughter and the future prospects of the family come to the fore in Servius Sulpicius Rufus's consolatory letter to Cicero on the death of Cicero's beloved Tullia (*Fam.* 248). The author notes what has been possibly taken from Tullia in her death: the prospects of marrying a distinguished husband and having children. In Servius Sulpicius Rufus's view, such a husband would have offered protection to a daughter. Her future children, particularly sons, would have preserved their patrimony and therefore ensured the financial viability of the family. In addition, they would have ensured the ongoing status of the family: a freeborn citizen's life of public office. Hopes for continuing financial and social status have been taken from Cicero in Tullia's death, however, contributing to what the author perceives as Cicero's already calamitous life. Her death is interpreted to symbolize much more than solely the loss of an individual. Tullia's loss is integrated into a broader narrative of loss in Cicero's civic life. In many of these examples, the cause of a cherished daughter's death or the condition of her corpse is not recorded and was possibly not of interest when commemorating a daughter's death.[80]

---

80. There are exceptions, such as the deaths of the thirteen-year-old girls, Ummidia Agathe and Publius Ummidius Primigenius, whose epitaph states that they were crushed to death in a Capitoline crowd (*CIL* 6.29436). Julia, the daughter of

4.6. Summary

The inscriptions, reliefs, and literature that have formed the focus of this chapter portray a fundamental role women, children, and families played in the early empire. Their images and stories were part of the material and literary landscape, taken up potentially in a mutual, dynamic shaping of the viewers or readers/hearers and the authors of the images. Those who generated texts and monuments that included references to women, children, and families generally aspired to some of the ideals of Roman society and expressed these aspirations publicly or to friends. At the same time, representations of women and children mediated ideas highly valued in Roman culture, potentially forming the consciousness of those who engaged with these depictions in the course of daily life. Images of women and children were not simply embellishments to a narrative or a family's monument. Instead, their presence communicated ideas that were considered particular to them; ideas concerning familial and imperial continuity and the promise of future prosperity, status, and power.

While examining the depictions of families and children in the narratives that some in Roman society were telling, the chapter has also provided specific insights into the significance of representations of females, particularly deceased daughters of wealthy, influential families. Even as children, their bodies carried the expectations of fertility and childbearing, and their corollaries of continuity and fruitfulness, to be fulfilled in marriage to a man of distinction. Like their mothers, their sexuality was constructed to promulgate the Roman values of modesty, chastity, compliance, and self-control. When remembered in death, daughters could become icons of these ideals. The deaths of these apparently much-loved figures not only triggered grief on account of their individual loss. They were also mourned because of their families' hopes that died with them. This is plain in the funerary rites and public monuments that recognized their deaths. At the same time, they remained overtly present in text and stone, continuing to affect the thinking of those who encountered them.

Caesar and wife of Pompey, died as a consequence of childbirth (Plutarch, *Pomp.* 53). Chariton uses descriptions of domesticated violence to narrate the cause of Callirhoe's apparent death in *Chaereas and Callirhoe* (*Chaer.* 1.4.12).

5
Images of Female Bodies in the Landscape of Late Second Temple Judaism

> Hear, you mountains, my lamentation, and behold, you hills, the tears of my eyes and be witnesses, you rocks, to the weeping of my soul.... But let not my life be taken in vain. May my words go forth to the heavens, and my tears be written before the firmament, in order that a father not venture to sacrifice a daughter ... and a ruler not let his only daughter be promised for sacrifice.
>
> —LAB 40.5

Having considered the depictions of females' bodies in Greco-Roman culture, our attention now turns to the bodies of dying and deceased women and female children in the world of late Second Temple Judaism.[1] To gain an insight into how depictions of the body of women and of female children functioned in this era, I will discuss their various representations in the works of Josephus and Philo, as well as in Jubilees and Liber Antiquitatum Biblicarum. I will also draw on Jewish funerary data from the turn of the era to provide further perspectives on how females were memorialized in death. Our particular concern will be to consider the significance of how women and female children were portrayed, particularly in relation to dying and death. It will be apparent that the bodies of females were often depicted in the context of the family, specifically in relation to marrying and bearing children. Their capacity to bear children ensured the continuity of a family's lineage and the preservation of Israel's identity. Female bodies were also portrayed in Second Temple literature in rela-

---

1. My focus is late Second Temple Judaism. For convenience, from this point on I will occasionally refer to this period as "Second Temple Judaism." In so doing, I refer to late Second Temple Judaism.

tion to suffering, violence, and death. These depictions often functioned to serve the apologetic purposes of writers in communicating their views on broader matters concerned with Jewish identity and the various intersections between Jews and non-Jews in the Greco-Roman world in which they lived.

5.1. The Image of the Family in Late Second Temple Times

The dominant paradigm for the depiction of females was in the context of family life. Given this, it is helpful to begin our discussion with some observations on the broader representations of families at the turn of the era. These will assist us to understand how the images of females possibly functioned.[2] In the funerary data of Jerusalem and Jericho in the first century CE and in the literary sources we analyze, the family was deemed a central social unit in Judaism. Individual family members were honored and familial ties were memorialized in the family tombs that dotted the geographical landscapes of Jerusalem and Jericho. In the literature of the Second Temple era, writers drew on various images of families to convey ideas about the significance of family life in Judaism and the roles that various family members performed within the family and the life of Judaism more broadly. The family was promoted by some as a fundamental ingredient in the construction of Jewish identity.[3]

As we observed in relation to Greco-Roman society, one of the ways we can discern the importance of family life among some Jews in the first century CE is in the way they memorialized their dead. For some Jews, family tombs were a witness to the value placed on familial bonds in death. The architectural plans and ossuary inscriptions of Jerusalem and Jericho during the first century CE reveal that many of the tombs located in those

---

2. I note Peskowitz's observation that there is no universal picture of the Jewish family. She states that the notion of family was a "plural concept" in the first few centuries CE, manifested in a diversity of "forms, configurations, living arrangements, and habitations in built environments, economic and geographic locations." See Miriam Peskowitz, "Family/ies in Antiquity: Evidence from Tannaitic Literature and Roman Galilean Architecture," in *The Jewish Family in Antiquity*, ed. Shaye J. D. Cohen, BJS 289 (Atlanta: Scholars Press, 1993), 14–15. What I am doing in this current study is noting patterns in the representations of families in the numerous sources I use.

3. I reiterate that the sources that are available to us are representative of particular contexts and do not necessarily indicate the reality of all Jews in the late Second Temple era.

areas were in fact family tombs. When a family member died, the corpse was placed in a family tomb. After their flesh had decomposed, the bones were laid in an ossuary. In several tombs, the ossuaries of family members were placed close together in the same loculus or chamber.[4] The placement of bones in an ossuary suggests the practice of initial individual burial, although the remains of more than one member were occasionally placed in a box.[5] This is particularly the case with small children (presumably siblings), and mothers and children, whose remains were sometimes located together in a single ossuary (*CIIP*, figs. 25, 59, 286, 298, 462, 566, 590).

The study of skeletal remains in burial caves in Jericho and Mount Scopus suggests that the majority of females who were buried at both sites were younger than their male counterparts. At Mount Scopus, for example, six of the twelve women who were buried were under twenty years old, in comparison to the one male who was of a similar age. The other six men at the site were over thirty years of age, while one woman could be identified in that age category.[6] This implies that women died earlier than men did. It suggests the precariousness of childbirth, and raises questions concerned not only with illness but also with familial violence.[7]

Women, men, and children were afforded similar burial rites according to the data in the tombs in Judea. Alongside the practice of placing their bones in ossuaries, many of the boxes of women, men, and children bear inscriptions. In Rachel Hachlili's calculations, about half of the inscriptions in family tombs belong to women. For both males and females, the inscriptions commonly feature the pattern "son of" or "daughter of" with the patronym generally included, although matronyms do (rarely) appear (*CIIP*, figs. 558.2, 592.1). The inscriptions indicate that mothers, fathers, sons and daughters, children and babies, including the unborn, were all interred in family tombs.[8] The respect afforded to parents is evident in

---

4. Hachlili, *Jewish Funerary Customs*, 302.

5. Hachlili, *Jewish Funerary Customs*, 235, 239.

6. Tal Ilan, *Integrating Women into Second Temple History* (Peabody, MA: Hendrickson Publishers, 2001), 208. She cites the report of Joe Zias, "Human Skeletal Remains from the Mount Scopus Tomb," *Atiqot* 21 (1992): 97–103. For the Goliath tomb at Jericho, Ilan cites Rachel Hachlili and Patricia Smith, "The Genealogy of the Goliath Family," *BASOR* 235 (1979): 67–70.

7. Ilan, *Integrating Women*, 208. Ilan also notes the evidence of domestic violence targeted at women at Giv'at Hamtivar (209–10). Contra Ilan, see Daniel R. Schwartz, "Did the Jews Practice Infanticide in Antiquity?," *SPhiloA* 16 (2004): 72.

8. For an example of a woman buried with her unborn fetus, see *CIIP*, fig. 25.

the inscriptions that often note the father of the deceased, sometimes noting his title, profession, or trade, and occasionally state the mother of the deceased.[9] Funerary and mourning rituals were usually carried out by sons rather than daughters. Nonetheless, women participated in public expressions of mourning, providing vocalized lamentations for the dead, as either relatives or professional keeners. Grief was conveyed in the bodily actions of hand clasping, beating one's chest, and chanting laments. The funerary data reveal how the relationships between father, mother, and children (sons and daughters) were valued in memorializing the dead. In addition, the data testify to a readiness among surviving family members, often located in the conjugal family network, to preserve the status and relational links within families and between generations. Hachlili suggests that the family tomb became akin to a house, an expression of respect for the resting place of the family.[10] In their burial, the bodies of the dead signified the bonds of family life.

The depictions of families played a significant role in the narrative literature of Second Temple times. The most explicit statements on the family emerge in the work of Philo. In his writing, the male was of primary importance in the family. Men took precedence over women in families, and sons took precedence over daughters as heirs (*Spec.* 2.123–124).

Despite the accent on the son, the virgin daughter also rated some mention in Philo's familial network. The security of a virgin daughter left without a dowry, for instance, was noted by Philo as a chief concern. Measures were to be taken by the males in the family to ensure that her maintenance and education were provided for and to avoid vulnerability in securing a marriage. In the absence of a dowry, she was to share equally in the property of the family (*Spec.* 2.125). If no male was able to provide for her maintenance and to arrange a marriage, the magistrate assumed the role to ensure she married within the tribe and that the family inheritance was preserved (*Spec.* 2.125–126). While a daughter's status and economic well-being were secured in an arranged marriage, Philo represented her as having little agency over what happened to her. How her life unfolded was understood to be at the behest of a male: either her father, brother, or

---

9. Hachlili notes that about 50 percent of the inscriptions refer to the name of the deceased and their family relationships, usually denoted by a patronym (*Jewish Funerary Customs*, 303).

10. Hachlili, *Jewish Funerary Customs*, 310.

the magistrate.¹¹ Philo's approach to the role of fathers and the welfare of the virgin daughter sought to ensure that the law would be observed. It also supported his broader view that Jewish mothers were instrumental in handing on Jewish status to their children.¹² In this way, the role of a father/guardian in protecting the status of a virgin daughter was critical to preserving Jewish culture and identity.

Fathers exercised a specific role in the Philonic family in relation to females. One of the dimensions to this role related to authority and control. Virgins or daughters were subject to their fathers while husbands made decisions for their wives (*Spec.* 2.23-25).¹³ This role of exerting control over females in the household was deemed necessary due to the inadequacies of females: a daughters' youth meant she lacked knowledge, and a wife suffered for "want of sense" (*Spec.* 2.24).¹⁴ A second dimension related to protection. The role of the father in Philo's framework was to protect the family. A wife of a priest, for example, who was left widowed and childless (and therefore elevated to the status of a virgin) had to return to the house of her father (*Spec.* 1.129-130). Otherwise desolate, she found "refuge" with her father.¹⁵

Marriage was a fundamental element in Philo's picture of the family. In his view, the goal of marriage was procreation (*Spec.* 3.113; 1.332). The children produced in marriage ensured the continuation of a family's name, lineage, and property, as well as the perpetuation of the human race

---

11. Loader, *Philo, Josephus, and the Testaments on Sexuality*, 239.
12. Maren R. Niehoff, "Jewish Identity and Jewish Mothers: Who Was a Jew according to Philo?," *SPhiloA* 11 (1999): 36.
13. I acknowledge that the use of Philo's *Special Laws* is an exception to the normal focus on narrative texts.
14. Loader, *Philo, Josephus, and the Testaments on Sexuality*, 237.
15. In Reinhartz's view, Philo's image of the absolute authority and control of the father in the household coheres with that of the Roman paterfamilias. The concept of the *patria potestas* was evident in Roman law, and in Egypt, in the first century CE. See Adele Reinhartz, "Parents and Children: A Philonic Perspective," in Cohen, *Jewish Family in Antiquity*, 76-77. Loader identifies a similar theme in Josephus's writings, "Josephus' world was one of powerful households, ruled mainly by male heads, subordinate but not unresourceful women, political and social pressures to affirm Roman order, including its hierarchical values of family, and the vicissitudes of imperial rule and its wrangle of regional appointees" (*Philo, Josephus, and the Testaments on Sexuality*, 367).

(*Spec.* 2.130, 133–134).¹⁶ In the Philonic system, it was the responsibility of parents to care for and rear their children appropriately. It was their duty to attend to the physical health of their children and to care for them in illness (*Spec.* 2.229–230), as well as provide for their tuition, clothing, and food (*Spec.* 2.232).

A key reference point for Philo's view on the family is the fifth commandment (*Spec.* 2.225–235). In his reading of the commandment, the father functioned as the authority figure and children were to be submissive. Children who did not submit to their parents' control could be corporally punished: beaten, degraded, and put in chains by their father. The law, in Philo's rhetoric, even permitted a father to execute his child so long as the child's mother had agreed to the application of the death penalty in a particular instance (*Spec.* 2.232).

Accompanying the responsibility of parents to rear their children was the corollary duty of children to honor their parents (*Spec.* 2.243–245). Parents participated in the immortal act of creation. To honor them was a duty second only to honoring God.¹⁷ To underscore this obligation, Philo argued that the consequence for the dishonorable act of physically harming a parent ought to be a death penalty, that is, stoning (2.243).¹⁸ By locating the basis for this argument in the fifth commandment, Philo presented his view of the family as the exemplification of the torah.¹⁹ In other words, for family members to relate to each other as Philo outlined was to embody the law. Those children who disregarded the law therefore "had forsaken

---

16. Accordingly, situations in which children predecease their parents are problematic for Philo. Potentially threatening the practical aspirations for familial continuity, they represent a disruption of what Philo considers the broader harmonious ideal of a cosmic order of which children surviving their parents is constituent (*Spec.* 2.130).

17. O. Larry Yarbrough, "Parents and Children in the Jewish Family of Antiquity," in Cohen, *Jewish Family in Antiquity*, 50. For similar thinking expressed by Josephus, see *C. Ap.* 2.206.

18. Josephus reveals similar views in *C. Ap.* 2.206; 2.217. See also the gradation of punishments from "orally admonishing" to stoning, followed by burial for rebellious youths who do not honor their parents in *A.J.* 4.260–264. Reinhartz speculates that Josephus's view on children may reflect the Roman idea of *patria potestas*. See Adele Reinhartz and Kim Shier, "Josephus on Children and Childhood," *SR* 41 (2012): 370.

19. Sly argues that Philo reveals the importance of parents as demonstrations of torah while concomitantly appealing to those ideals about the family that he shares with some non-Jews concerned with family stability. See Dorothy Sly, *Philo's Perception of Women*, BJS 209 (Atlanta: Scholars Press, 1990), 186.

their ancestral traditions and thus lost any right to live within the Jewish community."[20] Philo appears sympathetic to the execution of dissenting offspring on this basis. The family structure was pivotal to maintaining Jewish identity and the formation of obedient children under the controlling influence of the parents (particularly the father) was integral to the ongoing transmission of Jewish tradition.

5.2. Images of Women

According to numerous sources associated with Judaism at the turn of the era, the value of the woman was derived predominantly from her role in the family. One of the main ways in which this value found expression was in the importance attached to her marital status. This is evident in the inscriptional material associated with ossuaries during the first century CE in Jerusalem and Jericho, where there are many examples of women who were identified within a familial context and, more specifically, in relation to a significant male within a family. According to Hachlili, about half of the inscriptions in Jewish burial sites belong to women and these frequently mention the woman's marital status in the categories of wife, mother, or daughter. In some instances, women were named; Hachlili identifies 23 percent of those who are named in inscriptions as women. In other cases, they were unnamed and identified solely by their husband's name.[21]

There is little uniformity in the way that women are identified or how the relationships between the women and the rest of the family are noted in inscriptions. Instead, the inscriptions reveal a few distinct patterns. In

---

20. Maren R. Niehoff, *Philo on Jewish Identity and Culture*, TSAJ 86 (Tübingen: Mohr Siebeck, 2001), 176.

21. Hachlili, *Jewish Funerary Customs*, 312. There is a small sample of females whose inscriptions bear only their name, i.e., the inscriptions record only their name and no other associated person. If, as Hachlili rightfully argues, the most common way of burying a woman was to denote her marital status and her familial context, a question arises as to how we might understand this small sample. For example, where the bones are identified as an adult, not a child, an inscription could denote an unmarried adult female, a childless widow or, perhaps, a divorced woman. Some of the references may point to the remains of a male, not a female as is assumed. The inscriptions may also suggest that the marital status of females was not as significant across the board in first-century CE—at least in death—as some of the literature and larger sample of inscriptions appears to represent.

some instances, unidentified women were buried with a named male. In such cases, the only indicator that a woman's remains were in the ossuary was the presence of female bones (*CIIP*, fig. 54.3). Some unnamed women were buried with a named, specific male family member (*CIIP*, fig. 30). In other instances, women were named and were buried alone in an ossuary. They were identified in the inscription in relation to a husband (*CIIP*, fig. 72.1), and/or father (*CIIP*, fig. 342.1), or sometimes their father-in-law. Some named women were buried with their named husbands (*CIIP*, fig. 412.2b). In many instances, husbands and wives were buried in separate ossuaries, albeit in close proximity in the one family tomb, suggesting they died at different times from each other.[22] There was diversity in how adult females were buried, but they were generally identified in relation to a male.

The inscriptions further suggest that while women were regularly identified in relation to husbands and sons, they were also identified in relation to children and siblings. This indicates another fundamental way in which the value of some women in the Jewish homeland of the first century CE found expression: through the recognition of their capacity to bear children. We find, for example, inscriptions that attest to burial arrangements in which named or unnamed women were buried with named or unnamed children. These children are identified as the woman's own children by labeling the woman as the mother (*CIIP*, figs. 98, 517). There are also examples of named women being buried together as mother and daughter, or as sisters (*CIIP*, figs. 590.1a, 590.2b). Taken together, the inscriptional data and the location of women's remains in family tombs— while not uniform—demonstrates that in death some mothers and wives were memorialized as important figures in the familial network. Their identity, in the main, was associated with the males in their families, be they fathers, husbands, sons- or fathers-in-law, and/or with their children.[23]

---

22. Hachlili, *Jewish Funerary Customs*, 312.

23. Funerary material in the diaspora postdates the first century CE. Nonetheless, many inscriptions continue to name women and female children in death. Women are regularly identified without naming a significant male member. Equally, there is evidence that they are identified in relation to their sons and fathers (and in some cases mothers and daughters). Erwin Ramsdell Goodenough, *The Archeological Evidence from the Diaspora*, vol. 2 of *Jewish Symbols in the Greco-Roman Period* (New York: Pantheon, 1953). There is also evidence of women being identified in relation to honorable, civic activities or to labels concerning honorable, public roles, held by their husbands (Goodenough, *Archeological Evidence*, fig. 721).

5. Images of Female Bodies in Late Second Temple Judaism 155

When we turn to some of the literature of the late Second Temple period, we also find an emphasis on the depiction of women as conceivers and bearers of children. One place this is apparent is in the genealogies of Jubilees and Liber Antiquitatum Biblicarum. Genealogies map out the chronological succession of generations or ancestors as well as the relationships between individuals and groups in one entire, extended family over time.[24] More than chronicles of descent, the way in which genealogies were constructed in the Jewish tradition could communicate specific ideas and theologies.[25] When placed within narratives that contained uncertainty or tension, for example, they could function to suggest stability and order.[26] In particular, genealogies played an important role where it was necessary to define the community.[27] Given Israel considered itself to be a particular kinship group within the societies in which it existed, genealogies enabled some Jews to situate themselves within the ethnic mix of their broader context and concomitantly to grant honor to the family's identity, while at the same time singling out specific individuals for note.

The author of Jubilees firmly locates women in the roles of conceivers and bearers of children in the recounting of ancestry through genealogies. Wives and mothers are identified as being instrumental in the movement of family life through the generations. Their significance is primarily identified in relation to the man who married them and the children they subsequently produced. In the narration of the descendants of Adam in Jub. 4:7–15, for example, a male is named, described as "taking" a named woman as his wife. She is subsequently identified in terms of bearing a son for her husband. The father assumes the role of naming the child. Accordingly, in 4:15, the author narrates, "Mahalalel took for himself a wife, Dinah, the daughter of Baraki'el, the daughter of his father's brother, as a wife. And she bore a son for him in the third week in the sixth year. And he called him Jared." This quotation exemplifies a model for describing the begetting of generations that was replicated throughout the narra-

---

24. Frederick J. Murphy, *Early Judaism: The Exile to the Time of Jesus* (Peabody, MA: Hendrickson, 2002), 53.

25. Lester L. Grabbe, *Yehud: A History of the Persian Province of Judah*, vol. 1 of *A History of the Jews and Judaism in the Second Temple Period*, LSTS 47 (London: T&T Clark, 2004), 80.

26. Robert B. Robinson, "Literary Functions of the Genealogies of Genesis " *CBQ* 48 (1986): 595–608.

27. Murphy, *Early Judaism*, 53, 406.

tive. The following demonstrates the general formula that the author of Jubilees employed, albeit with minor variations: "... *took* a wife and *her name* was..., *daughter of...*, son of.... And in the ... year *she bore a son for him* [and on fewer occasions, a daughter] and *he* called him" (emphasis added).[28] The author clearly presents the woman in the context of family relationships. While identified by name in the narratives of ancestry, she could also be considered as a passive participant in much of the generative activity: she is taken by the male as a wife; she bears children for him; and is mostly portrayed as insignificant in the naming of the child.[29]

Providing the woman with a name was not so much a matter of acknowledging her individual identity as it was her broader significance in the family line. Marriages were critical to preserving Jewish identity and genealogies bore witness to a desire to create boundaries when defining the community's identity.[30] One of the concerns of the book of Jubilees is the preservation of Jewish identity in the midst of a hellenizing culture. Sexual relations with foreigners were understood to pose a threat to Jewish identity, while endogamous marriages were perceived as a vehicle for ensuring the purity of the line. This is reflected in how females were identified in the lists of the ancestors. They were named and their pedigree identified by noting their fathers and grandfathers. The identity of the wife and mother in the genealogy of Jubilees was a vehicle for reinforcing the role that women understood to play in ensuring the stability and purity of the Jewish familial network.[31]

The author of Liber Antiquitatum Biblicarum paints a similar picture of women, constructing genealogies that represented women first and foremost as bearers of children throughout the succession of Israelite generations.[32] Formulas appear that bear semblance to those observed in

---

28. Other instances include Jub. 4.16, 20, 27, 28; 8.1, 5–8; 10.18; 11.1, 7–8, 9–11, 14–15; 12.10.

29. I am not working from the original text of Jubilees in this study. I therefore recognize that any comments I make on the language of Jubilees and its insight to thinking in the first century CE are considered circumspect in nature.

30. Murphy, *Early Judaism*, 79.

31. Betsy Halpern-Amaru, *The Empowerment of Women in the Book of Jubilees*, JSJSup 60 (Leiden: Brill, 1999), 17, 19; VanderKam, *Jubilees*, 115.

32. The genealogies in Liber Antiquitatum Biblicarum are an example of Ps-Philo's rewriting of the Bible. Pseudo-Philo adds comments and names to Gen 4–5. Many of the names do not appear anywhere else in the Jewish tradition. This multiplication of names, in Murphy's view, is a strategy to present the author as an expert who knows

Jubilees. In the genealogies from Cain to Lamech (2.1–10), of the sons of Noah (4.1–17), and from Canaan to Egypt (8.1–4), we again note a general pattern by which a man takes a named daughter of another man as his wife; the wife bears sons and (in fewer numbers) daughters to her husband; and the sons and daughters are sometimes named.[33]

Sarah, Hagar, Rebecca, Leah, Zilpah, Billah, Rachel, and Dinah are central characters in the narrative of Liber Antiquitatum Biblicarum. Each is described in terms of her role in conceiving and bearing children, with an emphasis on the producing of sons. One key to understanding the significance of their motherhood for the author is suggested in the narration of the flood in chapter 3. In the directions that God gives for the construction of the ark, Noah is directed to take his wife and sons, and the wives of his sons into the ark (Jub. 3.4). The ensuing direction to Noah to take seven clean male and female birds "so that their seed can live on the earth" (Jub. 3.4) perhaps implies that the directive to take sons and their wives is also for the purpose of procreation and to ensure ongoing lineage. Viewed in this context, Liber Antiquitatum Biblicarum recognized these mothers as important agents in the continuity of Israel.[34]

The identification of Jewish mothers with the ongoing existence of Israel through the bearing of children is also evident in Josephus's writing. In his interpretation of the rescue of the infant Moses, Josephus draws on specific images of women's bodies and their associated functions to describe the nurturing of the infant (*A.J.* 1.224–227). Thermuthis arranges for an Egyptian woman to breast feed the abandoned child. Upon Moses rejecting this gesture, the king's daughter—on the advice of Mariam— orders a "Hebrew woman" to suckle the child in the hope that "it would take the breast of one of its own race." Josephus then describes the infant as "gleefully..., fastened upon the breast." The image of Moses taking and fastening onto the breast of his Hebrew mother, juxtaposed

---

the details of biblical history well, thus inspiring confidence in those who read Liber Antiquitatum Biblicarum (*Pseudo-Philo*, 30).

33. Pseudo-Philo notes the birth of more sons than daughters in all the genealogies. The author also reverses the biblical order of Gen 4 and 5, with the genealogy of Seth in ch. 1 and that of Cain in ch, 2 (Jacobson, *Pseudo-Philo's Liber Antiquitatum Biblicarum*, 1:293).

34. In the figure of Deborah, Pseudo-Philo reworks the image of a Jewish woman as a mother. Her status as a mother is defined not by her childbearing capacity but by her reputation as the holy, judicious leader of Israel (LAB 33.1–6).

with his rejection of the breast of the Egyptian woman, is central to the continuation of the story of Moses and the Hebrew people. It suggests the perceived importance of Jewish mothers in ensuring the survival of the people.[35]

Another dimension to the portrayal of women as wives and bearers of children is the concentration on notions of female fertility. In Jubilees, the author identifies the belly and the womb of Rebecca as the corporeal spaces in which Esau and Jacob were sown and from which they emerged (Jub. 35.18–27). Philo draws on the image of the womb in *Spec.* 3 to affirm the place of women's bodies in the gestation of children. He describes the womb metaphorically as a "laboratory of nature," a physical receptacle in which the creature takes shape (*Spec.* 3.33). The image is evoked again in *Spec.* 3.107–109 alongside that of the womb as an artist's studio, in which the forming offspring lies like a "statue" waiting to be released from its confinement. Both images of the pregnant woman are corporeal, depicting the woman's body as a room in which the unborn child develops. Other than providing the bodily space in which growth occurs, however, no other formative contribution is made by the woman. The seed from which life is derived, the procreating force (σπερματικοὺς τόνους), is not derived from the woman's body (3.33). Instead, the source of conception is associated with the male body.

Liber Antiquitatum Biblicarum takes notions of female fertility further in the usage of the image of the womb. Sarai is described in terms of her sterility—her inability to conceive offspring—prompting Abram to take Hagar who consequently bears a son for him (LAB 8.1). Images of Sarai's infertility are conjured up in terms of environmental barrenness, "that rock of mine that is closed up" (LAB 23.5–6). This association between barrenness and the infertility of the woman's body is illustrated in the idea of being closed up, with the image of the open or closed womb. Those who have closed wombs are sterile, and those with open wombs give birth (LAB 23.7).

Liber Antiquitatum Biblicarum depicts the Lord as the determiner of whether a womb is open or closed (LAB 23.7). In the hymn of Deborah,

---

35. Given the role of women and children in the life of the people, Josephus describes the consequences for those men who abuse the bodies of women leading to the miscarriage of unborn children, "destruction of the fruit of her womb" (*A.J.* 4.278). The violence enacted on women is not deemed inherently evil except in that which it implies for the potential depletion of the people.

the author extols the Lord who gave Isaac two sons "from a womb that was closed up" (LAB 32.5). In the narration of Samson's birth, Eluma is identified in terms of infertility, described as "sterile and did not bear children to [Manoah]" (LAB 42.1). Her husband attributes this state to the Lord who has "shut up your womb so that you may not bear children," thus prompting a desire to seek out another wife for fear that he will die without offspring (LAB 42.1–2). As the story progresses, Eluma approaches the Lord enquiring whether it is on her account, or her husband's, or indeed both, that they are unable to produce children. The Lord, through an angel, responds by indicating that it is Eluma who is sterile, "you are the womb that is forbidden so as not to bear fruit" (LAB 42.3). In response to Eluma's voice and her tears, however, the Lord opens her womb to enable her to conceive and bear a son, which she is to name Samson (LAB 42.3).

Notions of fertility and infertility play a role in the characterization of Hannah. In the prayer of Hannah and the birth of Samuel in Liber Antiquitatum Biblicarum, Hannah is taunted daily by Peninnah, the fertile second wife of her husband, Elkanah, on account of her sterility, which becomes for Hannah a source of intense sadness (LAB 50.2). Applying another ecological metaphor for barrenness, Peninnah describes the sterile Hannah as a "dry tree" (50.1). Hannah attributes the state of having an open and closed womb to God (50.4). Her transition to a state of fertility through God's intervention is not as explicit as in the case of Eluma, however the author implies some divine association given the priest's knowledge that a prophet had been foreordained to be born of Hannah (LAB 50.7–8). In this trope of the open and closed womb, women's bodies are deemed responsible for the inability to conceive and bear offspring. The infertile state of a woman's body is therefore insufferable. The transformation to a fertile body is attributed to God. The Lord is depicted as having power over the womb, including the formation of the child in the womb (23.7). Women's own vocal and emotional supplications prompt God to bring about changes to their physical state to that of a fertile womb. This in turn elevates their status in the narrative to that of the bearer of offspring.[36]

The author of Jubilees also employs images of female fertility. This is evident in Rebecca's blessing of Jacob. Her blessing is described partly in the physical characteristics of prayer: she lifts her face toward heaven;

---

36. The trope appears also in Jubilees in the descriptions of Rachel, Leah, and Zilpah and the births of children (Jub. 28.9–24).

spreads out the fingers of her hands; opens her mouth and blesses God; places her two hands upon the head of Jacob; and kisses him (Jub. 25.11–23). In 25.19, the author adopts images that are specific to female fertility and nursing, "The womb of the one who bore you likewise blesses you; My affection and my breasts are blessing you." What marks Rebecca as unique in Jubilees *is* her role as the bearer of offspring. As Betsy Halpern-Amaru notes, Rebecca's role is linked to the immediate generation and she is the assertive partner in comparison to Jacob in matters to do with the family.[37] It is her body, associated with her fertility and childbearing, that is a site and source of blessing in the family.

Liber Antiquitatum Biblicarum employs the images of the womb and female breasts to elaborate on the significance of the role of Hannah for Israel. In LAB 51.1, she is described as nursing Samuel until he reaches two years when she weans him. At this time, she presents Samuel to Eli, the priest, who draws out both Samuel's and her broader significance. It is through her childbearing—embodied in the image of her womb, as the writer notes—that the tribes have gained advantage. Conjuring up images of lactation, the author describes Hannah's breast milk as a spring-like source of nourishment for a collective Israel, "a fountain for the twelve tribes" (LAB 51.3). Her breastfeeding of Samuel, in particular, is pivotal in the raising of the child who will bring wisdom and law to the people. (LAB 51.3). In other words, her breast milk and her breastfeeding are a means of unifying and nourishing Israel. The future bonds of Israel are attributed to Hannah.[38]

Given that women's capacity to bear children was recognized as a means of ensuring the continuity of the people of Israel, it is not surprising to find that their sexuality and fertility could also be perceived as a danger to the stability of Jewish identity. One of the ways in which this attitude was revealed in the first-century CE was through the depictions of sexual activity between Jews and non-Jews. A specific case in point is the threat to priesthood that Josephus raises in *Against Apion*. Josephus narrates

---

37. Halpern-Amaru, *Empowerment of Women*, 62.

38. Joan E. Cook, "Pseudo-Philo's Song of Hannah: Testament of a Mother in Israel," *JSP* 5 (1991): 103–14; Cynthia R. Chapman, *The House of the Mother: The Social Roles of Maternal Kin in Biblical Hebrew Narrative and Poetry*, ABRL (New Haven: Yale University Press, 2016), 135–38; Jacobson suggests that the image of Hannah as a nursing mother "is testimony to God's goodness and power" (*Pseudo-Philo's Liber Antiquitatum Biblicarum*, 2:1100).

how, in times of war, priests compiled records of surviving Jews. Of the women who survived, those who had been taken captive were prohibited from marrying priests in the fear that they had had frequent intercourse with "foreigners" (*C. Ap.* 1.34). John Barclay notes the important function that marriage played in producing male children to continue the priestly line. Maintaining the purity of the priesthood was of particular interest to Josephus given his own role as a priest. It is not surprising therefore that we encounter his attitudes to the "taboo of ethnic mixing" that would have compromised the integrity of Jewish ritual life.[39] A woman who had engaged in sexual relations with an uncircumcised man was considered defiled (Lev 21:7). When women were taken captive, they were generally raped, leaving them unsuitable as potential wives for priests in Josephus's account.[40] Josephus does not incorporate ideas about how women responded to this prohibition in his narration. How women thought about such a directive appears of no interest. Instead, the focus rested on the perceived violation that came about when captive Jewish women engaged sexually with foreigners and the implications of this in relation to subsequent marriages to priests and maintaining a "pure and unadulterated" priestly lineage (*C. Ap.* 1.30).

Liber Antiquitatum Biblicarum provides a more elaborate critique of sex with foreigners in his narration of the fate of the Levite Bethac's unnamed concubine (LAB 45). Upon entering Nob, Bethac/Beel and his concubine are dragged out by the inhabitants of the city. While Bethac is cast off, the concubine is abused until she dies. The reason given for this fatal violence is that she has transgressed her man at one time with the Amalekites. Because of this, God has consigned her to the abuse of sinners (LAB 45.3). Her violated, dead body represents opposition to the act of sleeping with the enemy as it were. As the episode continues, the concubine's body is further violated by Bethac in the description of a horrific dismemberment. Finding his concubine dead, he puts her on his mule, hurries away and comes to Cades, takes her body, cuts it up, and sends it around to the twelve tribes as a sign of Israel's wickedness (LAB 45.4). Beel undertakes this act as a unifying gesture to Israel to act against potential ongoing wickedness and the threats this poses to the continuation of

---

39. Barclay, *Against Apion*, 25 nn. 125 and 126.
40. Notably, Josephus's first wife was a captive. The author, of priestly descent himself, justifies his marriage on account of the woman still being a virgin (*Vita* 414; Barclay, *Against Apion*, 27 n. 143).

Israel (LAB 45.5). In this example, the concubine functions as an "object of divine punishment." It is through the violence enacted on her body that God carries out divine retribution.[41] Her physical violation and death is depicted as acceptable on the basis of her activity with the Amalekites. She embodies the sin of wrongful sexual relations. As a measure of the gravity of this sin, her dead body is not given a burial but violated further through dismemberment and, in its mutilated, divided parts, functions as an instrument of warning to the tribes.[42]

A precursor to the representation of the concubine is that of Tamar (LAB 9). Her story is cited by the figure Amran in his speech opposing the elders' prohibition on sexual intercourse with one's wife on account of the Egyptians' plans to enslave Israelite females (LAB 9.1). Tamar's deceit of her father-in-law and her subsequent sexual engagement with him, resulting in pregnancy, is commended by Amran. Tamar's actions are not labeled pejoratively as "fornication" but, instead, as the correct alternative to having intercourse with non-Jews. They demonstrate her unwillingness to "separate from the sons of Israel" (LAB 9.5). In accordance with the covenant, Tamar will produce Israelite offspring, rendering her actions superior to the elders' proposal to remain childless (LAB 9.2). Amran argues that, as Tamar has survived, so too will Israel endure beyond any assault by the Egyptians. His line of reasoning finds favor with God and the covenant between God and Israel stands (LAB 9.3, 7, 8). Tamar's sexual activity and subsequent motherhood reveal her as "an agent in God's governance of Israel's destiny."[43] Her fertility, when directed toward Israel and away from foreigners, facilitates the bonds between God and Israel.

---

41. Betsy Halpern-Amaru, "Portraits of Women in Pseudo-Philo's *Biblical Antiquities*," in *"Women Like This": New Perspectives on Women in the Greco-Roman World*, ed. Amy-Jill Levine, EJL 1 (Atlanta: Scholars Press, 1991), 100.

42. The concubine's dismembered body also functions to unite the twelve tribes (45:5). In this way, her dismembered body shifts from being an object of divine punishment to a positive "agent in God's governance of Israel's destiny" (Halpern-Amaru, "Portraits of Women," 100).

43. Halpern-Amaru, "Portraits of Women," 100. For further observations on the figure of Tamar in Amran's speech, particularly in light of Ps.-Philo's treatment in terms of female sexuality, see Donald C. Polaski, "On Taming Tamar: Amram's Rhetoric and Women's Roles in Pseudo-Philo's Liber Antiquitatum Biblicarum," *JSP* 13 (1995): 79–99.

Bearing the enemy's or a foreigner's children is deemed so negatively that the author uses the term "miscarriage" in relation to children who are the fruit of such relationships. Pseudo-Philo writes:

> The wombs of our wives have suffered miscarriage; our fruit is delivered to our enemies. And now we are lost, and let us set up rules for ourselves that a man should not approach his wife lest the fruit of their wombs be defiled and our offspring serve idols. For it is better to die without sons until we know what God may do. (LAB 9.2)

The outcome of these mixed relationships is imaged as the destruction of the physical life contained in the womb. This destruction occurs not on account of any physical injury that may be enacted on the enslaved woman, but in relation to the notion that offspring born from intercourse with gentiles are considered defiled and oriented to idol worship.

A second dimension to the notion that women's sexuality and fertility poses a threat within Judaism reveals itself in the depictions of foreign women in relation to Jewish men. The perceived danger of foreign women attracts comment by Philo who associates them with leading Jewish men away from their religious observances to "unholy conduct in public" (*Spec.* 1.57). The perceived capacity of foreign women to lead men to spurn their own religion and turn to the practices of foreign rites prompts Philo to label them as an "instructor in wickedness" (*Spec.* 1.56). In addition, it is the basis upon which Philo depicts a man "with admirable courage" who "slew without qualm" a foreign woman alongside her Jewish male counterpart as he attended to the foreign woman's lesson (*Spec.* 1.56–57). Philo's narrative serves as an insight into a perception that the threat presented by foreign women lay in their capacity to lead men beyond Judaism, signified in the worship of idols. A serious state, Philo appears to justify the murder of both offenders.

In Jubilees, the threat that foreign women posed by virtue of their fertility is clear. In instructing Jacob on marriage, Rebecca unambiguously directs her son not to take a wife from the daughters of Canaan (Jub. 25.1). The basis for her opposition is derived from the perceptions of the sexuality of foreign women: They engage in fornication and lust, which are associated with impurity (Jub. 25.1). Instead, Rebecca instructs him to take a wife from her own patrilineage, "her father's house," and therefore from Israel (Jub. 25.3). Such a relationship will ensure that Jacob will be blessed by God, which will find expression in the procreation of Israelite children, "a righteous generation and a holy seed" (Jub. 25.3).

A presupposition of Jubilees is that the identity of Israel is defined by the covenant. The markers of this covenant include circumcision and endogamous marriages.[44] The value of such marriages, as we have seen, lies in their capacity to maintain the purity and continuity of Israel. Conversely, sexual relations with foreign women are not only understood to defile Israel but, at the same time, they threaten its existence through the unholy offspring that intermarriage generates. It is this ability to pervert the life of Israel that renders the fertile bodies of foreign women as sites of danger.[45]

5.3. The Bodies of Children

Given the emphasis on family and the role of women as mothers and wives, we can expect depictions of children to perform specific functions within this paradigm. Among the voices of the first century CE, the language used to identify children included that of the fetus, of babies, of infants, of children as offspring or descendants, and of sons and daughters. The ages of children seldom appear in the literature we view. Where they do appear, they enhance the picture that the writer is painting of each child. Josephus, for example, notes the age of Sethos as five years old (*C. Ap.* 1.245). When this label is coupled with the description of protecting the child by putting him into the care of a beloved friend, the image that is created is one of childhood vulnerability.[46] In *A.J.* 12.190 Hyrcanus is labeled as thirteen years old alongside the descriptor of being a "young lad." Together, these labels paint a picture of youthfulness, which then underscores the accompanying description of his extraordinary competence, "his natural courage and intelligence … great superiority and enviable qualities." The ages of children appear even more rarely in the epigraphic material.[47] In literary

---

44. Mary Anna Bader, *Tracing the Evidence: Dinah in Post-Hebrew Bible Literature*, StBibLit 102 (New York: Lang, 2008), 107.
45. The gravity of the corruption of idol worship is also translated in Ps.-Philo in the representation of women's and men's bodies. See the descriptions of violence enacted upon Micah and his mother, Dedila, for their involvement with idols (LAB 44.9). Also, Orpah, the mother of Goliath, is represented in relation to her worship of the gods of the Philistines. Her allegiances eventually lead to the slinging and beheading of her son at the hands of David (LAB 61.7-9).
46. Similarly, *A.J.* 9.142.
47. Hachlili cites the ages of two males in the Goliath tomb in Jericho as aged four (*Jewish Funerary Customs*, 323). Ages appear in later Jewish burial inscriptions

cases, at least, chronological age is noted alongside other descriptors to enhance the characterization of specific children.

Instead of using chronological age as a common indicator of a stage in life, childhood is described in relation to different stages of young people's lives and is associated with various phenomena peculiar to those times. Philo, for example, describes the fetus becoming a human being when all the limbs are fully grown and intact (*Spec.* 3.107–109). Infancy is denoted by the wearing of swaddling clothing or bands as well as the propensity for learning dishonesty within the household (*Spec.* 4.57–58).[48] Childhood is associated with naiveté as well as the potential for cruel play.[49] Children could be considered inadequate in comparison to adults. In his bid to gain imperial authority, Gaius describes his chief rival—the child Tiberius—as one in need of "guardians, teachers, and tutors" (*Legat.* 26).[50] Philo presents Gaius as employing the ideas of childhood inadequacy to craft his argument for succession.

When the discussion shifts to images of older children, the categories by which writers refer to males and females diverge. For males, there is a period between childhood and being an adult. Philo refers to the cousin of Gaius as a male child passing into the phase of being a "stripling" (*Legat.* 23).[51] Older girls, however, receive no such label to denote a period of transition. Instead, their progression beyond childhood is routinely marked by their eligibility to marry. Philo describes this time as the point in which the female is in adolescence or in her prime in relation to childbearing (*Spec.* 3.81).[52] Alas, it is not possible to identify an exact age at which girls married. Tal Ilan points out that no inscriptions in the first century CE

---

in the diaspora, spanning from the age of infants up to those who are sixty years old (Goodenough, *Archeological Evidence*, 2).

48. Philo, *Spec.* 4.57–58 refers to children at birth being "from the cradle." The term used, σπάργανον, can also refer to swaddling clothes.

49. To be sure, *Legat.* 1 uses the image of a child, παῖς, and an infant, νήπιος, metaphorically to connote child-like innocence or perhaps, immaturity; a lack of sense and, as yet, unaware of how life works in terms of nature and fortune. Also *Flacc.* 36, which refers to both children (νήπιος) and youths (μειράκιον) treating the lunatic Carabas as a play thing.

50. The term νήπιος refers to a very young child.

51. Philo uses the term παῖς, which indicates a child, and μειράκιον, which denotes a stripling.

52. The Loeb translation of "τῆς ἀκμῆς καιρόν" uses the term *adolescence* to refer to the girl who is unmarried. The term may connote being in one's prime.

refer to the age at which girls married.[53] The rabbinic literature of Palestine and the west diaspora talks of men marrying around the age of thirty and girls from fifteen to twenty years old, while earlier ages are noted in the writings from Babylonia. These texts, however, often indicate a perceived ideal, rather than the reality of when girls married.[54]

Overall, while representations of children appear in the literature, they do not feature as prominently as adults do. Nor do their bodies attract the degree of explanation that the adults do. In addition, writers seldom tell their narratives from the perspectives of children. The reader/hearer rarely glimpses what children see, hear, think, or feel. They are commonly represented as passive, and in terms of what is done to them. They seldom talk but are talked *about*. It is to this talk of children that we now turn to glean some of the ideas that writers in the first century CE reveal about children through depictions of their bodies.

5.3.1. Children as Valued

Children were valued in some of the literature of the Second Temple era. Their worth was located primarily in their capacity to continue the lineage of their families and therefore to ensure the continuity of Israel. This is illustrated in the importance attached to the circumcision of Jewish infant males as an identity marker of Judaism (A.J. 1.214).[55] It is also exemplified in the naming of sons and daughters throughout the genealogies of Liber Antiquitatum Biblicarum and Jubilees.[56]

At a figurative level, the image of children is taken up to connote the collective people of Israel. In Jub. 2.26–30 the "children of Israel" are commanded to keep the Sabbath: to guard it and sanctify it to ensure that Israel will not be uprooted from the land (Jub. 2.26–8). They are not permitted

---

53. Ilan, *Integrating Women*, 213.

54. Satlow, *Jewish Marriage*, 131–32; Ross S. Kraemer, "Jewish Mothers and Daughters in the Greco-Roman World," in Cohen, *The Jewish Family in Antiquity*, 104–5.

55. Josephus also refers to the important role of children in looking after the welfare of aged parents (A.J. 1.186–188).

56. Reinhartz and Shier observe three further characteristics of this appreciation in Josephus's description of the three-year-old Moses, two of which relate to the physicality of the infant: beauty (A.J. 2.231), intellectual superiority (A.J. 2.230), and physical stature (A.J. 2.230; "Josephus," 367–68). They also note similar themes in Philo, *Mos.* 1.5.18–21.

5. Images of Female Bodies in Late Second Temple Judaism 167

to eat, drink, work, draw water, or to move goods in or out of a house (Jub. 2.29–30). The author of Jubilees associates the "children of Israel" with the ritual life and covenantal commitment of Israel.[57] This image differs from that of the "children of men," a term that the author uses in relation to evil and to contrast with the virtues of Israel (Jub. 4.24; 50.10). Noah adjures "my children" to "hear and do justice and righteousness.... To build for yourselves cities ... and plant in them every plant that bears fruit" (Jub. 7.34–35). For the author of Jubilees the image of children is co-opted in the construction of metaphors that relate to upholding the covenant and ensuring the future stability of Israel.

Rather than taking up terms related to children to develop metaphors for Israel, Philo speaks of the value of children through the metaphors of ritual imagery of "first fruits" (*Spec.* 1.137–138). This imagery is future-oriented. The first-born son receives particular attention as the first produce of a marriage. He is consecrated as a first fruit to celebrate the realization of the blessings of parenthood and the hope of further blessings (*Spec.* 1.138.).[58]

While Philo recognizes that "first fruits" are generally offered from among people's possessions, he expands this notion by asserting that parents offer the first fruits that come from their very bodies and souls in the generation of children. Philo explains that children are separable from their parents but also inseparable, "joined to them by kinship of blood, by the thoughts and memories of ancestors, invisible presences still alive among their descendants, by the love-ties of the affection which unites them, by the indissoluble bonds of nature" (*Spec.* 1.137–138). The continuity between parents and their offspring is both corporeal through the kinship of blood/αἵματα, and noncorporeal, in the thoughts and memories of the ancestors. This continuity through the generations therefore is embodied in children. In Philo's framework, children are the conduit through which the life of the ancestors endures.

---

57. This image of the "children of Israel" in relation to the covenant is expanded in Jubilees to include observing the feast of Shavuot (6.19), guarding the number of years in the 364-day calendar (6:32), not breaching the covenant (31.21), not lying with one's mother-in-law and therefore becoming defiled (41:26), in the escape from Egypt Israel is referred to as "children of Israel" (48.9–19), in relation to the Passover (49.1–23), in relation to keeping the Sabbath (50.1–13).

58. The status of the first-born son also receives attention in the characterization of Jacob in Jub. 2.20.

Conversely, children can also be a source of defilement. Liber Antiquitatum Biblicarum also presents the image of children as "fruit of the womb," identifying children as the produce of a woman's body. Rather than produce to be consecrated, in the recount of Amran and the birth of Moses the author speaks of the anxiety concerning females who have been possibly taken as Egyptian wives and slaves (LAB 9.1–2). Their offspring bear the possibility of defilement and the worship of idols. While children hold a significant role in the continuity of Israel, like their mothers, they also potentially pose risks to the ongoing life of Israel.[59]

5.3.2. The Deaths of Children

The mourning of children's deaths provides a second indicator of the value by which some children were held in the first century CE. In Jerusalem and Jericho, we find burial sites in which children are identified. They are commonly located in the tombs of families, and interred in ossuaries or coffins usually with others but sometimes alone (*CIIP*, fig. 116.1). Children appear as named and unnamed in the inscriptions commemorating their death. Indicators of their childhood status include the size of the remains and/or the size of the ossuary.

In the *Corpus Inscriptionum Iudaeae/Palestinae*, I have counted at least six boxes of small children or infants—male and female—who were interred alone. The smaller-sized ossuaries are usually taken to indicate that the box was intended for an infant or small child. There are a further nine boxes which have the remains of small children and adults. If buried with others, children are usually interred with a parent, and most often a mother, but there is also evidence of children being interred together (*CIIP*, fig. 47). Hannah Cotton posits that some of the boxes containing a mother and a very small infant possibly suggest evidence of mothers and children either dying in birth, dying during the birth of a still-born baby, or dying within a short time after birth (*CIIP*, figs. 279.3(b), 298). It is impossible to know, however, why or how children died. No indicators of the causes of death are provided in the inscriptions for children. Possibilities such as disease or illness, an accident or abuse are not noted. What the data does attest to is that for some Jews the burial of children was deemed important.

---

59. As we have observed, this view is subsequently rejected by Amran, who advocates sexual relations with wives in the ensuing verses of the chapter.

Some of the children who are buried in family tombs are remembered with great affection. In the Goliath Family Tomb in Jericho, for instance, we find the remains of an infant and a child. Both are named, with the term of endearment, "cinnamon," or sweet (as in sweet fragrance) added to the infant's inscription (Goliath Family Tomb, ossuaries XVI and XXII).[60] Similarly, the term "saffron" or "κρόκος" appears on an inscription in a small ossuary built for children, located north of the Damascus Gate (*CIIP*, fig. 249). It is another term of endearment and possibly communicated the poignancy with which the death of the child(ren) was felt. The child is otherwise not named, with the inscribed nickname testifying to the affection with which they were to be regarded in death.

The description of infants and children in relation to death is also evident in the literature. Their deaths are commonly attributed to violence, usually taking the forms of infanticide, abortion, and exposure. In the rhetoric of *Spec.* 3 Philo exploits imagery of murdered infants to assert his view on the superiority of the Mosaic law. Giving the impression that exposure was widely practiced beyond Judaism, Philo clearly rejects the practice, labeling it with terms such as "sacrilegious," "monstrous cruelty and barbarity" (*Spec.* 3.110, 115).[61] He employs graphic language to bring the grisly nature of exposure close to the reader/hearer. Infants' bodies are stifled and throttled of their first breath, thrown into a river or sea with a weight, exposed in a desert, consumed by animals that eat human flesh. The body is described as dismembered and eaten in fragments, and labeled in animalistic terms as a *carcass*. He translates the horror of exposure through the language of food and feasting. This common imagery is turned on its head with descriptions of animals consuming babies' bodies: beasts "feast unhindered on the infants, a fine banquet provided by … those who above all others should keep them safe, their fathers and

---

60. Hachlili, *Jewish Funerary Customs*, 229, 290.

61. There is debate as to whether or not Jews practiced infant exposure and infanticide in Philo's time. Niehoff argues that they did (*Philo*, 171). Reinhartz is more speculative than Niehoff. Adele Reinhartz, "Philo on Infanticide," *SPhiloA* 4 (1992): 42–58. Schwartz argues that there is no evidence to prove or deny that Jews practiced infanticide and infant exposure, or that Jews condoned these practices ("Jews Practice Infanticide," 91–93). Niehoff points out nonetheless, that child exposure was practiced by Greeks living in Roman Egypt during the first century CE. In light of this, Philo may have been affirming the superiority of the Jewish law in defending the rights of children to survival (Niehoff, *Philo*, 168).

mothers" (*Spec.* 3.115). Philo's assessment of the practice is clearly conveyed through these abhorrent descriptions. The role of parents, in Philo's view, was to protect their young, not murder them. The basis for Philo's criticism of exposure is the law of Moses.[62] His rhetoric on infant exposure contributes to his wider assertion that the Mosaic law distinguished Jews as moral and spiritual exemplars within the broader cultural mix in which they existed.[63] The law's emphasis on parents protecting children from death (infanticide and exposure) was utilized by Philo to set Jews apart from their neighbors.

Descriptions of child sacrifice present a further aspect to the image of children in relation to death. This is illustrated in Liber Antiquitatum Biblicarum's account of the sacrificing of Isaac, which appears within the hymn of Deborah (LAB 32.2-4). Isaac is labeled as the "fruit of [Abraham's] body," clearly establishing him as the child of Abraham. It is God who commands Abraham to offer his son as a holocaust. The author describes Isaac as compliant in the activity. He is given a voice and the words placed on his lips are words of acceptance. Moreover, Isaac is depicted as understanding that his sacrificial death casts him as blessed above others and a model for future generations. As the story progresses, and Abraham binds his son's feet to kill him, God's voice intervenes and stops the sacrifice from being carried through.

We can make two observations in this account. First, Liber Antiquitatum Biblicarum represents child sacrifice to underscore the relationship between Abraham and God. The order for the sacrifice is attributed to God, and likewise, the order to refrain from the slaughter. By its end, the story rejects the idea of child sacrifice as a final sign of Abraham's fidelity to God, but the authority of God and Abraham's obedience to God are established. Second, the child Isaac is painted as a model for the people of the willingness to die in order to fulfil God's designs. He is a paradigm of one who is obedient even in the face of death.[64]

---

62. The basis for Philo's opposition to infanticide and exposure is Exod 21:22–25 LXX, which concerns the prohibition against feticide.

63. Maren R. Niehoff et al., "Philo," in *Early Judaism: A Comprehensive Overview*, ed. John J. Collins and Daniel C. Harlow (Grand Rapids: Eerdmans, 2012), 272.

64. See the comments on the figure of Isaac in Cheryl Anne Brown, *No Longer Be Silent: First Century Jewish Portraits of Biblical Women*, Gender and the Biblical Tradition (Louisville: Westminster John Knox, 1992), 94–99.

5.3.3. "Women and Children"

Some of the writers of the first century CE combine representations of women and children through the cluster "women and children" or "wives and children." The expression is repeated in the works of Philo, Liber Antiquitatum Biblicarum, and Josephus, functioning to indicate a collective group of Jews.[65] In *Life*, for example, Josephus applies the cluster in his description of the collective group of Jews who are murdered by the Syrians: "The inhabitants of the surrounding cities of Syria proceeded to lay hands on and kill, with their *wives and children*, the Jewish residents among them" (*Vita* 25, emphasis added).[66] Indeed, references to women and children are predominantly employed in relation to dying and death throughout the writings of Philo and Josephus in order to communicate the authors' ideas about the scale, brutality, and opposition to the violence enacted on Jews in times of conflict.[67]

A key function of depictions of the suffering and death of women and children is to signify the defeat of Jews. This is often conveyed in their characterization as captives. The sacking and pillaging of Sekella (Ziklag) in *A.J.* 6.357–360, for example, involves wives and children being taken as captives. Their capture prompts grief among David and his male confreres. The effect on David is physical. He rends his clothes, wails and laments with his friends, and tears fail him (*A.J.* 6.357–358). Equally, his comrades are depicted as angry, expressed in the description of their desire to stone David for the capture of their wives, for which they hold him responsible (*A.J.* 6.358). Josephus clearly presents the capture of wives and children as a grave occurrence to be mourned, and concomitantly implies a powerlessness on the part of fathers and husbands. Taken together, these helpless men and their captured wives and children embody defeat.

The representation of defeat is graphic in *C. Ap.* 2.53. "All the Jews in the city" are arrested, with their "wives and children," by Ptolemy Physcon.

---

65. E.g., LAB 5.1–8; 23.2; 36.1; *A.J.* 4.20; 19.349; *C. Ap.* 2.181.

66. He repeats the expression to conjure up the image of a widespread massacre of the Jewish population in *Vita* 61. See also *B.J.* 3.202 in which children and women with infants in their arms are clustered with old men. Also, *Vita* 166; *C. Ap.* 181; *A.J.* 4.20; 20.90.

67. Caryn A. Reeder, "Gender, War, and Josephus," *JSJ* 46 (2015): 65–85; Reeder, "Pity the Women and Children: Punishment by Siege in Josephus's *Jewish War*," *JSJ* 44 (2013): 174–94.

The addition of the cluster wives and children accentuates the completeness of Ptolemy's actions on all Jews.[68] Josephus describes what is done to their bodies. They are exposed naked and put in chains, to be trampled to death by elephants (*C. Ap.* 2.53). Bound in chains, exposed and powerless in the face of a brutal death, they embody what it meant to be a captive. This treatment is labeled as an "enormity" by the concubine Ithaca, who adjures Ptolemy to refrain (which he does and consequently repents; *C. Ap.* 2.55). Josephus thus represents the treatment of the Jews as inhumane. The addition of women and children magnifies the horror, complementing Ithaca's description of the capture in terms of an enormity.[69] The humiliating defeat of the Jews is brutal and comprehensive.

As the depiction of the defeat by Ptolemy Physcon reveals, a related function of the depiction of women and children in narratives of conflict is to augment the scale and brutality of warfare. In Josephus's reading of 2 Kgs 8.10 in *A.J.* 9.91, we encounter images of children being dashed against rocks while pregnant women are ripped open. These images are used alongside statements of men being slain and cities burnt. It is the brutalization of children and pregnant women that receive the lurid descriptions. Along similar lines, in *A.J.* 5.29–30 women and children are singularly identified with the inhabitants in the deathly destruction of the city.[70] In both cases, the singling out of this cluster intensifies the cruelty targeted at all Jews.

The motif is especially evident in Josephus's *Jewish War* where depictions of the suffering of women and children abound.[71] In *B.J.* 2.306–308, as the city is raided under the direction of Florus, Josephus singles out women and children as part of the total number of the victims who were "arrested ... scourged ... and crucified" (*B.J.* 2.307). He intensifies the picture by adding that even infants endure the violence (*B.J.* 2.307). In *B.J.*

---

68. The phrase "women and children" might otherwise be considered superfluous given the author's previous indication that "all Jews" had been rounded up (*C. Ap.* 2.53).

69. All the same, in the attack of Tiberius by the Galileans Josephus appears to justify the capture of women and children and all (*Vita* 99).

70. The exception in this destruction is Rahab and her family (*A.J.* 5.30). See also *Vita* 25.

71. For the observation that Josephus wrote *Jewish War* to combat the portrait of the "Judean character" as "weak and womanish," see Steve Mason, "Essenes and Lurking Spartans in Josephus' *Judean War*," in *Making History: Josephus and Historical Method*, ed. Zuleika Rodgers, JSJSup 110 (Leiden: Brill, 2007), 229.

4.79–81, women and children are identified among the multitude that suicides in the ravine in response to the advance of the Romans on Gamla. The desperate deaths en masse are horrific, demonstrated in Josephus's detail that they even made the previous slaughter of Jews by Romans appear mild (*B.J.* 4.80).[72]

In *B.J.* 5.512–514, Josephus uses images of women's, children's, babies', and youth's bodies to paint a horrific picture of the siege of Jerusalem. Sealing off the city results in a famine that, in Josephus's representation, has a specific impact on families and the household (*B.J.* 5.512). Women and babies are portrayed as exhausted.[73] Employing the language of graphic realism, the famine manifests itself in the bodies of children and youths who are swollen with hunger, and who roam in public places in a ghost-like demeanor. Josephus describes them as already appearing as if they were dead: the term εἴδωλον refers to something that is an image of itself, the phantom of a dead man (*B.J.* 5.513). Overcome by their suffering, they eventually die wherever they fall, and not necessarily in the confines of the household. Indeed, the Jewish household appears to be destroyed; it is no longer a place of protection, nurturing, and familial bonds, but is a place in which women and babies perish, and older children leave in order to (unsuccessfully) find succor.

The scenes that Josephus paints in *Jewish War* conjure up images of violent warfare. Co-opting women and children into these images magnifies the harshness and pathos of his account of the siege of Jerusalem. Generally depicted as being at the mercy of others, women and children are represented as bearing the brunt of the conflicts taken up by their men. Their inclusion conveys the notion that warfare is not played out by men in faraway places. It surrounds and enters cities, destroying households and the lives of all Jews, regardless of age, stage in life, and sex.[74]

---

72. According to Atkinson, there is no archaeological evidence to support Josephus's account of a mass suicide of Jews at Gamla. Instead, Josephus's account "demonstrates the bravery and obstinacy of the the Jewish population … [and concomitantly] highlights the superiority of the Roman legions. … [while distinguishing the] demagogues from their own numbers, who lead the populace to their own destruction." See Kenneth Atkinson, "Noble Deaths at Gamla and Masada?," in Rodgers, *Making History*, 362–66.

73. The weakness of women and babies in this verse is underscored in Josephus's addition of the "aged" to this cluster of groups. He graphically describes the aged as corpses in the alley (*B.J.* 5.513).

74. Reeder, "Pity the Women and Children," 184–90.

In a similar vein, the motif "women and children" appears in Philo's accounts of conflict in *Flaccus*. He coopts the cluster to embody the effects of the famine imposed on Jews by the Alexandrians, describing women and young infants–γύναια καὶ τέκνα νήπια—perishing before the eyes of their men (*Flacc.* 62–64). The term γύναιον and the addition of "καὶ τέκνα νήπια" in particular connoted weakness and helplessness.[75] In *Flacc.* 68, he narrates the violent death of entire families. Spelling out the various members of the households, he lists the presence of wives and infants, in addition to husbands and parents, "whole families, husbands with their wives, infant children with their parents" (*Flacc.* 68). In other words, the loss embraces the heads of households and the driving force in procreation, those who bear and rear children, and children themselves. In light of Philo's emphasis on the continuity of the population, this particular lineup suggests the all-encompassing vulnerability of the future community in the conflict.

Philo's description of the violence enacted on the bodies of family members is graphic and lurid. They are set on fire, and when the wood runs out, they slowly die by being smoked to death. Their bodies become a "painful and most heart-rending spectacle" (*Flacc.* 68). Philo explains they are burnt in the middle of the city, and for those for whom there is insufficient wood to burn, their gruesome bodies "lay promiscuously half-burnt" (*Flacc.* 68). Philo conveys the widespread destruction of the grisly slaughter by using terms that encompass each pole of the human life span: old age and youth. These groups that, when combined, signify the bonds that link the past (old age) and the future of the community (youth) are destroyed. The response of the Jews themselves during their suffering is not described by Philo. There is no mention of screaming or wailing, for instance. Instead, Philo describes what he views as the state of the bodies to accentuate the excessive violence enacted on them. From Philo's perspective, the Jews are victims of Alexandrian brutality that is merciless and extensive.[76]

---

75. According to van der Horst, γύναιον also functioned as a term of endearment. When employed to denote weakness and helplessness, it could carry pejorative connotations. Pieter van der Horst, *Philo's Flaccus: The First Pogrom; Introduction, Translation and Commentary*, PACS 2 (Leiden: Brill, 2003), 163.

76. In his argument against killing substitutes when prosecuting criminals, Philo co-opts images of innocent women and children in the graphic scenes of public humiliation and torture (*Spec.* 3.153–68).

5. Images of Female Bodies in Late Second Temple Judaism   175

A function of these images of brutal and far-reaching suffering and death is to offer an assessment of those who commit these acts. Women and children in Josephus's writing, for example, serve as a tool for the author to interpret the actions of others.[77] Their suffering and death form a recurring theme in his narrative, exploited in his rhetoric of warfare to advance his own colored perspective on particular events and people. His depiction of the killing of women and children at Masada in *Jewish War* is a further case in point (*B.J.* 7.392–394).[78] Rather than allowing their wives and children to be captured and dishonored or slayed by the Romans, the fathers and husbands at Masada, at the exhortation of Eleazar, kill their families and themselves (*B.J.* 7.392–394). Josephus narrates the account from the perspective of the fathers. Poignantly, he describes them "caressing and embracing their wives" and taking their children up in their arms, "clinging in tears to those parting tears" (*B.J.* 7.391).[79] No lurid representation is provided for their subsequent actions; the men are singularly described as slaying their wives and children by their own hands (*B.J.* 7.394). The hands of affection become hands of destruction, killing the beloved and weak who appear passive throughout the ordeal.[80]

In an earlier episode in *Jewish War*, we read of Josephus's opposition to suicide in conflict (*B.J.* 3.362–382). When we turn to the scene at Masada, however, Josephus appears to present the collective suicide (and matricide and filicide) from a different angle.[81] In the speech put onto the lips

---

77. Reeder, "Pity the Women and Children," 186–88.
78. There are no other extant literary accounts of this event from antiquity. Honora Howell Chapman, "Masada in the First and Twenty-first Centuries," in Rodgers, *Making History*, 87 n. 22. The credibility of Josephus's account of the Masada event is the subject of scholarly scrutiny. See Atkinson, "Noble Deaths," 349–71; Shaye J. D. Cohen, "Masada: Literary Tradition, Archaeological Remains and the Credibility of Josephus," *JJS* 28 (1982): 385–405; Jan Willem van Henten, "Noble Death in Josephus: Just Rhetoric?," in Rodgers, *Making History*, 204 n. 28.
79. Reeder notes that suicide rather than surrender were signs of manliness. Faced with the dishonor and violence of being captured, a man could only protect his family through his own violence ("Gender, War, and Josephus," 74).
80. A similar but more detailed narrative appears in *B.J.* 2.475 in which Simon the Jewish renegade murders his wife, children, and aged parents with a sword. In *Flacc.* 68, one of the ways in which Philo criticizes the murder of the Jews is by emphasizing childhood innocence. The Alexandrians show no pity for the "innocent years of childhood."
81. On the ambiguity of Josephus's attitude to suicide in conflict in *Jewish War*, see van Henten, "Noble Death," 215.

of Eleazar, the leader of the sicarii at Masada asserts that, with a Roman victory imminent, it is a *divine necessity* that the men kill themselves and their wives and children (*B.J.* 7.387).[82] In other words, the crimes they previously committed on their own people have incurred the wrath of God.[83] They now pay the price according to God's authority, the "penalty ... to God ... through their own hands" (*B.J.* 7.333–334). In Josephus's account, the impending Roman assault on Masada and the suicide of the last remnant of resistant Jews are all part of God's plan.[84]

In addition to presenting the killing of wives and children as constituent of divine retribution, it is also possible that Josephus ennobles the acts of matricide and filicide. Eleazar argues that killing wives and children is preferable to submitting them to the violation and shame that accompanied foreign captivity (*B.J.* 7.321, 334). In this way, to the Greco-Roman mind of a noble death, Josephus ensures that the Jews at Masada appear as brave in suicide and honorable in the slaying of their own women and children while concomitantly remaining faithful to their God by suffering the divine judgement that has condemned them to such a death.[85] The tragic killing of wives and children therefore becomes instrumental in Josephus's depiction of Eleazar and his colleagues as noble in the face of their own foolishness.

---

82. For observations on the use of the term ἀνάγκην ("necessity") in *Jewish War*, see Mark Andrew Brighton, *The Sicarii in Josephus's Judean War: Rhetorical Analysis and Historical Oberservations*, EJL 27 (Atlanta: Society of Biblical Literature, 2009), 112–14; Nicole Kelley, "The Cosmopolitan Expression of Josephus's Prophetic Perspective in the Jewish War," *HTR* 97 (2004): 257–74. On the various scholarly approaches to the designation "sicarii," see Brighton, *Sicarii*, 1–18.

83. Josephus attributes the suicides and atrocities of the revolt to the sicarii and other rebels, not to priestly leaders (Atkinson, "Noble Deaths," 357–58).

84. John M. G. Barclay, Steve Mason, and James S. McLaren, "Josephus," in Collins and Harlow, *Early Judaism*, 299.

85. Brighton makes the distinction that the sicarii are presented as noble but not heroic or examples of "supreme virtue" (*Sicarii*, 115–19). On the depiction of deaths as noble in Josephus's writings, see van Henten, "Noble Death," 195–218. Atkinson argues that the suicides at both Gamla and Masada are presented by Josephus as noble deaths: "Josephus' stories gave the defenders of Masada and Gamla some dignity in the face of overwhelming might, ... [and] allowed him to blame their defeat upon God. The Romans were invincible,... because God had willed it so." The suicides at both Gamla and Masada are not exemplary however as they are the result of the foolishness of a select few Jews (Atkinson, "Noble Deaths," 365–66).

That the sicarii's slaying of wives and children is not rendered completely honorable is suggested in Josephus's detail that two older women and five children saved themselves from the slaughter by escaping (*B.J.* 7.400–401). Josephus describes one of the women as superior in "sagacity and training" in comparison to other women (*B.J.* 7.399). Upon finding her and the others in the cavern, the Romans pay attention to her "lucid" recount of the episode (*B.J.* 7.405). These survivors are not considered cowards for avoiding death but instead are deemed wise.[86]

Even less redeeming than the portrait of the sicarii at Masada is Josephus's depiction of his nemesis John of Gischala. In an attempt to outwit Titus and his men who had made allowances for Jews in Gischala to observe Sabbath before seizing their town, John presses "a multitude" to flee to Jerusalem (*B.J.* 4.106). The "mob" keeps pace with John for twenty furlongs but then falls behind while he continues to flee (*B.J.* 4.107). In *B.J.* 4.106, 108, Josephus casts John of Gischala in poor light for deserting women and children on account of his fear of captivity and its implications for his own life.[87] He represents John's flight as pitiless, suggested in the emotive sound of lamenting women and children (*B.J.* 4.108).[88] The portrait of suffering and grieving women and children forms part of Josephus's broad critique of the destructive actions undertaken in the face of Roman subjugation and Jewish resistance in *Jewish War*. In the case of his arch enemy John, the motif intensifies Josephus's hostile view of the man.

Perhaps the most confronting of Josephus's accounts of condemnation is that concerning the treatment of Mary and her baby in *B.J.* 6.206–212. Mary, daughter of Eleazar from Bethezuba, flees to Jerusalem only to become caught up in the siege. Contending with the hunger associated with the famine brought on by the siege and driven by anger, Mary is depicted as murdering, cooking, and eating her infant son. She then offers the remains to the Jewish rebels who are drawn into the scene when they enquire into the odor that is produced as the baby is cooked. Josephus's portrait of mother and infant is both horrifying and poignant. It functions in a threefold fashion to judge harshly the Jewish rebels, to underscore the innocence of Titus who consequently destroys the temple in Jerusalem,

---

86. Chapman, "Masada in the First and Twenty-first Centuries," 99.

87. James S. McLaren, *Turbulent Times? Josephus and Scholarship on Judaea in the First Century CE*, JSPSup 29 (Sheffield: Sheffield Academic, 1998), 97.

88. See also *B.J.* 1.313.

and to elicit compassion for all the Jews who suffered as a result of the rebels' actions.[89]

When we read the account with an awareness of the body, the apologetic agenda of Josephus is evident. There are numerous elements in the episode that bear this out. First, as Honora Howell Chapman points out in her analysis of this episode, Mary is only one of two women who are given voice—direct speech—in *Jewish War*.[90] Mary's speech is directed to the baby to whom she outlines the reasons for sacrificing her child: to provide food; to avenge the rebels; and to be a testimony to others of the suffering being endured (*B.J.* 6.208). The hunger that has precipitated her act is palpable, with the famine being described as having "coursed through her intestines and marrow" (*B.J.* 6.205). So, too, the anger it has aroused. Josephus uses the term σπλάγχνα to describe the "fire of rage" that drives her (*B.J.* 6.204). This term, connoting both the innards and the womb, conveys the visceral nature of Mary's fury.[91] One of the features of Greek drama was the granting of women a voice through direct speech. Chapman notes that Josephus draws a direct line between the story of Mary and Greek drama by placing direct speech on her lips. Likewise, the depiction of a mother driven by anger and necessity to commit an unnatural act situates the episode within the realms of Greek tragedy.[92] The tragic desperation embodied in this mother figure augments the sense of pathos in Josephus's account.

Second, the account of what is done to the infant relays the appalling suffering of the innocent. The baby is slain by his mother (κτείνω), roasted (ὀπτάω), and is half-devoured (κατεσθίω, *B.J.* 6.208). This image of the sacrificed child embodies those Jews whose lives had been sacrificed as a result of the decisions of the rebels.[93] Identifying the child as an "infant at the breast" (παῖς ὑπομάστιος, *B.J.* 6.205) particularly amplifies the picture of the vulnerable and innocent victim. The suffering and pain of innocent Jews is projected onto the body of Mary's infant son to draw pity from the

---

89. Honora Howell Chapman, "Spectacle and Theater in Josephus's *Bellum Judaicum*" (PhD diss., Stanford University, 1998), 58–120.

90. The other instance occurs in book 1.584. For comment, see Chapman, "Spectacle and Theater," 99–101, and corresponding nn. 119–25.

91. Chapman, "Spectacle and Theater," 95.

92. E.g., the figure of Medea in Euripides's *Medea* (Chapman, "Spectacle and Theater," 96).

93. Chapman, "Spectacle and Theater," 195.

hearer. Together, the representations of both Mary and her baby as victims embody the pain and tragedy of war.

The purpose of this shocking but poignant scene in Josephus's account is perhaps apparent in the ensuing lines of text. In his negative assessment of the rebels, Josephus describes the rebels, while horrified at what they see, as tempted to eat the remains of the child, "scarcely yielding even this food to the mother" (*B.J.* 6.212).[94] The Romans, on the other hand, are moved with pity and their hatred of Jews is thus further fueled (*B.J.* 6.214–215), eventually paving the way for the devastation of Jerusalem and the burning of its temple. The innocent Jews of Jerusalem pay a hefty price for the actions of the rebels. The trope of the suffering mother and child as tragic, innocent victims therefore becomes a fundamental element in how Josephus communicates his take on the Jewish War and the destruction of the temple.

While Josephus condemns the actions of the rebels, his view on the innocence of the Romans is not without reservation. He casts judgment on the violence of the Romans in terms of their excessive use of force. Illustrating their brutality, in book 3 of *Jewish War* Josephus depicts the Romans during their nocturnal assault on the inhabitants of Jotapata. Hit by a stone, the dismembered skull of a man is described as catapulted "three furlongs" away. A pregnant woman is struck "on the belly" as she leaves her house in the early morning, resulting in the "babe in her womb" being flung "half a furlong away" (*B.J.* 3.245–247). The force of the violence is intensified in the description of the length by which the body parts are flung. The addition of the woman and unborn child, resonating with other examples we have already examined, augments the sense of pathos and spread of the Roman assault. Moreover, in light of Josephus's statements in *A.J.* 4.278 on forced miscarriages as murder and signifying a threat to the ongoing life of the population, the death of the expected child is especially poignant. Neither Romans nor Jews are beyond reprieve in *Jewish War*. Josephus condemns both through the depictions of what is done to the bodies of women and children.

One final association with the depiction of women and children in narratives of warfare concerns the expression of emotion. The cluster is often employed to describe the embodiment of fear and grief. In *Flaccus*, as Castus searches the houses of Jews for arms, women and children

---

94. Chapman, "Spectacle and Theater," 108.

are described as clinging to their men, bathed in tears in fear of being taken captive (*Flacc.* 87). The men are described as showing consternation, ἔκπληξις, but it is the description of the bodily response of the women and children that takes the emotion of the scene to an extreme. Their fear and vulnerability are illustrated in the use of the verb, ἐμπλέω, "to become entangled in another, to cling." Others do not cling to them; instead, their bodies merge with those of their men for protection. The depth of their fear is underscored in the use of the verb ῥέω to depict the gushing of their tears.

In Josephus's works, associations with the voice are evoked to explain the grief or fear of suffering women and children. He describes the "fearful shrieks" of women in *B.J.* 3.248 upon hearing the thud of dead bodies falling off the wall. Wailing and weeping, families flee Titus in *B.J.* 4.71. In *B.J.* 4.108 he describes women and children as lamenting after being deserted by John of Gischala, and intensifies their despair with the term δεινός, "dreadful." Josephus interprets the distress of the Hebrews of Exod 14:10, singling out the women and children who are again characterized by their "wailing and lamentations," ὀδυρμός, when faced with the possibility of death (*A.J.* 2.328).

Notions of weakness, defeat, helplessness, suffering, fear, and grief are all closely associated with the motif "women and children" in the works of Josephus and Philo. Indeed, in our analysis of women and children's bodies in the narratives of war, they embody these notions. The writers reveal a sense in which these elements are gendered as well as related to one's status in the household, as wife and child. These notions are feminized or are the domain of the young. By extension, they are not generally considered part of the realm of the man and the masculine. There are men who exhibit these, not least Josephus's opponent, John of Gischala, who is depicted as deserting the helpless out of fear of his own life. In so doing, he embodies the emasculated man.[95]

Before drawing our discussion of children in late Second Temple Judaism to a close, it is necessary to talk about one final story. The story is a single occurrence among the voices we are examining. It is an account of an ill child resulting in what appears to be death and the outpouring of grief leading to a physical restoration to life. We find such an account in *A.J.* 8.325–327, in which Josephus narrates the story of Elijah reviving

---

95. Reeder, "Gender, War, and Josephus," 78–79.

the widow's son (1 Kgs 17:17).[96] The story concerns a boy, labeled by the term παῖς, the son of the widow. His illness is described in terms of him ceasing to breathe and appearing as if he were dead. The latter detail is Josephus's addition and, while still implying uncertainty as to whether or not the child has deceased, nevertheless augments the seriousness of the boy's condition as well as presaging the prophet's ability to address the dire situation.[97] The child's apparent death stirs grief in his mother. Josephus embellishes the account in 1 Kgs 17:17 by inserting descriptions of the woman's grief.[98] She expresses her sorrow in physical terms, through cries and weeping. Her suffering is vocalized. In addition, Josephus portrays her as injuring herself with her hands (*A.J.* 8.325). The representation of the boy resonates with themes we have previously identified: the death of children and the grief it prompts. Here we observe that the mourning of children also takes on a physical dimension in Josephus's representation of the child's mother.

As the story progresses, the prophet encourages the woman with a promise that he will restore the child to life. The term ζάω is used, conjuring the notion of living (*A.J.* 8.326). This is an expansion of 1 Kgs 17:19 and emphasizes the prophet's ability to restore the child.[99] In both 1 Kgs 17:19 and *A.J.* 8.326, the mother hands her child over to Elijah/the prophet. The child is carried by the prophet into the setting of the restoration: a chamber in the house—the room where the prophet had resided—and is set on the bed. The restoration itself is physical although there is no interaction between the bodies of the boy and the prophet. This depiction contrasts with the account in 1 Kgs 17:21b in which the biblical author inserts the bodily description: "Then he stretched himself upon the child three times, and cried out to the Lord, 'O Lord my God, let this child's life come into

---

96. Feldman notes, however, that Josephus omits the restoration from the dead of the Shunammite woman's son in 2 Kgs 4:34. See Louis H. Feldman, *Josephus's Interpretation of the Bible*, HCS (Berkley: University of California Press, 1998), 212.

97. In 1 Kgs 17:17, the child is only described as having "no breath left in him." Christopher T. Begg and Paul Spilsbury, *Judean Antiquities Books 8–10*, FJTC 5 (Leiden: Brill, 2005), 91 n. 1220. Hogan states that Josephus seems to suggest a little further in the text that the boy has died, and that his choice of this story of uncertain status may have reflected a desire for the story to sound credible to his readership. See Larry P. Hogan, *Healing in the Second Temple Period*, NTOA 211 (Fribourg: Universitätsverlag; Göttingen: Vandenhoeck & Ruprecht, 1992), 216.

98. Begg and Spilsbury, *Antiquities Books 8–10*, 91 n. 1221.

99. Begg and Spilsbury, *Antiquities Books 8–10*, 91 n. 1224.

him again.'"[100] Instead, in Josephus's account the prophet vocalizes his prayer for God to send breath into the body again to bring life. The boy is thus restored, conveyed in the use of ἀναβιόω, "to return to life" (*A.J.* 8.327).

Josephus provides no details of the boy's physical condition to signify that he has been revived. Instead, he narrates God's perspective on the boy's situation to validate the child's restoration. He describes God, upon hearing Elijah's prayer, being stirred by mercy and compassion, κατοικτείρω (*A.J.* 8.327). Underscoring God's agency in the restoration of the child, God feels pity for both the mother and the prophet, although not the child. Nevertheless, Josephus notes that the child is brought back to life "beyond expectation" (*A.J.* 8.327). The source of the extraordinary restoration is God, who speaks with Elijah (*A.J.* 8.327).[101] Louis Feldman notes that Josephus generally deemphasizes miracles in his rewriting of biblical accounts.[102] Despite this tendency for playing-down the miraculous, Josephus apparently saw it important to retain the story of the restoration of an apparently deceased child in *Antiquities*. While he preserved the actions of the prophet taking the child to a location in a room in the house and placing him on a bed, he embellished the account with details that heighten the gravity of the boy's condition and the mother's grief, and represent the roles of the prophet and God in restoring the child's life.

Up to this point, we have considered various depictions of women and children in Second Temple Judaism. Our investigation now turns to the specific category of unmarried females. In Josephus's interpretation of the

---

100. Begg and Spilsbury, *Antiquities Books 8–10*, 91 n. 1227.

101. Pseudo-Philo depicts the state of being raised from the dead. In LAB 64, Samuel is raised by the witch of Endor. The reader is aware that Samuel has died (64.1). The witch refers to him as a "divine being," not a human being, when he appears after his death with Saul (64.6). This is on account of his physical appearance. He is clothed "in a white robe with a mantle placed over it, and two angels leading him." As raised from the dead, he retains a corporeal form that is clothed. He can communicate. Indeed, the mantle is indicative of his previous human life (64.6). Yet, the robe, its color, and the presence of angels who lead Samuel indicate to the witch he has taken up an altered, although not wholly physically different, state.

102. In the case of *Antiquities*, this is possibly due to the non-Jewish readership (Feldman, *Josephus's Interpretation*, 210, 212). Indeed, Feldman observes that Josephus is more interested in Elijah as a prophet than in the miracles he works in the biblical tradition. See Louis H. Feldman, *Studies in Josephus' Rewritten Bible*, JSJSup 58 (Leiden: Brill, 1998), 300.

defeat of the Benjaminites in *A.J.* 5.165, he notes that, while all of military age, including women and children, were massacred, four hundred *unmarried women* were saved. On this occasion, this particular category is singled out. Indeed, in many instances unmarried females are a separate category that attracts a distinctive commentary. Given they are treated as a separate group, a specific examination of the interpretation of unmarried women's bodies in first-century Judaism warrants our attention.

5.4. Daughters and Virgins

The final category to consider is that of daughters and virgins. While we can assume that daughters and female children were subsumed into the category of children and the cluster "women and children," they also feature as a separate category in the material and literary data. Two labels are used when referring specifically to females who are not married. The first of these, παρθένος, "virgin," distinguished a female from a wife and/or mother. Philo, for instance, uses γυνή to indicate a woman or wife, παῖς for a child, and παρθένος to denote the female who is not a wife/woman (*Legat.* 227).[103] The second label, θυγάτηρ, denoted a daughter or female descendant. It could be also used to denote females who were not yet married, although it was not applied exclusively in this way.[104] In both cases, each label associated females within the context of family and kinship.

The meaning and importance of the label παρθένος is evident in the works of Philo and Josephus. The emphasis on virginity as the absence of sexual activity is apparent throughout much of Philo's discussion of unmarried women and it is the state of their bodies—their chastity—that is significant.[105] One way this interpretation comes to the fore is in Philo's discussion of gender and space. In *Embassy* Philo describes the layout of houses comprising various chambers that are designated for either women or men (*Legat.* 357–358). In *Special Laws* he elaborates on the design,

---

103. I note Reinhartz's view, contra the LCL translation, that Philo only uses παῖς in reference to male children. When he refers to female children, he applies the term, θυγάτηρ (Reinhartz, "Parents and Children," 64–65).

104. E.g., it may also refer to married women when the status of the woman in relation to her father is being accentuated.

105. Philo explains the notion of virginity as the abandonment of the body and its associations with fertility, sexual activity, and childbearing in his allegory in *Congr.* 7 (Sly, *Philo*, 71–72; Loader, *Philo, Josephus, and the Testaments on Sexuality*, 53).

explaining that men are permitted outdoors in public while women are best suited for the indoors or areas not far from the house (*Spec.* 3.169–171). Ideally, in Philo's view, women ought to seek seclusion. The outer door of the house was the boundary marker for mature women while the middle door was the boundary for the virgin, παρθένος. She was ensconced in the center of the home.

Whether Philo's description of the domestic seclusion of females, including virgins, was a reality in Alexandria is questionable. Living in seclusion was an expensive lifestyle that required wealth to maintain. William Loader argues that this practice would have been applicable only, if at all, in affluent households where females were not required to contribute to the economic and social viability of the household.[106] The activities of poorer households that could not afford servants to carry out errands in public, or manage with females not working in areas beyond the perimeter of the house, are not reflected in Philo's descriptions. Moreover, in Philo's time Alexandrian women were not restricted in their movements but, to the contrary, were visible in the public domain.[107]

Instead, Philo's view is more than likely to have reflected an ideal not necessarily based in reality, in order to advance his own ideas concerning females and their relationship to males.[108] Women were to practice self-control and restraint like their male counterparts. They were best located in the household where they could be controlled by men and bear children. This attitude also aligned Philo with the views of the Roman elite in Alexandria (and away from the views of the Egyptians) who valued female modesty, which was characterized by shying away from the male

---

106. Loader, *Philo, Josephus, and the Testaments on Sexuality*, 34.

107. Van der Horst, *Philo's Flaccus*, 180. Van der Horst also notes that Seneca shares similar sentiments to Philo in relation to the seclusion of women in *Cons. Helv.* 19.6.

108. Loader, *Philo, Josephus, and the Testaments on Sexuality*, 34; Sly, *Philo*, 197–98. Peskowitz argues that the notion of gendered spaces does not necessarily bear out in the architecture of all Jewish homes in the Galilee region either. She observes that in Galilee there was an overlapping of domestic and work-related spaces in the architecture that suggests that these were interrelated in the household. Furthermore, she notes that the structural overlaps in Roman Galilean architecture may indicate that people lived in close proximity to each other, sharing cisterns, rooftops, and even workspaces, possibly borrowing tools for trades, communally sharing eating times and observances of Shabbat (Peskowitz, "Family/ies in Antiquity," 31, 33–34).

5. Images of Female Bodies in Late Second Temple Judaism

world of public affairs and retreating into the seclusion of the house.[109] In light of this, unmarried daughters were best placed well into the interior of the home where their bodily chastity could be protected.[110] The role of an unmarried daughter's parents was to protect their daughter who would eventually marry a man who expected his wife to be a virgin at the time they married (*Spec.* 3.80-82).[111]

The status of the bodily chaste daughter is also a focus in Josephus's writing. In his representation of the marriage laws in *A.J.* 4.244-248, a virgin (of freeborn and honest parents) is desirable for a young man. Upon marrying, if she is found not to be a virgin, she may be stoned to death.[112] Priests were permitted to marry only virgins (*A.J.* 3.227). Likewise, the king discerned a wife from a selection of beautiful virgins (*A.J.* 11.196).[113] In this worldview, the protection of a daughter from illicit sexual activity was paramount if she was to secure a reputable man for marriage.

Contrary to this view, virgin daughters do, however, engage in sexual activity that is represented as acceptable. In *A.J.* 11.198-201, the virgin Esther has intercourse with the king as part of his selection process for a wife. This is deemed acceptable to Josephus.[114] While there are portraits of sexually active unmarried females, tensions are nevertheless apparent in the narrative. At the beginning of *Antiquities*, virgin daughters are depicted as having intercourse with their father in order to maintain the existence of the race. While the action appears

---

109. Niehoff, *Philo*, 103-4.

110. Philo argues that women ought not to go the gymnasium to gaze on naked male bodies. This note, while consistent with Philo's opposition to women appearing in public places, may also imply that, indeed, Jewish women were present in the public realm of the gymnasium (*Spec.* 3.176-177).

111. Sly, *Philo*, 200. Loader observes that Philo's value for self-restraint, modesty, and control was indicative of his engagement with a Greco-Roman culture beyond Judaism that held similar values. In this way, a good Jewish woman could both observe the law and accommodate Roman ideals (Loader, *Philo, Josephus, and the Testaments on Sexuality*, 32-34).

112. Female slaves and prostitutes are considered to have ignoble passion and lacking in decorum and rank, and even to possess an abused body in the case of the prostitute. These states do not produce offspring that are virtuous (*A.J.* 4.245).

113. Also Abishag (Abisake) in *A.J.* 7.343-344; 8.5.

114. Indeed, he provides rich detail on how her body, already described as beautiful, is prepared for sexual relations with the king. Accentuating the role of fragrance and touch in enhancing the physical beauty of females, she is anointed with an abundance of spices and costly unguents "such as women's bodies need" (*A.J.* 11.200).

justifiable, there is an uneasiness in this representation, which Josephus signals in his description that they "[took] care to elude detection" (*A.J.* 1.205). In a later episode in *Antiquities,* Josephus describes how Solymius deceitfully substituted his daughter to sleep with Joseph for a foreign female dancer. He does this to prevent Joseph from breaching the law (*A.J.* 12.187–190). The tension in the depiction is revealed in Josephus's words: "he had chosen to *dishonour his own daughter* rather than see [Joseph] fall into disgrace, and so Joseph, commending him for his brotherly love, married his daughter and by her begot a son named Hyrcanus" (*A.J.* 12.189). There are two sources of angst—the dishonor wrought on the daughter and the dishonor Joseph will bring on himself. The latter trumps the former.

Both of these accounts present an uneasy intersection of principles: the continuity of the people, and the honor of Joseph in terms of the law on foreign wives, set against the value for Jewish women to engage in sexual intercourse within a suitable marriage only, and the ideal of protecting an unmarried Jewish girl's honor. In both accounts, the latter two stances are secondary to the former principle. Josephus promotes the stability of the people and the honor of Joseph over against female bodily chastity and the virgin's honor. In addition, in the first account, the daughters are depicted as having bodily agency; they choose and act to remedy their situation and the reader is made aware of their thoughts as a way of justifying their actions. In the second account, the story is told from the perspective of Joseph and Solymius. The daughter expresses no agency, and what she thinks or feels is of no interest to the author; the issue is Joseph's honor.

5.4.1. Sexual Violation of Daughters

Earlier in the chapter, we considered a narrative in which a woman specifically suffered sexualized and domesticated violence (LAB 45). Accounts containing sexual violence are not the reserve of stories involving adult females. There are also narratives that depict the sexual violation of young, unmarried daughters. These, too, serve the broader rhetorical purposes of the various first-century authors.

As in the case of women, the sexual violence enacted on unmarried females' bodies usually took the form of rape. It was generally criticized by writers. Philo labels rape a criminal offense (*Spec.* 3.65). In such a case, the male can subsequently ask the girl's family for permission to marry her. It is the father who agrees—or not—to the request for the girl.[115] If the father refuses, the perpetrator must pay a monetary fine, a dowry. If he accepts the offer, they are to marry immediately to ensure the rape appears as an act of love, not lust (*Spec.* 3.66–71). The girl exercises no agency in Philo's account of rape, neither in the act itself nor in the resolution that is subsequently reached. What she thinks or feels, and what has occurred to her is not of interest in Philo's discussion of the penalties for the crime. His focus rests on the negotiations between the girl's father/guardian and the abuser.

Another account of the rape of a daughter and virgin is narrated by Josephus in *Antiquities* (*A.J.* 7.162, 167–171). In this episode, Tamar is described as a daughter, a virgin, and in terms of her physical beauty (*A.J.* 7.162). On account of this prized status, she is "guarded closely" (*A.J.* 7.163). Her character is domesticated, evident in the physical actions of food preparation and cooking that are ascribed to her (*A.J.* 7.167). The rape of Tamar is also domesticated, carried out by her brother in her home (*A.J.* 7.170).

Unlike Philo's references to the rape of virgin daughters, Tamar has both voice and bodily agency in the face of the violence enacted on her. She voices her opposition to Amnon's sexual advances and her disgust at his insistence that she leave his room for others to witness her shame (*A.J.* 7.169). She responds in pain and sorrow at the indignity with which her body has been mistreated. This pain and sorrow is embodied in Tamar's actions. It includes tearing off the clothes that once signified her status as a virgin, pouring ashes on her head, crying aloud, and bewailing the violence that she has suffered (*A.J.*7.171). Her expressions of sorrow and shame take place in the public domain, not the domestic space where her identity was first centered. In Josephus's account, unrestrained lust leads to violence and is a cause of social shame and grief.[116]

The rape of another virgin daughter, Dinah (Gen 34), is narrated in Jubilees and Liber Antiquitatum Biblicarum. In the latter, the account of the rape of Dinah by Shechem, the son of Hamor the Hurrite, is sparse.[117] The act is depicted as a form of humiliation for Dinah and after her brothers kill the "whole city," they remove her (LAB 8.7). While the comprehensiveness

---

115. In the case where a father is unavailable, a judge takes his place (*Spec.* 3.71).
116. Loader, *Philo, Josephus, and the Testaments on Sexuality*, 297.
117. Halpern-Amaru, "Portraits of Women," 91; William R. G. Loader, *The Pseudepigrapha on Sexuality: Attitude towards Sexuality in Apocalypses, Testaments, Legends, Wisdom, and Related Literature* (Grand Rapids: Eerdmans, 2011), 264.

of the killing implies a seriousness by which the rape is perceived, there is no account of Dinah's perspective.

The author of Jubilees, on the other hand, elaborates further on the episode. The image of the violated female child at the hands of foreigners is exploited to make a statement concerning Jewish identity. The sexuality of the virgin daughter plays a central role in the author's vision of Israel. The author explains that Dinah, the daughter of Jacob, was snatched away to the house of Shechem, where the son of Hamor, the Hivite, lay with her and defiled her (Jub. 30.2). The cruelty of the act is suggested in the double description of Dinah as "little" and "only twelve years old," implying she is a child and suggesting, therefore, that the act is rape, not a tryst between older figures who were lovers (Jub. 30.2).[118] Unlike the account of Gen 34, the author of Jubilees does not describe the Shechemite as being in love with Dinah nor as willing to undergo circumcision (Gen 34:3, 8, 2). The insertion of the girl's age in light of these excised details of the Shechemite's disposition functions to portray the foreigner unsympathetically as a callous perpetrator of a shocking act, a depiction that is further underscored in the angry response of Dinah's brothers to the act.[119]

While the heinous nature of the act is apparent in the text, the author brings to the fore the more significant offense of the act in the labeling of Dinah as "defiled" and "polluted" (Jub. 30.2, 5). Not just a family member whose sexual violation humiliates her family, Dinah is the daughter of Jacob and an esteemed daughter of Israel. What happens to her body, therefore, is significant (Jub.30. 5). Raped by a foreigner, the Shechemite's defilement of her body brings shame to the whole of her people, the scale of which is reflected in the comprehensive killing of every Shechemite man. In other words, the nature of the offense shifts from the brutal rape of a child to the defilement of Israel.[120]

As part of a discussion on the preservation of Jewish identity, highlighting sexual intercourse between a daughter of Israel and an outsider

---

118. The descriptor of Dinah as a little girl of twelve years old is not in Gen 34. The author of Jubilees has inserted this detail.

119. Bader, *Tracing the Evidence*, 108; Helena Zlotnick, *Dinah's Daughters: Gender and Judaism from the Hebrew Bible to Late Antiquity* (Philadelphia: University of Pennsylvania Press, 2002), 71–72.

120. William R. G. Loader, "Attitudes towards Sexuality in Qumran and Related Literature—and the New Testament," *NTS* 54 (2008): 352.

5. Images of Female Bodies in Late Second Temple Judaism   189

as a source of pollution is a central concern of this account, and reinforces the author's stance toward endogamous marriages.[121] As a little girl of twelve years old, Dinah's place is expected to be at home with her father Jacob and her brothers, and her trajectory in life is to marry and maintain the integrity of the Jewish line.[122] In this episode, the author of Jubilees warns about the dangers that the sexuality of virgin daughters pose and the gravity of sexual transgressions with foreigners.[123]

5.4.2. Daughters, Dying, and Death

Daughters are also recognized in the funerary data of the first century CE. In the family tombs in Jerusalem and Jericho, many daughters, often named, are identified in relation to their fathers. A formula is used, similar to those applied to the commemoration of sons, that identifies a daughter and then notes a patronym. The identification of daughters is sometimes personalized by the inclusion of a name, for example, Shalom, the daughter of Yeḥoḥanan (*CIIP*, 78).[124] Of course, this form of identification does not automatically denote an unmarried woman. There are other options for interpreting the name of a female with a patronym.[125] It may have indicated that a female was widowed or divorced and had subsequently returned to her father's house. This is best understood considering the customary practice of a woman moving to her husband's household when they married and therefore usually being buried in his family's tomb. Alternatively, it could have signaled that a female was unmarried and therefore buried in her father's tomb.

Whatever the marital status of the females buried in these tombs, their status as the daughter of a specific father and head of the household was worthy of note. Further, they were considered deserving of a burial in the family tomb and were commemorated with an inscription, be they

---

121. Bader, *Tracing the Evidence*, 107; Loader, "Attitudes towards Sexuality," 343; Zlotnick, *Dinah's Daughters*, 58.
122. Zlotnick, *Dinah's Daughters*, 58.
123. Zlotnick, *Dinah's Daughters*, 74.
124. In other instances, females are identified without any reference to offspring, a husband, or a father. Their marital status is difficult to ascertain except that, most likely, they would have been known to those who buried them.
125. Hachlili, *Jewish Funerary Customs*, 315; Tal Ilan, *Jewish Women in Greco-Roman Palestine* (Peabody, MA: Hendrickson, 1995), 52 n. 23.

identified by their own name in that inscription, or not. Their death was mourned and their bodily remains were honored. They were remembered as an integral part of the familial network in their death. Finally, if they were unmarried, the noting of females in relation to their father cohered with a notion that is evident in the literary data, which positioned fathers (or other males) in a patriarchal system as the guardians of unmarried daughters. The ties between fathers and unmarried daughters continued in the memorialization of their deaths.

In the literature of the late Second Temple, accounts concerned with the deaths of specific unmarried daughters are rare.[126] There are two instances, however, where the story of the death of a young daughter is incorporated into the broader narrative of the author. Both Josephus and Liber Antiquitatum Biblicarum each present renderings of the sacrifice of Jephthah's daughter (Judg 11:29–40). It will become apparent that while the relationship between fathers and unmarried daughters is a characteristic of both accounts, it is secondary to the focus on the death of the daughter. In both cases, the interpretation of the girl's death functions to advance ideas particular to each author.

In *A.J.* 5.263–266, Jephthah's daughter is labeled with the term παρθένος and is depicted in terms of her youth (*A.J.* 5.264, 265). The author clearly projects the picture of a young, unmarried girl. To fulfil an oath made by her father to God, the girl is sacrificed through burning (*A.J.* 5.263, 265). The picture that Josephus paints of the relationship between Jephthah and his daughter resonates in part with some of the depictions of fathers and daughters we have already encountered. He has influence over the life and death of his unmarried daughter, and she is obedient to her father. Her impending death is widely lamented: Jephthah "wails in anguish" and the girl "bewails her youth with her fellow citizens" (*A.J.* 5.264, 265). While Jephthah is fond of his daughter, the girl willingly accepts her fate "without displeasure" not only to obey her father, but because it ensures the liberation of her people (*A.J.* 5.265). In her death, she is the ideal young female who gives up her life for the good of her people. In this way, Josephus's portrait of Jephthah's daughter shares some of the characteristics of deceased young daughters who were

---

126. Irrespective of how a person dies, corpses could be deemed sources of ritual impurity in ancient Judaism. Corpse impurity, however, does not emerge as a strong theme among any of the voices we are examining. Josephus briefly discusses the state in *C. Ap.* 2.205.

depicted as idealized women in Greco-Roman society.[127] Through her death, she is cast as a role model.[128]

Despite this picture of obedience, the sacrifice of Jephthah's daughter is critiqued harshly in Josephus's account. Altering the version of the account as it appears in the biblical tradition (Judg 11:29–40), Josephus inserts details to indicate that the girl's sacrificial death is unjustified on the basis of the very tenets of Judaism: "a sacrifice neither sanctioned by the law nor well-pleasing to God" (*A.J.* 5.266). This additional detail enables the account to counter anti-Jewish accusations that child sacrifice was an acceptable practice among Jews.[129] In this way, Josephus's account of the girl's death holds two contrasting values in tension: the exemplar of the young daughter who willingly subordinated her life to that of the welfare of her people and the opposition to claims that child sacrifice was affirmed by Jews.

In LAB 39–40, the depiction of Jephthah's daughter's sacrificial death also functions as an exemplar. Liber Antiquitatum Biblicarum does not supply details of the girl's death but instead emphasizes her disposition and the emotions that surround her fate. While the episode is prompted by the vow of Jephthah, it is his daughter who becomes the chief protagonist in chapter 40.

Corresponding with many of the depictions of deceased daughters of eminent men we have already observed, Jephthah's daughter's death is lamented for the lost opportunity to marry. The lamenting begins before her death, however, and it is the girl herself—named Seila—who is represented as the voice of grief through her words and weeping (LAB 40.5).[130] While the narrative starts out with Seila dispassionately telling her father that she willingly accepts her destiny (LAB 40.2), the parental focus shifts as she invokes her mother—an alteration made by Liber Antiquitatum Biblicarum—in the lament over her impending death (LAB 40.6).[131] In

---

127. E.g., Pliny, *Ep.* 5.16. Brown, *No Longer Be Silent*, 125.

128. Van Henten views Josephus's depiction of Jephthah's daughter as an example of the "noble death" motif, "a patriotic death, not unfamiliar to the death for the fatherland of ... Euripides' heroes" ("Noble Death," 213).

129. Brown, *No Longer Be Silent*, 125.

130. The naming of the daughter as "Seila" only appears in Liber Antiquitatum Biblicarum. It may mean "she who was demanded," or perhaps "she who was borrowed" (Jacobson, *Commentary on Pseudo-Philo's Liber Antiquitatum Biblicarum*, 2:960–61).

131. For observations on the "distance" between the father and daughter, and the "intimacy and shared grief" between mother and daughter, see Cynthia Baker,

Seila's lamentation, images of the materiality of weddings are transformed into matter associated with death: "The blend of oil that you have prepared must be poured out, and the white robe ... the moth will eat, the crown of flowers may it wither up, the coverlet woven of hyacinth and purple ... let the worms devour it" (LAB 40.5–7).[132] The focus of the grief is her lost future as a wife.

Despite this picture of grief, she is concomitantly depicted as electing to observe the will of God whom Liber Antiquitatum Biblicarum depicts as inviting the death of Jephthah's first born (39.11). She is "a willing martyr."[133] Her death is presented as a means of freeing her people. It is an honorable death signified in the detail that the author uses to describe how Seila's death is mourned. The children of Israel lament (LAB 40.8). All the virgins of Israel bury the daughter of Jephthah and weep for her. Children and females typically vocalize the community's grief. In her death, she is accorded four days for annual memorial and, like other matriarchs and patriarchs, a tomb with her name (LAB 40.8–9). She is to be remembered in death for a sacrifice that establishes her greatness in Israel.[134]

"Pseudo-Philo and the Transformation of Jephthah's Daughter," in *Anti-Covenant: Counter-Reading Women's Lives in the Hebrew Bible*, ed. Mieke Bal, BLS 22 (Sheffield: Almond Press, 1989), 197–98, 201–2.

132. As Jacobson notes, "the theme of bridal chamber becoming tomb is common in Greek literature." He cites Sophocles, *Ant.* 891 (*Commentary on Pseudo-Philo's Liber Antiquitatum Biblicarum*, 2, 974). See also Baker, "Pseudo-Philo," 200–202; Pieter van der Horst, "Deborah and Seila in Ps-Philo," in *Messiah and Christos: Studies in the Jewish Origins of Christianity; Presented to David Flusser on the Occasion of His Seventy-Fifth Birthday*, ed. Ithamar Gruenwald, Shaul Shaked, and Gedaliahu G. Stroumsa, TSAJ 32 (Tübingen: Mohr Siebeck, 1992), 116.

133. Jacobson, *Commentary on Pseudo-Philo's Liber Antiquitatum Biblicarum*, 2:961.

134. In the literature of the Second Temple period, a respect for the dead is apparent in the descriptions of burials, at least among the more eminent figures. The deaths and burials of men and women who are deemed significant in Israel are recounted in detail. They are buried in close proximity to, or in the same geographical locations as their deceased forefathers and foremothers. See Jub. 23.1–7; 32.33–34; 34.15–17; 35.1–8; 36.21–24; 45.13–15; 46.5–8; LAB 24.1–6; 29.1–4; 43.1–8; 64.1. It is only Moses who is buried by God's own hands—not human hands—in a concealed tomb that will be disclosed when God returns to earth (LAB 19.1–16). Their corpses are not cremated. Their bones are buried (Jub. 35.21–22; 46.5–6, 9–10). In *Flacc.* 61–62 the bodies of those who are killed by the enemy are deserving of a burial. Mourning is also described. In Liber Antiquitatum Biblicarum, e.g., various periods of mourning

Cheryl Brown identifies numerous insights into Liber Antiquitatum Biblicarum's reading of the sacrifice of Seila, which enable us to appreciate the possible import of this deceased female figure in the narrative.[135] Like Isaac, Seila is a willing sacrifice (LAB 18.5).[136] Her acquiescence to her fate is not tantamount to blind submission to divine will however. As Cynthia Baker points out, Seila exercises a degree of "volition"; she chooses to be sacrificed according to how she perceives her divinely ordained destiny (LAB 40.3). Her choice is communicated in her speech to Jephthah and implied in the ensuing lament that Liber Antiquitatum Biblicarum puts on her lips.[137] Unlike Isaac, however, Seila's sacrifice is actually carried out, resulting in a death that is considered efficacious (LAB 40.2) and precious before God (LAB 40.5). She has sacrificed her life for her people and her death is valued because of the freedom it has guaranteed them (LAB 40.2).[138] Brown also observes the metaphorical use of the terms *daughter* and *virgin* for Jerusalem and the temple more broadly in Jewish literature, particularly in relation to the destruction of the Second Temple.[139] In light of this, she argues that Liber Antiquitatum Biblicarum exploits this temple imagery to represent the virgin daughter Seila's death as a symbol of Israel's suffering in the past. The mourning rites attached to the girl's death indicate the far-reaching significance that the author attributes to the virgin daughter's sacrifice.[140]

---

are explicitly assigned to the deaths of matriarchs and patriarchs. Representations of sound and emotion are woven into scenes of mourning. Families weep when a member dies, an act that encompasses the body, sound, and emotion. See Jub. 17.10; 23.6; LAB 9.2; 10.1.

135. Brown, *No Longer Be Silent*, 95–117.

136. Brown posits that Pseudo-Philo views the death of Seila within the framework of the doctrine of the Akedah (*No Longer Be Silent*, 99, 125). See also van der Horst, "Deborah and Seila," 114–15.

137. Baker notes that Pseudo-Philo modifies the Judges account by casting Seila as an "independent and noble heroine" rather than a victim of child sacrifice ("Pseudo-Philo," 195, 202–5).

138. Also Murphy, *Pseudo-Philo*, 166.

139. "Virgin daughter of Zion" in Lam 2:1, 3; "virgin daughter of Judah" in Lam 1:15; Jerusalem as "weeping for its only-begotten daughter," Bar 4:16 (Brown, *No Longer Be Silent*, 113).

140. Brown, *No Longer Be Silent*, 115–17. Baker notes that the description that Seila will "rest in the bosom of her mothers" is unique to Liber Antiquitatum Biblicarum and contrasts with the often-used imagery of "sleeping with the fathers" (LAB 40.4; 33.6; Baker, "Pseudo-Philo," 202).

In Brown's view, it is plausible that the composer of Liber Antiquitatum Biblicarum reinterpreted the account of Jephthah's daughter's death in order to enable the people to make sense of the destruction of Jerusalem and the temple. In this way, Seila's story became a vehicle for supporting Liber Antiquitatum Biblicarum's argument that this catastrophic event of destruction—on the face of it, threatening the life and future of Israel—was part of God's plan for the Jewish people. Of course, Brown's interpretation is dependent on a post-70 CE dating of the text, on which there is no consensus.[141] Even if the text is situated in a pre-70 CE context, the story of Seila remains powerful. Frederick Murphy notes, "The hymn dwells on the real cost to Seila of her obedience to God's will. It is not just death but the loss of the potential of her young life that is in question, yet she is most insistent on the inevitability of her sacrifice."[142] Through the portrait of Seila, Liber Antiquitatum Biblicarum communicates the notion that choosing to observe one's divinely ordained destiny was a noble act, albeit marked by loss and sorrow.

5.5. Summary

From the preceding discussion, the role and function of depictions of females is best understood in light of the conceptualization of the family, and the place of the familial network in promoting Jewish identity. Given the importance of children in ensuring the ongoing life of the Jewish people and their traditions, the association of women with nurturing and enabling the transmission of the tradition was prominent. Females were specifically valued for their role as wives, mothers, and conceivers of children. References to sexuality and fertility often dominated accounts containing representations of females. Within this framework, virgin daughters were particularly prized as potential instruments for ensuring the stability and future integrity of Judaism. In the realia of the funerary

---

141. Jacobson, *Pseudo-Philo's Liber Antiquitatum Biblicarum*, 1:253. I acknowledge that there is no consensus for a dating of Liber Antiquitatum Biblicarum either before or after 70 CE. For observations on dating, see Jacobson, *Pseudo-Philo's Liber Antiquitatum Biblicarum*, 1:199–209.

142. Murphy, *Pseudo-Philo*. While noting the debate on the dating of Pseudo-Philo, Murphy situates the text in a pre-70 CE period based on the "balance of evidence" (*Pseudo-Philo*, 6). For a critique of the notion that Seila is obedient to God's will, see Baker, "Pseudo-Philo," 195–209.

data, they were remembered in death and were buried within the family tomb. Their identity in relation to their father was a particular feature in how they were memorialized, although their bones could be interred with those of various members depending on the circumstances of their death. In the literature, the relationship between daughters and fathers (and/or brothers and guardians) was also a feature. Fathers were depicted as exercising great control of their daughters. In the rhetoric of Philo, their lives could be controlled right down to their movement throughout the household. For Josephus and Liber Antiquitatum Biblicarum, fathers influenced their daughter's lives right down to matters of life and death.

Another feature of the depiction of females in the late Second Temple period was the way in which the tensions of the time were projected onto their bodies. Be they adults or children, females embodied the vexed issues concerned with Jewish and non-Jewish interrelations, mostly characterized through depictions of sexual and domestic violence. These accounts often served as grim warnings against mixing with foreigners, especially in terms of sexual activity, for the dangers this posed to Jewish identity and life. The tragic suffering of innocent Jews was also communicated in the painful violence and death ascribed to women and children. Often cast as the victims of conflict, accounts of violence involving women and children brought the horror and poignancy of conflict up close to the reader. Their images functioned to condemn those deemed responsible for the brutal acts. Commonly depicted as weeping, wailing, and screaming, the emotive representations of women and children were used to voice the fear and grief that authors associated with the violent times in which they lived and that they sought to address. Images of women and children, and females in general, functioned as vehicles for conveying the views of authors on the various issues that dominated their own lives. Women and female children were part of the cultural landscape. While seldom given a voice of their own, they were certainly noticed and discussed, in both life and death.

6
Raising Jairus's Daughter

Then he put them all outside, and took the child's father and mother and those who were with him, and went in where the child was.
—Mark 5:40

Ideas about the body in Greco-Roman and Jewish experience in the first century CE have been analyzed in chapters 4 and 5. Particular attention was given to those ideas concerning girls, including their representations as dying and dead figures. The examination generated insights that suggest alternative ways of reading the raising of Jairus's daughter when we take into consideration the role and function of representations of the body. Drawing on those insights, this chapter will examine Mark 5:21–24, 35–43, bringing into focus how the story resonates with and diverges from other ideas in the first century CE. While my focus is on the body of Jairus's daughter, I also draw into the discussion the images of other characters' bodies in the episode. Reading the depiction of the child's body requires us to analyze how it relates to the representation of others in the scene. As we observed in chapters 4 and 5, the images of the body of women and female children were used in conjunction with other figures in the Jewish and Greco-Roman sources. They functioned to convey more than that which pertained to the individual female. The analysis that ensues will provide a new approach to the reading of Jairus's daughter that indicates how the story helps to elucidate some key themes in the broader narrative.

When the story of Jairus's daughter is read within a first century CE milieu, several aspects of the account particularly stand out. These are:

1. The function of location;
2. The representations of father, daughter, and mother;
3. The restoration of a dead, unmarried daughter;

198   Jairus's Daughter and the Female Body in Mark

4. The interaction of bodies to restore a daughter's life;
5. The representation of Jesus as a figure of authority;
6. The notion of family.

I will argue that, when read with an awareness of the role of the body, the story of Jairus's daughter illuminates the significance of the household and family for those who identified with Jesus. Indeed, it is through focusing on the representation of the body in both the story and in the context of the first century CE, that our attention is drawn to the story of Jairus's daughter being about family. I will demonstrate that the hearer would have comprehended the story in terms of family above and beyond any other consideration. Having established this case, I will then discuss how a hearer in the first century CE may have situated this story within the broader narrative of the gospel. It will become apparent that the story could have functioned to illuminate other episodes concerning children, the household, and family.

6.1. The Function of Location

The first part of our discussion considers how a hearer may have engaged with the settings of Mark 5:21–24, 35–43 and the associated expectations, roles, and behaviors in those settings. The locations that are identified throughout Mark 5:21–24, 35–43 are integral to an understanding of the story as it unfolds. The narrative begins outdoors in a public space and then shifts indoors, to a domestic space. From the outset, in this open location, the hearer immediately encounters a man of status, an ἀρχισυνάγωγος, a synagogue leader. This is not a minor detail; the label is heard four times in the story (5:22, 35, 36, 38). Inscriptional data suggest that this title could have indicated patronal figures (including non-Jews) who donated to the restoration of a synagogue, as in the case of Julia Severa's synagogue in Akmonia in the late first-century.[1] An inscription related to the construction of a synagogue in Jerusalem before 70 CE further suggests instances in which the title may have been handed down through families.[2] More generally, the title is understood to have

---

1. *CIJ* 766, quoted in Tessa Rajak and David Noy, "Archisynagogoi: Office, Title and Social Status in the Greco-Jewish Synagogue," *JRS* 83 (1993): 91, no. 20.
2. *CIJ* 1404, quoted in Rajak and Noy, "Archisynagogoi," 91, no. 25.

been honorific, denoting a recognized status within and beyond the Jewish community.³

Mapping the characterization of Jairus to this approach to the role of the synagogue leader, it is possible to conceive of Jairus as an eminent public figure. This image of a distinguished father being identified with his daughter resonates with many of the representations of fathers we have noted in the previous chapters. Similarly, as we have observed, the daughters of fathers who occupied a social position were also present in narratives and public relief in the first century CE.

The application of the name Jairus (Ἰάϊρος) may further reinforce this depiction. The name appears only once throughout the entire episode; it is also taken up at the outset to identify the protagonist alongside the designation of ἀρχισυνάγωγος (5:22). The name appears in the Old Testament and also appears in at least two literary sources of the first century CE.⁴ In *Antiquities*, Josephus invokes the name Jair, the minor judge of Judg 10:3–5. Josephus's portrayal of this figure is positive: He is identified as both a successful leader of Israel and a father.⁵ He is "blessed" on account of his extensive male progeny (*A.J.* 5.254). He has thirty sons who are physically adept as "excellent horsemen." This familial fruitfulness is paralleled by the suggestion of stable leadership, signified in the note that

---

3. According to Rajak and Noy, the title did not necessarily denote a person of powerful authority within the synagogal system. Instead, its significance more often lay in its acceptance in the civic context. Most of the data cited by the authors postdate the first century CE ("Archisynagogoi," 75–93).

4. In the Old Testament: (1) As son of Manasseh (Num 32:41; Deut 3:14; 1 Kgs 4:13; (2) A minor judge of Israel (Judg 10:3–5); (3) A Benjamite in the line of Esther's guardian, Mordechai (Esth 2:5); and the father of Elhanan who killed Goliath's brother, Lahmi (1 Chr 20:5, although see 2 Sam 21:19). Robert G. Boling, "Jair," *ABD* 3:615. In Judg 10:3–5, Jair is a minor judge who is depicted as having status and wealth. Susan Niditch, *Judges: A Commentary*, OTL (Louisville: Westminster John Knox, 2008), 121. Webb asserts that the descriptions of Jair convey a time of "prosperity" and "peace" as well as associating him with "prestige." See Barry G. Webb, *The Book of the Judges: An Integrated Reading*, JSOTSup 46 (Sheffield: Sheffield Academic, 1987), 160, 161. According to Butler, Jair "represents the strength of East Jordan tribes." Citing Schneider, he notes that Jair is portrayed in Judges as a powerful figure associated with the elite. See Trent C. Butler, *Judges*, WBC 8 (Nashville: Nelson, 2009), 260, 261. In Esther, the author includes the name Jair in the genealogy of Mordechai to emphasize his Jewish lineage (Esth 2:5). See Carol M. Bechtel, *Esther* IBC (Louisville: Westminster John Knox, 2002), 30; Linda M. Day, *Esther*, AOTC (Nashville: Abingdon, 2005), 45.

5. Beavis, "The Resurrection of Jephthah's Daughter," 53, 54.

Jair ruled for twenty-two years. Josephus's favorable rendering of Jair is further evident in his description that Jair died at an old age and received an honored burial (*A.J.* 5:254). Josephus promotes Jair as an honorable leader and father, a personification of the ideal father who contributed to the continuity of Israel.

The name Jair is also taken up in LAB 38.1–4. The author's portrait of this figure is diametrically opposed to that of Josephus's, describing Jair as building a sanctuary to Baal and deceiving the people.[6] Rather than drawing a picture of a man who signified the stability and prosperity of Israel, the author conveys the image of a poor leader who not only could not resist idolatry, to the contrary he promoted it and deceived the people.[7] Liber Antiquitatum Biblicarum enlists this distinct portrait of Jair in his advocacy for the preservation of the integrity of Israel's worship.

It is not possible to know what the name Ἰάϊρος may have conjured up among those who heard the story. The references in *Antiquities* and Liber Antiquitatum Biblicarum imply that for a Jewish person of the first century CE, the name Jairus was not necessarily unusual. If Josephus and Liber Antiquitatum Biblicarum are any indication, the name may have evoked various connections with the traditions of Israel, and opened up several ways of thinking whenever a person encountered the name. For Jews accustomed to family tombs where patronyms—sometimes including the father's title and profession—identified the deceased female, the identification of Jairus the synagogue leader in a story about a dying daughter may not have been extraordinary either. As we noted in chapter 5, in Jerusalem and Jericho females could be identified by their father and the head of the household in inscriptions in the first century CE. Jairus's identity in the story may have functioned along similar lines, conveying his primacy as the father and providing an identity and status for his daughter. Indeed, at the beginning of the story all that we know about the identity of the girl is dependent entirely on her father.

The news of the synagogue leader's daughter's death also occurs outside, in public. In Mark 5:35, "some people" associated with the synagogue leader arrive while Jesus is still speaking with the bleeding woman (5:35) implying that the disciples and the crowd are still present in the scene. In

---

6. Christopher T. Begg, *Judean Antiquities Books 5–7*, FJTC 4 (Leiden: Brill, 2005), 62 n. 688.

7. Frederick J. Murphy, "Retelling the Bible: Idolatry in Pseudo-Philo," *JBL* 107 (1988): 276.

this public setting, the people tell the synagogue leader that his daughter is dead. At this stage, Jairus is still referred to as ἀρχισυνάγωγος. His depiction as an eminent public figure remains evident when he is informed of his daughter's death. As we have noted on several occasions, the public recognition of the deaths of members of prominent families was a feature of the first century CE landscape.

As the setting shifts to the house of the synagogue leader, a hearer encounters further familiar images. In the first instance, Jairus's daughter and her mother are located within a domestic context. Both females appear in the narrative at 5:40 when Jesus takes the girl's father and mother, and the three disciples to the site in the house where the deceased child lies.[8] In light of our observations in chapters 4 and 5, this domestic location appears stereotypical of females and therefore is unsurprising.[9] It also coheres with the location of other representations of sick females who had families: Peter's mother-in-law (Mark 1:29–30) and the daughter of the Syrophoenician woman (Mark 7: 30). In addition, the localizing of the mother and her dead daughter in the home may have corresponded with the perceived duty of the immediate family to prepare the body of the dead for its burial (Josephus, *C. Ap.* 2.205; Pliny, *Nat.* 7.176–178; Cicero, *Leg.* 2.59–64).[10] Earlier, in Roman mythology, there is an instance in which a mother is specifically depicted as closing the eyes and bathing the wounds of a dead son (*Aen.* 9.486–489). A similar image appears in the later writings where a mother is portrayed as catching the final kiss of her child (Cicero, *Verr.* 2.5.118).

The presence of mourners at the house, in particular women, was also a familiar image. In the late republic and early empire, groups called the *libitinarii* were paid to undertake funerary arrangements and families hired keeners to mourn. This is depicted in the funeral scene on the

---

8. At 5:40 Jairus is no longer identified as "Jairus" or "synagogue leader" but exclusively as the father of the child.

9. In describing the *good death*, Noy argues the best scenario for a young person or child to die was at home with the parents, peacefully. He cites an image on a sarcophagus dating from the mid-second to the early third century CE in which a child is located in a domestic setting, appearing asleep in a bed with the parents at the end of a bed and female mourners in attendance. See David Noy, "'Goodbye Livia': Dying in the Roman Home," in Hope and Huskinson, *Memory and Mourning*, 1, fig. 1.1.

10. Valerie M. Hope, *Death in Ancient Rome: A Source Book*, Routledge Sourcebooks for the Ancient World (London: Routledge, 2000), fig. 3.12, a second century CE marble sarcophagus depicting a child's deathbed.

Haterii monument in which a deceased woman, (possibly Hateria or one of her daughters) lies on a couch in the atrium of the house, attended by female and male musicians and mourners.[11] While both women and men undertook the task of hired mourners, women were frequently associated (disparagingly) in the literary material with the physical signs of grief. *Praeficae* were hired female mourners who wept, tore out their hair, and cried out (Lucilius 29.995–996). Women wailed (Lucan, *Bell. civ.* 2.21–28) and made noisy lamentations (Livy 22.55.6; Plutarch, *Comp. Per. Fab.* 17.7).

While Jairus is identified by his role as synagogue leader and father outside in the public space, once Jairus enters the house the identifiers ἀρχισυνάγωγος and Ἰάϊρος do not reappear. Instead, from 5:40 onward Jairus is solely identified as the girl's father, πατήρ.[12] This modification of nomenclature occurs at the same time in which the girl's mother is introduced into the story, and when both parents go to where their dead daughter lies (along with Jesus and the three disciples).[13] The relabeling of Jairus as "father" together with the appearance of the mother and deceased daughter thus enables another common familial image to emerge in the account: the triad of mother-father-child. As we have already observed, the depiction of a triadic family structure on Roman funerary monuments that incorporated children was one of various ways in which images of families were constructed in the first century CE. It was not unusual. Its significance lay more with conveying ideas about the social status and lost aspirations of a family than its size and precise membership or the loss of a specific individual. From this perspective, the account starts out as a common representation of a family whose hopes were dying (and had died) with their daughter.

---

11. See also Pliny the Elder, *Nat.* 7.176–178; Graham, "Memory and Materiality," 32; Jennifer Trimble, "Figure and Ornament, Death and Transformation in the Tomb of the Haterii," in *Ornament and Figure in Graeco-Roman Art: Rethinking Visual Ontologies in Classical Antiquity*, ed. Nikolaus Dietrich and Michael Squire (Berlin: de Gruyter, 2018), 327–52.

12. Note the progression of the narrative and the use of nomenclature for Jairus in relation to the designation of space: in 5:38 they come to the house of the "synagogue leader"; in 5:39 Jesus enters the house and addresses the mourners; at 5:40 in the house Jesus takes the child's "mother and father and those who were with him" and goes to the location of the deceased child in the house.

13. The girl has been described as dead earlier in 5:35.

6.2. The Representations of Father, Daughter, and Mother

The image of Jairus as a devoted father conforms to other contemporaneous depictions of fathers that routinely appeared in the material and literary landscapes. This image is expressed in various forms throughout the episode. When Jairus initially sees Jesus, he falls at his feet and exhorts him repeatedly to attend to his daughter (5:22–23). Placing himself in close proximity to Jesus, he potentially obstructs any interaction between Jesus and others, in order to direct Jesus's attention to his daughter's plight. At the same time, the description of Jairus throwing himself, πίπτω, at the feet of Jesus, conjures up the image of a supplicant (Chariton, *Chaer.* 1.9.4–5).

The imagery of supplication appeared on Roman coins in the first century CE. The *supplicatio/adoratio* types of coins depicted provinces appealing to Rome for favor, often conveyed through the image of a woman or man kneeling with hands reaching out to the Roman conqueror (*BMC* 1.8 nos. 43–4; *BMC* 2.147 no. 652).[14] The kneeling gesture implies that the figure to whom the appeal is targeted is a king. The *supplicatio/adoratio* coin was disseminated up until 18 BCE, then reemerged under the rule of Emperor Vespasian after a hiatus of eighty-five years. In the case of the Markan passage, it is possible that a hearer perceived the gestures of Jairus as those of supplication. The gesture conveys a sign of respect for Jesus as well as reinforcing the powerful position of Jesus in the relationship.

If this physical positioning of Jairus in relation to Jesus embodies the superior and inferior statuses of Jesus and Jairus respectively, as some scholars argue, then the synagogue leader can be understood to forgo his dignity and status as an eminent figure in order to urge the popular healer to save his daughter.[15] Jairus's gesture may also have been judged negatively as an excessive act of desperation among those who valued the moderation of emotions. Given the comments by some Roman authors about women and expressions of emotion, this public display of emotion by Jairus raises questions about what is being conveyed (Plutarch, *Cons. ux.* 4; Tacitus, *Ann.* 15.63). The action certainly conveys the image of a

---

14. Jane Cody, "Conquerors and Conquered on Flavian Coins," 103–23 in *Flavian Rome: Culture, Image, Text*, ed. Anthony Boyle and William J. Domink (Leiden: Brill, 2003), 102–23.

15. Brendan Byrne, *A Costly Freedom: A Theological Reading of Mark's Gospel* (Collegeville, MN: Liturgical Press, 2008), 1; Hooker, *Saint Mark*, 148.

despairing father. At the same time, the verb used to denote Jairus's words to Jesus, παρακαλέω, possibly reinforced the picture of a desperate father, beseeching Jesus for help.[16] The language that describes Jairus's relationship to the child conveys an image of deep affection. The label that the father applies to his daughter as he exhorts Jesus is the term θυγάτριον, "little daughter." The diminutive form of θυγάτηρ, the term referred to the size of the girl and her status as a child, but it's also plausible that the term brought to mind a term of endearment.[17] In fact, both meanings work together to reinforce the picture of Jairus as the devoted father. The image of the dying female child typically evokes vulnerability and pathos, allowing Jairus's words and actions to convey a picture of the protective father, dedicated to his daughter's welfare.

The image of the devoted father of a dying or deceased daughter resonates with other representations of fathers faced with the loss of a daughter. As noted in chapters 4 and 5, Pliny describes Fundanus, the father of Minicia Marcellae, being in a state of sorrow at the death of his daughter (*Ep.* 5.19). Likewise, the representation of a despairing Cicero at the death of his daughter, Tullia (*Att.* 12.14). To honor his deceased daughter, Hemocrates constructs a large public tomb for Callirhoe and fills it with a cache of riches (*Chaer.* 6.3–5). In Josephus's narration of the death of Jephthah's daughter, the prospect of the girl's death, brought about by Jephthah's own vow, is a source of grief for her father (*A.J.* 5.264). In the case of Mark 5:21–24, 35–43, the term θυγάτριον, a form of endearment, possibly connoted Jairus's affection and care, further underlining the portrait of paternal loyalty in the face of a young, dying daughter.

The mother of the child is introduced later into the story at 5:40, at the same point at which Jairus is denoted solely as the girl's father. Like the majority of women in the gospel, she is identified by familial language.[18] Indeed, she is defined exclusively by her relationship to the child (5:40). In

---

16. The verb, παρακαλέω, may denote calling another to one's aid—including calling one's friends, or demanding, begging, or exhorting another. It suggests the act of begging or exhorting Jesus in healing contexts in Mark (1:40; 5:10, 12; 6:56; 7:32; 8:22).

17. Betsworth, *Reign of God Is Such as These*, 101; Francis, *Adults as Children*, 7; Gundry, "Children in the Gospel of Mark," 147–48; Gundry, *Mark*, 267.

18. Mark 1:29–31; 3:31; 6:14–29; 7:24–31; 10:1–12; 12:18–22, 40–44; 13:12, 17–19; and Mary the mother of Joses in 15:40, 42–47; and 16:1–8. Exceptions: the woman who anoints Jesus (14:1–11), Mary Magdalene and Salome (15:40, 42–47; and 16:1–8), and arguably the bleeding woman (5:25–34).

addition, located at the house of the synagogue leader, her role is domesticated, as are those of most of the mothers in Mark, with the exception of Mary, the mother of Joses.[19] It is Jairus, rather than his wife, who has spoken and acted for his daughter. What she thinks or feels is possibly perceived to have required no explaining. Her perspective may have been well understood by the first-century audience, and/or of no interest. At best, her presence completes the picture of the familial triad whose fundamental structure and future trajectory had been disrupted with the premature death of a beloved daughter and child.

As we have observed in chapters 4 and 5, the experience of female children dying was commonplace in the first century CE. Representations of dying and deceased daughters were part of the literature of first century CE, and equally dotted the material landscape in funerary reliefs and epitaphs of both Jews and non-Jews. It was not unusual for girls between the ages of eight and fourteen years old to die, nor to be remembered in death for having died at those ages. In a survey of funerary inscriptions in *CIL* 4, for example, the majority of dedications to deceased female children is found in the age group from eleven to thirty years old, highlighting the grief associated with the loss of a female who would have presumably mothered future generations.[20]

While some daughters were named in death, others were not. In death, their public identity was customarily defined by their association with family. In the case of the funerary material in Jerusalem and Jericho, their relationship to their fathers was particularly worthy of note, signified in the use of patronyms to identify many daughters in their burial places in family tombs. The identity of deceased unmarried females or female children was located in their families. Their lives and deaths were part of familial and social memory.

For a hearer of the first century CE, the presentation of a twelve-year-old daughter who had died corresponded with conventional ways of depicting the death of a girl. A hearer would not necessarily have been surprised upon first encountering this story. The constant use of diminutives to label the girl, placed not only on Jairus's lips but taken up also throughout the account, emphasized her stage in life. She is referred to as

---

19. Unlike the Syrophoenician mother, the mother of Jairus's daughter is silent and passive (7:24–30).

20. Jeremy McInerney, "Interpreting Funerary Inscriptions from the City of Rome," *Journal of Ancient History* 7 (2019): 172.

ταλιθά, "little girl," κοράσιον, "little girl or maiden," and παιδίον, "child or infant" (5:41). At the age of twelve, she was not an infant but her location in the family's home suggested she was not married and living with a husband. She was a child.

The hearer is not given specific causes of the daughter's condition. No details are given as to how she came to be dying. Despite this lack of detail, Markan scholars today almost unanimously suppose she was ill as a result of disease, given the story's placement alongside the story of the bleeding woman and the attention given to sick bodies more broadly.[21] Her dying body is certainly represented as being in a liminal state. In this way, she is like the boy, also in Jewish territory and whose father acts on his behalf. He, too, appears to be a corpse in 9:26 and is subsequently restored by Jesus. Yet, the condition of Jairus's daughter is not described with the graphic detail of illness and corporal suffering that characterize the boy's condition (9:17, 18, 26).

The girl's body becomes a site of healing and transformation, nevertheless, as do other sick bodies in the gospel. As we noted in chapter 2, to be sick or to inhabit a body that did not function as it was perceived it ought, was not regarded propitiously in the gospel. The preferred state of the body was one in which a person was no longer suffering but upright and strong, awake and alive. By the end of the story, regardless of whether the child was understood to be literally dead or in some form of sleep, the author unambiguously depicts her as awake and living (5:43).

Apart from sickness, there are other ways that a hearer may have thought about the girl's condition. It is possible that, given the references to physical violence throughout the gospel, while never a reference point in commentary on this story, a hearer may have considered ill treatment of some sort resulting in the girl's untimely death. Violence, be it domesticated, sexualized, and/or in the context of warfare certainly featured in stories of females in the broader milieu. We also noted in chapter 4, the epitaph of two thirteen-year-old females who were crushed to death in a crowd (*CIL* 6.29436). Notwithstanding the possibilities of either sickness, an accident, or abuse, there are no markers in 5:21–24, 35–43 on which even to speculate if and how a hearer may have thought about the daughter's condition. At the most,

---

21. For an exception, see Murphy, who raises possible options such as sickness, abuse, and an accident (*Kids and Kingdom*, 121).

the absence of detail is consistent with much of the Greco-Roman and Jewish material data wherein the cause of female children's deaths is often not noted.[22]

What is clear is that a key issue in the story is the daughter-child's death. She is initially presented as dying (Mark 5:23), followed by people notifying the synagogue leader that she has died (Mark 5:35). They recommend that he trouble Jesus the teacher no more, underscoring the finality of her state. In other words, there is no further hope for her revival. Once at the house, the synagogue leader sees mourners who are already expressing grief for his deceased daughter (Mark 5:38). In a typical scene that marked the death of a person who was understood to have lived a good life, mourners are located at the house of the deceased, weeping and wailing. Conventional representations are conjured up of people vocalizing their grief through sound, volume, and lament, communicating the household's sorrow.

As we have observed, images of weeping and wailing, while on the one hand voicing a community's grief, were simultaneously criticized among some writers as excessive displays of emotion that undermined their need for self-restraint. This is particularly the case when commenting on the emotions expressed by females. Jesus reprimands the mourners for their show of grief, disparagingly labeling it as noise in his question to them: "Why do you make a commotion and weep?" (5:39).[23] Disapproval

---

22. It is possible hearers may have associated the death of the twelve-year-old girl with ideas about the lost hopes for fertility, marriage, and childbearing. Perhaps the story brought to mind notions concerning the loss of the continuity of ancestral lineage and unrealized aspirations for future prosperity in the family. These themes were certainly prominent among Jewish and Greco-Roman voices representing females in the first century CE. Such associations would certainly heighten the tragedy of the story. They might also cohere with the description of Jairus's despair and his preparedness to humiliate himself publicly by throwing himself down and begging (5:22–23). While possible, a hearer does not encounter explicit references to marriage and/or childbearing, unlike the material we examined in chs. 4 and 5. In addition, the term παρθένος is never employed as a label for the girl, unlike Jewish and Greco-Roman voices who consistently used the term when referring to females who had reached a stage in life in which they were considered eligible to be married. While a hearer may have projected notions of marriage and fertility onto the child-daughter, it is difficult to know with any certainty.

23. The term θορυβέω indicates to make a noise or uproar. They also make the physical sound of laughing at Jesus (καταγελάω, 5:40).

of mourning already has been signaled with the mourning scene in 5:38 when he labels the sight that Jesus beholds at the synagogue leader's house with the term, θόρυσον, denoting a riot or commotion. His objection is not, however, a defense of the value of a person's capacity to control their emotions. At no stage are the mourners specifically identified as female. Instead, Jesus qualifies his disapproval of their grief in his following statement that the girl is not dead, but sleeping (5:39).

The grief of the mourners is not refuted because it is excessive. It is dismissed by Jesus because it is misguided, signaled in his corrective that the girl is sleeping. What might have been understood by the term καθεύδω, "to sleep," is an ongoing point of discussion in the scholarship, as we noted in chapter 2. It is a term that was used in the Jewish and Greco-Roman literature of the first century CE when narrating stories of death. The composers of both Liber Antiquitatum Biblicarum and Jubilees employed the image when recounting the deaths of the patriarchs and a matriarch. Part of the formulaic portrayal of the deaths of key figures of Israel was to describe them as *sleeping with the fathers*. Liber Antiquitatum Biblicarum applied the image to the deaths of Moses, Joshua, Kenaz, Zebul, and Gideon (LAB 19.1–16; 28.1–10; 29.1–4; 35.4). Likewise, the author of Jubilees used the image of sleeping with the fathers when narrating the death of Jacob (Jub. 45.13–15).[24] Not the reserve of male figures, the descriptor was also employed by Pseudo-Philo in the narration of the death of Deborah, the "mother of Israel" in his remarks that she rested with the fathers (LAB 33.6). Liber Antiquitatum Biblicarum describes her death as bodily, as "going in the way of all flesh" (33.2). Her physical existence has come to an end. The reference to her sleeping with the fathers reinforces her honorable status in death.

Yet while Liber Antiquitatum Biblicarum used the term in relation to the end of physical life, it was also applied alongside allusions to the afterlife. In the account of Moses's death, God says to Moses, "I will raise you up and your fathers from the land of Egypt where you sleep and you will dwell in the immortal dwelling place that is not subject to time" (LAB 19.12–13). In this case, sleep refers to death but with a promise of resurrection and eternal life.[25] What this meant for the body is uncertain in the

---

24. Jubilees does not use the image when referring to the deaths of women, although key female figures are described as being buried in proximity to each other (Jub. 19.1–9; 32.30, 33–34; 34.15–17; 35.20–22; 36.21–24).

25. Jacobson, *Pseudo-Philo's Liber Antiquitatum Biblicarum*, 1:248.

text, and is complicated further in LAB 19.16 where God buries Moses, an act that is then followed by mourning angels going "before" Moses. Noting the complication, Howard Jacobson explains, "there is some kind of body/soul split here: Moses's body is buried, his soul is led to some other world. On the other hand, this does not seem to jibe well with the explicit statement that after his death Moses will sleep."[26]

The sleep motif is developed further in the prayer of Hannah. Liber Antiquitatum Biblicarum distinguishes the death of the righteous as a form of sleep, while the wicked simply die. Having died, the wicked perish whereas the just who sleep are then freed (LAB 51.5). In this instance, sleep implies a real death but not necessarily an absolute one. It is associated with a notion of liberation or resurrection. In contrast, death is absolute for the wicked.[27] While it is not clear how resurrection or the afterlife was understood, Jacobson's observations best sum up the author's approach to "sleep." While sleep connoted death, Pseudo-Philo "believed firmly that life did not end with the death of a human's body and that in some fashion God would distinguish between the righteous and the unjust."[28] Life could continue despite the death of the body.

Chariton also adopts the comparison between sleep and death in the narration of Callirhoe's apparent death.[29] Having been assaulted by her husband, Callirhoe takes on the "appearance of death" (*Chaer.* 1.5.1). The implications of her appearance are developed further as Chariton uses the imagery of sleep to denote the girl's unconscious state. As she lies upon her bier, she is compared to the "the sleeping Ariadne" (*Chaer.* 1.6.2). When she eventually regains life, Chariton describes her as if awakening from sleep (*Chaer.* 1.8). In both cases, the author uses the term καθεύδω to denote a state of unconsciousness. The hearer is under no apprehension about the condition of Callirhoe. She is alive and the image of sleep is employed to reinforce this picture. Her apparent death, of which the

---

26. Jacobson, *Pseudo-Philo's Liber Antiquitatum Biblicarum*, 1:249.

27. Liber Antiquitatum Biblicarum shares motifs of death as sleeping in the earth with the apocalyptic books of 4 Ezra and 2 Baruch. Daniel J. Harrington, "Pseudo-Philo," *OTP* 2:302.

28. Jacobson, *Pseudo-Philo's Liber Antiquitatum Biblicarum*, 1:250.

29. For another comparison of sleep and death in the narrative of a young person's death, see the death of Sarpedon in Homer, *Il.* 16.528–531; noted by Dennis R. MacDonald, *The Homeric Epics and the Gospel of Mark* (New Haven: Yale University Press, 2000), 66–69.

hearer knows otherwise, is the dramatic catalyst for the ensuing narrative of tragic romance.

Considering the death of Jairus's daughter with these voices in mind, a hearer may have formed a picture of this daughter and child as now deceased after having lived a good life and with the possibility of being raised up after a period of death, signaled in the use of the term καθεύδω. Alternatively, when bearing in mind Chariton's use of the image of sleeping and death for a female, a person might have perceived the synagogue leader's daughter to be giving the appearance of having died.[30] Depending on the context of each hearer, both readings may have been possible, although the scope of readership and audience for Chariton remains a matter of debate.[31] At this point, the voices that sounded in the first century CE offer no decisive clarity to the debate that currently dominates discussions of the term καθεύδω in Mark 5:39. Instead, they increase the contextual layers that possibly intersected with this story of a child and daughter who died in her familial context.

6.3. The Restoration of a Child

Stories of dying and deceased daughters were interwoven into the larger narratives that some in Judaism and Roman society told of themselves. We have already observed that among the literary voices, the death of these daughters was most often a consequence of being violated, sacrificed, or murdered. In their death, their corpses were dismembered, or anointed, possibly cremated, and buried with particular funerary rites and with

---

30. For an analysis of young girls appearing dead in the medical literature, see Helen King, "Once Upon a Text: Hysteria from Hippocrates," in *Hysteria beyond Freud*, ed. Sander L. Gilman et al. (Berkeley: University of California Press, 1994), 3–90. Also, the third century CE text Philostratus, *Vit. Apoll.* 4.45. For examples of approaches that draw on medical literature, see D'Angelo, "Gender and Power," 83–109; Fischbach, *Totenerweckungen*, 163–64; Wainwright, *Women Healing/Healing Women*, 112–23.

31. E. Bowie, "Literature and Sophistic," in *The High Empire: AD 70–192*, ed. Alan K. Bowman, Peter Garnsey, and Dominic Rathbone, 2nd ed., CAH 11 (Cambridge: Cambridge University Press, 2000), 909; Thomas Hägg, "Orality, Literacy, and the 'Readership' of the Early Greek Novel," in *Contexts of Pre-Novel Narrative: The European Tradition*, ed. Roy Eriksen, Approaches to Semiotics 114 (Berlin: Mouton de Gruyter, 1994), 47–74. For women as possible hearers, see Stephanie West, "Κερκίδος Παραμύθια? For Whom Did Chariton Write?," *ZPE* 143 (2003): 63–69.

varying degrees of grief and lamentation. Their deaths carried symbolic weight. The death of Jephthah's daughter in Liber Antiquitatum Biblicarum, for example, was presented as efficacious (LAB 39–40). Seila was a model of a willing martyr for the good of the people.

The story of Jairus's daughter is not, however, a story concerned only with death. While the standard image of mourners appears in the narrative of Jairus's daughter's death, the account does not progress to a point in which funerary rites were included. Instead, the narrative shifts away from a story of death to a story of restoration. This twist in a story of death was not novel in the literature of the late Second Temple period. There is one specific story of restoration that has particular resonance with the story of Jairus's daughter. As noted in chapter 5, in *A.J.* 8.325–327, Josephus retains the story of the restoration of a child in the raising of the widow's son (1 Kgs 17:17). Josephus's narration has some resonance with the story of the girl. While a young son is the object of the prophet's actions, Josephus employs the diminutive παιδός, evoking the image of a young, possibly cherished child. The gravity of the child's condition is also emphasized. Having become ill, the boy stops breathing and seems to be dead. His apparent death triggers grief in the child's mother, the widow. This suffering, πάθος, is conveyed through the voice of the mother who utters her cries of grief (*A.J.* 8.325). Elijah urges the mother to give her son over to him, which she does. Like Jesus, Elijah restores the child's life in a chamber within the mother's house, and the family of mother and son is reinstated.[32] These resonances imply that the story of a restoration of a deceased child to its family may not have been unusual for some who encountered Mark's account.

Notwithstanding these resonances, there are points of difference with the story of Jairus's daughter. Putting aside the genders of both the mother and the son, and the note about the illness of the child, the portrait of Jesus differs from Josephus's representation of Elijah. Touch is not a means of transmitting power in Josephus's account. To the contrary, Josephus omits the reference to Elijah stretching out on the child's body three times (1 Kgs 17:21). The restoration of the son occurs through the prophet's cries to God. His recovery is denoted by the verb ἀναβιόω, "to return to life" (*A.J.* 8.327). In Josephus's narration, it is not Elijah who restores the child, but

---

32. The raising of Jairus's daughter in a house aligns the account with Old Testament/Jewish traditions of miracles of the dying (Pesch, *Das Markusevangelium*, 308–9).

God who has compassion and brings the child back to life. Indeed, in *A.J.* 8.326 it is Elijah who petitions God to give the child life (ζάω).

The story of the girl's restoration unfolds differently. The girl's transformation occurs as a result of Jesus's direct interaction with her and without any recourse to a divine being. No invocation of a deity, it is the father who begs Jesus to lay his hands on the girl in order that she may live (ζάω, Mark 5:23). It is the interface of Jesus's body and voice with the girl that restores life (5:41). The hearer encounters an image whereby the restoration of life is not the domain of a deity working through a prophet, but where Jesus himself is presented as a source of life, made manifest most particularly in his body. Restoration to life occurs through engagement with Jesus's body.

6.4. The Interaction of Bodies to Restore a Daughter's Life

In the early Roman Empire, some families chose to represent their relationships as intimate and interconnected on monuments and reliefs. The gestures of touch between figures could be understood to signify family ties. This is apparent in the funerary stela of the Florius family in the first-century CE. Three adults and a child feature on the relief with a male and a female figure thought to be the husband and wife linking hands.[33] This gesture of taking each other's hands may have connoted marriage, while the bonds that existed between parents and children could also be expressed through actions involving hands and touch. We also observed the significance of such gestures on the Sertorii relief and the Ara Pacis in Rome.[34] In the northern and southern processions of the Ara Pacis, for example, the children Lucius Gaius, Gaius Caesar, and Gnaeus Domitius

---

33. Funerary stela of Florius family, Capua, first century CE (Rawson, "Children and Childhood," 90, fig. 1.19). While the stela is in Capua, Rawson notes that of the five hundred images she has collected throughout Italy, eighty of these are located outside of Rome and Ostia. She observes that they are difficult to differentiate according to regions given the lack of variation among the representations.

34. The Sertorii relief is in Larsson Loven, "Children and Childhood," 307–8, fig. 15.4. For the southern and northern processions of the Ara Pacis in Rome, see Rossini, *Ara Pacis*, 58–59. For an example in a nuclear family, see Kleiner, *Roman Group Portraiture*, fig. 66. For an example of how the marital relationship is accentuated when parents join right hands, see Kockel, *Porträtreliefs stadtrömischer Grabbauten*, 532, nos. C3, F11, F12, and L20. See also Müller, "Dextrarum Iunctio," doi:10.1002/9781444338386.wbeah22079. On funerary reliefs, the motif of the handclasp could connote fidelity in death, or notions of reunion in the afterlife. Glenys

Ahenobarbus are depicted as grasping the togas of the adults in the family line. In the southern frieze the child Germanicus, in full toga and bulla, grasps the hand of Antonia Minor, signifying the ties between generations that would ensure the continuity of the imperial family and the empire.[35]

Gestures involving hands and touch also appear throughout the Markan narrative. Jesus's body—most often his hands and fingers—are integral in the process of altering bodies that are sick, or perceived to be not functioning appropriately.[36] As Jairus exhorts Jesus to make his daughter well, he draws on the image of laying hands on an ill person in order to restore that person. Jesus's hands and the girl's body are understood to be a locus of healing in the episode.

In addition, the gesture of grasping hands is employed in descriptions of Jesus's healing activities, particularly the healing of family members. In the case of Simon's mother-in-law, Jesus grasps her hand, κρατέω, and raises her up to restore her body (Mark 1:31). The verb is repeated in Mark 9:27 when Jesus grasps the hand of the boy who had been possessed by an unclean spirit and raises him. Likewise, Jesus grasps Jairus's daughter by the hand and raises her up in Mark 5:41. Gestures involving the hands and touch, signs that could connote familial bonds, are not the domain of parents or sons-in-law in these stories, although they clearly occur in accounts that involve family members. Instead, these gestures are attributed to Jesus. It is possible that, as each person is restored, an image of Jesus that is brought to mind is not only of a healer, but also as the person with whom bonds have now been forged. In the case of Jairus's daughter, not only have new bonds been created through physical interaction, Jesus's body has become the means for bridging the chasm between death and life.

6.5. The Representation of Jesus as a Figure of Authority

In addition to the activity of forging new bonds, the actions of Jesus throughout Mark 5:21–24, 35–43 present Jesus as the central authority

---

Davies, "The Significance of the Handshake Motif in Classical Funerary Art," *AJA* 89 (1985): 627–40.

35. Rossini, *Ara Pacis*, 50–53.

36. Mark 1:40–45; 3:7–12; 6:5; 7:32–37 (includes saliva); 8:22–26 (includes saliva); 9:27. In 5:24–35 and 6:56 others touch Jesus via his clothing, which mediates Jesus's healing power. Instances of no bodily interaction are Mark 1:32–33; 7:25–30; 10:46–52.

figure in the account. Jairus's demands that Jesus place his hands on his daughter are met with a characteristically hasty Markan response. What is uncharacteristic is Jesus's action: Jesus goes with Jairus to the house where the girl lies. The verb ἀπέρχομαι, "to depart on their way to another location," is used to describe their move to the house. Unlike other characters in the gospel, Jairus and Jesus go together. We do not encounter the standard image of people following Jesus. Instead, the prominent figure, Jairus, and Jesus appear to move jointly. In addition, this is also the only story in the gospel in which Jesus is depicted as traveling to an ill person. The standard representation is of a person being brought to Jesus, or Jesus happening upon them as he moves through the regions.[37]

While the physical movement of Jesus and Jairus to the house where the dying girl lies may allow for the interruption of the bleeding woman in 5:25, it also marks a significant transition in the representations of both of the male protagonists in the episode. Both men set off together but as they arrive at the house, οἶκος (5:38), the roles of both figures alter dramatically.[38] The author reveals this change in three ways. First, once the pair reaches the house, Jairus no longer speaks. The father-figure who exhorted Jesus repeatedly to heal his daughter is silent while Jesus becomes the commanding figure who exercises voice. He is depicted as speaking forthrightly on five occasions: First, when Jairus is informed that his daughter has died, Jesus dismisses the grim news by telling the leader to "not fear, only believe" (5:36). Second, when Jesus enters the house, he speaks directly to the mourners, refuting their belief that she is dead (5:39). Third, he speaks specifically to the little girl and tells her to get up (5:41). Fourth, he expressly charges the disciples, parents, and possibly the child to tell no one what has occurred (5:43). Lastly, he tells the disciples and the girl's parents to give her something to eat (5:43). The picture of Jesus in this account corresponds with the standard Markan portrait of Jesus that we noticed in chapter 3: a man whose speech acts, often monological, communicated a demanding and commanding figure.

Second, as the environmental settings within the episode shift so too do the characterizations of both male figures. The episode starts in an open, crowded public space, then transitions to outside the house where the mourners and the girl's mother gather, before moving into the house

---

37. In Mark 7:29–30 the healing occurs remotely.
38. The term οἶκος may denote a house, household, or family.

from where the mourners are ejected, and finally progresses to the space inside the house where the dead child lies. In a funnel-like fashion, the space through which Jesus and Jairus move tapers, from the public outdoors, to the domestic and private space, until they arrive at the specific place within the house where the child is located.[39] The place of the restoration to life is within the house.

The movement through these environments reflects the changes in both men's roles. The closer Jesus gets to the house the more influence he assumes. Once Jairus and Jesus reach the house, Jesus adopts the role of the sole authority figure, taking control of the household. He is depicted as single-handedly deciding who stays in the house and who is expelled. Despite what might be deemed as a fitting, even moving, expression of sorrow at the death of the daughter, Jesus asserts the authority to eject the mourners from the household. He effectively privatizes the domestic space, regulating who is able to be present in the household, and who must leave it, at a time of heightened emotion. He enacts an authority that enables him to bring adult males—presumably unknown to the girl—into the chamber of the house where the young female lies. Indeed, in 5:40 he has even assumed the power to take the parents of the girl into their own house where their own daughter lies dead. He has the power to influence the fate of the girl, usually the dominion of a paternal figure, which he exerts. In the final verse, he exercises the authority to tell the girls' parents, along with Peter, James, and John, to feed the restored daughter (5:43).

The command to feed the girl is a bewildering request. Among the voices we have heard, rearing children was commonly understood to be the purview of parents and involved feeding them and tending to their welfare. It would seem unnecessary to tell parents to feed their own child, especially in a family in which the child had been a cherished member. Just as perplexing is the inference that the disciples are possibly included in the command to feed the daughter. Given the story is set in a household, and that the girl's parents are present, it appears superfluous to suggest that the disciples, along with Jairus and the girl's mother, are told to give her something to eat.

This brings us to the third point. As Jesus's authority in the house intensifies, Jairus's authority appears to diminish. The contraction of influ-

---

39. Zwiep refers to a "telescoping of the spatial settings" (*Jairus's Daughter*, 240).

ence is conveyed through the labels that are applied to Jairus throughout the course of the account. He is referred to by name only once in 5:22. In the same verse, he is identified as a leader of the synagogue and a father. His identity as a synagogue leader is maintained from 5:35–39. From the moment at which Jesus ousts the mourners from the household and moves to the site in the house where the child lies, Jairus is no longer referred to as a synagogue leader. He is solely labeled as the father of the child. The new labeling of Jairus in terms of πατήρ in 5:40 strips away contextual layers associated with the title ἀρχισυνάγωγος. Instead, the story develops into an account that deals primarily with the family, house, and household. By the conclusion of the episode both Jairus and his wife, however, are no longer even referred to as the mother and father of the girl, but are subsumed into a grouping with the three disciples who are also rendered unnamed in 5:43.

In addition to the application of various labels, the diminishing authority of Jairus appears in the decline of the character's physical agency and the absence of any further speech acts following his exhortation to Jesus in 5:23. As the story progresses, it is Jesus whose voice prevails as decisive and demanding. The representation of the public figure and father who obstructed Jesus at the beginning of the account and then moved together with Jesus to his house shifts to that of a man who no longer undertakes any further activity once they reach his house, other than what Jesus commands him to do. Of course, this diminished role could be an index of Jairus's mounting grief given the deterioration of his daughter. Jairus had agency while his daughter was alive and he sought help. After hearing she has died, his agency is less significant. Notwithstanding this possibility, the closer Jairus's proximity to his own house, the less authority he is pictured to possess in comparison to Jesus. Once death occurs, Jesus is the focus of the two men.

In sum, while the episode begins with a common scenario relating the death of a beloved child and daughter, as the story progresses a shift appears in these standard representations whereby notions of the family are significantly modified. The image of Jesus taking over the authority of the household of a man of civic status, deciding who is entitled to remain and who must be expelled from the house and enacting such a decision, disrupts the more conventional view of the household in which the parents, particularly the father, were the central authority figures. The image of Jesus ejecting those who voice the family's grief at the loss of a cherished child ignores—perhaps even dispenses with—the significance of the dynamics through which families articulated ideas about their identity and status.⁴⁰

When we consider the traditional role of the devoted father that was discussed in the previous chapters, the depictions of Jesus and Jairus could now be understood to alter who functions as the father in the episode. In her analysis of Markan representations of daughters, Betsworth examines the image of Jesus as the protector that emerges in the account of Jairus's daughter. Jesus adopts the paternal role of preserving the welfare of the child that was initially performed by Jairus. Acting as the father figure, Betsworth contends that Jesus inaugurates a new family that now comprises the girl, her parents, the disciples, and Jesus himself.⁴¹ Betsworth's remarks resonate in part with the observations in our own examination.

Although our analysis has primarily focused on how bodies were imaged, it has likewise revealed that while it was often the father or male guardian who was perceived to hold the fate of a daughter in his hands—including her life and death in some examples—it is Jesus who ultimately determines the life of this girl, not her father. By 5:40, Jairus appears to no longer possess the authority to determine who enters the chamber where his daughter lies. Indeed, the once concerned father could be understood as irrelevant when Jesus brings three adult males into the presence of the girl. This shift in authority reinforces the notion that Jesus assumes the role of the father of the house.⁴²

Jesus not only dominates the household, but the leader and father is represented as showing no opposition to the transfer of his authority to Jesus.⁴³ Kahl insightfully notes that Jairus is depicted as never challenging Jesus's domination of the domestic space. She examines the role of

---

40. The relationship between Jesus and Jairus does not replicate a patron-client association either. Given that his daughter has been raised to life, Jairus is not in a position to reciprocate this gesture. See Adriana Destro and Maura Pesce, "Fathers and Householders in the Jesus Movement: The Perspective of the Gospel of Luke," *BibInt* 11 (2003): 229.

41. Betsworth, *Reign of God Is Such as These*, 115.

42. Bolt observes that in the second half of the account, Jesus is the subject of all the verbs. In Bolt's view, the text is not focused on Jairus's faith, but with the portrait of Jesus as one who raises a dead child to life, and primarily with Jesus's identity as the one who defeats death (*Jesus' Defeat of Death*, 178). See also *Chaer.* 5.8.8–9, where Callirhoe's guardian is a male figure who is not her biological father.

43. I include the labels of *synagogue leader* and *father* here. The term synagogue leader is used when Jesus enters the house (5:38–39). The term father is used at 5:40

Jairus in what she interprets as the dispute, "die Kontroverse," between Jesus and the mourners.[44] Prior to the interaction between Jesus and the grieving party, the synagogue leader has been informed of his daughter's death. Kahl highlights the lack of response—emotional or otherwise—of the synagogue leader to the news: He is not represented as joining the lamenting voices; he says and does nothing. Reading along with the narrative, this absence of a reaction is unusual given his desperation at the beginning of the episode. Jairus's silence is equally irregular when we recall the value placed on grieving the loss of daughters and children that has emerged in our own analyses of families in the first century CE. Of course, this lack of representation of emotion may have harmonized with Roman ideas about moderating displays of excessive emotion. But Kahl also observes that neither does the father support what she considers to be the mourners' derision of Jesus at 5:40 when Jesus states that the girl is not dead but asleep. Instead, Jairus appears passive as he proceeds further into the house with Jesus. This depiction of Jairus's silence possibly further conveyed the shift in authority in the family. In conflict with the broader household, Jesus overpowers the mourners by ejecting them from the house and in so doing assumes the leadership of the household without resistance from Jairus.[45]

The displacement of Jairus by Jesus as the household leader becomes a key to understanding the episode when it is considered in the light of notions of the family. A person acquainted with the idea of the family as a fundamental social unit, associated with notions of hope, prosperity, and stability, and among some Jews with ongoing lineage and the preservation of identity, would be well placed to notice an alteration of this image in the story of Jairus's daughter. Jesus now stands at the head of the household. He is the overarching authority figure who determines who enters and what happens in the house. The familial triad still exists of course. There is no indication that the relationship of father-mother-daughter ceases to exist. The daughter is restored to life but the structure to which she is

---

after Jesus has cast out the mourners from the synagogue leader's house (5:40a) and they move to where the dead girl lies.

44. Kahl, "Jairus und die verlorenen Töchter Israels," 73.

45. Kahl, "Jairus und die verlorenen Töchter Israels," 74. Kahl also argues that Jairus's alignment with the position of Jesus, over against the position of the mourners, indicates the leader has the faith with which Jesus encouraged him in 5:36.

restored differs from the one in which she died.⁴⁶ Her family is now part of a household that Jairus does not lead, but where Jesus prevails, and of which her family is a constituent part.

It is worth noting that there is no indication that Jairus forgoes or maintains his attachment to the role of ἀρχισυνάγωγος. The title is simply omitted as the household configuration changes. Once Jesus and Jairus are inside the house, the label ἀρχισυνάγωγος does not reappear. Malbon argues that the raising of Jairus's daughter can be understood as part of the synagogue versus house dichotomy that she associates with Mark: the *house* takes over the function of the *synagogue*, with power no longer residing with the synagogue leader but with Jesus in the house.⁴⁷ Kahl avoids this particular dualism but generates another one, albeit far more subtle: *die alten Hausgemeinschaft des Jairus* and *die neue Hausgemeinschaft*. The old household is associated with the destructive forces of death, while the new household is related to the raising of the daughter, and the power of the resurrection over death.⁴⁸ Each dimension in Kahl's dichotomy correlates respectively with old and new ways of belonging to the synagogue. The old household believes in the omnipotence of death, while the new, arising out of the faith of the synagogue leader (and therefore not antithetical to the law), symbolizes Israel granting household rights to Jesus.⁴⁹

In my view, there is another way to understand the shifts in household authority that does not have recourse to constructing such dualisms. By 5:42, Jairus is no longer labeled as either ἀρχισυνάγωγος or πατήρ, but he is subsumed into the collective *they* who were amazed and bewildered. His role as a father becomes irrelevant—but not necessarily abolished—as the authority of the household transfers to Jesus. There is no detail about Jairus leaving his family or relinquishing his status as ἀρχισυνάγωγος. At the end of the episode he is not sent anywhere by Jesus, nor does he up and follow him. Indeed, a hearer of the account might assume that Jairus is directed, along with the others who remained in the house, to undertake the domestic duty of feeding the child. In light of this, we might say that civic and religious status in addition to one's place in the biological family

---

46. In this way, the portrayal of Jairus's daughter differs from Callirhoe who is eventually restored to her former married life.
47. Elizabeth Struthers Malbon, *Narrative Space and Mythic Meaning in Mark* (San Francisco: Harper & Row, 1986), 132–33.
48. Kahl, "Jairus und die verlorenen Töchter Israels," 74.
49. Kahl, "Jairus und die verlorenen Töchter Israels," 75.

may continue to exist in 5:21–24, 35–43. Indeed, the synagogue leader's belief in Jesus—embodied in his pleas (5:23) and later demanded by Jesus (5:36)—are important factors in the first half of the episode. Rather than a case of the synagogue being surpassed by the household, or the old as being overtaken by the new, the situation could be described as individuals simply being incorporated into the household of Jesus as they were.

In addition, not all who constituted the household at the time of the girl's death remain members in the reconfigured household. Notwithstanding the possible emotional attachments that the grieving party may have had with the trio, the members who mourned have been removed by Jesus from the household. While the composition of the household appears to be pared back when those who grieve are expelled, the picture of the household a hearer now encountered encompasses new members: the three disciples are incorporated into the reconfigured household (5:37–43). The presence of Peter, James, and John in the intimate space of the house where the girl lies suggests that they too may be considered part of the reconstituted household structure.[50] In other words, biological ties do not appear to determine membership in the refashioned household in this story. Rather, a person is admitted on the basis of how they respond to the authoritative voice of Jesus.

We observed in chapter 4 that the marriage of daughters and their relocation to their husband's household was presented as a means of the girl's family securing status and stability or pursuing a political agenda. In the case of males, sons could be adopted by families for the purpose of attaining civic status with its concomitant social rewards (*Ann.* 1.2–3). In this way, membership in Roman families could be seen as fluid in some instances in the pursuit of status and familial viability. In a similar way, membership of the household of Jesus could be seen as fluid in Mark 5:21–24, 35–43. The mother, father, and child, as well as the three disciples are now incorporated into a new family. Upon becoming a member of the household, their identity is associated with their affiliation to Jesus.

It is not the negotiations of the father, however, that determine the new family to which one belongs. While Jairus is initially instrumental in securing Jesus's interest, it is the response to Jesus's commands that qualifies a person to take their place as kin. Jesus's directive to give the raised

---

50. The three named figures also accompany Jesus and are in close proximity to him in the transfiguration (9:2–13), sitting at the Mount of Olives discussing signs of the end times (Mark 13), and at Gethsemane during the passion (14:33–42).

child something to eat may have been perplexing for some who understood a parent's role to perform this duty. In the Philonic system, a parent's responsibility was to provide food for their children (*Spec.* 2.232). In some of the Greco-Roman and late Second Temple sources, women were depicted in terms of feeding others: breastfeeding infants (*CIL* 6.19128; Josephus, *A.J.* 1.224–227; LAB 51.3) and preparing food (*A.J.* 7.167). Jesus's directive has a dual function of positioning him as an authoritative, paternal figure while suggesting that those who now take their place in the house follow his commands. As head of the household, Jesus directs others to feed the child. No longer the domain of the woman, the nurturing role may be performed by any member of the household.

Integral to the idea of the household being refashioned is the power of Jesus to restore life. One way of approaching this notion is in relation to conceptualizations of the male body concerning reproduction. In Philo's description of procreation in *Spec.* 3, the womb is depicted in terms of a physical receptacle, a laboratory, in which the creature takes shape (*Spec.* 3.33). It is like a workshop in which the creature that inhabits the space is molded.[51] While the female incubates human life, it is the life force of the male that spawns life (*Spec.* 3.33). The father provides the seed while the woman's body is likened to a field that is impregnated with seed. Likewise, in *Spec.* 1, Philo talks of circumcision as assisting the male genitals to provide the fertility of offspring (*Spec.* 1.3–7). In these approaches, the procreating force is associated with the male body. It is the domain of fathers to generate life with their bodies, which women then nurture with their bodies.

Along similar lines, gendered ideas of the body appear in Liber Antiquitatum Biblicarum in its allusions to fertility, procreation, and child-bearing. Drawing on the imagery of agriculture, the seed is used as a metaphor for the offspring of Abram. The seed is given by God to Abram as a sign of the enduring generations who will live according to the covenant that God establishes with Abram (LAB 8). Extending the metaphor, the children who are born as a result of their father's seed, are labeled "the fruit of the womb" (LAB 9.2; 42.3; 50.2). Resonating with the imagery of Philo, the man's body contains seed that is the life force and a woman's body is the fertile site in which the seed takes hold and grows.

---

51. The womb is imaged as an artist's studio in *Spec.* 3.107–109.

In the account of Jairus's daughter, the fruit of the seed of the synagogue leader has died. Reading the story with Philo's and Liber Antiquitatum Biblicarum's imagery in mind, Jairus's life force may be understood to have come to an end in the death of his daughter. Her restoration to life comes about, however, not through any direct intervention involving her parents, particularly her father, but through interaction with the body and voice of Jesus. His body is depicted as a source of life; contact between the girl's body and that of Jesus's brings about transformation to a state of living. From this perspective, it is possible to conceive of Jesus as appropriating the role as the life force of the family.[52] The death of Jairus's daughter can be understood to mark the end of the primacy of the conventional familial structure in the narrative. Her transformation to life and to a different household structure is not explicitly associated, however, with Jesus's sexuality or with procreation. It is, nevertheless, brought about through the interaction with Jesus's own body—his touch and authoritative and creative voice—that produces a different approach to family whereby the fundamental life force is associated with Jesus.

The girl does not metamorphose into another bodily form in this transformation. Labeled as neither an apparition nor a ghost, she retains her embodiment as a twelve-year-old child that is able to walk about and eat, like others her age (5:42–43).[53] The term ἐγείρω is used to command the little girl to get up (5:41). The same verb is also used in relation to the raising of Jesus (14:28, 16:6). While it is possible that hearers of the account noticed the overtones of Jesus's resurrection in Jairus's daughter's transformation from a deathly state to life, it is also conceivable that they acknowledged her transformation as denoting physical restoration. Not

---

52. I thank Professor John Barclay for drawing my attention to the possibility that Jesus becomes associated with the perception of the male as providing a life force.

53. Pesch, *Das Markusevangelium*, 311; Betsworth, *Reign of God Is Such as These*, 50. The girl's return to her former body contrasts with the depiction of Jesus as a ghost-like figure in 6:45–52. For an analysis of the ghostly image of Jesus as a phantasma/ φάντασμα, see Choi's discussion of 6:45–52 (*Postcolonial Discipleship of Embodiment*, 63–84). I also note the observation of Sue Kossew that ghost-like appearances may function as tropes that signify hope in texts concerning suffering. Kossew, "Women Writing Pain: Recent Australian Fiction and the Representation of Gendered Violence" (paper presented at Translating Pain: An International Forum on Language, Text and Suffering, Monash University, Caulfield, Australia, 12 August 2015). For a perspective on the notion of metamorphosis in the New Testament, see George Aichele and Richard Walsh, "Metamorphosis, Transfiguration, and the Body," *BibInt* 19 (2011): 253–75.

exclusive to 5:41, the verb ἐγείρω is used in various forms in accounts that deal with the alteration of an ill body to a state of wellness (1:31; 2:12; 3:3; 9:27; 10:49). It commonly describes the actions of persons as soon as they are cured: they get up. The term ἀνίστημι, "to cause to arise," is taken up in a similar vein to signify the girl's return (5:42).[54] By the end of the account, the initial request that Jairus made to Jesus in Mark 5:23 that his little daughter be saved from death (σῴζω) and live or be in full strength (ζάω) is accomplished (5:43).

The hearer also encounters the description of the three disciples and the girl's parents in a state of ecstasy, "overcome with amazement" (Mark 5:42). The use of the verb ἐξίστημι suggests the group are out of their senses or disembodied, "'standing outside' of their everyday reactions to events."[55] This reaction is replicated in other instances in which the preceding events have left people puzzled and Jesus's ensuing actions have prompted amazement (2:12; 3:21; 6:51). Likewise, in 5:21–24, 35–43 the misalignment of the mourners' grief with Jesus's capacity to restore the dead to life leads to a reaction of amazement. In addition, the reaction is one of ἔκστασις or ecstasy (5:42). The only other time this noun is heard is in the description of the trembling women as they flee the empty tomb (16:8). Their experience of the absent corpse and the news of Jesus being raised from the dead leaves them displaced from their own normal reality. In the case of 5:21–24, 35–43 the restoration of the girl from death to life elicits the same sense of displacement from reality. This underscores the extraordinary nature of what has occurred. In both cases, when bodies are understood to transcend the boundaries of death and life, people are transferred into a new reality.

In essence, the restoration of Jairus's daughter departs from the typical narrative that was told of dying and deceased daughters in the first century CE. At first blush, the story appears as one in which a dead child was restored to life and given back to her parents and the life of the household.[56] In this way, both the child's life and her family were simultaneously physically restored; a narrative detail that diverged from the standard accounts about the deaths of daughters. What lies at the heart of this story when it

---

54. The term ἀνίστημι is also used to describe the restoration of the corpse-like son in 9:27.

55. Marcus, *Mark 1–8*, 363.

56. Murphy, *Kids and Kingdom*, 72. See also Gundry, "Children in the Gospel of Mark," 161.

is read with an awareness of the body, however, is not merely the corporeal restoration of the girl (as remarkable as that act is). Rather, reading the story with the body in mind opens up the possibility that a hearer encountered the notion of a reconfigured household, and Jesus's role in that structure as the authoritative, paternal figure. If that is the case, it is conceivable that the restored daughter and her parents were understood to be incorporated into a broader conceptualization of household; a household whose life force was derived from the body of Jesus, rather than the traditional father of the house. The new household was one in which the gap between death and life was bridged.

6.6. The Notion of Family

Our engagement with the Jewish and Greco-Roman voices of the late Second Temple period and the early Roman Empire respectively has allowed us to expand the possibilities of how the story of Jairus's daughter may have been heard in the first century CE. We now proceed a step further to examine how a hearer might have situated the account within the broader narrative of Mark's Gospel. The previous insights that have been gleaned concerning the notion of the reconfigured household have implications for how a hearer may have understood what constituted a family and household. To think of family as an entity that was primarily bound by biological ties and led by the traditional father figure appears to be problematic, given that our approach to Jairus's daughter suggests that the conventional family structure was altered by Jesus. As we have seen, it is plausible that some common ideas concerning the roles and membership of households and families could have had a bearing on the understanding of Jesus as the head of the household. Given this, we would expect to see other instances in the narrative in which a hearer of Mark might have reason to rethink notions concerning the make-up and function of families with Jesus as the fundamental reference point.

There is a view that the image of the family in Mark's Gospel is a disruptive one. Rather than seeing the notion of family as nonproblematic or profamily, there is recognition that ideas about what constituted family in relation to Jesus are revised in the narrative, and that the resulting picture can be regarded as devaluing natural kinship ties.[57] Perceived to

---

57. Stephen P. Ahearne-Kroll, "'Who Are My Mother and My Brothers?' Family

be threatened, the conventional family in the gospel is understood to be "endangered by the impact of Jesus and his gospel."[58] The gospel is labeled as "anti(conventional) family" and as "relativiz[ing] ... household ties and kinship-related identity."[59] While little of the scholarship that proposes such a view considers familial imagery in the story of Jairus's daughter, my reading confirms and extends this line of argument.[60]

Leif Vaage, for example, takes up various images of family in the gospel to argue that the Markan Jesus practices "an alternate domesticity as the model for early Christian discipleship."[61] The alternate model he proposes includes "socially liminal characters" such as the bleeding woman (5:23–34) and children (9:36; 10:13–16).[62] Despite the potential implications for the account of Jairus's daughter, Vaage does not draw on this story in his argument. On the other hand, in Katrina Poetker's study of Markan families, there is a reference to Jairus's daughter. Nonetheless,

---

Relations and Family Language in the Gospel of Mark," *JR* 81 (2001): 1–25; George Aichele, "Jesus' Uncanny 'Family Scene,'" *JSNT* 21.74 (1999): 29–48; Stephen C. Barton, *Discipleship and Family Ties in Mark and Matthew*, SNTSMS 80 (Cambridge: Cambridge University Press, 1994); Adriana Destro and Mauro Pesce, *Encounters with Jesus: The Man in His Place and Time* (Minneapolis: Fortress, 2012), 102–25; Bonnie Miller-McLemore, "Jesus Loves the Little Children? An Exercise in the Use of Scripture," *JCR* 1 (2010): 1–35; Murphy, *Kids and Kingdom*, 111–29; Katrina M. Poetker, "'You Are My Mother, My Brothers, and My Sisters': A Literary-Anthropological Investigation of Family in the Gospel of Mark (PhD diss., Emory University, 2001); Poetker, "Domestic Domains in the Gospel of Mark," *Direction* 24 (1995): 14–24; Leif E. Vaage, "An Other Home: Discipleship in Mark as Domestic Asceticism," *CBQ* 71 (2009): 741–61; John H. Elliott, "Household/Family in the Gospel of Mark as a Core Symbol of Community," in *Fabrics of Discourse: Essays in Honor of Vernon K. Robbins*, ed. David B. Gowler, L. Gregory Bloomquist, and Duane F. Watson (Harrisburg, PA: Trinity Press International, 2003), 36–63. Contra (in part) Gundry who proposes a positive interpretation of children and family in Mark's Gospel ("Children in the Gospel of Mark," 143–76). See also Peter Balla, *The Child-Parent Relationship in the New Testament and Its Environment* (Peabody, MA: Hendrickson, 2005), 130–56.

58. Poetker, "You Are My Mother, My Brothers, and My Sisters," 172.

59. Quotations from Vaage, "Other Home," 741; Barton, *Discipleship and Family Ties*, 122, respectively.

60. Some scholars do treat the account of Jairus's daughter in studies of specific subcategories that relate to familial contexts, such as *daughters* and *children*: Betsworth, *Children in Early Christian Narratives*, 48–52; Betsworth, *Reign of God Is Such as These*, 101–15; Murphy, *Kids and Kingdom*, 72, 121–22.

61. Vaage, "Other Home," 756.

62. Vaage, "Other Home," 742.

she is of the view that the girl resumes her role in the household with no changes to the family and household structure as a result of her return to life and the family's encounter with Jesus.[63] Further, Poetker identifies Jesus as a "senior householder" more broadly in the gospel but draws no comparison with the portrayal of Jesus's role in Jairus's household.[64] In contrast to this position, the examination we have undertaken thus far leads to a stronger conclusion.

Bearing in mind the insights that have surfaced in our analysis, in this final section we turn to a series of Markan images of family and household. When these are considered with notions of the body in mind, it becomes clear that the account of Jairus's daughter contributes its own particular dimension to the overall picture of family and household in the narrative, and therefore warrants inclusion in scholarly discussions of this theme. The following discussion is broken into two parts. Part one examines the various images of family and household that a hearer could have conceivably observed in the narrative. I establish that the notion of a reconfigured household corresponds to other representations of the family and household within the spectrum of the narrative. Given this consistency, part two considers membership of the new household, with a specific focus on women and children.

6.6.1. Representations of Family

Images and language of the family permeate the Markan narrative. Any person who engaged with the gospel in the first century CE encountered various ideas about families and households that both resonated with and diverged from the representations we have examined. I will address five perspectives that are particularly evident. First, a hearer may observe that family life and biological ties are affirmed. Second, despite this acknowledgement, the ties that bind family life may also be understood to be loosened. Third, the bonds between Jesus and his family of origin can be seen to be severed in preference for a notion of family that differs from that defined by genetic ascent. Fourth, the image of family wherein Jesus

---

63. Poetker, "You Are My Mother, My Brothers, and My Sisters," 164–65. Balla ventures further, however, noting that in using "daughter" Jesus's claim to authority may be implied. Balla does not develop this idea further (*Child-Parent Relationship*, 122–23).

64. Poetker, "You Are My Mother, My Brothers, and My Sisters," 200.

is completely absent is associated with corruption and death. Lastly, the upheaval of the end time is signified in the implosion of the conjugal family, accompanied by images of labor and birth and suggestions that Jesus had overcome the power of Satan. I will treat each of these observations separately and draw in connections with the story of Jairus's daughter.

First, at one end of the spectrum, a hearer of Mark's Gospel could find an affirmation of family life and the biological ties that forged familial relationships. Some characters that are healed, for instance, are sent back to their families and homes, or are restored in a domestic context (1:29–31; 5:19; 7:24, 30; 8:26).[65] We have noted that marriage was an important factor in the fabric of first century life for many of the voices we have considered in both the early empire and late Second Temple Judaism. In Mark 10, the hearer encounters ideas about the importance of marriage. In a milieu in which marriage could be understood as a way of preserving the purity of Jewish identity, with a particular focus on the status of a woman's body in relation to marriage (e.g., Jub. 30.2), a hearer is presented with a notion of marriage as the fusion of two separate bodies into one body (Mark 10:7-9). God is the subject of the act of joining these bodies, and together they form a new entity, one flesh, σάρξ (10:8). As one body, they are unable to be divided.[66] Moreover, given that God has done the joining of the two, no person can undo what God has brought together (10:9). To divorce and marry another therefore is not possible.[67] Remarrying is labeled as "adultery," μοιχάω, and therefore possibly heard as a breach of the law.[68] The notion of an "indissoluble marriage" is linked to sexual intercourse, an experience that is associated with the divine.[69]

In the same chapter, Jesus alludes to the commandment to love one's father and mother in his response to a question of what one must do to inherit eternal life (10:19; see also 7:10). The importance placed on the

---

65. Vaage, "Other Home," 752–55.
66. I am conscious that Mark does not use a term for marriage here. I am using it in my analysis to differentiate from the act of divorce/ἀπολύω.
67. On divorce in Judaism and Greco-Roman contexts contemporaneous with Mark, see Yarbro Collins, *Mark*, 459–65.
68. This is possibly a rider to the call of male disciples to leave all behind—including family and household—and follow Jesus. See Mary Rose D'Angelo, "Roman Imperial Values and the Gospel of Mark: The Divorce Sayings (Mark 10:2–12)," in *Women and Gender in Ancient Religions*, ed. Stephen Ahearne-Kroll, Paul A. Holloway, and James A. Kelhoffer, WUNT 263 (Tübingen: Mohr Siebeck, 2010), 78.
69. Marcus, *Mark 8–16*, 712.

commandment to honor one's parents has resonance with contemporaneous Jewish voices. Philo also reinforces the importance of the fifth commandment, reflecting his broader concern for maintaining the population of Israel. He maps parents' capacity to bring to birth and raise a "nonbeing" to what God has accomplished in the world: "Parents, in my opinion, are to their children what God is to the world" (*Spec.* 2.224–225). In other words, to honor parents is to honor God (also Josephus, *C. Ap.* 2.206). In Mark 10:19, the commandment to honor parents in a list of commandments deals specifically with right relations between people. Perhaps, as Peter Balla suggests, giving special emphasis to the relationship between parents and children, the commandment is placed last in the list.[70] In any case, those who encountered this passage were offered ideas that echoed a normative stance within the literary landscape of Judaism of the faithful commitment of offspring to their mothers and fathers.

Second, while a person may have perceived family life to be affirmed in the narrative, they would also have encountered the image of conventional familial ties being loosened. The depictions of the disciples at the beginning of the gospel occupy a position somewhere in between the portraits of loyal family relations bound by biological ties and images of the destruction of families that are encountered later in chapter 13. From chapter 1 the hearer comes across Simon and his brother Andrew, and James son of Zebedee and his brother John (1:16–20). The context has a clear familial element with both pairs of men designated as brothers (1:16, 18) with the added patronym further denoting the identity of James and John (1:18). All four are identified as fishermen, located in Jewish territory by the Sea of Galilee. Their familial and work lives appear as intertwined: each pair works together as brothers; James and John are located in the fishing boat with their father Zebedee, as well as the hired men (1:19–20).

No sooner does the hearer encounter this image than Jesus invites the men to follow him. The men's response to Jesus's words is both immediate and physically discernible: "immediately they left their nets and followed him" (1:18) and "they left their father Zebedee in the boat with the hired men, and followed him" (1:20). To follow Jesus involved a degree of separation from the domestic realm: leaving behind one's

---

70. Balla, *Child-Parent Relationship*, 120.

work life, the family's livelihood, and one's father.⁷¹ The familial network is not completely severed, however. While leaving the place of family ties and livelihood, they follow Jesus as brothers.⁷² Nonetheless, from the beginning of the narrative, the biological family or the family of one's origin no longer appears as the core structure in which those who associate with Jesus necessarily express their identity. Rather, the identity of those who follow Jesus is generally enacted through some separation from one's family.

The depiction of family separation is starker in Mark 10. In a discussion concerning the difficulty for the wealthy to enter the kingdom of God, Peter voices that the disciples have already let go of everything in order to follow Jesus (10:28). Jesus considers Peter's remarks in 10:29. In Jesus's words, leaving everything involves leaving house, family, and fields for "my sake and the sake of the good news" (10:29). He clarifies family as: brothers, sisters, mother, father, and children.⁷³ The separation is comprehensive. As well as the material resources a man possesses, it is the ties to household and family that a male disciple may be required to sever in order to identify with Jesus: a father may be forced to forsake his children for the sake of the good news. In other words, to follow Jesus may have required a detachment from some of the conventional relationships that afforded a man identity and status.

At the same time, in forsaking one's biological family, a disciple may move into another form of family. This family also comprises "houses, brothers and sisters, mothers and children, and fields" (10:30). It will not be immune to persecutions in this life, but will receive "eternal life" in the coming age (10:30). While a disciple may encounter a cost in following Jesus, the new family they will receive in return—a hundredfold in size—will be oriented to eternal life.⁷⁴

The father figure does not appear in the list of those whom the new family comprises. John Donahue attributes this absence to two possible factors. First, God could be understood to be the only father (cf. 11:25; 14:36). Second, it reflects an antipatriarchal stance that "indicates the radically egalitarian nature of the Markan community.... Mark's new

---

71. Barton, *Discipleship and Family Ties*, 62.
72. Ahearne-Kroll, "'Who Are My Mother and My Brothers?,'" 10.
73. Terms for children: τέκνα/τέκνον. Note also that Mark does not refer to a person's spouse.
74. Ahearne-Kroll, "'Who Are My Mother and My Brothers?,'" 22.

family is to be characterized by the renunciation of dominating power and by mutual service."[75] When the account is read in light of the story of Jairus's daughter, Donahue's options appear less plausible. In becoming the authority figure in the reconfigured household, Jesus could be understood to appropriate a father-like role to himself. Furthermore, in usurping the authority of the house, the resulting structure is not completely discontinuous with ideals held more broadly in society. John Elliott's broad observations are apposite: "At no point in Mark [is there] an explicit critique of the family as such, let alone of patriarchy. Jesus assumes the traditional family structure along with familial roles and responsibilities throughout his teaching, with no mention of eliminating social disparities."[76]

Contrary to the egalitarian explanation that Donahue provides, the household now appears dominated by Jesus.[77] Rather than to one's biological parents, a person's ultimate loyalty is to be directed to Jesus, whose authority is partly constructed in traditional patriarchal terms.[78] The reference to "hundredfold" members (Mark 10:30) reinforces the notions of continuity and vitality in this household, ideas that were also integral to Greco-Roman and Jewish perspectives on family. The household that Jesus heads will have many members, a sign that it flourishes.

While a hearer may have speculated about the repercussions of such changes for the family, they are not explicit in the narrative. There are no allusions to the feelings or perceptions of any of the family members to the alterations to the familial structure, nor does the author provide details of how the remaining "brothers, sisters, mother, father, and children" might subsequently go about their lives.[79] A hearer might have imagined the possible consequences for wives, children, and perhaps aging parents when the father/husband's obligations to his family's welfare were not the main priority. The absence of such detail appears

---

75. Donahue, *The Theology and Setting of Discipleship in the Gospel of Mark* (Milwaukee, WI: Marquette University Press, 1983), 43.

76. Elliott, "Household/Family," 55. Note that Elliott does not treat the raising of Jairus's daughter in any detail.

77. Against Vaage, "Other Home," 747.

78. Elliott, "Household/Family," 62.

79. Miller-McLemore, "Jesus Loves the Little Children?," 21; Murphy, *Kids and Kingdom*, 68–102. See also David C. Sim, "What About the Wives and Children of the Disciples? The Cost of Discipleship from Another Perspective," *HeyJ* 35 (1994): 373–90.

anomalous given that the perceptions and motivations of various characters are often disclosed in the narrative.[80] A hearer may have been disturbed by the choice of an individual to dismiss their father and household leader in order to identify with Jesus. If a hearer had concerns, they are not reflected in the narrative. Instead, the emphasis lies in how a detachment from one's family of origin may have been necessary to advance the good news. The disciple's duty to his family was outstripped by his choice of allegiance to Jesus.[81] The image of a newly formulated family with various members may have assuaged any sense of disruption or loss of the conventional family.

Third, in Mark 3 and 6, a hearer encounters depictions of the separation of Jesus from his own biological family and the emergence of alternative ways to articulate what constituted family for those who identified with him. In chapter 3, the location of a person determines their membership in Jesus's family. Those who are inside the house, in close physical proximity to Jesus, personify membership in Jesus's family, in addition to obeying God's will. Biological ties no longer define the identity of Jesus's family. Throughout the chapter, Jesus's family, comprising mother and brothers, is physically displaced and Jesus is repositioned within a different familial structure. In 3:19–20, Jesus moves to the domestic setting of the house, οἶκος, where a crowd prevents him and his disciples from eating. Upon hearing this, Jesus's family goes out to restrain him, κρατέω, in the belief that he has gone out of his mind, ἐξίστημι (3:21).[82] This description of being out of one's mind could connote a person afflicted by demon possession, a depiction of Jesus reinforced by the ensuing remarks of scribes (3:22–30). Jesus's response to his family's accusations is severe. He accuses them of blasphemy and condemns them to a state of eternal sin (3:29).[83] By the conclusion of chapter 3, Jesus and the crowd are inside the house, οἶκος, while his family

---

80. Fowler, *Let the Reader Understand*, 121. For examples in which a character's perceptions, questions, and motivations are revealed, see 4:10; 5:28; 6:20, 26; 8:14–21; 9:10; 16:3; for references to characters' emotions, see, e.g., 9:30–32, 10:24, 11:18; 15:10.

81. Miller-McLemore describes it as a "subordination of family and children to mission" ("Jesus Love the Little Children?," 22).

82. I follow Sim, who disputes the translation that suggests other "people" label Jesus as "out of his mind," instead of Jesus's own kin. See David C. Sim, "The Family of Jesus and the Disciples of Jesus in Paul and Mark: Taking Sides in the Early Church's Factional Dispute," in Wischmeyer, Sim, and Elmer, *Paul and Mark*, 87, 89.

83. Sim, "Family of Jesus," 88.

is outside.[84] The hearer is presented with an unambiguous image of Jesus as distinct from his family of origin.

While Jesus's biological family appears displaced, the setting of 3:31–35 is nonetheless both familial and domestic. Representations of physical positioning and speech possibly functioned to convey notions about the shifting identity of Jesus's family. Positioned outside, Jesus's biological family sends for and calls to him (3:31). In contrast, the crowd who is inside and in close proximity to Jesus—sitting around him in a circle—is able to speak to Jesus directly (3:32). While Jesus's mother and brothers are depicted as sending and calling for him, no words are put on their lips. Indeed, their efforts are ineffectual as Jesus pays no attention to them whatsoever, providing no response to their call. Instead, he directs his attention to those positioned physically close to him, talking to the crowd inside the house (3:32). His response identifies the members of his family: those who sit around him inside the house and who do the will of God (3:35).[85] In addition, Jesus's new family embraces many who may be designated as a "brother and ... mother" including a reference to "sister" (3:35). Females, other than mothers, are included in this reconceptualized family.[86]

A hearer may have discerned resonances with the story of Jairus's daughter. It is possible that the story implied that membership of the household now included a female child. The mother, father, and daughter, as well as the three disciples are located inside the house in close proximity to Jesus, while others had been ejected outside (5:40). It is plausible that those who encountered both stories understood that issues concerning who constituted family were being addressed through the depictions of various figures that were positioned in close physical proximity to Jesus inside the household. [87]

---

84. For similar comments on the use of the spatial language of outside/inside in relation to notions of family in 3:21–35, see Ahearne-Kroll, "'Who Are My Mother and My Brothers?,'" 14. Also, Elizabeth Struthers Malbon, *Narrative Space*, 130.

85. Donahue, *Theology and Setting of Discipleship*, 35; Vaage, "Other Home," 747. See also Barton, *Discipleship and Family Ties*, 123. On the relationship between Jesus's biological family and the scribes from Jerusalem in 3:22, see Elliott, "Household/Family," 48–49.

86. Barton, *Discipleship and Family Ties*, 74.

87. While Jesus has identified a new household that he leads, at the same time he is portrayed as plundering the household, οἰκία, of Satan, in the intercalated parable of 3:27 (Poetker, "You Are My Mother, My Brothers, and My Sisters," 167). See also Elizabeth E. Shively, *Apocalyptic Imagination in the Gospel of Mark: The Literary and Theological Role of Mark 3:22–30*, BZNW 189 (Berlin: de Gruyter, 2012), 41–83.

Biological ties, including those that once bound Jesus's family, were no longer determinative.[88]

In 6:1–6a, it is not only Jesus's immediate family but also the extended kin in Nazareth from whom Jesus is separated. At the beginning of the chapter, Jesus is located in his "hometown," πατρίς, in Nazareth (6:1). In the synagogue, his kinfolk who hear him are affected by his teaching, amazed at his wisdom (σοφία) and the deeds of power (δύναμις) being done by his hands (6:2). His own people notice both the substance of his speech acts and the power he embodies. The amazement of the people shifts, however, to a sense of being scandalized, "an obstacle to coming to faith" (6:3).[89] This response is based on the identification of Jesus as a carpenter and in terms of his biological family whom the people know. It is not possible that a man of such status and origins could possess wisdom and power as he does.[90] Jesus is thus rejected among many of his kin, in his own hometown, and in his own house (6:4). He is rendered powerless among his own people (6:5–6) on account of their unbelief and is reduced to curing only a few people through his hands. The biological family of Jesus is thus constructed as a site of unbelief, contributing to a broader picture of familial rupture and mutual rejection.

As we have observed, the membership of families could change in Greco-Roman society in the first century CE. Sons, for example, were adopted to advance an individual's or family's prospects (e.g., Cicero, *Tusc.* 1.32; *RIC*, 72, nos. 404. 405). In this way, representations of the changing membership of Jesus's family to advance the good news may not have been entirely unfamiliar to some. Given the publicly lauded role of motherhood in the early empire, the ousting of Jesus's mother may nevertheless have been an anomaly for some hearers of Mark (Tellus panel; *CIL* 6.323232-6).

When we consider the changing depiction of family in relation to late Second Temple Judaism, some divergences appear. According to the

---

88. Note also the location and proximity of Jesus's biological family to the scribes in the intercalated text of 3:22–30 (Barton, *Discipleship and Family Ties*, 76–78; Shively, *Apocalyptic Imagination in the Gospel of Mark*, 189, 54, 82). Fassnacht discusses the notion of proximity to Jesus in 5: 21–43 and the implications for the reader who was/ is no longer in physical proximity to Jesus ("Konfrontation mit der Weisheit Jesu," 105–24, esp. 114–20, 122).

89. Yarbro Collins, *Mark*, 291, also nn. 218–19.

90. Marcus notes the similarity of the people's reaction in 6:2 and the scribes in 3:20–30 (*Mark 1–8*, 379).

voices we considered in chapter 5, genetic ascent and familial ties were important. The genealogies in Jubilees, for example, that mapped the ties between generations, noting a woman's pedigree in the progression of each generation, functioned to emphasize the identity and boundaries of a community. Beyond Jubilees, the importance of family life was often epitomized in the portrayals of women who were routinely characterized as wives and mothers. They were fundamental to maintaining Jewish identity and transmitting faith. In the funerary data of Jerusalem and Jericho, we also observed that some Jews memorialized the bonds of family life in the construction of family tombs. For hearers familiar with these depictions, the representation of Jesus's family as no longer defined by genetic ascent or the conjugal family implies a departure from some of the ideas that were present in the context of a first century CE hearer. The shift in how people identified themselves in relation to Jesus could be substantial.

Fourth, in 6:17–29 a hearer encountered the depiction of a family wherein Jesus is absent. This family, deprived of the presence of Jesus, is associated with corruption and death. In a recall of the circumstances surrounding John the Baptizer's beheading, the common image of the familial triad is again evoked. In this portrait of father, mother, and child, Herodias is labeled as wife (6:18) and mother (6:24, 28). Herod, recognized as king (6:14), is also identified in terms of his marriage to Herodias (6:17–18), and his relationship to his daughter (θυγάτηρ, 6:22). [91] In the same verse, the daughter is also labeled κοράσιον. The diminutive of κορή, the term could connote the image of a little girl or an unmarried girl. In either case, the girl's dependency on her family is suggested by this term and her parents' authority is thus underscored.

Another indicator of the familial context is the setting of the episode. A hearer encountered a banquet scene, connoted using the term συνανάκειμαι, which conveyed an image of a Mediterranean dining scene with guests reclining on couches (6:22). By the time of the early empire, we find children depicted in dining scenes of elite families during special occasions, along with their mothers and fathers.[92] In a discussion of the placement of guests at a dinner, Plutarch notes that the children or the wife

---

91. The death of the baptizer is also narrated in Josephus, *A.J.* 18.116–119. Note that Josephus does not implicate Herodias and her daughter in the baptizer's death. See Ross S. Kraemer, "Implicating Herodias and Her Daughter in the Death of the Baptizer: A (Christian) Theological Strategy?" *JBL* 125 (2006): 321–349.

92. Suetonius, *Claud.* 32; Rawson, *Children and Childhood*.

of a host may be located on couches near him (*Mor.* 619). A hearer may not have been surprised, therefore, to find Herod's daughter/unmarried girl in the scene of Herod's birthday banquet. The presence of children at dinner parties, however, is mostly considered unfavorable in the writings of the time. Plutarch, for example, discusses women and children being exposed to inappropriate entertainment during these events that is "disruptive of an orderly mind" (*Mor.* 712). Quintilian considers the dinner party a place in which children are exposed to "obscene songs; things are to be seen that it is shameful to name" (*Inst.* 1.2, 8–9). In other words, the dinner party provides children of elite families with a formation in immorality according to these writers. The location of 6:17–29, therefore, possibly functioned as a key to understanding the representation of this family as immoral.

The depiction of the bond between Herodias and her daughter suggests further associations with immorality. There are two themes that emerge in the literary sources that shed light on how the relationships between mothers and daughters in elite families were constructed by some writers. One theme concerns portraying the ideal daughter as obedient to her mother. There were expectations that mothers would ensure their daughters obtained an education, that they formed their daughters for marriage and motherhood, and that they supported them in times of crises (Plutarch, *Pomp.* 9; Cicero, *Clu.* 12–14).[93] A girl's mother, therefore, exerted power over her daughter, who was expected to submit to her mother's authority. As Suzanne Dixon observes, however, the characterizations of mothers in these relationships were often far from the exemplar of Roman motherhood. This is illustrated in Plutarch's portrayal of Caecilia Metilla who instructs her pregnant daughter, Aemilia, to divorce in order to marry Pompey (*Pomp.* 9). While reflecting social ideals about the authoritative mother and obedient daughter, Plutarch passes judgment on Caecilia Metilla's exercise of power, suggesting that some mothers in elite families formed their daughters in immoral behavior, contributing in this case to "tyranny" and ultimately leading to the death of Aemilia during childbirth (Plutarch, *Pomp.* 9; also Juvenal, *Sat.* 14). In this way, Plutarch's idea of the inappropriate use of maternal authority and a daughter's subsequent submission to such power became associated with political corruption and tragedy.

---

93. Suzanne Dixon, *The Roman Mother* (Florence: Routledge, 2013), 215–20.

The other theme that emerges concerns the depiction of solidarity between mothers and daughters to serve the political agenda of a mother. An example of this representation is evident in Tacitus's description of Julia Livia and her mother, Livillia, in *Ann.* 4.60. Tacitus casts the women as schemers, conspiring to accuse Nero, Julia Livia's husband, of treason. Julia Livia divulges to her mother the nocturnal ramblings of her husband that serve to build a case against Nero. In Tacitus's narrative, mother and daughter are collaborators in a mire of imperial politics with Julia Livia confiding in her mother and Livilla using her daughter for her own political ends.[94]

What is evident in the description of these themes is their resonance with the depictions of Herodias and her daughter in Mark 6:17–29. The hearer encountered a portrait of a commanding mother and her deferential daughter. The daughter, upon being asked to request whatever she wishes (6:21), leaves the room seeking her mother's direction (6:24). The question she poses to her mother is delivered in the deliberative subjunctive, indicating she expects an answer from her mother. Accordingly, Herodias instructs her daughter directly (6:24). Herodias co-opts her daughter to participate in an act that ends in the grisly death of an innocent man. The compliant daughter indulges her mother further with the added request that the baptizer's head is presented to her on a platter (6:25, 28). As a result, the representation of the relationship between Herodias and her daughter reflects the pattern we observed earlier, whereby a mother works through her daughter to advance her own agenda (6:19, 20).

One further detail that possibly reinforced a sense of immorality associated with this family is the note that the girl danced for Herod in a way that pleased him (6:22). Given what we observed earlier of Plutarch's and Quintilian's criticisms of children being present at banquets, a hearer may have perceived that the dance was sexual in nature and inappropriate for an unmarried girl of an elite family to engage in. This depiction is not explicit in the passage, however. Further, while there is evidence that children danced in both public and domestic settings, these children are generally slaves or freed persons, of which Herodias's daughter is neither.[95] Certainly, the *puella* (maiden) of early imperial love poetry was described in terms of her erotic dance that aroused the desire of the poet, casting the unmarried girl as a mistress and muse, or a courtesan (Ovid, *Am.* 2.4.23–32; Mar-

---

94. Dixon, *Roman Mother*, 226.

95. *IK* 44.200; *CIL* 12.188. Ruth Webb, *Demons and Dancers: Performance in Late Antiquity* (Cambridge: Harvard University Press, 2008), 59–67.

tial, *Epigr.* 14.203.1–2). In Mark 6:22, there are no clear markers, however, to signify that the girl's dance is erotic and that Herod's reaction to the dance is sexual. In contrast to the explicit detail of amatory poetry of the time, there is no description of the girl's dance whatsoever. And the term used to indicate that Herod is pleased by the girl, ἀρέσκω (6:22), does not expressly denote sexual pleasure, unlike the term ἡδονή. Instead, ἀρέσκω could simply connote being agreeable or acceptable to another. Images of elite women dancing at banquets nonetheless feature in the literature of the early empire and were constructed, in the main, as immoral and dangerous (Tac. *Ann.* 11.31.10). Their depictions served the purpose to contrast what was perceived as the ideal Roman woman, thereby critiquing the families to which the women belonged. In this sense, it is possible to see that the unmarried girl of 6:17–29 and her family were understood to be immoral.

There is, however, another perspective to the perception of dancing girls that is found in the funerary data of the early empire. The epitaphs on some stelae of deceased girls provide a different picture from the one we have discovered in the literary material. The funerary inscriptions, commissioned by the parents or patron of a deceased girl, eulogize the abilities and intellect of young girls who excelled in the arts, including music and dance.[96] Some of the features of these inscriptions are useful for our exploration of 6:17–29. First, the dancing girls who are given an epitaph are depicted as unmarried and under the authority of an adult. This status is indicated on epitaphs where the ages of the deceased girls—between eleven and fifteen years—are noted. Many of the dancers are also identified as a *puella*, a young unmarried girl or maiden. Second, the girls are depicted in death as being admired by adoring fathers for their dancing abilities. We find an example of this in the epitaph of freedwoman, Licinia Eucharis, dating to the late republic or early empire:

> Learned woman, cultivated in all the arts. She lived fourteen years. Hey you, with a wandering eye, who look at the house of death, hold your step and scan my epitaph, which the love of my father gave to his daughter, where the remains of her body lie. (*CLE* 55)

Unlike the literature, which associates dancing with the erotic and immoral, the epitaphs suggest that unmarried girls who danced were remembered

---

96. Zoa Alfonso Fernandez, "Docta saltatrix: Body Knowledge, Culture, and Corporeal Discourse in Female Roman Dance," *Phoenix* 69 (2015): 304–33.

in honor. They were publicly memorialized as a beloved daughter and praised for their dancing abilities. It is possible, therefore, that those who encountered the story of Herodias's daughter, immersed in such a material environment, brought a mindset that cast the young girl (κοράσιον) as located within Herod's household and admired by Herod for her dancing prowess. While a hearer may not have necessarily associated the young girl with a courtesan, they would have understood her to be, nonetheless, planted firmly in this unscrupulous family.

We are now at a point where we can draw some comparisons between this episode and the story of Jairus's daughter. It is clear that both episodes deal with depictions of families in which the figure of a daughter is a focus. Each daughter is explicitly identified as living under the authority of parental figures, denoted in each case by the term κοράσιον. Both girls are valued by their parents. The physicality of both daughters is also in the foreground of each passage. Herodias's daughter's capacity to please Herod through dance prompts the king publicly to make an oath to the young girl that is excessive (6:23) and that he must uphold to maintain honor among his guests (6:26). The pledge ultimately leads to death. Conversely, the body of Jairus's daughter, as we have already seen, is associated with a transition from suffering and death to life.

The representations of father-figures in each episode also require explanation. Jairus and Herod, located in familial contexts, are portrayed as eminent public figures who exert authority over others. Jairus's demands that Jesus heal his daughter are met with a hasty response from Jesus, and both men set off for the synagogue leader's house (5:22–24). Herod's commands lead to death (6:27). If we accept the argument that I expounded earlier in this chapter, the depiction of Jesus in 5:35–43 is also that of a father-figure who exerts authority in a reconfigured household. In contrast to Herod, Jesus's commands (and touch) restore life (6:41). Herod exercises authority over people whereas Jesus exercises authority over death itself. The household of Herod, where Jesus is absent, is associated with corruption, immorality, and the death of an innocent man. The figure of Herodias's daughter, unmarried and therefore a symbol of the future aspirations of this household, suggests a family on a trajectory of destruction. The representation of Jairus's daughter, on the other hand, implies a household whose trajectory is oriented to life beyond suffering. The hearer of the Markan narrative could have no misunderstanding as to what constituted the exemplar family—the one in which Jesus was the authority figure.

Finally, in Mark 13 the hearer encounters depictions of the complete destruction of the biological family. Images of familial violence are used to describe the signs of the end times. Children are represented as both victims and perpetrators of fatal, domesticated violence: "Brother will betray brother to death, and a father his child, and children will rise against parents and have them put to death" (13:12). The relationship between the child or offspring and father, πατήρ and τέκνον, will be characterized by betrayal at the instigation of the father. The noun, γονεῖς, is in the plural, so it possibly relates to both mother and father. It is in the masculine plural, however, so it could refer to the fathers of those children who rise up. The relationship between parents and children will nevertheless be marked by fatal violence with the death of parents at the behest of the children.[97]

In 13:17, the maternal imagery of pregnant and nursing bodies conveys the suffering that will occur:

> Woe to those who are pregnant and to those who are nursing infants in those days! Pray that it may not be in winter. For in those days there will be suffering, such as has not been from the beginning of the creation that God created until now, no, and never will be. (Mark 13:17–19)

As we observed in chapter 5, in the writings of Josephus and Philo, the violence enacted upon wives and children and their subsequent suffering was part of the rhetoric of war. One of the ways it functioned was to augment the picture of brutality and suffering experienced by Jews. The context of Mark 13 is the future end time, not the retelling of an event that had occurred in the storyline. Nevertheless, as Peter, James, John, and Andrew question Jesus about the sign of "When all these things are about to be accomplished," images of the devastation of families at their own hands convey a scene of a future disaster (13:4). Pregnant and nursing mothers are especially singled out as victims of these extreme times. These figures, associated with nurturing life, are typically described in terms of suffering and vulnerability. On the other hand, children, usually portrayed as the objects of adults' actions, are represented in this instance as active participants in the destruction of their own families. There is a reversal of the image of children as innocent victims (Josephus, *B.J.* 2.307; 5.512–514;

---

97. Jesus is the only other character who is consigned to death where forms of θάνατος are used: by the chief priests and scribes (10:33) and by "all of them," i.e., chief priests, elders, and scribes (14:64).

7.392–394; *C. Ap.* 2.53; *A.J.* 5.29–30; 9.91; Philo, *Flacc.* 62–64, 68) to their representation as perpetrators of violence against their own kin, an image that possibly conjured up ideas about the comprehensive disordering that would accompany the end times.

Despite the picture of disorder and destruction that is painted in 13:12, imagery related to childbirth appears earlier in 13:8 to provide some momentary reassurance amidst the events of the last days. The image of the pain experienced by a woman in labor, ὠδίν, not only suggested the suffering that was thought to signify the end time.[98] The reference to birth pains may also have communicated ideas about the eventual trajectory of the upheaval. Given the connotations of continuity and stability that were often associated with children, it is conceivable that the use of this image, while presaging the beginning of the last days, also evoked a glimmer of future hope beyond the destruction.[99]

This latter point returns us to the story of Jairus's daughter and the notion of the reconfigured household that, under the authority of Jesus, inaugurated a promise of hope. It is also possible that a hearer who encountered this story understood that the household was one in which Satan, the force of death, was conquered. To consider this idea, first we need to examine two images that appeared on coins in the late republic/early empire. One of these coins, labeled the *restitutio* coin, commonly depicted a male Roman leader raising a conquered female to a standing position.[100] The image of the female personified a Roman city or state. The scene conveyed the idea that the leader had the power to restore or liberate others. The other coin is the *fides* coin. The image on the coin featured a male and female clasping hands to denote a partnership, albeit an unequal one. The larger figure, the male, signified the superior status of Roma and the smaller, female figure was understood as the inferior Italia. The clasping of hands indicated a partnership between the once warring armies while also conveying where power ultimately resided.[101] Another image that often appeared on the *fides* coin, associated with the female,

---

98. The image of birth pains in eschatological writing is common (Marcus, *Mark 8–16*, 877–78).

99. On the apocalyptic or eschatological character of Mark 13:7–8, see Yarbro Collins, *Mark*, 605–6.

100. *RRC*, 510.1; *BMC* 1.359, no. 258–59; *BMC* 2.118 no. 549; *BMC* 186 no. 768. Cody, "Conquerors and Conquered," 103–23.

101. *RRC*, 403.1; *BMC* 2.68.

was the cornucopia representing abundance. No longer the subdued captive of the *supplicatio* coins we noted earlier, in the *fides* coinage the female represented the restored city as a partner who offered prosperity to Rome.

The images on these coins are instructive for considering how some people may have thought about the representation of Jairus's daughter and Jesus. A hearer who was familiar with the imagery on the coins encountered a scene in Mark 5:40-42 whereby the powerful ruler, Jesus, liberated the conquered people, personified in Jairus's daughter. As the powerful liberator, Jesus clasped the hands of the girl, raising her to a standing position (5:41, 42). Mapping the depiction of the restored daughter onto the ideas that were communicated via the *fides* coins, the image of Jairus's daughter connoted ideas about the promise of life that those who were liberated by Jesus brought into the new household.

The use of this imagery raises the question of what, or whom, Jesus conquered in the narrative of Mark's Gospel. Up to this point, I have argued that it is plausible that a hearer in first century CE understood that Jesus conquered suffering and death. Now I would like to expand this idea. In 5:40, the hearer encountered the verb ἐκβάλλω, "to cast out." This verb is associated with casting out demons (1:34, 39; 3:15, 22; 6:13; 7:26; 9:18, 28, 38) and Satan (3:23) throughout the narrative of Mark's Gospel. While not explicit in 5:40, it is possible that those who knew the narrative could hear the resonances that linked the reference to driving out mourners (3:40) with previous and later statements about the expulsion of demons. In this way, it is conceivable that the story of Jairus's daughter contributed to the idea that Jesus's power over death signified his power of Satan. Hearers were familiar with the idea that the new family and household of Jesus was one in which Satan had been forced out and the house plundered (3:19-35). It may be that the hearer in the first century CE perceived the raising of Jairus's daughter as the plundering of the household of Satan and the establishment of a new household promising life.[102]

In sum, the reading of the story of Jairus's daughter that was outlined earlier in the chapter enriches some of the representations of the family that feature in the rest of the narrative. While a hearer may have noted conventional beliefs and attitudes associated with the family throughout the narrative, at the same time they would have also observed a shift in

---

102. Elizabeth E. Shively, "What Type of Resistance? How Apocalyptic Discourse Functions as Social Discourse in Mark's Gospel," *JSNT* 37 (2015): 381-406.

the ideas about who constituted a family for those who identified with Jesus. A person's family of origin was no longer a chief locus of identity and status. Instead, one's identity was shaped by their location within the household of Jesus. As 5:21–24, 35–43; and 3:31–35 explicitly reveal, one of the markers of belonging to this household was physical proximity to Jesus—being inside the house with Jesus, sitting around him, listening to his words. Indeed, a household in which Jesus was absent was a household of death and hopelessness. Moreover, the household of Jesus signified that the household of Satan had been finally destroyed.

6.6.2. A Woman and Children in the Household of Jesus

Having established that the story of Jairus's daughter could have been heard as the reconfiguring of the household with Jesus as the authority figure, and that biological ties no longer determined membership in the family of Jesus, we now consider who else may have been included in the refashioned household. It is beyond the scope of this thesis to provide a comprehensive analysis of this theme. Instead, given our focus on women and female children, we will consider five episodes that illuminate how household membership may have been understood by a first century CE hearer and how these insights can be understood to relate to the story of Jairus's daughter. In line with the Jewish setting of 5:21–24, 35–43, the first three episodes are located in Jewish territory and feature Jesus interacting with children (9:33–37; 10:13–16; 9:14–29). In the fourth episode, the geographical setting moves to gentile territory, with the introduction of the Syrophoenician woman and her child-daughter (7:24–30). The fifth episode shifts away from a focus on children to concern the healing of an ill woman (5:23–35).

In Mark 9:36 and 10:16, the hearer encounters stories about the inclusion of children in the household. In our earlier discussion of representations of the body in Mark's narrative in chapter 2, we noted that in both 9:36 and 10:16 Jesus is depicted as touching children. In both cases, he takes children in his arms and hugs them. In 10:16, the gestures extend to laying hands on the children and blessing them. We also observed that each episode occurred in a house where the children were separated by Jesus from the other adults and repositioned in close proximity to him. In the case of 9:36, this repositioning located them also amid the disciples. We further recognized that the tactile gestures ascribed to Jesus, in tandem with teachings about hospitality (9:37) and to whom the reign of God belongs (10:14), and who may enter it (10:15), possibly identified children within the fold of those associated with Jesus.

Returning to these passages now in light of the examination of 5:21–24, 35–43, we note various overlaps between the story of Jairus's daughter and the depictions of Jesus and children in 9:33–50 and 10:13–16. In each account, the children are referred to in terms of diminutives, possibly connoting terms of endearment and/or the size and life-stage of the child.[103] The setting of each episode is inside, in a house. In each house, Jesus directs the physical interaction with children and the role of parents appears irrelevant. Indeed, in 9:33–50 and 10:13–16 there is no explicit reference to parents whatsoever, unlike 5:21–24, 35–43. Instead, children are positioned by Jesus away from the other adults in the house and in closer proximity to him and the disciples (9:36). While it is impossible to know what a hearer gleaned from these accounts, it remains plausible that in each instance the conventional representation of a family led by a father-figure was now coopted to depict how children and adults related to Jesus. Within this context, the images of children potentially functioned as symbols of continuity and hope in a household now controlled by Jesus and associated with the reign of God.

Of course, a clear difference between the scenes of Mark 9:36 and 10:16 and 5:21–24, 35–43 is the focus on the death and restoration of the child-daughter in the latter passage. The possible import of images of liminal bodies associated with the household of Jesus has become apparent in our study of 5:21–24, 35–43. When we consider the healing of the son possessed by a spirit, we observe overlaps with and divergences from the story of Jairus's daughter. Nonetheless, the episode affirms some of our insights concerning the role of children in the household.[104]

A person who encountered 9:14–29 in the first century CE, having already heard 5:21–24, 35–43, might have observed some differences between both episodes. The setting of the story, while presumably in Jewish territory, is outside (8:27; 9:2). It is a father who advocates on behalf of his son, with his initial request for healing directed at the disciples who are depicted as ineffective (9:18). Perhaps the location was not unusual for

---

103. In 9:36 and 10:13, the term παιδίον is used.

104. For the view that 5:21–24, 35–43 is concerned with maturing to womanhood rather than a focus on childhood, see Moloney, *Mark*, 111. Oppel recognizes the raised daughter as an autonomous figure within the family, about to become a woman (*Heilsam erzählen*, 105).

a first-century hearer given the episode centers on a father and his son, rather than the stereotypical domestic context of women. The boy's condition is identified; he is possessed by a spirit, leaving him unable to speak. The effects of the spirit on his body are graphically described (9:20, 22). The boy appears to be dead, like a corpse, as a result of Jesus's intervention, commanding the spirit to exit the boy (9:26).

Alongside these differences, there are various overlaps with 5:21–24, 35–43. The diminutive παιδίον is heard when describing the relationship between the father and the son.[105] The loyal father is depicted as concerned for the welfare of his beloved boy, resonating with the representation of Jairus as well as other depictions of fathers in the first century CE (e.g., Quintilian, *Inst.* 6.3–14). The father, like Jairus, is also portrayed as powerless in altering the condition of the son. Instead, it is Jesus whose authoritative commands over the forceful spirit enable physical transformation (9:25).

Once the spirit exits the boy, the hearer encounters the now familiar image of a child who appears dead (9:26; 5:35). Indeed, it is the onlookers who make this declaration (9:26; 5:35).[106] Although the story suggests the boy is not dead, a hearer may have recollected the actions of Jesus in 5:41, in the image of Jesus grasping the boy by the hands and lifting him up (9:27). He is pulled "out of the grasp of death."[107] The terms κρατέω and ἐγείρω are heard again, in addition to the image of hands and touch to denote new ties (9:27). At the end of the pericope, the verb ἀνίστημι is also reheard to depict the boy as standing (9:27). When mapped to the story of Jairus's daughter, the story of the restored son may have underscored the image of the household as bridging the gap between death and life.[108] It is a place where even long-term suffering and the power of spirits is abolished. In addition, the implied inclusion of the restored son may have reinforced notions of familial strength and continuity.

---

105. It may not have been clear whether this story dealt with a child or older male. The boy is described as having suffered since childhood, 9:21. This may have reinforced the severity of the disease. On this, and on "epilepsy" as the "child's disease," see Marcus, *Mark 8–16*, 654.

106. On the question of faith in the pericope and possible links between 5:36 and 9:23–24, see Marcus, *Mark 8–16*, 661–64. For another view on the faith of the father, see Moloney, *Gospel of Mark*, 184–85.

107. Marcus, *Mark 8–16*, 664.

108. On links between 9:27, 5:41–42, and Christian resurrection, see Marcus, *Mark 8–16*, 664–65; Moloney, *Gospel of Mark*, 185.

When we shift our analysis to the story of the Syrophoenician woman and her daughter (7:24–30) we can observe a new perspective on what membership of the reconfigured household may have constituted for a gentile woman's daughter who suffered demon possession. I make three observations concerning how a hearer may have understood this story. Each observation is derived from the depiction of characters and activities in domestic settings.

The first domestic setting that a hearer encounters is that of the house where the identity of the gentile woman and her daughter is revealed (οἰκία, 7:24). This is also the place where interaction between Jesus and the woman takes place. Reminiscent of the depictions of Jairus in 5:22–23, the woman is in close physical proximity to Jesus when she advocates for her ill child. Her desperation is conveyed in her gesture of supplication, bowing at the feet of Jesus (προσπίπτω, 7:25). The diminutives put on her lips as she refers to her ill child possibly connote both the girl's status as a child and the affection with which she is held by her mother (θυγάτριον, 7:25; παιδίον, 7:29).

The woman's and child's identity differs significantly from that of Jairus and his daughter, however. While common for a woman to be depicted in a domestic context, the emphasis in describing this woman also falls along gender, religious, and ethnic lines: she is a "woman," a "gentile" of "Syrophonician origin" (7:26). Her role as mother is implied through the designation of the child as her "daughter" (θυγάτηρ, 7:25, 29). Together, the woman and her daughter are both defined by an affiliation with gentile origins and territories.[109] In addition, the woman is depicted as approaching Jesus without any other family members, notably the father of the child. The child is described in terms of her condition. She is possessed by an unclean spirit (7:25–26). Little detail is offered about her other than the life force within her (πνεῦμα, 7:25) is associated with demons. Furthermore, the child is not present in the house with Jesus and her mother, but (presumably) is located in her own home.

The second domestic context is a metaphorical one. The woman's request that Jesus cast out the demon from her daughter is met with rejection (7:26–27). Jesus can be heard to declare that he has come to address the needs of his own people rather than those of the gentiles. He invokes

---

109. On socioeconomic tensions between Galilean Jews and Tyrian gentiles, see Marcus, *Mark 1–8*, 462.

the language of children, τέκνον, to talk about his role to feed his Jewish kin, rather than the woman and her daughter whom he refers to as little dogs (κυνάριον, 7:27).[110] The woman transforms the application of this imagery, however. She shifts the image of simply throwing food to dogs to a domestic context whereby household dogs eat the crumbs that fall from a table.[111] In other words, gentiles are depicted as eating the leftovers in the household that Jesus feeds. The woman's words thereby suggest an expansion of the household to include gentiles even if the positioning at the table is not identical to those of the Jewish members, which Jesus affirms (7:29).

The third setting is that of the woman's and daughter's house. Unlike the story of Jairus's daughter, Jesus never physically interacts with the child. Indeed, she is healed from a distance. The hearer learns that the demon has departed through the authoritative words of Jesus (7:29) and the description that her mother finds her at home lying on her bed with the demon gone (7:30). Akin to 5:21–24, 35–43, however, there is no mention of other siblings, a possible indicator to those familiar with Greco-Roman depictions of family, that the story was concerned with the status and identity of the family, rather than its individual members. This raises the question of what the physical distance between the location of the girl and that of Jesus might have suggested.

In light of 5:21–24, 35–43, it is possible that a hearer understood the restoration of the girl to signify an extension of the paternal role of Jesus. The absence of a father-figure in the depiction of the mother and daughter is possibly addressed through the actions of Jesus.[112] Once inhabited by a life force associated with demons, the child—like Jairus's daughter—has now been transformed by the life force of Jesus. In addition, his authority and power now bridge the gaps—geographical, religious, and ethnic—that separate those wishing to be included in the household he leads.

We now move our focus from children to an adult, to consider the relationship of the story of the bleeding woman (5:25–34) to the raising of Jairus's daughter. This provides us with another perspective on what it

---

110. Children could refer to a collective Israel, e.g., Jub. 2.26–30. On the imagery of dogs, see Alan H. Cadwallader, *Beyond the Word of a Woman: Recovering the Bodies of the Syrophoenician Women* (Adelaide: ATF, 2008).

111. Yarbro Collins, *Mark*, 367.

112. Jesus is the girl's "protector" and "guardian" (Betsworth, *Reign of God Is Such as These*, 133).

may have meant to be a "daughter" in the household of Jesus (5:34). Four observations of 5:25–34 form the focus of our discussion, which I will treat separately while drawing together some connections to 5:21–24, 35–43.

First, it is clear by now that, according to various voices we have considered throughout this study, women were predominantly represented in the context of family in the first century CE. Given this, it is noteworthy that in the story of the bleeding woman familial and domestic life are not explicitly mentioned. The woman is not represented as a mother, wife, sister, or daughter. The common markers that provided a woman with status and identity are absent. Instead, she is depicted as acting unaccompanied, albeit within a crowd.

Second, the woman is portrayed as physically ill and suffering. The hearer is told that for twelve years she had suffered from a blood flow (5:25).[113] For those accustomed to the myriad stories of female suffering, the labeling of her condition as μάστιξ (5:29), a term connoting whips, scourges, and torment, may have signaled pain and despair. The detail that her sickness had been occurring for twelve years may have also suggested to some in a first century CE audience that she was dying. In ancient medicine, the prolonged period and incurability of a disease could indicate its severity and the person's proximity to death.[114] The impression that she was dying is also implied in the note that she was deteriorating, and no longer possessing the finances to fund more treatment by physicians

---

113. As noted in ch. 1, scholars routinely assume that the woman suffers from a form of gynecological bleeding based on a reading of the term ῥύσει αἵματος in Lev 15:24 and 15:33. In the ancient world, the meaning of the term was ambiguous, however. On the term in ancient medical literature, see Annette Weissenrieder, *Images of Illness in the Gospel of Luke: Insights of Ancient Medical Texts*, WUNT 2/164 (Tübingen: Mohr Siebeck, 2003), 241–44; see also, Soranus, *Gyn.* 1.46. For alternative approaches to the woman's sickness, see D'Angelo, "Gender and Power," 83–109. In Matthew's Gospel, see Amy-Jill Levine, "Discharging Responsibility: Matthean Jesus, Biblical Law and Hemorrhaging Woman," in *Feminist Companion to Matthew*, ed. Amy-Jill Levine and Marianne Blickenstaff (Sheffield: Sheffield Academic, 2001), 70–87. In Luke's Gospel, see Weissenrieder, *Images of Illness in the Gospel of Luke*, 227–95. On Greco-Roman notions of bodily fluids and their relationship to ideas of balanced/unbalanced bodies, see Jennifer Schultz, "Doctors, Philosophers, and Christian Fathers on Menstrual Blood," in *Wholly Woman, Holy Blood: A Feminist Critique of Purity and Impurity*, ed. Kristin De Troyer (Harrisburg, PA: Trinity Press International, 2003), 100. See also Candida R. Moss, "The Man with the Flow of Power: Porous Bodies in Mark 5:25–34," *JBL* 129 (2010): 508–11.

114. Weissenrieder, *Images of Illness in the Gospel of Luke*, 253.

(5:26). In addition, she is described as having suffered at the hands of physicians (5:26). The term used to convey her suffering, πάσχω, appears only two other times in the gospel, when Jesus portends his own fate in the predictions of the suffering of the Son of Man (8:31; 9:12). Through the use of this term, her suffering body is possibly mapped to the eventual suffering of Jesus.[115]

Third, while the woman's state is one of illness and suffering at the hands of others, this is only a partial picture. As the story progresses, the woman emerges as a figure that possesses agency and whose body becomes a site of transformation. Not thwarted by the pressing crowd that occupies the scene, nor rendered completely hopeless by her condition, she is depicted as actively seeking healing from Jesus. Taking advantage of her close proximity to Jesus, she comes up behind and touches his cloak (5:27).[116] As she touches his clothing, the source or spring (πηγή) of her flowing blood dries up (ξηραίνω) and she is healed (5:29). Her healing is bodily—her blood flow stops and her suffering is over, which is conveyed to the woman in her own sense of her body (5:29). At the beginning of the account, she desired to be freed of her sickness or preserved from death, denoted by σῴζω (5:28). At the end of the account, the hearer is given two signs that she has been saved. First, the woman's own body tells her she has been healed; she has a felt sense (5:29).[117] Second, Jesus, using the term σῴζω, authoritatively confirms that she has been saved from death (5:34). In addition, using the language of health, ὑγιής, he reinforces what she and the hearer would have already known, she has been healed of her disease (5:34).

As the woman has corporeal knowledge of her healing, so too Jesus demonstrates a capacity for corporeal knowledge of the woman's healing. Jesus comes to know that power has issued forth from his body: "Immediately aware that power had gone forth from him" (5:30). The term used, δύναμις, refers to power, strength, and authority.[118] It is power that the woman takes from Jesus when she touches his clothing. It is a form of

---

115. Wainwright, *Women Healing/Healing Women*, 119–20.
116. As others do in 6:56.
117. Wainwright, *Women Healing/Healing Women*, 120.
118. On the term δύναμις in relation to Aristotle's ideas of the male body, virility, and procreation, see Emanuela Bianchi, "Aristotelian *Dunamis* and Sexual Difference: An Analysis of *Adunamia* and *Dunamis meta Logou* in *Metaphysics* Theta," *Philosophy Today* Supplement (2007): 89–97.

power that transforms the state of her prolonged bleeding body to a state of healing and peace (εἰρήνη, 5:34). With such power, Jesus is depicted as possessing an authority to free bodies in extreme states of sickness that cause suffering. While not explicitly returning the dead to life, as in the case of 5:41-42, Jesus is presented nonetheless in 5:24b-34 as one who had the power to restore life in those who were fading.

Fourth, once the healed woman makes herself known to Jesus, he identifies her as "daughter" (5:34). The depiction of the woman as suffering from illness, especially in its corporeal detail, and then being restored resonates strongly with the general portraiture of ill people in the gospel. The representation of the woman's plight differs, however, from that of Jairus's daughter. Those who engaged with the story of the woman encountered her suffering body, her corporeal agency, and her restoration to health and peace. In the case of Jairus's daughter, the hearer is not made aware of the cause and symptoms of the child's condition. Instead, what unfolds is the girls' transition from death to life and the concomitant evolution of the reconfigured household. Yet, this latter dimension to the story of Jairus's daughter may heighten the hearer's awareness of another label that Jesus applies to the woman who is healed: θυγάτηρ, "daughter" (5:34). Jesus takes up the language of family to refer directly to the woman once she is healed. As in the case of Jairus and his family, the woman with faith in Jesus (5:34), and located in close proximity to him (5:27-28), may be understood to be transferred by Jesus into a familial network in which he is the paternal figure.[119] The absence of a domestic context at the beginning of the account is now addressed as the woman is brought into the familial fold of Jesus.[120]

---

119. The label *daughter* is explained by some scholars who focus on the Markan sandwich structure on the basis that the woman observes the will of God (Mark 3:35; Miller, *Women*, 60-61). Betsworth notes a social basis: "*God's* family ... [of] those on the margins," of which God is the authority figure, the paterfamilias, and Jesus functions as the woman's guardian (Betsworth, *Reign of God Is Such as These*, 103-7, 115). Moloney identifies Mark 3:7-6:6a as "Jesus and his New Family." The woman is brought into "a chosen people of God." There is no exploration of the woman being brought into the household or family of Jesus as it relates to the account of Jairus's daughter (Moloney, *Mark*, 108; nor in Donahue and Harrington, *Mark*, 176; Marcus, *Mark 1-8*, 360, 69).

120. According to Kahl, the bleeding woman is the first daughter of the family of God in which old family ties no longer count. The woman is a marginalized charac-

The story of Jairus's daughter—with its picture of the household being led by the authoritative figure of Jesus—potentially provides another context by which the hearer may have understood the restoration of the woman. Read with notions of the reconfigured household in mind, the woman's story emerges as another facet of the symbolization of family. The account can be understood to concern a woman, whose faith enabled her body to be transformed from a site of constant blood and suffering to a site of peace and health, taking her from an apparently solitary existence of despair into a familial relationship with Jesus. As a consequence of her transformation, the woman is given a place in the household in which Jesus is the source of life and authority.[121] Her inclusion suggests a bridge between suffering, peace, and health that is enabled through physical engagement with the power of Jesus. This resonates with the encompassing story of Jairus's daughter where Jesus's body is the bridge between life and death in the new household. Taken together, the specific inclusion of women and children in the newly formed family could communicate its hopes for continuity.

Before drawing the discussion to a close, I wish to digress briefly from the topic at hand in order to make a comment concerning the structure of Mark 5:21–43. The focus we have taken with the raising of Jairus's daughter also opens up new possibilities to approaching the structure of the Markan sandwich. At one level, both stories in 5:21–43 resonate respectively with slightly different themes that are articulated more broadly in the gospel. The story of Jairus's daughter interacts with other iterations of the theme of family and household in the gospel. The story of the bleeding woman can be understood to have broader links with those episodes that depict the ill and suffering. In this way, the two accounts that form the sandwich can each be seen to have their own particular relationship to the broader narrative. Indeed, an overemphasis on the analysis of the sandwich technique may hinder how the reader today notices the resonances of both stories within the wider narrative. Certainly, it appears that a comprehensive exploration of the family/household dimension of the story of Jairus's

---

ter, a "lost daughter of Israel," and her designation as daughter brings her into a new family, paving the way for the restoration of Jairus's daughter. Both females become sisters, not rivals ("Jairus und die verlorenen Töchter Israels," 69, 71, 75, 76).

121. Contra Poetker, who argues that there are no changes to family relations and household structures in any Markan healings (*You Are My Mother, My Brothers, and My Sisters*, 164–66).

daughter has been absent in current treatments of the intercalation where the analysis of the story of the bleeding woman is the focal point.

On another level, our examination has revealed that what may be regarded as the so-called framing story, the account of Jairus's daughter, can function as an interpretive lens to the story that it frames. Or, put differently, 5:21–24, 35–43 can be seen to "wrap around" the story of the bleeding woman.[122] This approach identifies the three layers that are commonly attributed to the sandwich technique: two outer layers and an inner layer. Our study suggests that it is plausible to view the outer layers as enfolding the inner layer.[123] In so doing, the outer layers confer on the inner layer an additional significance that it alone cannot convey.

This interpretation of the sandwich technique differs from that whereby a complete story is understood to be inserted into another story, with the focus on the insertion or interruption.[124] As noted in chapter 2, this approach is prevalent in studies of Mark 5:21–43. It is typified by Edwards who argues that the inserted story "is the standard by which the flanking material is measured, the key to the interpretation of the whole."[125] In the examination of the story of Jairus's daughter in this study, we have found that the scope for understanding the sandwich technique has widened to include another approach. This approach reveals that there is more to be discovered when both episodes are also viewed through the lens of the framing story.

6.7. Summary

Reading from the vantage point of a first century CE hearer opens up new insights into the story of Jairus's daughter. When read with an awareness of the body, and in light of the Jewish and Greco-Roman voices of Mark's age, the story no longer remains secondary to what is often regarded as the main game, the story of the bleeding woman in 5:25–34. Instead, the

---

122. Scott G. Brown, "On the Composition History of the Longer ("Secret") Gospel of Mark," *JBL* 122 (2003): 104 n. 44. Scott suggests that this "wrapping around" approach to an intercalation, while generally unusual, may be plausible and applicable to Mark 11:12–25. See also Telford, *Barren Temple*, 40–49.

123. In his treatment of 3:20–35, Elliott suggests a similar approach ("Household/Family," 49).

124. Brown, "Mark 11:1–12:12," 78. See also John R. Donahue, *Are You the Christ? The Trial Narrative in the Gospel of Mark*, SBLDS 10 (Missoula, MT: Society of Biblical Literature, 1973), 42.

125. Edwards, "Markan Sandwiches," 216.

account of Jairus's daughter conveys specific ideas about Jesus and those who identified themselves with him. The story can be seen to take its place within the spectrum of Markan depictions of the family, particularly resonating with those portraits in which the biological family appears subordinate to (or taken to its extreme, is replaced by) a domestic network that centers on the authoritative figure of Jesus. Yet, the story also brings its own particular perspective to this discourse on family in its elucidation of the role of Jesus as the authority figure and source of life in the household. Indeed, the power of Jesus to restore life in the household is located in his very own body, and restoration occurs when the child's body interacts with his. The picture of the reconfigured household with Jesus as its life-source becomes a powerful optic to view the healing of the bleeding woman. She is not only healed of her bloody suffering, she is also restored *to* the household that Jesus leads, joining the ranks of the disciples, and the girl and her parents.

The familial structure that Jesus establishes in Jairus's daughter's story, while led by Jesus, nevertheless appears to retain some of the stereotypical characteristics of families and households that populated the literary and material landscapes of the first century CE. A male authority figure remains the head of the house and those inside the house operate within the dominion of the leader. Jesus can be understood to operate in a way that builds on, rather than overturns, conventional family power dynamics. On the one hand, the portrait of the young daughter and child resonates with those that are generally featured in the broader milieu. She is recognized as a constituent part of the household structure, co-opted, along with her father and mother and the three disciples, to mediate ideas about the identity and status of the household of Jesus.

On the other hand, in a narrative in which the depictions of bodies function as vehicles for conveying meaning, the figure of Jairus's daughter can be seen to exercise great agency. Our focus on the representation of her body opens up the possibility that in their most liminal states, bodies are potentially sites of life and hope. Ultimately, the death of the daughter-child appears neither associated with desperation and despair nor lost aspirations. Grief and death, while part of the course, do not appear final in Mark 5:21–24, 35–43. Instead, the story of the girl suggests that they form part of the trajectory of inaugurating a new household at whose center is Jesus. This is a household that can be understood to include men, women, and children, and gentiles and Jews. It encompasses geographical territories. It transforms bodily limitations. Interaction with Jesus body—a body which itself will realize the transition from death to being raised in Mark 16:1–8—bridges the chasm between grief, death, and life, a key feature of the household in 5:21–24, 35–43 according to our reading. Not only is illness and suffering transformed but the person in the most liminal, hopeless of states, death, comes to embody the Markan trajectory of hope.

7
Conclusions

This book sets forth a reading of the story of Jairus's daughter that takes the image of a dying, dead, and restored little daughter as its focus. It explains the possible import of this image for a person who encountered Mark's account in the first century CE. More specifically, it addresses the question of the significance of depictions of the body in the story of the raising of Jairus's daughter and how a hearer in the first century CE might have constructed meaning about this passage given the cultural milieu they inhabited.

In posing these questions, the approach to Mark 5:21–24, 35–43 that is taken departs from the ways in which the story of Jairus's daughter is commonly treated. As I note in chapter 1, a considerable deposit of the scholarship on Mark 5:21–24, 35–43 examines this story in the context of the account of the healing of the bleeding woman, 5:23–34. There is a consensus that together both episodes exemplify the so-called Markan sandwich technique. Across a range of methodologies and approaches, the account of Jairus's daughter is read primarily in light of this technique. What is apparent when the story of Jairus's daughter is read within the frame of the sandwich technique are two patterns. One of these patterns concerns the parallels that are drawn between the stories of Jairus's daughter and the bleeding woman. Scholars frequently identify numerous parallels between both episodes, which invariably discuss motifs including gender and sexuality, menstruation, (in)fertility, and disease; issues concerning the possible status of being ritually impure; as well as assertions concerning Jesus's power over death.

A second pattern in the reading of the story of Jairus's story in light of the sandwich technique is the identification of contrasts between both episodes. Scholars regularly draw contrasts between the characterizations of the bleeding woman and the synagogue leader and his daughter. In so doing, the story of the woman frequently dominates the analysis, becoming the hermeneutical key for understanding the whole of 5:21–43. This approach often produces a dualistic understanding of the relationship between both episodes, with the bleeding woman generally emerging in analyses as the superior character to Jairus and the girl. In a Markan reversal of social conventions, the unnamed, poor, outcast woman is deemed a role model for the named synagogue leader who represents the Jewish establishment and his precious daughter. As a consequence of this approach, the interpretation of the account of Jairus's daughter is frequently controlled and limited by the analysis of the bleeding woman's account.

Yet not all insights are classified into sets of parallels and contrasts. Some scholars, while still using the sandwich technique as the general framing structure for examining 5:21–24, 35–43, identify themes that are unique to the story of Jairus's daughter, rather than attempting to correlate every detail of the passage with that of the account about the bleeding woman. Some commentators, for example, interpret Jairus as a positive role model of Judaism and the exemplification of a devoted parent, rather than a privileged member of the synagogue whose faith is lacking in comparison to that of the woman's. Others discuss the significance of the girl being raised from the dead, deliberating over whether or not she is dead or sleeping, and resuscitated or resurrected. The insights that arise as a result of addressing these questions are not necessarily contingent on a reading of the story of the bleeding woman. Indeed, the ongoing discussion across commentaries and studies concerning the significance of the dying-deceased-restored girl suggest that new approaches to examining the story can be explored in order to consider further the import of the story.

While the dominant paradigm for reading 5:21–24, 35–43 is through the lens of the sandwich technique, there are other ways to examine the story. Some scholars analyze the account without considering its relationship to the story of the bleeding woman at all. Instead, they use various frames of reference to consider the passage. Studies exist that examine the account within the context of the overall narrative of the gospel and in relation to the articulation of themes within the broader biblical tradition. The topics of discussion range widely from the exploration of ideas related to sleeping, death, and resurrection to recent studies concerning the portrayals of daughters, children, and families in Mark and the biblical tradition generally.

In line with these shifts in the examination of 5:21–24, 35–43, this study analyzes the account of Jairus's daughter using new frames of reference. In so doing, the aim of the study is not to negate the role of the Markan sandwich technique for Markan studies. Instead, I argue that we need to open up further ways of considering the story of Jairus's daughter, rather than limiting our analyses to the current parameters that generally dominate how the passage is read. To this end, I present an approach that understands the significance of the story of Jairus's daughter without the interpretation of 5:25–34 controlling how the story of Jairus's daughter is read. In this approach, I take seriously the role and function of the body in the narrative. While some scholars have examined 5:21–24, 35–43 according to broad Markan or biblical themes, none has specifically considered the significance of depictions of the body throughout the gospel and how the account of the dying, deceased, and restored little daughter contributes to this understanding. This study fills that lacuna.

Fundamental to this study is my observation that the body is an important element in the Gospel of Mark. In chapter 3, I note how the body is depicted throughout the narrative, arriving at the conclusion that representations of the body can be understood to function as mediators of meaning throughout the gospel. This conclusion is based on my assessment of representations of the body in the narrative. I investigate the types of bodies that are represented, how those bodies are described, which actions bodies perform and what actions are enacted on bodies.

There are a number of ways in which representations of the body play a role in the narrative of the gospel. The insights of this investigation reveal that those who are ill, which encompasses the sick, the disfigured, and the impaired, form a dominant group. Their conditions are described in corporeal terms, with some characters painted in explicit detail as pictures of physical suffering. While prominent, ill bodies are not desirable in the narrative and cures are constantly sought.

In the desire for curing ill bodies, the body is portrayed as a site of transformation. Bodies are sites in which sickness and suffering are healed and life is preserved. The transformation of these bodies usually occurs through physical interaction—generally touch or speech—between the body of Jesus and those who are sick or have malfunctioning bodies. The alterations that occur as a result of a person's engagement with Jesus have a strong corporeal dimension; the changes are physically perceptible. The stories of transformation suggest that the preferred state is a healthy, living body, without impairment or disfigurement. Interaction with Jesus's body is the source of this change.

Another type of body that dominates the narrative is that characterized by violence, suffering, and death. The gospel contains images of people either meting out physical violence or those whose bodies are marked by violence. Graphic descriptions of violated bodies and the treatment of dead bodies potentially bring ideas concerning suffering, violence, and death up close to a hearer in first century CE. Notable among these depictions is the representation of the passion and death of Jesus. The final events leading up to Jesus's death are portrayed in a series of graphically narrated violent actions that culminate in a death that is described in terms of physicality and pain. The narration of the burial of Jesus's dead body draws on sensory acts that involve sight, movement, touch, and smell. Paradoxically, given the ubiquity of bodies throughout the entire narrative, the gospel draws to a close with the reference to the absent body of Jesus. The body of Jesus, a focal point in the retelling of his passion, death, and burial, is depicted as no longer located in the place where it ought to have been—the tomb. Framed by references to being raised and seen, the mention of the absence of Jesus's corpse possibly connotes a view that Jesus continues to exist beyond violence, pain, and death, albeit uncertain in terms of his physicality (16:7).

Expressions of emotion also have a corporeal dimension in the narrative. Feelings of compassion, fear, courage, and grief are described throughout the narrative in terms of bodily acts or sensations. Emotions function to interpret the actions committed by and upon the body in the unfolding narrative. Experiences of betrayal, suffering, violence, and death are interpreted through expressions of fear and grief. The lost, hungry, and diseased encounter a portrait of Jesus as one physically moved by these states who acts to alter them. To take responsibility for the dead body of Jesus and afford it honor is lauded as an embodiment of courage.

When we examine bodies in terms of what they do in the narrative, we notice that many characters are depicted in terms of sensory functions. Activities related to speech, hearing, sight, touch, and movement feature predominantly, while references to the senses of taste and smell are rare (9:1; 14:4; 16:1). Acts related to orality dominate the gospel, and generally take the form of commands, questions, and requests. The use of commands often functions to portray a character's power. Jesus's commands, for example, accentuate his power over the destructive forces of nature, unclean spirits and illness, and even over death itself.

The preoccupation with speech and voice give rise to an emphasis on the aurality of those who engage with Jesus. This is expressed in the references to ears and hearing. The faculty of hearing is primarily concerned with the process of perception and is constructed in such a way so as to identify those who understand Jesus and those who do not. Similarly, references to eyes and sight are also related to acts of perception. Allusions to seeing Jesus often suggest that a character not only recognizes Jesus physically, but also perceives Jesus's ability to act in a particular way that is connected to ideas about Jesus's identity.

Another significant sensory act that plays a part is the gesture of touch. In addition to bodily interaction as a means of altering sick and malfunctioning bodies, some gestures involving touch embody Jesus's teachings on who is included in the reign of God. A case in point is Jesus's tactile approach to children. Acts of taking children up in his arms, depicted in tandem with teachings on hospitality and the reign of God, identify children within the fold of those associated with Jesus.

Given my view that depictions of the body in the gospel are vehicles for communicating or enhancing ideas, the study takes the body of Jairus's daughter—the body of a dying, deceased, and restored female—as its focus. The observations I have made about the role and function of the body in the narrative up to this point have been mine. As such, they ask questions as to what a person in the first century CE may have noticed when they encountered the story of Jairus's daughter. With this in mind, in chapters 3–6 the study shifts from my reflections as a twenty-first century reader to consider how a person in the first century CE may have heard the story, and what meaning they may have attached to representations of the body. I examine the depictions of women and female children that were present in the world of the first century CE to gain insight into the ideas and mindsets that would have influenced a person's encounter with the story. In other words, I examine the intersections between the portrait of Jairus's daughter and the ideas and images concerning women and children that were part of the world in which hearers of the story in the first century CE lived.

Establishing a context in which to analyze the representations of women and children in the world of a hearer of Mark's story in the first century CE is a vexed issue. In chapter 3, I consider the various starting points for examining the images and ideas that influence a person's encounter with the gospel. One of these is based on locating the provenance of Mark. While much has been written on the topic of Markan provenance, to date there is no scholarly consensus or conclusive evidence for one specific location. Bearing this uncertainty in mind, I approach the context of a hearer based on what *is known* about Mark: It is a story that is both set and composed in the first century CE; it is set geographically in the Jewish homeland of the first century CE; it is a narrative that reaches beyond Judaism, possessing traces of Greco-Roman culture. In other words, the narrative of Mark bears the imprints of an affiliation with Judaism and a location in Greco-Roman culture in the first century CE.

In light of these three interrelated contextual certainties, this study takes seriously the Jewish and Greco-Roman sources containing references to women and children in the first century CE that are currently available. Using these sources, I undertake a historical investigation of the temporal context of a hearer of Mark's account. By temporal context, I mean the rich fabric of texts, customs, and practices that constituted the world of hearers in the first century CE. The attention given to a range of voices across the landscape of the time provides glimpses of how some people talked about the place of women and female children, and the ways in which they constructed their bodies. The language and imagery that are examined are drawn from both written and visual sources. These reveal some of the beliefs and attitudes that would have been brought to bear on the thinking of a person who encountered the story of Jairus's daughter in the first century CE.

In using the term *hearer/hearers,* I recognize that various people may have encountered the Gospel of Mark, hailing from different circumstances, yet all existing within a Greco-Roman setting. It is plausible that some who engaged with the story of Jairus's daughter may have had connections to Judaism. Others would have been gentiles, participants in Greco-Roman society and culture, who perhaps possessed no or negligible knowledge of Jewish thought and practice. All would have been hellenized in particular ways by virtue of the Greco-Roman world they inhabited. The term hearer on the one hand acknowledges this shared setting while, on the other hand, recognizes the diverse subcultures and societies that were constituent of the setting and with which groups and individuals would have had affiliations.

To gain insight into the images and language of Greco-Roman culture, in chapter 4 I focus specifically on the representations of women and female children that were present in the early Roman Empire, including those of dying and deceased females. I glean these representations from a range of extant sources that reveal information about some of the ideas and mindsets concerning females in the first century CE. The written sources encompass works by Cicero, Tacitus, Juvenal, Pliny the Younger, Plutarch,

Quintilian, Suetonius, and Chariton. The material sources are drawn from inscriptions and reliefs on honorary and funerary monuments, as well as coins. These sources reveal a first-century world in which images of the family were highly visible in the public domain. The conjugal family is a common feature in depictions of the family, with the triad of father-mother-child (either a son or daughter) appearing as emblematic of family life. Images of family members physically interacting through the touch of hands are understood to signify familial bonds. In the case of the Roman imperial family, physical interaction between children and adults is understood to communicate ideas about the future stability and continuity of the family and the empire. Images of children prove important elements in the representations of families in the early empire. I argue that they function as symbols of hope, mediating ideas about a family's status and their aspirations for the future.

Infant and child mortality are also common experiences in the first century CE. In both written and visual sources, the deaths of children are mourned. The deaths of some daughters of wealthy or eminent families are noted in written sources, or memorialized on epitaphs and reliefs on funerary monuments that populate the public landscape. In these representations, daughters are often depicted as being held in great affection in death by their parents. The memorials and written accounts of daughter's deaths voice the grief of family members and friends over the loss of a beloved daughter, but they can also be understood to convey the aspirations that are lost in the death of a female child. The qualities that some authors associate with idealized Roman women, for example, are used in some cases to describe the attributes of the female child who has died, thus forgoing any future development of their potential. It is not uncommon to note the age at which a daughter dies. The death of the twelve-year-old Minicia Marcellae, for instance, is recorded in an inscription. Pliny also notes her death (as not yet fourteen years old), reinforcing her status as unmarried and chaste. In so doing, he grieves her lost opportunity for marriage and childbearing, female capacities that are highly valued in the data we examine. Marriage to a reputable man and bearing children could contribute to the stability and continuity of the family and the empire.

The depictions of women and female children in sources within late Second Temple Judaism provide further insights into some of the ideas that were part of the milieu of a hearer of Mark's narrative in the first century CE. The analysis of these images is the focus of chapter 5. The sources I examine comprise selected narratives from the writings of Philo and

Josephus as well as Liber Antiquitatum Biblicarum and the book of Jubilees. While composed in a Greco-Roman world, these sources are derived from authors who adhered to a Jewish religious affiliation. The material sources are drawn from inscriptional data from Jewish burial sites in Jerusalem and Jericho in the first centuries BCE and CE. Upon examination of these sources, I argue that the depictions of women's and girls' bodies function to mediate ideas concerning the continuation of Jewish familial lineage and life. At the same time, the myriad representations of the suffering, violation, and death of Jewish women and children are understood to function as vehicles for communicating the authors' assessments of the actions undertaken by others.

In the written and material sources I examine, the family is depicted as a significant social unit in late Second Temple Judaism. In death, familial bonds are memorialized, with evidence of children and adults being buried together in family tombs in Jerusalem and Jericho in the first century CE. In the written sources, marriage is considered fundamentally important. Its purpose is primarily to generate children who guarantee the continuity of the family name, lineage, and property, as well as ensuring the stability and future of the people of Israel. Fathers are depicted as holding prime place of importance in the family, which includes asserting authority and control over their daughters as a means of protecting them. Women are portrayed, in the main, in the context of the family, as wives and mothers. The written sources regularly comment on their (in)fertility and their principal role in conceiving and bearing children. Women's capacity for bearing children is viewed as instrumental to the ongoing existence of Israel. The often-applied label for children, "fruit of the womb," exemplifies the generative role that women's bodies are expected to play for those who compose texts in late Second Temple times.

Unmarried females also play a role in the familial constructs of late Second Temple Judaism. They are regularly labeled as παρθένος ("virgin") or θυγάτηρ ("daughter, descendent, unmarried female"), associating them with expressions of family life. On funerary epitaphs, unmarried daughters (or daughters not named in relation to husbands), are identified with their father via a patronym. Writers often comment on the importance of a daughter's body being chaste before she marries. Along these lines, Philo makes references to domestic architecture in secluding virgin daughters in order to keep them chaste. While not necessarily reflecting the realia of daily living, Philo's rhetoric nonetheless suggests the importance he places on the bodily state of the unmarried female and its future function in preserving Jewish identity—a sentiment shared broadly within the sources I consult.

Chapter 6 also illustrates how depictions of women's and children's bodies are used to communicate ideas about Jewish identity and relations with non-Jews. Women are painted as the victims of sexual and domesticated violence, their stories often characterized by the use of graphic detail. As a cluster, "women and children" are frequently described as people who suffer and die, often as a result of violence in warfare. Representations of the violence enacted on women's and children's bodies and the suffering they voice, serve various functions. They work rhetorically to augment the scale of suffering experienced by Jews. They are a means of casting judgment on those who inflict violence, or of passing judgment on the consequences of activities carried out by fellow Jews. The descriptions of suffering and violence endured by women and children give voice to the grief of the community in response to the violent acts enacted on all Jews. The representations of suffering and corporeal violation function to communicate writers' attitudes to the actions of Jews and non-Jews alike.

Stories of unmarried daughters are also characterized by physical violence. The reworking of the story of Jephthah's daughter in Liber Antiquitatum Biblicarum, for instance, illustrates how the sacrifice of a much-loved daughter could serve as a symbol of an efficacious death. The narration of the rape of the unmarried, twelve-year-old Dinah by the Shechemite in Jubilees is seen to serve the ideological purposes of the author. The violation of the twelve-year-old's chaste body is depicted as representing a threat to the future purity of the family's lineage in terms of an exclusive association with Israel. In this way, the story functions to underscore the author's own preference for endogamous marriages and the antithetical stance toward engagement with non-Jews.

Finally, two further representations of death are specifically noted among the biblical stories reworked by authors in Second Temple times. The first of these reveals that the detailed story of the seeming death and restoration of a child through divine intervention was still in circulation in the first century CE (Josephus, *A.J.* 8.325–327). The second reference is related to the notion of sleep. The image of being asleep is used metaphorically in the late Second Temple era to signify the state of death. To be described in death as sleeping suggests a figure was to be remembered in a favorable light. It could also connote the possibility of being raised up after a period of death.

Having explored the language and imagery of women's and children's bodies that forms the experience of a person in the first century CE, in chapter 6 I examine how these inform an encounter with the story of Jairus's daughter. I argue that the focus on the body of the dying, deceased, and restored female child leads to observations about the household and family. It opens up further possibilities for understanding how the notion of the household and family in the gospel may have been heard in the first century CE. While I do not assume a direct line between the aspects of the first century CE I have observed and that which a hearer of Mark might have brought to the text, there is overlap nonetheless between many features of the episode and the depictions of daughters that populate the first-century milieu of Mark. These overlaps include: the image of a beloved dying and deceased daughter of an eminent man, identified by the use of a patronym; her death occurring in a familial context, denoted not only by her location in the house but also in the use of the conventional image of the familial triad of father-mother-child; the daughter dying at home with her death noted outside, publicly by people from the household and then mourned at the house. At first blush, the story could be understood to connote ideas concerning the loss of hope, generativity, and sense of future embodied in a female child's death. The story clearly diverges from this motif, however, in the girl's restoration to life. The body that symbolizes a loss of hope is restored to a living child-daughter's body. When read within the temporal context of a hearer of Mark, the story of the girl's death is instrumental in communicating a narrative of life and future hopes.

But the account is also concerned with the situation *to which* the child is restored. I argue that the story is focused on the family and household into which Jairus's daughter is raised. Furthermore, I contend that the story would have been heard in this way in the first century CE. From the moment people from the household state publicly that Jairus's daughter has died, Jesus assumes an authoritative and creative role in the episode. Indeed, once Jairus and Jesus arrive at the synagogue leader's house, Jesus appropriates for himself the authority of the household. This authority is observed in three ways. First, upon entering the house, Jesus is the only figure who speaks, and his speech acts are commands or requests. Second, once inside the house, Jesus is the sole figure who decides who stays in the house and who is expelled, not Jairus—the father of the household and a man of social standing—as convention might have dictated. Jesus asserts the authority to eject the mourners from the household and to bring three adult males—presumably unknown to the girl—into the chamber of the house where the young female lies. Indeed, in 5:40 he even assumes the power to take the parents of the girl into their own house where their own daughter lies dead. Third, while the fruit of the seed of the father has died, it is through interaction with Jesus's body that the girl is restored to life. Jesus's body is thus conceived as the source of life in the household.

In this image of the reconfigured household, a hearer encounters the image of a household that both overlaps with and diverges from some of the conventional images of the time. While the conjugal family stays intact in the episode, it is now Jesus—not the traditional father-figure—who is the head of the household. Moreover, while some members of the former household are expelled, other distinct figures (Peter, James, and John) are now incorporated at Jesus's command, suggesting that biological ties do not determine membership in Mark's refashioned structure. I affirm that this reworking of the household image takes its place within the spectrum of Markan representations of children, the family, and the household, particularly as they pertain to discipleship. It addresses in part questions concerning what constitutes family and household for those who identify with Jesus's authority.

The study demonstrates the centrality of the image of the daughter's body in this story. In so doing, it confirms the fruitfulness of shifting the vantage point from which the passage is read. For someone encountering this episode in the first century CE, notions of hope, generativity, and continuity, which were routinely projected onto females' bodies, are reworked to tell a story of hope among those who identify with Jesus and are well acquainted with death. One of the consequences of reading the passage in view of the Markan sandwich is that some scholars focus on the maturation of the girl as a result of her restoration. My interpretation differs from those readings that place more of an emphasis on womanhood rather than on the daughter's status as a child. Instead, I affirm that the emphasis on her as a twelve-year-old child and daughter is wholly significant. The presence of the twelve-year-old child in the reconfigured household could be heard to signify that the household is one of future life and promise. This usage of the image of a child, in turn, resonates with other instances whereby children can be seen as integral to conceptualizations of the reign of God. In this story, the reference to the child not only suggests that children are included in the βασιλεία like their adult counterparts, in addition, the image of the child-daughter is the key to advancing beliefs about future hope and continuity for those who currently know sorrow, loss, and death in the household of Jesus. Such a conclusion validates the importance of being open to new perspectives for reading the account of Jairus's daughter.

In a narrative where the body functions as a mediator of meaning, I demonstrate that the body of Jairus's daughter has agency. Like the representations of many women and children that were part of the world of the first century CE, this study reveals how the little daughter's image influences questions about what defined families and households among those who identified with Jesus and possibly lived with experiences of suffering, illness, violence, and death. It is through her representation that a hearer is aware that bodies in their most liminal states are sites of life and signs of future hope. Through the account of Jairus's daughter, a hearer traces a trajectory from loss and grief to hope that is associated with the household of Jesus. Indeed, through the imagery of the girl's death and restoration it is possible to see the household as an entity inclusive of not only women and children, but one in which the chasm between life and death is bridged. This is a fundamental characteristic of the household that becomes apparent only through this episode. Further, it is through engagement with the body of Jesus—who is depicted as overcoming the breach of death himself in 16:6—that this bridging of death and life becomes possible, eliciting the same response as 16:8, ἔκστασις, the transference to a new reality. In this way, the household of the child-daughter that is depicted in 5:21–24, 35–43 can be mapped to the new reality of the death and raising of Jesus.

It is not possible to know with certainty what a hearer contemplated when they encountered the story of the child-daughter. This study is significant, however, because I affirm that the story of Jairus's daughter makes its own contribution to the broader motifs encountered in the gospel concerning notions of the body, of children, the family and household, of loss, death, restoration, and hope. The novel approach I have taken has offered another way to frame the discussion of the story. The image of Jairus's daughter has been able to rise again and to stand on her own two feet. Indeed, the significance of the role and function of the female child in the account is such that it calls into question the long-established titling of the story, "the raising of Jairus's daughter." In my view, this designation can be understood to dismiss the import of the child in the story and suggest a disposition among interpreters to accentuate the synagogue leader/father at the expense of his daughter. A title that better bespeaks the significant role of this child-daughter now warrants further consideration (if, indeed, a title ought to be used at all).

The study is significant in other ways. First, it examines the contribution that the story of Jairus's daughter makes to the role and function the body plays throughout the Gospel of Mark. This is an aspect of the story and the gospel that has received little attention. Given the current interest in the image of the body in Mark, and the approaches and methodologies that scholars apply are varied, the fruits of this study suggest further investigation into the depictions of the body in literary and material sources in the first century CE might enrich the work concerning conceptualizations of the body in Mark. More specifically, the insights gained from examining the story of Jairus's daughter suggest that a reading of the story of the bleeding woman along similar lines may also prove fruitful. Reading the story in dialogue with the depictions of women's bodies in the first century CE might generate new readings of this well-mined account, and provide new insights into its relationship to the little girl's story and the rest of the Markan narrative.

Second, the study demonstrates how a focus on the body leads to further insight into children and families. It expands the understanding that the gospel would have been heard as addressing issues of loss, death, and grief. The study reveals that these concerns had a physical dimension, that children and families could be associated with such issues, and that experiences related to loss, death, and grief were not the end point but a locus for hope.

Third, the study has demonstrated the importance of expanding the vista from which Mark 5:21–24, 35–43 is read today. As already observed, widening the interpretive lens beyond the Markan sandwich, the most common way the account is treated, has allowed us to discover some distinctive features of the household and family that a person in first century CE would have heard. In addition, resisting the temptation to consider the story through the optic of a theory of Markan provenance with its predetermined assumptions has enabled an examination of the temporal context of Mark. This focus has permitted a new data set to be brought into dialogue with Mark's story. The data have been particularly instructive for contemporary commentary on Mark 5:21–24, 35–43. When attention is given specifically to the depictions of women and female children in first century CE, notions of ancient Jewish ritual purity, a fundamental feature of 5:21–43 for many scholars, are not emphasized. While applying a theory of Markan provenance produces rich hermeneutical fruit, it may now be appropriate to explore further the possibilities for widening the explanatory palette of other episodes in Mark's narrative in light of its temporal context.

Admittedly, a limitation of the study is that given the abundance of sources from late Second Temple Judaism, only a selection could be analyzed. In addition, the Greco-Roman materials were predominantly affiliated with Rome due to their abundance and accessibility today. Future readings of Mark 5:21–24, 35–43 may be enriched by increasing the data sets that are brought into dialogue.[1]

Finally, the study has significance beyond an academic study of the past. While I proffer a reading of Mark 5:21–24, 35–43 based on an analysis of the past, that analysis is mine. As a historian, I have carefully attended to the words and images of the first century CE and brought them into dialogue with Mark 5:21–24, 35–43. The reading of Jairus's daughter that I consequently tender, while based on a close examination of primary sources, is also mine. The interpretation that is submitted is thus located in both the past and the present. As the book draws to a close, I wish to conclude therefore by identifying some areas that in my view are important for further reflection. They hold in mutual tension the dimensions of the past, the present, as well as the future.

Guided by the approach I have taken in this study, I am aware that the structure that Jesus establishes in the account retains some of the stereotypical characteristics of households that populated the literary and material landscapes of the first century CE. A male authority figure remains the head of the house and those inside the house operate within the dominion of the household leader. All of their actions are determined by the new leader, Jesus. The portrait of the child-daughter continues to correspond to those that generally featured in the broader milieu. She is recognized as a constituent part of the household structure and her image may be understood to have had an active role in forming a hearer's ideas of the identity of the household.

Yet apart from the fact of her being a child-daughter, the girl herself appears to be of no interest. Her character is not ascribed a voice, or thoughts or feelings. In this way, hers is unlike the portrayal of the bleeding woman, whose thoughts and feelings are clearly disclosed to the reader. The portrait of the girl also contrasts with many other adult characters to which Mark has ascribed emotions, perceptions, and speech throughout the work. Instead, her image can be understood to be co-opted, along with

---

1. This raises questions, however, concerning the existence of an extensive range of sources for women and children beyond those identified with Rome.

her father's and mother's and the three disciples', to mediate ideas about the identity and status of the household of Jesus. In this way, her depiction overlaps with those of other children throughout the gospel. With the exception of Herodias's daughter, children are not afforded speech, nor are they attributed perceptions and emotions. Such representations, consonant with many of the depictions of children throughout the first century CE, sheds light on what adults thought in Mark's milieu: While cherished by their parents and functioning as important symbols of their family's identity, what children themselves experienced, thought, or felt appeared of little interest or required no comment. Their images could have agency.

These insights raise tensions in a twenty-first-century world that increasingly values the voice of children. During the period in which this project was undertaken, for example, two contemporary representations of children particularly attracted the attention of many Australians. In the first case, a series of photographic and video images revealed the treatment of some children who were incarcerated in juvenile justice centers in remote parts of the Northern Territory of Australia.[2] In the second case, the past sexual abuse of children was recounted through verbal and written accounts during the Royal Commission into Institutional Responses to Sexual Abuse in Australia.[3] Both cases, in my view, highlighted (among many things) the problems that arise in modern culture when the voices, experiences, and perceptions of children are silenced in preference to those of adults. The public reaction in both cases signified in part the growing acknowledgment of the voice of children in contemporary culture.

A question that arises from this study of the story of Jairus's daughter, therefore, concerns how a reader is to approach the account in a modern context that increasingly values the voice of children and has witnessed the consequences of when those voices are suppressed.[4] Further work is required to explore a contemporary hermeneutic that could be helpful for institutions, for instance, who pore over Mark's stories of children, which

---

2. Australian Broadcasting Commission, "Australia's Shame," https://www.abc.net.au/news/2016-07-25/australias-shame-promo/7649462.

3. Australian Commonwealth Government, "Royal Commission into Institutional Responses to Child Sexual Abuse," https://www.childabuseroyalcommission.gov.au/.

4. On questions concerning biblical texts that "may be used to legitimize attitudes that show a lack of respect for children," see Annemie Dillen, "Good News for Children? Towards a Biblical Hermeneutic of Texts of Terror," *ITQ* 76 (2011): 164–82.

do not, in fact, reflect a time in which the voices of children resounded in text.

A further question arising from this study is how images of children's corporeality in Mark's Gospel function either as a help or hindrance (or both) to elucidating further the values by which children's bodies are viewed today. This question is potentially significant for Christian organizations that, in Australia, both historically and presently have had a shaping influence on children's lives, including attitudes to their bodies.

Even the very conceptualization of Jairus's daughter as symbol of hope for the future is not without its possible dangers. On the one hand, her image functions as a positive symbol. At the same time, however, it runs the risk of reinforcing the myriad ways children are commodified or instrumentalized in the twenty-first century, including in church-related institutions, for what they will contribute in the future as adults rather than seeing childhood as having an inherent value.

In the reading I have put forward in this book, the image of Jairus's daughter rises to take its place within the greater story of Mark's Gospel as it was heard in the first century CE. We might say that the hermeneutical questions that the girl's story raises are, figuratively speaking, part and parcel of the complex job of raising this child. Raising children is an expansive and formative experience. Likewise, further critical engagement with the story of Jairus's daughter will open up new insights into both the past world of Mark and the present world in which the story of this little daughter is read and heard today.

Bibliography

Ahearne-Kroll, Stephen P. "'Who Are My Mother and My Brothers?' Family Relations and Family Language in the Gospel of Mark." *JR* 81 (2001): 1–25.
Aichele, George. "Jesus' Uncanny 'Family Scene.'" *JSNT* 21.74 (1999): 29–48.
Aichele, George, and Richard Walsh. "Metamorphosis, Transfiguration, and the Body." *BibInt* 19 (2011): 253–75.
Amerding, Carl E. "The Daughter of Jairus." *BSac* 105 (1948): 56–58.
Amjad Ali, Christine. "Faith and Power in the New Community: Jairus' Daughter and the Woman with the Haemorrhages." Pages 132–35 in *Affirming Difference, Celebrating Wholeness: A Partnership of Equals*. Edited by Ranjini Rebera. Hong Kong: Christian Conference of Asia Women's Concerns, 1995.
Atkinson, Kenneth. "Noble Deaths at Gamla and Masada?" Pages 349–71 in *Making History: Josephus and Historical Method*. Edited by Zuleika Rodgers. JSJSup 110. Leiden: Brill, 2007.
Australian Broadcasting Commission. "Australia's Shame." https://www.abc.net.au/news/2016-07-25/australias-shame-promo/7649462.
Australian Commonwealth Government. "Royal Commission into Institutional Response to Child Sexual Abuse." https://www.childabuseroyalcommission.gov.au/.
Bader, Mary Anna. *Tracing the Evidence: Dinah in Post-Hebrew Bible Literature*. StBibLit 102. New York: Lang, 2008.
Baker, Cynthia. "Pseudo-Philo and the Transformation of Jephthah's Daughter." Pages 195–209 in *Anti-Covenant: Counter-Reading Women's Lives in the Hebrew Bible*. Edited by Mieke Bal. BLS 22. Sheffield: Almond Press, 1989.
Baldwin, Barry. *Suetonius*. Amsterdam: Hakkert, 1983.
Balla, Peter. *The Child-Parent Relationship in the New Testament and Its Environment*. Peabody, MA: Hendrickson, 2005.

Barclay, John M. G. *Against Apion*. FJTC 10. Leiden: Brill, 2007.
Barclay, John M. G., Steve Mason, and James S. McLaren. "Josephus." Pages 290–321 in *Early Judaism: A Comprehensive Overview*. Edited by John J. Collins and Daniel C. Harlow. Grand Rapids: Eerdmans, 2012.
Barton, Stephen C. *Discipleship and Family Ties in Mark and Matthew*. SNTSMS 80. Cambridge: Cambridge University Press, 1994.
Beard, Mary, John North, and Simon Price. *Religions of Rome*. 2 vols. Cambridge: Cambridge University Press, 1998.
Beavis, Mary Ann. *Mark*. Paideia. Grand Rapids: Baker Academic, 2011.
———. "The Resurrection of Jephthah's Daughter: Judges 11:34–40 and Mark 5:21–24, 35–43." *CBQ* 72 (2010): 46–62.
Bechtel, Carol M. *Esther*. IBC. Louisville: Westminster John Knox, 2002.
Becker, Eve-Marie, Troels Engberg-Pedersen, and Mogens Müller, eds. *Mark and Paul: Comparative Essays, Part II; For and Against Pauline Influence on Mark*. BZNW 199. Berlin: de Gruyter, 2014.
Begg, Christopher T. *Judean Antiquities Books 5–7*. FJTC 4. Leiden: Brill, 2005.
Begg, Christopher T., and Paul Spilsbury. *Judean Antiquities Books 8–10*. FJTC 5. Leiden: Brill, 2005.
Betsworth, Sharon. *Children in Early Christian Narratives*. LNTS 521. London: Bloomsbury, 2015.
———. *The Reign of God Is Such as These: A Socio-literary Analysis of Daughters in the Gospel of Mark*. LNTS 422. London: T&T Clark, 2010.
Bianchi, Emanuela. "Aristotelian *Dunamis* and Sexual Difference: An Analysis of *Adunamia* and *Dunamis meta Logou* in *Metaphysics* Theta." *Philosophy Today* Supplement (2007): 89–97.
Boling, Robert G. "Jair." *ABD* 3:614–15.
Bolt, Peter. *Jesus' Defeat of Death: Persuading Mark's Early Readers*. SNTSMS 125. Cambridge: Cambridge University Press, 2003.
Bomford, Rodney. "Jairus, His Daughter, the Woman and the Saviour: The Communication of Symmetric Thinking in the Gospel of St Mark." *PrT* 3 (2010): 41–50.
Bonneau, Normand. "Suspense in Mark 5:21–43: A Narrative Study of Two Healing Stories." *Thf* 36 (2005): 131–54.
Boring, M. Eugene. *Mark: A Commentary*. NTL. Louisville: Westminster John Knox, 2006.
Bowie, E. "Literature and Sophistic." Pages 898–921 in *The High Empire: AD 70–192*. Edited by Alan K. Bowman, Peter Garnsey, and Dominic

Rathbone. 2nd ed. CAH 11. Cambridge: Cambridge University Press, 2000.
Branch, Robin Gallaher. "Literary Comparisons and Contrasts in Mark 5: 21–43: Original Research." *IDS* 48 (2014): 1–9.
———. "A Study of the Woman in the Crowd and Her Desperate Courage (Mark 5:21–43)/'n studie van die vrou tussen die menigtes en haar desperate dapperheid (Mark 5:21–43)." *IDS* 47 (2013): 1–13.
Braund, Susanna Morton. "Juvenal." In *Oxford Companion to Classical Civilization*. Edited by Simon Hornblower, Antony Spawforth, and Esther Eidinow. 2nd ed. Oxford: Oxford University Press, 2014. https://tinyurl.com/SBLPress4534a3.
Breytenbach, Cilliers. "Current Research on the Gospel according to Mark: A Report on Monographs Published from 2000–2009." Pages 13–32 in *Mark and Matthew I: Comparative Readings; Understanding the Earliest Gospels in Their First-Century Settings*. Edited by Eve-Marie Becker and Anders Runesson. WUNT 1/271. Tübingen: Mohr Siebeck, 2011.
Brighton, Mark Andrew. *The Sicarii in Josephus's Judean War: Rhetorical Analysis and Historical Observations*. EJL 27. Atlanta: Society of Biblical Literature, 2009.
Brown, Cheryl Anne. *No Longer Be Silent: First Century Jewish Portraits of Biblical Women*. Gender and the Biblical Tradition. Louisville: Westminster John Knox, 1992.
Brown, Scott G. "Mark 11:1–12:12: A Triple Intercalation?" *CBQ* 64 (2002): 78–89.
———. "On the Composition History of the Longer ('Secret') Gospel of Mark." *JBL* 122 (2003): 89–110.
Butler, Trent C. *Judges*. WBC 8. Nashville: Nelson, 2009.
Bynum, Caroline Walker. *Fragmentation and Redemption: Essays on Gender and the Human Body in Medieval Religion*. New York: Zone, 1992.
———. *Resurrection of the Body in Western Christianity, 200–1336*. New York: Columbia University Press, 1995.
Byrne, Brendan. *A Costly Freedom: A Theological Reading of Mark's Gospel*. Collegeville, MN: Liturgical Press, 2008.
Cadwallader, Alan H. *Beyond the Word of a Woman: Recovering the Bodies of the Syrophoenician Women*. Adelaide: ATF, 2008.
———. "Sometimes One Word Makes a World of Difference: Rethinking the Origins of Mark's Gospel (Mk 1:38)." Paper presented at the

research seminar for the Centre for Biblical and Early Christian Studies at Australian Catholic University. Melbourne, 4 May 2017.
Campbell, Charles L., and Johan Cilliers. *Preaching Fools: The Gospel as a Rhetoric of Folly*. Waco, TX: Baylor University Press, 2012.
Capps, Donald. "Curing Anxious Adolescents through Fatherlike Performance." *Int* 55 (2001): 135–47.
———. "Jesus the Village Psychiatrist: A Summary." *HvTSt* 66 (2010): 1–5.
Chapman, Cynthia R. *The House of the Mother: The Social Roles of Maternal Kin in Biblical Hebrew Narrative and Poetry*. ABRL. New Haven: Yale University Press, 2016.
Chapman, Honora Howell. "Masada in the First and Twenty-first Centuries." Pages 82–102 in *Making History: Josephus and Historical Method*. Edited by Zuleika Rodgers. JSJSup 110. Leiden: Brill, 2007.
———. "Spectacle and Theater in Josephus's *Bellum Judaicum*." PhD diss., Stanford University, 1998.
Chariton. *Callirhoe*. Translated by G. P. Goold. LCL. Cambridge: Harvard University Press, 1995.
Choi, Jin Young. *Postcolonial Discipleship of Embodiment: An Asian and Asian American Feminist Reading of the Gospel of Mark*. New York: Palgrave Macmillan, 2015.
Cicero. *Works*. Translated by H. Grose Hodge, J. E. King, Clinton W. Keyes, and D. R. Shackleton Bailey. 7 vols. LCL. Cambridge: Harvard University Press, 1928–2009.
Cody, Jane. "Conquerors and Conquered on Flavian Coins." Pages 103–23 in *Flavian Rome: Culture, Image, Text*. Edited by Anthony Boyle and William J. Dominik. Leiden: Brill, 2003.
Cohen, Sande. *Academia and the Luster of Capital*. Minneapolis: University of Minnesota Press, 1993.
Cohen, Shaye J. D. "Masada: Literary Tradition, Archaeological Remains and the Credibility of Josephus." *JJS* 33 (1982): 385–405.
———. "Menstruants and the Sacred in Judaism and Christianity." Pages 273–300 in *Women's History and Ancient History*. Edited by Sarah B. Pomeroy. Chapel Hill: University of North Carolina Press, 1991.
Collins, Adela Yarbro. *Mark: A Commentary*. Hermeneia. Minneapolis: Fortress, 2007.
Constantine, David, Rodney Pybus, Noel Connor, and Barry Hirst. *Talitha Cumi*. Newcastle upon Tyne: Bloodaxe, 1983.
Cook, Joan E. "Pseudo-Philo's Song of Hannah: Testament of a Mother in Israel." *JSP* 5 (1991): 103–14.

Cotter, Wendy. "Mark's Hero of the Twelfth-Year Miracles: The Healing of the Woman with the Hemorrhage and the Raising of Jairus' Daughter." Pages 54–78 in *A Feminist Companion to Mark*. Edited by Amy-Jill Levine and Marianne Blickenstaff. Sheffield: Sheffield Academic, 2001.

Craig, Christopher P. "Quintilian." In *The Oxford Encyclopedia of Ancient Greece and Rome*. Edited by Michael Gagarin. Oxford: Oxford University Press, 2010. https://tinyurl.com/SBLPress4534a2.

Crossley, James G. *The Date of Mark's Gospel: Insight from the Law in Earliest Christianity*. JSNTSup 266. London: T&T Clark, 2004.

Culpepper, R. Alan. *Mark*. SHBC 20. Macon, GA: Smyth & Helwys, 2007.

Dalgaard, Kasper. "The Four Keys of God: Mark 4:35–6:44 and the Midrash of the Keys." *Hen* 33 (2011): 238–49.

D'Angelo, Mary Rose. "Gender and Power in the Gospel of Mark: The Daughter of Jairus and the Woman with the Flow of Blood." Pages 83–109 in *Miracles in Jewish and Christian Antiquity: Imagining Truth*. Edited by John C. Cavadini. Notre Dame Studies in Theology 3. Notre Dame: University of Notre Dame Press, 1999.

———. "Roman Imperial Family Values and the Gospel of Mark: The Divorce Sayings (Mark 10:2–12)." Pages 59–83 in *Women and Gender in Ancient Religions*. Edited by Stephen P. Ahearne-Kroll, Paul A. Holloway, and James A. Kelhoffer. WUNT 263. Tübingen: Mohr Siebeck, 2010.

Danker, Frederick William. *The Concise Greek-English Lexicon of the New Testament*. Chicago: University of Chicago Press, 2009.

Davies, Glenys. "The Significance of the Handshake Motif in Classical Funerary Art." *AJA* 89 (1985): 627–40.

Day, Linda M. *Esther*. AOTC. Nashville: Abingdon, 2005.

Dench, Emma. "Beyond Greeks and Barbarians: Italy and Sicily in the Hellenistic Age." Pages 294–310 in *A Companion to the Hellenistic World*. Edited by Andrew Erskine. BCAW. Malden, MA: Blackwell, 2005.

Destro, Adriana, and Mauro Pesce. *Encounters with Jesus: The Man in His Place and Time*. Minneapolis: Fortress, 2012.

———. "Fathers and Householders in the Jesus Movement: The Perspective of the Gospel of Luke." *BibInt* 11 (2003): 211–38.

Dewey, Joanna. "Jesus' Healings of Women: Conformity and Nonconformity to Dominant Cultural Values as Clues for Historical Reconstruction." *BTB* 24 (1994): 122–31.

Dillen, Annemie. "Good News for Children? Towards a Biblical Hermeneutic of Texts of Terror." *ITQ* 76 (2011): 164–82.

Dixon, Suzanne. "From Ceremonial to Sexualities: A Survey of Scholarship on Roman Marriage." Pages 245–61 in *A Companion to Families in the Greek and Roman Worlds*. Edited by Beryl Rawson. BCAW. Chichester: Wiley-Blackwell, 2011.

———. *Reading Roman Women: Sources, Genres, and Real Life*. London: Duckworth, 2001.

———. *The Roman Mother*. Florence: Routledge, 2013.

Docherty, Susan E. *The Jewish Pseudepigrapha: An Introduction to the Literature of the Second Temple Period*. Minneapolis: Fortress, 2015.

Donahue, John R. *Are You the Christ? The Trial Narrative in the Gospel of Mark*. SBLDS 10. Missoula, MT: Society of Biblical Literature, 1973.

———. *The Theology and Setting of Discipleship in the Gospel of Mark*. Milwaukee, WI: Marquette University Press, 1983.

Donahue, John R., and Daniel J. Harrington. *The Gospel of Mark*. SP. Collegeville, MN: Liturgical Press, 2002.

Driscoll, Martha. *Reading between the Lines: The Hidden Wisdom of Women in the Gospels*. Ligouri, MO: Liguori, 2006.

Dube Shomanah, Musa W. "Talitha Cum! A Postcolonial Feminist and HIV/AIDS Reading of Mark 5:21–43." Pages 115–40 in *Grant Me Justice! HIV/AIDS and Gender Readings of the Bible*. Edited by Musa W. Dube Shomanah and Rachel Angogo Kanyoro. Pietermaritzburg, South Africa: Cluster; Maryknoll, NY: Orbis Books, 2004.

Dwyer, Timothy. "Prominent Women, Widows, and Prophets: A Case for Midrashic Intertextuality." *Essays in Literature* 20 (1993): 23–30.

Dyson, Stephen L. "The Family and the Roman Countryside." Pages 431–44 in *A Companion to Families in the Greek and Roman Worlds*. Edited by Beryl Rawson. BCAW. Chichester: Wiley-Blackwell, 2011.

Edwards, Catharine. *Suetonius: Lives of the Caesars; A New Translation*. New York: Oxford University Press, 2000.

Edwards, James R. "Markan Sandwiches: The Significance of Interpolations in Markan Narratives." *NovT* 31 (1989): 193–216.

Edwards Harris, Steven. "On the Three Kinds of Resurrection of the Dead," *IJST* 20 (2018): 8–30.

Elliott, John H. "Household/Family in the Gospel of Mark as a Core Symbol of Community." Pages 36–63 in *Fabrics of Discourse: Essays in Honor of Vernon K. Robbins*. Edited by David B. Gowler, L. Gregory Bloomquist, and Duane F. Watson. Harrisburg, PA: Trinity Press International, 2003.

England, Frank. "Afterthought: An Excuse or an Opportunity?" *JTSA* 92 (1995): 56–59.

Fassnacht, Martin. "Konfrontation mit der Weisheit Jesu: Das Verhältnis von Wissen und Rettung dargestellt an der Wundergeschichte Mk 5,21–43." Pages 105–24 in *Die Weisheit—Ursprünge und Rezeption: Festschrift für Karl Löning zum 65. Geburtstag*. Edited by Karl Löning, Martin Fassnacht, Andreas Leinhäupl-Wilke, and Stefan Lücking. NTAbh 44. Münster: Aschendorff, 2003.

Feldman, Louis H. *Judean Antiquities 1–4*. FJTC 3. Leiden: Brill, 2000.

———. *Josephus's Interpretation of the Bible*. HCS. Berkley: University of California Press, 1998.

———. *Studies in Josephus' Rewritten Bible*. JSJSup 58. Leiden: Brill, 1998.

Fenton, Steve. *Ethnicity*. 2nd ed. Cambridge: Polity, 2010.

Fernandez, Zoa Alfonso. "Docta saltatrix: Body Knowledge, Culture, and Corporeal Discourse in Female Roman Dance." *Phoenix* 69 (2015): 304–33.

Fischbach, Stephanie M. *Totenerweckungen: Zur Geschichte einer Gattung*. FB 69. Würzburg: Echter, 1992.

Flory, Marleen B. "Dynastic Ideology, the Domus Augusta, and Imperial Women: A Lost Statuary Group in the Circus Flaminius." *TAPA* 126 (1996): 287–306.

Fonrobert, Charlotte Elisheva. *Menstrual Purity: Rabbinic and Christian Reconstructions of Biblical Gender*. Stanford, CA: Stanford University Press, 2000.

Fowler, Robert M. *Let the Reader Understand: Reader-Response Criticism and the Gospel of Mark*. Minneapolis: Fortress, 1991.

France, R. T. *The Gospel of Mark: A Commentary on the Greek Text*. NIGTC. Grand Rapids: Eerdmans; Carlisle: Paternoster 2002.

Francis, James M. M. *Adults as Children: Images of Childhood in the Ancient World and the New Testament*. Religions and Discourse 17. Bern: Lang, 2006.

Fredriksen, Paula. "Compassion Is to Purity as Fish Is to Bicycle and Other Reflections on Constructions of 'Judaism' in Current Work on the Historical Jesus." Pages 55–67 in *Apocalypticism, Anti-Semitism and the Historical Jesus: Subtexts in Criticism*. Edited by John S. Kloppenborg and John W. Marshall. JSNTSup 275. London: T&T Clark, 2005.

———. "Did Jesus Oppose the Purity Laws?" *BRev* 11.3 (1995): 18–25.

———. "What You See Is What You Get: Context and Content in Current Research on the Historical Jesus." *ThTo* 52 (1995): 75–97.

Friberg, Timothy, Barbara Friberg, and Neva F. Miller. *Analytical Lexicon of the Greek New Testament*. Grand Rapids: Baker, 2000.

Fullmer, Paul M. *Resurrection in Mark's Literary-Historical Perspective*. LNTS 360. London: T&T Clark, 2007.

Gardner, A. Edward. "Reading between the Texts: Minor Characters Who Prepare the Way for Jesus." *Enc* 66 (2005): 45–66.

Gerber, Jörg, and Vera Binder. "Hellenization." *BNP*. https://doi.org/10.1163/1574-9347_bnp_e506840.

Gill, Robin. "Health Care, Jesus and the Church." *Ecclesiology* 1 (2004): 37–55.

Gingrich, F. Wilbur. *Shorter Lexicon of the Greek New Testament*. Revised by Frederick W. Danker. 2nd ed. Chicago: University of Chicago Press, 1983.

Glancy, Jennifer A. *Corporal Knowledge: Early Christian Bodies*. New York: Oxford University Press, 2010.

———. "Jesus, the Syrophoenician Woman, and Other First Century Bodies." *BibInt* 18 (2010): 342–63.

Goodenough, Erwin Ramsdell. *The Archeological Evidence from the Diaspora*. Vol. 2 of *Jewish Symbols in the Greco-Roman Period*. New York: Pantheon, 1953.

Grabbe, Lester L. *Yehud: A History of the Persian Province of Judah*. Vol. 1 of *A History of the Jews and Judaism in the Second Temple Period*. LSTS 47. London: T&T Clark, 2004.

Graham, Emma Jayne. "Memory and Materiality: Re-Embodying the Roman Funeral." Pages 21–39 in *Memory and Mourning: Studies on Roman Death*. Edited by Valerie M. Hope and Janet Huskinson. Oxford: Oxbow, 2011.

Graver, Margaret. *Cicero on the Emotions: Tusculan Disputations 3 and 4*. Chicago: University of Chicago Press, 2002.

Greenblatt, Stephen. "Towards a Poetics of Culture." Pages 1–13 in *The New Historicism*. Edited H. Aram Veeser. New York: Routledge, 1989.

Grubbs, Judith Evans. *Woman and the Law in the Roman Empire: A Sourcebook on Marriage, Divorce and Widowhood*. London: Routledge, 2002.

Guelich, Robert A. *Mark 1–8:26*. WBC 34a. Dallas: Word, 1989.

Gundry, Judith M. "Children in the Gospel of Mark, with Special Attention to Jesus' Blessing of the Children (Mark 10:13–16) and the Purpose of Mark." Pages 143–76 in *The Child in the Bible*. Edited by Marcia C. Bunge. Grand Rapids: Eerdmans, 2008.

Gundry, Robert H. *Mark: A Commentary on His Apology for the Cross*. Grand Rapids: Eerdmans, 1993.
Haber, Susan. *"They Shall Purify Themselves": Essays on Purity in Early Judaism*. EJL 24. Atlanta: Society of Biblical Literature, 2008.
Hachlili, Rachel. *Jewish Funerary Customs, Practices and Rites in the Second Temple Period*. JSJSup 94. Leiden: Brill, 2005.
Hachlili, Rachel, and Patricia Smith. "The Genealogy of the Goliath Family." *BASOR* 235 (1979): 67–70.
Hägg, Thomas. "Orality, Literacy, and the 'Readership' of the Early Greek Novel." Pages 47–82 in *Contexts of Pre-novel Narrative: The European Tradition*. Edited by Roy Eriksen. Approaches to Semiotics 114. Berlin: Mouton de Gruyter, 1994.
Hallett, Judith P. "Women in Augustan Rome." Pages 372–84 in *A Companion to Women in the Ancient World*. Edited by Sharon L. James and Sheila Dillon. BCAW. Chichester: Wiley-Blackwell, 2012.
Halpern-Amaru, Betsy. *The Empowerment of Women in the Book of Jubilees*. JSJSup 60. Leiden: Brill, 1999.
———. "Portraits of Women in Pseudo-Philo's *Biblical Antiquities*." Pages 83–106 in *"Women Like This": New Perspectives on Women in the Greco-Roman World*. Edited by Amy-Jill Levine. EJL 1. Atlanta: Scholars Press, 1991.
Harrington, Daniel J. "Pseudo-Philo." *OTP* 2:297–377.
Harris, Murray J. *From Grave to Glory: Resurrection in the New Testament; Including a Response to Norman L. Geisler*. Grand Rapids: Zondervan, 1990.
Haynes, Katharine. *Fashioning the Feminine in the Greek Novel*. London: Routledge, 2003.
Hedrick, Charles W. "Miracle Stories as Literary Compositions: The Case of Jairus's Daughter." *PRSt* 20 (1993): 217–33.
Hens-Piazza, Gina. *The New Historicism*. GBS. Minneapolis: Fortress, 2002.
Henten, Jan Willem van. "Noble Death in Josephus: Just Rhetoric?" Pages 195–218 in *Making History: Josephus and Historical Method*. Edited by Zuleika Rodgers. JSJSup 110. Leiden: Brill, 2007.
Heslin, Peter. "Augustus, Domitian and the So-Called Horologium Augusti." *JRS* 97 (2007): 1–20.
Hogan, Larry P. *Healing in the Second Temple Period*. NTOA 211. Fribourg: Universitätsverlag; Göttingen: Vandenhoeck & Ruprecht, 1992.

Hooker, Morna D. *The Gospel according to Saint Mark*. BNTC. Peabody, MA: Hendrickson, 2009.
Hope, Valerie M. "Contempt and Respect: The Treatment of the Corpse in Ancient Rome." Pages 104–27 in *Death and Disease in the Ancient City*. Edited by Valerie M. Hope and Eireann Marshall. London: Routledge, 2000.
———. *Death in Ancient Rome: A Source Book*. Routledge Sourcebooks for the Ancient World. London: Routledge, 2007.
Hope, Valerie, and Janet Huskinson. *Memory and Mourning: Studies on Roman Death*. Oxford: Oxbow, 2011.
Horst, Pieter van der. "Deborah and Seila in Ps-Philo." Pages 111–17 in *Messiah and Christos: Studies in the Jewish Origins of Christianity; Presented to David Flusser on the Occasion of His Seventy-Fifth Birthday*. Edited by Ithamar Gruenwald, Shaul Shaked, and Gedaliahu G. Strousma. TSAJ 32. Mohr Siebeck: Tübingen, 1992.
———. *Philo's Flaccus: The First Pogrom; Introduction, Translation, and Commentary*. PACS 2. Leiden: Brill, 2003.
Hurtado, Larry W. "Oral Fixation and New Testament Studies? 'Orality,' 'Performance' and Reading Texts in Early Christianity." *NTS* 60 (2014): 321–40.
Huskinson, Janet. "Constructing Childhood on Roman Funerary Memorials." Pages 323–38 in *Constructions of Childhood in Ancient Greece and Italy*. Edited by Ada Cohen and Jeremy B. Rutter. Hesperia Supplements 41. Princeton: American School of Classical Studies at Athens, 2007.
———. "Picturing the Roman Family." Pages 521–41 in *A Companion to Families in the Greek and Roman Worlds*. Edited by Beryl Rawson. BCAW. Chichester: Wiley-Blackwell, 2011.
Iersel, Bas M. F. van. *Mark: A Reader-Response Commentary*. Translated by W. H. Bisscheroux. JSNTSup 164. Sheffield: Sheffield Academic, 1998.
Ilan, Tal. *Integrating Women into Second Temple History*. Peabody, MA: Hendrickson, 2001.
———. *Jewish Women in Greco-Roman Palestine*. Peabody, MA: Hendrickson, 1995.
Incigneri, Brian J. *The Gospel to the Romans: The Setting and Rhetoric of Mark's Gospel*. BibInt 65. Leiden: Brill, 2003.
Jacobson, Howard. *A Commentary on Pseudo-Philo's Liber Antiquitatum Biblicarum with Latin Text and English Translation*. 2 vols. AGJU 31. Leiden: Brill, 1996.

Jenkins, Keith. "Sande Cohen: On the Verge of Newness." Pages 270–94 in *At the Limits of History: Essays on Theory and Practice*. London: Routledge, 2009.
Josephus. *Works*. Translated by Henry St. J. Thackeray and Louis H. Feldman. 9 vols. LCL. Cambridge: Harvard University Press, 1926–1965.
Joynes, Christine E. "Still at the Margins? Gospel Women and Their Afterlives." Pages 117–36 in *Radical Christian Voices and Practice: Essays in Honour of Christopher Rowland*. Edited by Zoë Bennet and David B. Gowler. Oxford: Oxford University Press, 2012.
Juvenal and Persius. Translated by Susanna Morton Braund. LCL. Cambridge: Harvard University Press, 2004.
Kahl, Brigitte. "Jairus und die verlorenen Töchter Israels: Sozioliterarische überlegungen zum Problem der Grenzüberschreitung in Mk 5, 21–43." Pages 61–78 in *Von der Wurzel getragen: Christlich-feministische Exegese in Auseinandersetzung mit Antijudaismus*. Edited by Luise Schottroff and Marie-Theres Wacker. BibInt 17. Leiden: Brill, 1996.
Kazen, Thomas. *Jesus and Purity Halakhah: Was Jesus Indifferent to Impurity?* ConBNT 38. Winona Lake, IN: Eisenbrauns, 2010.
Kelley, Nicole. "The Cosmopolitan Expression of Josephus's Prophetic Perspective in the Jewish War." *HTR* 97 (2004): 257–74.
Kemmers, Fleur, and Nanouschka Myrberg. "Rethinking Numismatics: The Archaeology of Coins." *Archaeological Dialogues* 18 (2011): 87–108.
Kessler-Harris, Alice. "What Is Gender History Now?" Pages 95–112 in *What Is History Now?* Edited by David Cannadine. Basingstoke: Palgrave Macmillan, 2002.
Kiley, Mark. "Marcan Love, Sotto Voce." *BTB* 39 (2009): 71–76.
King, Helen. "Once Upon a Text: Hysteria from Hippocrates." Pages 3–90 in *Hysteria beyond Freud*. Edited by Sander L. Gilman, Helen King, Roy Porter, G. S. Rousseau, and Elaine Showalter. Berkeley: University of California Press, 1994.
Klawans, Jonathan. *Impurity and Sin in Ancient Judaism*. New York: Oxford University Press, 2000.
———. *Purity, Sacrifice, and the Temple: Symbolism and Supersessionism in the Study of Ancient Judaism*. Oxford: Oxford University Press, 2006.
Kleiner, Diana E. E. *Roman Group Portraiture: The Funerary Reliefs of the Late Republic and Early Empire*. New York: Garland, 1977.
Kockel, Valentin. *Porträtreliefs stadtrömischer Grabbauten: Ein Beitrag zur

Geschichte und zum Verständnis des spätrepublikanisch-frühkaiserzeitlichen Privatporträts. Mainz: von Zabern, 1993.

Kossew, Sue. "Women Writing Pain: Recent Australian Fiction and the Representation of Gendered Violence." Paper presented at Translating Pain: An International Forum on Language, Text and Suffering. Monash University, Caulfield, Australia, 12 August 2015.

Kraemer, Ross S. "Implicating Herodias and Her Daughter in the Death of the Baptizer: A (Christian) Theological Strategy?" *JBL* 125 (2006): 321–49.

———. "Jewish Mothers and Daughters in the Greco-Roman World." Pages 89–112 in *The Jewish Family in Antiquity*. Edited by Shaye J. D. Cohen. BJS 289. Atlanta: Scholars Press, 1993.

Kugel, James L. *A Walk through Jubilees: Studies in the Book of Jubilees and the World of Its Creation.* JSJSup 156. Leiden: Brill, 2012.

Laes, Christian. *Children in the Roman Empire: Outsiders Within.* Cambridge: Cambridge University Press, 2011.

Lamberton, Robert. *Plutarch.* Hermes Books. New Haven: Yale University Press, 2001.

Larsson Loven, Lena. "Children and Childhood in Roman Commemorative Art." Pages 302–21 in *The Oxford Handbook of Childhood and Education in the Classical World*. Edited by Roslynne Bell, Judith Evans Grubbs, and Tim Parkin. Oxford Handbooks. New York: Oxford University Press, 2013.

Lawless, Elaine J. "Transforming the Master Narrative: How Women Shift the Religious Subject." *Frontiers: A Journal of Women Studies* 24 (2003): 61–75.

Lawrence, Louise J. "Exploring the Sense-Scape of the Gospel of Mark." *JSNT* 33 (2011): 387–97.

———. *Sense and Stigma in the Gospels: Depictions of Sensory-Disabled Characters.* Biblical Refigurations. Oxford: Oxford University Press, 2013.

Leigh, Matthew. "Quintilian on the Emotions (*Institutio Oratoria* 6 Preface and 1–2)." *JRS* 94 (2004): 122–40.

Levine, Amy-Jill. "Discharging Responsibility: Matthean Jesus, Biblical Law and Hemorrhaging Woman." Pages 70–87 in *Feminist Companion to Matthew*. Edited by Amy Jill Levine and Marianne Blickenstaff. Sheffield: Sheffield Academic, 2001.

———. *The Misunderstood Jew: The Church and the Scandal of the Jewish Jesus.* New York: HarperOne, 2007.

Levine, Amy-Jill. "The Disease of Postcolonial New Testament Studies and the Hermeneutics of Healing." *JFSR* 20 (2004): 91–132 (including responses by Kwok Pui-lan, Musimbi Kanyoro, and Adele Reinhartz).

Levine, Lee I. *Judaism and Hellenism in Antiquity: Conflict or Confluence?* Seattle: University of Washington Press, 1998.

Loader, William R. G. "Attitudes towards Sexuality in Qumran and Related Literature—and the New Testament." *NTS* 54 (2008): 338–54.

———. *Philo, Josephus, and the Testaments on Sexuality: Attitudes towards Sexuality in the Writings of Philo and Josephus and in the Testaments of the Twelve Patriarchs*. Grand Rapids: Eerdmans, 2011.

———. *The Pseudepigrapha on Sexuality: Attitude towards Sexuality in Apocalypses, Testaments, Legends, Wisdom, and Related Literature*. Grand Rapids: Eerdmans, 2011.

López, Jorge Fernández. "Quintilian as Rhetorician and Teacher." Pages 307–22 in *A Companion to Roman Rhetoric*. Edited by William Dominik and Jon Hall. BCAW. Malden, MA: Wiley-Blackwell, 2007.

Louw, Johannes P., and Eugene A. Nida, eds. *Greek English Lexicon of the New Testament: Based on Semantic Domains*. 2nd ed. New York: United Bible Societies, 1989.

MacDonald, Dennis R. *The Homeric Epics and the Gospel of Mark*. New Haven: Yale University Press, 2000.

Malbon, Elizabeth Struthers. "Echoes and Foreshadowings in Mark 4–8: Reading and Rereading." *JBL* 112 (1993): 211–30.

———. *In the Company of Jesus: Characters in Mark's Gospel*. Louisville: Westminster John Knox, 2000.

———. "The Jewish Leaders in the Gospel of Mark: A Literary Study of Marcan Characterization." *JBL* 108 (1989): 259–81.

———. *Narrative Space and Mythic Meaning in Mark*. San Francisco: Harper & Row, 1986.

Maluleke, Tinyiko Sam. "Bible Study the Graveyardman, the 'Escaped Convict' and the Girl-Child: A Mission of Awakening, an Awakening of Mission." *International Review of Mission* 91 (2002): 550–57.

Manuwald, Gesine. *Cicero*. London: Tauris, 2015.

Marcus, Joel. *Mark 1–8: A New Translation with Introduction and Commentary*. AB 27A. New York: Doubleday, 2000.

———. *Mark 8–16: A New Translation with Introduction and Commentary*. AB 27B. New Haven: Yale University Press, 2009.

Marshall, Christopher D. *Faith as a Theme in Mark's Narrative*. Cambridge: Cambridge University Press, 1989.

Mason, Steve. "Essenes and Lurking Spartans in Josephus' *Judean War.*" Pages 219–61 in *Making History: Josephus and Historical Method*. Edited by Zuleika Rodgers. JSJSup 110. Leiden: Brill, 2007.

———. *Josephus, Judea, and Christian Origins: Methods and Categories*. Peabody, MA: Hendrickson, 2009.

———. *Life of Josephus*. FJTC 9. Leiden: Brill, 2001.

McFague, Sallie. *The Body of God: An Ecological Theology*. Minneapolis: Fortress, 1993.

McInerney, Jeremy. "Interpreting Funerary Inscriptions from the City of Rome." *Journal of Ancient History* 7 (2019): 156–206.

McIntyre, Gwynaeth. *A Family of Gods: The Worship of the Imperial Family in the Latin West*. Societas. Ann Arbor: University of Michigan Press, 2016.

McLaren, James S. *Power and Politics in Palestine: The Jews and the Governing of Their Land, 100 BC–AD 70*. JSNTSup 63. Sheffield: JSOT Press, 1991.

———. *Turbulent Times? Josephus and Scholarship on Judaea in the First Century CE*. JSPSup 29. Sheffield: Sheffield Academic, 1998.

McLaughlin, Raoul. *The Roman Empire and the Indian Ocean: Rome's Dealings with the Ancient Kingdoms of India, Africa and Arabia*. London: Pen & Sword, 2014.

McWilliam, Janette. "The Socialization of Roman Children." Pages 264–85 in *The Oxford Handbook of Childhood and Education in the Classical World*. Edited by Roslynne Bell, Judith Evans Grubbs, and Tim Parkin. Oxford Handbooks. New York: Oxford University Press, 2013.

Mendoza, Manuel Villalobos. *Abject Bodies in the Gospel of Mark*. Bible in the Modern World 45. Sheffield: Sheffield Phoenix, 2012.

Miller, Susan. *Women in Mark's Gospel*. JSNTSup 259. London: T&T Clark, 2004.

Miller-McLemore, Bonnie. "Jesus Loves the Little Children? An Exercise in the Use of Scripture." *JCR* 1 (2010): 1–35.

Milnor, Kristina. "Women and Domesticity." Pages 458–75 in *A Companion to Tacitus*. Edited by Victoria E. Pagán. BCAW. Oxford: Wiley-Blackwell, 2012.

Mirguet, Francoise. "Emotional Responses to the Suffering of Others: Explorations in Judeo-Hellenistic Literature." Paper presented at the Research Symposium. Harvard Center for Hellenic Studies, Washington DC, 26 April 2013.

Moloney, Francis J. *The Gospel of Mark: A Commentary*. Peabody, MA: Hendrickson, 2002.
Morello, Ruth. "Writer and Addressee in Cicero's Letters." Pages 196–214 in *The Cambridge Companion to Cicero*. Edited by Catherine Steel. Cambridge: Cambridge University Press, 2013.
Morgan, Teresa. *Roman Faith and Christian Faith: Pistis and Fides in the Early Roman Empire and Early Churches*. Oxford: Oxford University Press, 2015.
Moss, Candida R. "The Man with the Flow of Power: Porous Bodies in Mark 5:25–34." *JBL* 129 (2010): 507–19.
Moss, Candida R., and Joel S. Baden. *Reconceiving Infertility: Biblical Perspectives on Procreation and Childlessness*. Princeton: Princeton University Press, 2015.
Müller, Sabine. "Dextrarum Iunctio." In *The Encyclopedia of Ancient History*. New York: Wiley & Sons, 2013. http://dx.doi.org/10.1002/9781444338386.wbeah22079.
Murphy, Frederick J. *Early Judaism: The Exile to the Time of Jesus*. Peabody, MA: Hendrickson, 2002.
———. *Pseudo-Philo: Rewriting the Bible*. Oxford: Oxford University Press, 1993.
———. "Retelling the Bible: Idolatry in Pseudo-Philo." *JBL* 107 (1988): 275–87.
Murphy, James. *Kids and Kingdom: The Precarious Presence of Children in the Synoptic Gospels*. Eugene, OR: Pickwick, 2013.
Myers, Ched. *Binding the Strong Man: A Political Reading of Mark's Story of Jesus*. Maryknoll, NY: Orbis Books, 1988.
Myers, Ched, Marie Dennis, Joseph Nangle, Cynthia Moe-Lobeda, and Stuart Taylor. *Say to This Mountain: Mark's Story of Discipleship*. Maryknoll, NY: Orbis Books, 1996.
Niditch, Susan. *Judges: A Commentary*. OTL. Louisville: Westminster John Knox, 2008.
Niehoff, Maren R. "Jewish Identity and Jewish Mothers: Who Was a Jew according to Philo?" *SPhiloA* 11 (1999): 31–54.
———. *Philo on Jewish Identity and Culture*. TSAJ 86. Tübingen: Mohr Siebeck, 2001.
Niehoff, Maren R., David T. Runia, Gregory E. Sterling, and Annewies van den Hoek. "Philo." Pages 253–89 in *Early Judaism: A Comprehensive Overview*. Edited by John J. Collins and Daniel C. Harlow. Grand Rapids: Eerdmans, 2012.

Noy, David. "'Goodbye Livia': Dying in the Roman Home." Pages 1–20 in *Memory and Mourning: Studies on Roman Death*. Edited by Valerie M. Hope and Janet Huskinson. Oxford: Oxbow, 2011.

Oduyoye, Mercy A. "*Talitha qumi*: Celebrating Africa's Struggles against Structures and Cultures That Legitimize Exclusion and Inequalities; A Study of Mark 5: 21–24, 35–43." *RW* 58 (2008): 82–89.

Okure, Teresa. "Feminist Interpretation in Africa." Pages 76–85 in *Searching the Scriptures: A Feminist Introduction*. Edited by Elisabeth Schüssler Fiorenza. New York: Crossroad, 1993.

Olson, Kelly. "The Appearance of the Young Roman Girl." Pages 139–57 in *Roman Dress and the Fabrics of Roman Culture*. Edited by Jonathan C. Edmondson and Alison Keith. Phoenix Supplement 46. Toronto: University of Toronto Press, 2008.

Oppel, Dagmar. *Heilsam erzählen—erzählend heilen: Die Heilung der Blutflüssigen und die Erweckung der Jairustochter in Mk 5,21–43 als Beispiel markinischer Erzählfertigkeit*. BBB 102. Weinheim: Beltz Athenäum, 1995.

Parkin, Tim. "The Demography of Infancy and Early Childhood in the Ancient World." Pages 40–61 in *The Oxford Handbook of Childhood and Education in the Classical World*. Edited by Roslynne Bell, Judith Evans Grubbs, and Tim Parkin. Oxford Handbooks. New York: Oxford University Press, 2013.

———. "The Roman Life Course and the Family." Pages 276–90 in *A Companion to Families in the Greek and Roman Worlds*. Edited by Beryl Rawson. BCAW. Chichester: Wiley-Blackwell, 2011.

Pesch, Rudolf. *Das Markusevangelium*. HThKNT 2. Freiburg im Breisgau: Herder, 1977.

———. "Jaïrus (Mk 5:22/Lk 8:41)." *BZ* 14 (1970): 252–56.

Peskowitz, Miriam. "Family/ies in Antiquity: Evidence from Tannaitic Literature and Roman Galilean Architecture." Pages 9–36 in *The Jewish Family in Antiquity*. Edited by Shaye J. D. Cohen. BJS 289. Atlanta: Scholars Press, 1993.

Philo. *Works*. Translated by F. H. Colson. 10 vols. LCL. Cambridge: Harvard University Press, 1937–1965.

Pliny the Younger. *Letters, Volume I: Books 1–7*. Translated by Betty Radice. LCL. Cambridge: Harvard University Press, 1969.

Plutarch. *Works*. Translated by Bernadotte Perrin and Phillip H. De Lacy. 11 vols. LCL. Cambridge: Harvard University Press, 1914–1959.

Poetker, Katrina M. "Domestic Domains in the Gospel of Mark." *Direction* 24 (1995): 14–23.

———. "'You Are My Mother, My Brothers, and My Sisters': A Literary-Anthropological Investigation of Family in the Gospel of Mark." PhD diss., Emory University, 2001.

Polaski, Donald C. "On Taming Tamar: Amram's Rhetoric and Women's Roles in Pseudo-Philo's Liber Antiquitatum Biblicarum." *JSP* 13 (1995): 79–99.

Powell, Charles E. "The 'Passivity' of Jesus in Mark 5:25–34." *BSac* 162.645 (2005): 66–75.

Quintilian. *The Orator's Education, Volume III: Books 6–8*. Translated by Donald Russell. LCL. Cambridge: Harvard University Press, 2002.

Rajak, Tessa, and David Noy. "Archisynagogoi: Office, Title and Social Status in the Greco-Jewish Synagogue." *JRS* 83 (1993): 75–93.

Rawson, Beryl. *Children and Childhood in Roman Italy*. Oxford: Oxford University Press, 2003.

———. "Family and Society." Pages 610–23 in *The Oxford Handbook of Roman Studies*. Edited by Alessandro Barchiesi and Walter Scheidel. Oxford: Oxford University Press, 2010.

———. "The Iconography of Roman Childhood." Pages 205–32 in *The Roman Family in Italy: Status, Sentiment, Space*. Edited by Beryl Rawson and Paul Weaver. Oxford: Oxford University Press, 1997.

Reeder, Caryn A. *The Enemy in the Household: Family Violence in Deuteronomy and Beyond*. Grand Rapids: Baker Academic, 2012.

———. "Gender, War, and Josephus." *JSJ* 46 (2015): 65–85.

———. "Pity the Women and Children: Punishment by Siege in Josephus's *Jewish War*." *JSJ* 44 (2013): 174–94.

Reinhartz, Adele. "Parents and Children: A Philonic Perspective." Pages 61–88 in *The Jewish Family in Antiquity*. Edited by Shaye J. D. Cohen. BJS 289. Atlanta: Scholars Press, 1993.

———. "Philo on Infanticide." *SPhiloA* 4 (1992): 42–58.

Reinhartz, Adele, and Kim Shier. "Josephus on Children and Childhood." *SR* 41 (2012): 364–75.

Rhoads, David, Joanna Dewey, and Donald Michie. *Mark as Story: An Introduction to the Narrative of a Gospel*. 3rd ed. Minneapolis: Fortress, 2012.

Robinson, Robert B. "Literary Functions of the Genealogies of Genesis." *CBQ* 48 (1986): 595–608.

Rochais, Gérard. *Les récits de résurrection des morts dans le Nouveau Testament*. SNTSMS 40. Cambridge: Cambridge University Press, 1981.

Rose, Charles Brian. *Dynastic Commemoration and Imperial Portraiture in the Julio-Claudian Period*. Cambridge: Cambridge University Press, 1997.

Roskam, Hendrika N. *The Purpose of the Gospel of Mark in Its Historical and Social Context*. NovTSup 114. Leiden: Brill, 2004.

Rossini, Orietta. *Ara Pacis Guide*. Milan: Electa, 2007.

Rubin, Miri. "What Is Cultural History Now?" Pages 80–94 in *What Is History Now?* Edited by David Cannadine. Basingstoke: Palgrave MacMillan, 2002.

Rutgers, Leonard V. *The Hidden Heritage of Diaspora Judaism*. 2nd ed. BETL 20. Leuven: Peeters, 1998.

Sabourin, Leopold. "The Miracles of Jesus (III): Healings, Resuscitations, Nature Miracles." *BTB* 5 (1975): 146–200.

Saller, Richard. "The Roman Family as Productive Unit." Pages 116–28 in *A Companion to Families in the Greek and Roman Worlds*. Edited by Beryl Rawson. BCAW. Chichester: Wiley-Blackwell, 2011.

Sanders, E. P. "Jesus, Ancient Judaism, and Modern Christianity: The Quest Continues." Pages 31–55 in *Jesus, Judaism, and Christian Anti-Judaism: Reading the New Testament after the Holocaust*. Edited by Paula Fredriksen and Adele Reinhartz. Louisville: Westminster John Knox, 2002.

Satlow, Michael L. *Jewish Marriage in Antiquity*. Princeton: Princeton University Press, 2001.

Scarry, Elaine. *The Body in Pain: The Making and Unmaking of the World*. Oxford: Oxford University Press, 1985.

Schenck, Kenneth. *A Brief Guide to Philo*. Louisville: Westminster John Knox, 2005.

Schultz, Jennifer. "Doctors, Philosophers, and Christian Fathers on Menstrual Blood." Pages 97–116 in *Wholly Woman, Holy Blood: A Feminist Critique of Purity and Impurity*. Edited by Kristin De Troyer. Harrisburg, PA: Trinity Press International, 2003.

Schwartz, Daniel R. "Did the Jews Practice Infanticide in Antiquity?" *SPhiloA* 16 (2004): 61–95.

———. "Philo, His Family, and His Times." Pages 9–31 in *The Cambridge Companion to Philo*. Edited by Adam Kamesar. Cambridge: Cambridge University Press, 2009.

Schweizer, Eduard. *The Good News according to Mark*. Translated by Donald H. Madvig. Richmond, VA: John Knox, 1970.
Scott, Steven Richard. "Raising the Dead: Finding History in the Gospel Accounts of Jesus's Resurrection Miracles, Part One: The Synoptic Tradition." PhD diss., University of Ottawa, 2010.
Segal, Michael. *The Book of Jubilees: Rewritten Bible, Redaction, Ideology and Theology*. JSJSup 117. Leiden: Brill, 2007.
Selvidge, Marla J. *Woman, Cult, and Miracle Recital: A Redactional Critical Investigation on Mark 5:24–34*. Lewisburg, PA: Bucknell University Press; London: Associated University Presses, 1990.
Shelton, Jo-Ann. *Pliny the Younger: Selected Letters*. Mundelein, IL: Bolchazzy-Carducci, 2016.
Shively, Elizabeth E. *Apocalyptic Imagination in the Gospel of Mark: The Literary and Theological Role of Mark 3:22–30*. BZNW 189. Berlin: de Gruyter, 2012.
———. "What Type of Resistance? How Apocalyptic Discourse Functions as Social Discourse in Mark's Gospel." *JSNT* 37 (2015): 381–406.
Sibeko, Malika, and Beverley Haddad. "Reading the Bible 'with' Women in Poor and Marginalized Communities in South Africa." *Semeia* 78 (1997): 83–92.
Sim, David C. "The Family of Jesus and the Disciples of Jesus in Paul and Mark: Taking Sides in the Early Church's Factional Dispute." Pages 73–100 in *Paul and Mark: Comparative Essays Part I; Two Authors at the Beginnings of Christianity*. Edited by Oda Wischmeyer, David C. Sim, and Ian J. Elmer. BZNW 198. Berlin: de Gruyter, 2014.
———. "What about the Wives and Children of the Disciples? The Cost of Discipleship from Another Perspective." *HeyJ* 35 (1994): 373–90.
Sly, Dorothy. *Philo's Perception of Women*. BJS 209. Atlanta: Scholars Press, 1990.
Stadter, Philip A. "Plutarch and Rome." Pages 11–31 in *A Companion to Plutarch*. Edited by Mark Beck. BCAW. Malden, MA: Wiley-Blackwell, 2014.
Steegen, Martijn "'Little Girl, Get Up!': The 'Perspective of the Impossible' as Inspiration for Health Care Chaplains." Paper presented at the Annual Meeting of the Society of Biblical Literature. San Antonio, TX, 20 November 2016.
Steel, Catherine. "Introduction." Pages 1–6 in *The Cambridge Companion to Cicero*. Edited by Catherine Steel. Cambridge: Cambridge University Press, 2013.

Stein, Robert H. *Mark*. BECNT 2. Grand Rapids: Baker Academic, 2008.
Šterbenc Erker, Darja. "Gender and Roman Funeral Ritual." Pages 40–60 in *Memory and Mourning: Studies on Roman Death*. Edited by Valerie M. Hope and Janet Huskinson. Oxford: Oxbow, 2011.
Storey, Alan. "For the Healing of the Nation." *Sojourners Magazine* (May 2011): 30–35.
Story, J. Lyle. "Four Females Who Encounter Jesus." *Priscilla Papers* 23 (2009): 14–15.
Strauss, Mark L. *Mark*. ZECNT 2. Grand Rapids: Zondervan, 2014.
Suetonius. *Lives of the Caesars*. Translated by J. C. Rolfe. 2 vols. LCL. Cambridge: Harvard University Press, 1913–1914.
Swanson, Richard W. "Moving Bodies and Translating Scripture: Interpretation and Incarnation." *WW* 31 (2011): 271–78.
Swartley, Willard M. "The Role of Women in Mark's Gospel: A Narrative Analysis." *BTB* 27 (1997): 16–22.
Tacitus. *Works*. Translated by M. Hutton, Clifford H. Moore, and John Jackson. 4 vols. LCL. Cambridge: Harvard University Press, 1914–1937.
Taylor, Joan E., ed. *The Body in Biblical, Christian and Jewish Texts*. LSTS 85. London: Bloomsbury, 2014.
Telford, William R. *The Barren Temple and the Withered Tree*. JSNTSup 1. Sheffield: JSOT Press, 1980.
Theissen, Gerd. *The Gospels in Context: Social and Political History in the Synoptic Tradition*. Translated by Linda M. Maloney. Minneapolis: Fortress, 1991.
Tolbert, Mary Ann. *Sowing the Gospel: Mark's World in Literary-Historical Perspective*. Minneapolis: Fortress, 1989.
Toner, Jerry P. *Popular Culture in Ancient Rome*. Cambridge: Polity, 2013.
Toynbee, J. M. C. *Death and Burial in the Roman World*. Ithaca, NY: Cornell University Press, 1971.
Trainor, Michael. *Body of Jesus and Sexual Abuse: How the Gospel Passion Narrative Informs a Pastoral Approach*. Northcote, Australia: Morning Star, 2014.
Trimble, Jennifer. "Figure and Ornament, Death and Transformation in the Tomb of the Haterii." Pages 327–52 in *Ornament and Figure in Graeco-Roman Art: Rethinking Visual Ontologies in Classical Antiquity*. Edited by Nikolaus Dietrich and Michael Squire. Berlin: de Gruyter, 2018.
Uzzi, Jeannine Diddle. *Children in the Visual Arts of Imperial Rome*. New York: Cambridge University Press, 2005.

---. "The Representation of Children in the Official Art of the Roman Empire from Augustus to Constantine." PhD diss., Duke University, 1998.

Vaage, Leif E. "An Other Home: Discipleship in Mark as Domestic Asceticism." *CBQ* 71 (2009): 741-61.

Vander Stichele, Caroline. "Like Angels in Heaven: Corporeality, Resurrection, and Gender in Mark 12:18-27." Pages 215-32 in *Begin with the Body: Corporeality, Religion and Gender*. Edited by Jonneke Bekkenkamp and Maaike de Haardt. Leuven: Peeters, 1998.

VanderKam, James C. *The Book of Jubilees*. Sheffield: Sheffield Academic, 2001.

Wainwright, Elaine M. *Women Healing/Healing Women: The Genderization of Healing in Early Christianity*. Bible World. London: Acumen, 2006.

Wardle, Timothy. "Mark, the Jerusalem Temple and Jewish Sectarianism: Why Geographical Proximity Matters in Determining the Provenance of Mark." *NTS* 62 (2016): 60-78.

Watts, Rikki E. *Isaiah's New Exodus and Mark*. WUNT 2/88. Tübingen: Mohr Siebeck, 1997.

---. "Jesus and the New Exodus Restoration of Daughter Zion: Mark 5: 21-43 in Context." Pages 13-29 in *The New Testament in Its First Century Setting: Essays on Context and Background in Honour of B. W. Winter on His Sixty-fifth Birthday*. Edited by Peter J. Williams, Andrew D. Clarke, Peter M. Head, and David Instone Brewer. Grand Rapids: Eerdmans, 2004.

Webb, Barry G. *The Book of Judges: An Integrated Reading*. JSOTSup 46. Sheffield: Sheffield Academic, 1987.

Webb, Ruth. *Demons and Dancers: Performance in Late Antiquity*. Cambridge: Harvard University Press, 2008.

Weissenrieder, Annette. *Images of Illness in the Gospel of Luke: Insights of Ancient Medical Texts*. WUNT 2/164. Tübingen: Mohr Siebeck, 2003.

West, Stephanie. "Κερκίδος Παραμύθια? For Whom Did Chariton Write?" *ZPE* 143 (2003): 63-69.

Wilcox, Max. "Talitha Koum (I) in Mk 5:41." Pages 469-76 in *Logia: Les paroles de Jésus = The Sayings of Jesus; Mémorial Joseph Coppens*. Edited by Joël Delobel. BETL 59. Leuven: Leuven University Press, 1982.

Winn, Adam. *The Purpose of Mark's Gospel: An Early Christian Response to Roman Imperial Propaganda*. WUNT 2/245. Tübingen: Mohr Siebeck, 2008.

Wintermute, Orval S. "Jubilees." *OTP* 2:35–142.
Wischmeyer, Oda, David C. Sim, and Ian J. Elmer, eds. *Paul and Mark: Comparative Essays Part I; Two Authors at the Beginnings of Christianity*. BZNW 198. Berlin: de Gruyter, 2014.
Witherington, Ben, III. *The Gospel of Mark: A Socio-Rhetorical Commentary*. Grand Rapids: Eerdmans, 2001.
Wood, Susan E. *Imperial Women: A Study in Public Images, 40 BC–AD 68*. Mnemosyne Supplements 194. Leiden: Brill, 2000.
Woolf, Greg. "Romanization." *BNP*. http://dx.doi.org/10.1163/1574-9347_bnp_e1024530.
Yarbrough, O. Larry. "Parents and Children in the Jewish Family of Antiquity." Pages 39–60 in *The Jewish Family in Antiquity*. Edited by Shaye J. D. Cohen. BJS 289. Atlanta: Scholars Press, 1993.
Zanker, Paul. *The Power of Images in the Age of Augustus*. Translated by Alan Shapiro. Jerome Lectures. Ann Arbor: University of Michigan Press, 1988.
Zias, Joe. "Human Skeletal Remains from the Mount Scopus Tomb." *Atiquot* 21 (1992): 97–103.
Zlotnick, Helena. *Dinah's Daughters: Gender and Judaism from the Hebrew Bible to Late Antiquity*. Philadelphia: University of Pennsylvania Press, 2002.
Zwiep, Arie W. "Jairus, His Daughter and the Haemorrhaging Woman (Mk 5.21–43; Mt. 9.18–26; Lk. 8.40–56): Research Survey of a Gospel Story about People in Distress." *CurBR* 13 (2015): 351–87.
———. *Jairus's Daughter and the Haemorrhaging Woman: Tradition and Interpretation of an Early Christian Miracle Story*. WUNT 421. Tübingen: Mohr Siebeck, 2019.

Ancient Sources Index

Hebrew Bible/Old Testament		2 Samuel	
		21:19	199
Genesis			
4–5	156–57	1 Kings	
34	187–88	4:13	199
34:2	188	17:17	181, 211
34:3	188	17:19	181
34:8	188	17:21	211
		17:21b	181
Exodus			
14:10	180	2 Kings	
21:22–25	170	4:34	181
		8:10	172
Leviticus			
11:1–47	17	4 Kings (LXX)	
12:1–8	17	5:11	44
13:1–14:32	17		
15:1–33	17	Esther	
15:24	247	2:5	31, 199
15:25	13		
15:33	13, 247	Lamentations	
19:10–22	16–17	1:15	193
21:7	161	2:1	193
		2:3	193
Numbers			
19:11	17	Daniel	
32:41	31, 199	12:2	37
Deuteronomy		Deuterocanonical Books	
3:14	199		
		Baruch	
Judges		4:16	193
10:3–5	31, 199		
11:29–40	190–91	2 Maccabees	
11:34–40	33	3:26	54

-293-

4 Maccabees		34.15–17	208, 192
15:23	59	35.1–8	192
		35.18–27	158
Pseudepigrapha		35.20–22	208
		35.21–22	192
Jubilees		36.21–24	208, 192
2.1–10	157	41.26	167
2.20	167	45.13–15	192, 208
2.26–28	166	46.5–6	192
2.26–30	166, 246	46.5–8	192
2.29–30	167	46.9–10	192
4.1–17	157	48.9–19	167
4.7–15	155	49.1–23	167
4.16	156	50.1–13	167
4.20	156	50.10	167
4.24	167		
4.27	156	Ancient Jewish Writers	
4.28	156		
6.19	167	Josephus, *Antiquitates judaicae*	
6.32	167	1.186–188	166
7.34–35	167	1.205	186
8.1	156	1.214	166
8.1–4	157	1.224–227	157, 221
8.5–8	156	2.230	166
10.18	156	2.231	166
11.1	156	2.328	180
11.7–8	156	3.227	185
11.9–11	156	4.20	171
11.14–15	156	4.244–248	185
12.10	156	4.245	185
17.10	193	4.260–264	152
19.1–9	208	4.278	158, 179
23.1–7	192	5.29–30	172, 240
23.6	193	5.30	172
25.1	163	5.165	183
25.3	163	5.254	199–200
25.11–23	160	5.263–266	190
25.19	160	5.264	190, 204
28.9–24	159	5.265	190
30.2	188, 227	5.266	191
30.5	188	5.277	54
31.21	167	6.357–358	171
32.30	208	6.357–360	171
32.33–34	192	6.358	171
33–34	208	7.162	187

Ancient Sources Index 295

7.163	187	6.204	178
7.167	187	6.205	178
7.167–171	187	6.206–212	177
7.169	187	6.208	178
7.170	187	6.212	179
7.171	187	6.214–215	179
7.343–344	185	7.321	176
8.5	185	7.333–334	176
8.325	181, 211	7.334	176
8.325–327	180, 211, 263	7.387	176
8.326	181	7.391	175
8.327	182, 211	7.392–394	175, 240
9.91	172, 240	7.394	175
9.142	164	7.399	177
11.196	185	7.400–401	177
11.198–201	185	7.405	177
11.200	185		
12.187–190	186	Josephus, *Contra Apionem*	
12.189	186	1.30	161
12.190	164	1.34	161
18.116–119	234	1.245	164
19.349	171	2.53	171–72, 240
20.90	171	2.55	172
		2.181	171
Josephus, *Bellum judaicum*		2.205	190, 201
1.81	59	2.206	152, 228
1.313	177	2.206	152
1.584	178	2.217	152
2.306–308	172		
2.307	172, 239	Josephus, *Vita*	
2.475	175	25	171–72
3	179	61	171
3.202	171	99	172
3.245–247	179	166	171
3.248	180	414	161
3.362–382	175		
4.71	180	Liber Antiquitatum Biblicarum	
4.79–81	172–73	5.1–8	171
4.80	173	8	221
4.106	177	8.1	158
4.107	177	8.7	187
4.108	177, 180	9	162
5.512	173	9.1	162
5.512–514	173, 239	9.1–2	168
5.513	173	9.2	162–63, 193, 221

Liber Antiquitatum Biblicarum (cont.)

9.3	162
9.5	162
9.7	162
9.8	162
10.1	193
18.5	193
19.1–16	192, 208
19.12–13	208
19.16	209
23.2	171
23.5–6	158
23.7	158
24.1–6	192
28.1–10	208
29.1–4	192, 208
30	157
32.2–4	170
32.5	159
33.1–6	157
33.2	208
33.6	208
35.4	208
36.1	171
38.1–4	200
39–40	191, 211
39.11	192
40.2	191, 193
40.3	193
40.5	147, 191, 193
40.5–7	192
40.6	191
40.8	192
40.8–9	192
42.1	159
42.1–2	159
42.3	159, 221
43.1–8	192
44.9	164
45	161, 186
45.3	161
45.4	161
45.5	162
50.2	159, 221
50.7–8	159
51.1	160
51.3	160, 221
51.5	209
61.7–9	164
64	182
64.1	182, 192
64.6	182

Philo, *De congressu quaerendae eruditionis gratia*

7	183

Philo, *De opificio mundi*

118	59

Philo, *De specialibus legibus*

1.3–7	221
1.56	163
1.56–57	163
1.57	163
1.129–130	151
1.137–138	167
1.138	167
1.332	151
2.23–25	151
2.24	151
2.123–124	150
2.125	150
2.125–126	150
2.130	152
2.133–134	152
2.224–225	228
2.225–235	152
2.229–230	152
2.232	152, 221
2.243	152
2.243–245	152
3	158, 169
3.33	158, 221
3.65	186
3.66–71	187
3.80–82	185
3.81	165
3.107–109	158, 165
3.110	169

3.115	169–70	1:18	228
3.113	151	1:19	69
3.153–68	174	1:19–20	228
3.169–171	184	1:20	61, 73, 228
3.176–177	185	1:24	48, 66
4.57–58	165	1:25	50
		1:26	48
Philo, *De vita Mosis*		1:27	62
1.5.18–21	166	1:29–30	201
		1:29–31	49, 204, 227
Philo, *In Flaccum*		1:29–32	56
36	49	1:31	49, 51, 213, 223
62–64	174, 240	1:32–33	213
68	174–75, 240	1:34	49, 66, 241
87	180	1:39	66, 241
180	184	1:40	67, 204
227	183	1:40–44	23
		1:40–45	49, 213
Philo, *Legatio ad Gaium*		1:41	4, 59–60
23	165	2:5	50, 70
26	165	2:11	62
227	183	2:11–12	51
357–358	183	2:12	223
		2:13	49
Pseudo-Philo. *See* Liber Antiquitatum		2:14	61, 69, 73
Biblicarum		2:16–17	64
		2:18	64
New Testament		2:24–28	64
		3:1–6	47
Matthew		3:2	49
9:18–26	7	3:3	223
		3:5	50, 59, 62
Mark		3:7	73
1:1	66	3:7–12	213
1:2–3	66	3:7–6:6a	249
1:4	66	3:10	49
1:7	66	3:11	66
1:11	66–67	3:12	62, 66
1:13	65	3:13–14	61
1:14–15	66	3:13–19	52
1:14–4:34	39	3:15	241
1:16	69, 228	3:19–20	231
1:16–20	228	3:19–35	241
1:17	61	3:21	223, 231
1:17–18	73	3:21–35	232

Mark (cont.)
3:22	241
3:22–30	231
3:23	241
3:27	232
3:29	231
3:31	56, 204, 232
3:31–35	232, 242
3:32	232
3:35	232, 249
4:3–20	68
4:9	68
4:10	65
4:12	70–71
4:14–20	71
4:15	71
4:16–17	71
4:19	71
4:20	71
4:21–22	68
4:23	68, 77
4:35–41	40
4:39	62
4:40	57
4:44–45	71
5:1	83
5:1–20	50
5:2	70
5:3–20	49
5:5	48
5:6	70
5:7	66
5:8	50, 62
5:10	67, 204
5:12	67, 204
5:14	57
5:15	50
5:17	16, 67
5:18	67
5:19	227
5:20	63, 66
5:21–24	1–10, 31, 33–34, 41, 49, 197–98, 204, 206, 213, 220, 223, 242–44, 246–47, 251–53, 255–57, 266–68
5:21–43	3, 10, 12, 14–16, 18, 23, 25, 28, 46, 50, 250–51, 256, 267
5:22	32, 198, 216
5:22–23	203, 207, 245
5:22–24	238
5:23	32, 34, 49, 67, 207, 212, 216, 220, 223
5:23–34	10, 225, 255
5:23–35	242
5:24–34	21, 28
5:24–35	48, 213
5:25	13, 17, 214, 247
5:25–34	2, 10, 31, 41, 47, 49, 204, 246, 251, 257
5:26	48, 56, 248
5:27	49, 69, 248
5:27–28	249
5:28	49, 248
5:29	50, 247–48
5:30	28, 248
5:31	28, 70
5:33	57
5:34	15, 28, 63, 247–49
5:35	17, 36, 198, 200, 207, 244
5:35–39	216
5:35–43	1–10, 33–34, 39, 41, 49, 197–98, 204, 206, 213, 220, 223, 238, 242–44, 246, 247, 251–53, 255–57, 266–68
5:36	62, 198, 214, 220
5:37	73
5:37–43	220
5:38	198, 207, 214
5:39	3, 34, 36, 207–8, 210, 214
5:40	34, 197, 207, 216, 217, 232, 241
5:40–42	241
5:41	34, 38, 49–50, 63, 75, 206, 212–14, 222, 241, 244
5:41–42	3, 249
5:42	13, 34, 51, 223, 241
5:42–43	222
5:43	62–63, 206, 214, 216, 223
5:44	62
6:1	73
6:1–6a	16

Ancient Sources Index

6:2	49	7:25–30	49, 213
6:2–3	64	7:26	67, 241, 245
6:3	60	7:26–27	245
6:5	13, 49, 213	7:27	68, 246
6:6	66	7:29	68, 245–46
6:7–11	62	7:29–30	214
6:8–9	62	7:30	201, 227
6:12	66	7:31	82
6:13	49, 241	7:32	49, 67, 204
6:14	54, 234	7:32–37	49, 213
6:14–29	56–57, 204	7:33	49
6:16	54	7:34	50, 63
6:17–29	234, 236–37	7:35	50
6:18	234	7:36	63
6:19	68, 236	8:2	59, 60
6:20	236	8:6	62
6:21	236	8:8	71
6:22	73–74, 234, 236–37	8:10	82
6:23	74, 238	8:11	65
6:24	68, 234, 236	8:17	71
6:24–28	57	8:18	71
6:25	67, 68, 236	8:22	67, 204
6:26	58, 74, 238	8:22–26	47, 49, 213
6:27	52, 64, 238	8:23	49, 70
6:28	64, 68, 234, 236	8:24	70
6:29	53	8:24–25	50
6:34	59	8:25	70
6:37	62, 65	8:26	227
6:39–40	62	8:27	243
6:41	238	8:31	38, 56, 248
6:45–52	57	8:34–37	52
6:49	57	9:1	43, 258
6:50	57, 62	9:2	243
6:51	223	9:2–13	220
6:56	49, 67, 204, 213, 248	9:3	54
7:1	83	9:7	67, 68
7:1–23	23	9:9	38, 63
7:5–13	64	9:10	38, 65
7:10	227	9:11	65
7:14	69	9:12	56, 248
7:24	227, 245	9:14–29	242–43
7:24–30	242, 245	9:17	32, 206
7:24–31	50, 56, 204	9:17–27	49, 50
7:25	32, 68, 69, 245	9:18	48, 206, 241, 243
7:25–26	245	9:20	48, 244

Mark (cont.)	
9:22	48, 244
9:25	50, 62, 244
9:26	48, 206, 244
9:27	38, 51, 213, 223, 244
9:28	65, 241
9:31	38, 52
9:32	57
9:33	73
9:33–37	242
9:33–50	72, 243
9:36	72, 225, 242–43
9:37	72, 75, 242
9:38	73, 241
9:42	55
9:42–50	52, 55
9:43	55
9:43–47	55
9:45	55
9:47	55
10:1–2	65
10:1–12	56, 204
10:2	64, 65
10:7–9	227
10:8	227
10:9	227
10:13	72, 243
10:13–16	72, 225, 242, 243
10:14	59, 70, 72, 75, 243
10:15	72, 75, 243
10:16	72, 242–43
10:17	65
10:19	223, 228
10:21	62, 69
10:22	58
10:26	65
10:28	229
10:29	229
10:30	229–30
10:32	73
10:33	239
10:34	38
10:35	67
10:38	67
10:46	69
10:46–52	49, 213
10:47	66–67, 69
10:48	66, 69
10:49	58, 223
10:51	69
10:51–52	69
10:52	50, 63, 69, 73
11:12–25	251
11:15	52
11:17	69
11:18	57
11:25	229
11:27–33	64
12:1–12	52, 56
12:3	56
12:4	56
12:5	56
12:7	56
12:8	56
12:9	56
12:10	56
12:12	57
12:13	65
12:13–15	64
12:14	65
12:15	65
12:18–20	56
12:18–22	64, 204
12:18–27	54
12:23	38
12:25	38
12:28	32, 65
12:36	54
12:40	56
12:40–44	204
12:41–44	56
13	81, 220
13:4	65, 239
13:7–8	240
13:7–9	52
13:12	204, 239–40
13:14–15	81
13:12–19	52
13:17–19	56, 204, 239
13:36	37

14:1–11	61, 204	15:43	53, 58
14:3	57	15:46	53
14:3–9	71	15:47	53, 82
14:4	258	16:1	54, 61, 82, 258
14:4–5	65	16:1–8	53, 82, 204, 253
14:8	57	16:5	54, 55
14:9	65	16:6	222, 266
14:10	32	16:7	55, 82, 258
14:19	58	16:8	55, 57
14:27	52	16:9	82
14:28	82, 222		
14:32–42	37	Luke	
14:33	58	8:40–56	7
14:33–42	220		
14:34	58	Acts	
14:36	229	1:10	54
14:47	52	10:30	54
14:48	52		
14:51	73	1 Corinthians	
14:54	73	15:6	37
14:55	65		
14:61	65	1 Thessalonians	
14:62	54	5:10	37
14:64	239		
14:66–72	56	Revelation	
14:67	70	6:11	54
14:72	58	7:9	54
15:1–5	52		
15:2	65	Rabbinic Works	
15:5	52		
15:8	67	Hekhalot Rabbah	18
15:11	67		
15:13–14	64	Early Christian Writings	
15:13–15	64		
15:16–24	52	Eusebius, *Ecclesiastical History*	
15:21	82	3.39.14–15	78
15:29–30	53	6.14.6	78
15:34	58–59, 63		
15:37	53	Greco-Roman Literature	
15:38	70, 80		
15:39	66, 70	Chariton, *De Chaerea et Callirhoe*	
15:40	57, 82, 204	1.1.7–8	138–39
15:40–41	82	1.4.12	145
15:41	73	1.5.1	209
15:42–47	57, 204	1.6.2	209

Chariton, *De Chaerea et Callirhoe* (cont.)		Juvenal, *Satirae*	
1.8	209	6	97, 137
1.9.4–5	203	6.114–140	120
3.8.3	141	6.140–150	121
5.8.8–9	217	6.415	116
6.3–5	204	6.435–477	116
8.6.8	134	6.590–600	121
		14	235

Cicero, *Brutus*
211   116, 122

Lucan, *De bello civili* (*Pharsalia*)
2.21–28   202

Cicero, *De legibus*
2.59–64   201

Martial, *Epigrams*
14.203.1–2   236–37

Cicero, *De republica*
6.14   115

Ovid, *Amores*
2.4.23–32   236

Cicero, *Epistulae ad Atticum*
12.14   204

Philostratus, *Vita Apollonii*
4.45   12, 44, 210

Cicero, *Epistulae ad familiares*
248   144
249   142

Pliny the Elder, *Naturalis historia*
7.176–178   201–2

Cicero, *Epistulae ad Quintum fratrem*
3.1   135

Pliny the Younger, *Epistulae*
3.16   117, 123
5.16   127, 140–41, 143, 191
5.19   204
7.19   136

Cicero, *In Verrem*
2.5.118   201

Cicero, *Orationes philippicae*
9.16–17   113

Plutarch, *Comparatio Lycurgi et Numae*
3   136–37
4   138
3.1–7   115
4.2–5   115
77   116

Cicero, *Pro Cluentio*
12–14   235
27   130
28   130

Plutarch, *Comparatio Pericles et Fabius Maximus*
17.7   202

Cicero, *Tusculanae disputationes*
1.32   109–10, 233
1.33   110

Plutarch, *Consolatio ad uxorem*
4   122–23, 203
9   143
9b   116

Homer, *Iliad*
16.528–531   209

Ancient Sources Index

9c	116
611c	116
611d	116
8	140

Plutarch, *Moralia*
619	234–35
712	235

Plutarch, *Numa*
9	137

Plutarch, *Pompeius*
9	235
48	138
53	140, 145

Quintillian, *Institutio oratoria*
1.2	235
1.8–9	235
6	96
6.3	130
6.3–14	244
6.7	130
6.10	131
6.11	131
6.12–13	130

Seneca, *De consolatione ad Helviam*
19.6	184

Sophocles, *Antigone*
891	192

Soranus, *Gynaecology*
1.46	247
3.26	12
3.28	12

Suetonius, *Caligula*
7	127–28
8–10	128
10	137

Suetonius, *Divus Claudius*
32	234

Tacitus, *Annales*
1.10.5	114
3.1–2	123
3.1–3	123
4.60	236
11.34	120
11.38	120–21
15.23	134–35, 140, 144
15.63	116–17, 203

Tacitus, *Germania*
19	121
20.1	119

Tacitus, *Historiae*
4.53	127

Valerius Maximus, *Facta et Dicta Memorabilia*
5.4	127

Vergil, *Aeneid*
9.486–489	201

Modern Authors Index

Ahearne-Kroll, Stephen P. 224, 229, 232
Aichele, George 222, 225
Alfonso Fernandez, Zoa 237
Ali, Christine Amjad 27–28, 35
Amerding, Carl E. 38
Amoah, Elizabeth 20
Atkinson, Kenneth 173, 175–76
Australian Broadcasting Commission 269
Australian Commonwealth 269
Baden, Joel S. 14
Bader, Mary Anna 164, 188–89
Bakhtin, Mikhail 90
Baker, Cynthia 191–94
Baldwin, Barry 97
Balla, Peter 225–26, 228
Barclay, John 161, 176, 222
Barton, Stephen C. 225, 229, 232–33
Beard, Mary 120
Beavis, Mary Ann 1, 4, 18, 24, 33, 79, 83–84, 199
Bechtel, Carol M. 199
Becker, Eve-Marie 86
Begg, Christopher T. 181–82, 200
Betsworth, Sharon 2, 4, 11, 14, 28, 32, 34–35, 38, 46–47, 68, 72–74, 204, 217, 222, 225, 246, 249
Bianchi, Emanuela 248
Binder, Vera 86
Bock, Darrel L. 17
Boling, Robert G. 99
Bolt, Peter 2, 39, 217
Bomford, Rodney 11, 27
Bonneau, Normand 11
Boring, Eugene 11, 19, 34, 36, 41

Bowie, E. 210
Bowman, Alan K. 210
Branch, Robin Gallaher 13, 15–16, 18, 26–27, 38
Breytenbach, Cilliers 78
Brighton, Mark Andrew 176
Brown, Cheryl Anne 170, 191, 193–94
Brown, Scott G. 10, 251
Butler, Trent C. 199
Byrne, Brendon 203
Cadwallader, Alan H. 81, 246
Campbell, Charles L. 18–19
Capps, Donald 1, 13, 44–45
Chapman, Cynthia R. 160
Chapman, Honora Howell 175, 177–79
Chilton, Bruce 17
Choi, Jin Young 52, 222
Cilliers, Johan 18–19
Cody, Jane 203
Cohen, Sande 84
Cohen, Shaye J. D. 21, 175
Cook, Joan E. 160
Cotter, Wendy 24
Cotton, Hannah 168
Craig, Christopher P. 96
Crossley, James 85
Culpepper, R. Alan 12, 15, 20, 36, 38, 44
D'Angelo, Mary Rose 12–13, 23–24, 44, 210, 227, 247
Dalgaard, Kasper 4, 39
Danker, Frederick William 71
Davies, Glenys 212
Day, Linda M. 199
Dench, Emma 86
Destro, Adriana 217, 225

Modern Authors Index

Dewey, Joanna 10, 18, 78, 91
Dillen, Annemie 269
Dixon, Suzanne 110, 115–16, 121, 137, 139, 235–36
Docherty, Susan E. 92
Donahue, John 17–20, 79, 229–30, 232, 249, 251
Driscoll, Martha 31–33
Dwyer, Timothy 28–29
Dyson, Stephen L. 111
Edwards, Catharine 97
Edwards, James R. 12, 25–26, 251
Elliott, John H. 225, 230, 232, 251
Elmer, Ian J. 86
Endberg-Pedersen, Troels 86
England, Frank 13
Erker, Darja Šterbenc 123
Fassnacht, Martin 27, 233
Feldman, Louis H. 93, 181–82
Fenton, Steve 103
Fernández López, Jorge 96
Fischbach, Stephanie 2, 39–40, 210
Flory, Marleen B. 114
Fonrobert, Charlotte Elisheva 21
Fowler, Robert M. 10, 231
France, R. T. 3, 11–12, 18, 31, 36–39, 79
Francis, James 34–36, 40, 204
Fredriksen, Paula 21–22
Friberg, Barbara 54
Friberg, Timothy 54
Fullmer, Paul 4, 37
Gardner, A. Edward 19
Gerber, Jörg 86
Gill, Robin 11
Gingrich, F. Wilbur 58
Glancy, Jennifer A. 91, 104
Goodenough, Erwin Ramsdell 154, 165
Grabbe, Lester L. 155
Graham, Emma Jayne 53, 139, 202
Graver, Margaret 109
Greenblatt, Stephen 89–90
Grubbs, Judith Evans 14
Guelich, Robert 11, 38
Gundry, Judith 4, 15, 34–36, 41, 204, 223, 225
Gundry, Robert 3, 14, 16, 44, 204
Gurtner, Daniel M. 17
Hääg, Thoams 210
Haber, Susan 12–13, 17, 21
Hachlili, Rachel 99, 149–50, 149–50, 153–54, 164, 169, 189
Haddad, Beverly 18, 25
Hallett, Judith P. 133
Halpern-Amaru, Betsy 156, 160, 162, 187
Harrington, Daniel 17–20, 79, 209, 249
Harris, Murray J. 4, 36, 41
Harris, Steven Edwards 38
Haynes, Katharine 97
Hedrick, Charles 1, 37
Hens-Piazza, Gina 87, 90, 106
Heslin, Peter 112–13
Hogan, Larry P. 181
Hooker, Morna 3, 17, 31, 37, 79, 203
Hope, Valerie 117, 139–41, 201
Hurtado, Larry W. 78
Huskinson, Janet 101, 117, 125, 132–33, 139–41
Ilan, Tal 149, 165–66, 189
Incigneri, Brian J. 79–80, 83
Jacobson, Howard 94, 157, 160, 192, 194, 208–9
Jenkins, Keith 84
Joynes, Christine E. 1, 29
Kahl, Brigitte 11, 17, 23–25, 217–19, 249
Kanyoro, Musimbi R. A. 20
Kazen, Thomas 15, 21
Kelley, Nicole 176
Kemmers, Fleur 100
Kessler-Harris, Alice 88–89
Kiley, Mark 4
King, Helen 210
Klawans, Jonathan 21–22
Kleiner, Diana E. E. 133, 212
Kockel, Valentin 125, 212
Kossew, Sue 222
Kraemer, Ross S. 166, 234
Kristeva, Julia 90
Kugel, James L. 94
Laes, Christian 101, 112, 129, 140

Lamberton, Robert 96
Larsson Loven, Lena 72, 101, 126, 132, 212
Lawless, Elaine 17, 46
Lawrence, Louise J. 43, 49, 61, 63, 68–69, 105
Leigh, Matthew 96
Levine, Amy-Jill 21–23, 247
Levine, Lee I. 87
Loader, William R. G. 92, 151, 183–85, 187–89
Louw, Johannes P. 54
MacDonald, Dennis R. 209
Malbon, Elizabeth Struthers 2, 4, 15–18, 32, 219, 232
Maluleke, Tinyiko Sam 2, 35, 39
Manuwald, Gesine 96
Marcus, Joel 3, 11, 18, 31, 37–38, 54–55, 79, 81–82, 84, 223, 227, 233, 240, 244–45, 249
Marshall, Christopher D. 27
Mason, Steve 93, 172
McFague, Sallie 105
McInerney, Jeremy 205
McIntyre, Gwynaeth 114
McLaren, James S. 93, 177
McLaughlin, Raoul 61
McWilliam, Janette 143
Michie, Donald 10, 78, 91
Miller-McLemore, Bonnie 225, 230–31
Miller, Neva F. 54
Miller, Susan 2, 11–13, 16–17, 25–27, 38, 46–47, 249
Milnor, Kristina 96, 114
Mirguet, Francoise 59–60
Moloney, Francis 11, 13–14, 17–18, 54–55, 64, 66, 73, 78–79, 243–44, 249
Morello, Ruth 96
Morgan, Teresa 87–88
Morton Braund, Susanna 97
Moss, Candida R. 14, 247
Müller, Morgens 86
Müller, Sabine 125, 212
Murphy, Frederick J. 94, 155–56, 193–94, 200, 206, 223, 225, 20

Murphy, James 4, 33–37, 45–46, 73
Myers, Ched 13, 17, 26, 29, 37
Myrberg, Nanouschka 100
Nida, Eugene A. 54
Niditch, Susan 199
Niehoff, Maren R. 151, 153, 169–70, 185
North, John 120
Noy, David 198–99, 201
Oduyoye, Mercy 1, 35
Okure, Teresa 20
Olson, Kelly 132
Oppel, Dagmar 2, 11, 14, 37, 243
Parkin, Tim 33, 111, 127, 129
Pesce, Maura 217, 225
Pesch, Rudolf 1, 3, 31, 36–37, 40, 211, 222
Peskowitz, Miriam 148, 184
Poetker, Katrina M. 225–26, 232, 250
Polaski, Donald C. 162
Powell, Charles E. 17
Price, Simon 120
Rajak, Tessa 198–99
Rawson, Beryl 100–101, 111–12, 115, 118–19, 121, 125–26, 134–35, 141–42, 212, 234
Reeder, Caryn A. 93, 171, 173, 175, 180
Reinhartz, Adele 151–52, 166, 169, 183
Rhoads, David 10, 78, 91
Robinson, Robert B. 155
Rochais, Gérard 2, 15, 36, 40
Rose, Charles Brian 113
Roskam, Hendrika N. 80, 82–83
Rossini, Orietta 112–13, 119, 125, 212–13
Rubin, Miri 88
Rutgers, Leonard V. 99
Sabourin, Leopold 1, 36, 38
Saller, Richard 110–11
Sanders, E. P. 21–22
Satlow, Michael 14, 166
Scarry, Elaine 67, 69
Schenck, Kenneth 92
Schultz, Jennifer 247
Schwartz, Daniel R. 92, 149, 169
Schweizer, Eduard 38, 44, 46

Scott, Steven Richard	2, 14, 40–41	Webb, Barry G.	199
Segal, Michael	94	Webb, Ruth	236
Selvidge, Marla	17, 28	Weissenrieder, Annette	247
Shelton, Joanne	98	West, Stephanie	210
Shier, Kim	152	Wischmeyer, Oda	86
Shively, Elizabeth E.	232–33, 241	Wilcox, Max	1, 37
Shomanah, Musa W. Dube	15	Winn, Adam	79–80
Sibeko, Malika	18, 25	Witherington, Ben, III	27
Sim, David C.	86, 230–31	Wood, Susan E.	102
Sly, Dorothy	152, 183–85	Woolf, Greg	87
Smith, Patricia	149	Yarbro Collins, Adela	16, 21, 31, 44, 54, 79–80, 83, 91, 227, 233, 240, 246
Spilsbury, Paul	181–82		
Stadter, Philip A.	96	Yarbrough, O. Larry	152
Steegen, Martijn	1	Zanker, Paul	119
Steel, Catherine	96	Zias, Joe	149
Stein, Robert H.	3, 12, 14–16, 24, 35–37, 44	Zlotnick, Helena	188–89
		Zwiep, Arie	9, 11–12, 14, 30, 34, 215
Storey, Alan	20		
Story, J. Lyle	19		
Strauss, Mark	11–12, 14, 17, 19, 35, 38, 40		
Swanson, Richard	46		
Swartley, Willard	2, 25, 28, 38		
Taylor, Joan	8		
Telford, William R.	10, 251		
Theissen, Gerd	81–82		
Tolbert, Mary Ann	10–11, 16		
Toner, Jerry P.	92		
Toynbee, J. M. C.	120, 122		
Trainor, Michael	105		
Trimble, Jennifer	202		
Uzzi, Jeannine Diddle	106, 113, 125		
Vaage, Leif	225, 227, 230		
Van der Hoorst, Pieter	174, 184		
Van Henten, Jan Willem	175–76, 191		
Van Iersel, Bas M. F.	11–12, 27–28, 37		
VanderKam, James C.	94, 156		
Vander Stichele, Caroline	54		
Villalobos Mendoza, Manuel	52		
Wainwright, Elaine	2, 14, 24, 38, 45, 54, 103, 210, 248		
Walker, Caroline Bynum	103, 105		
Walsh, Richard	222		
Wardle, Timothy	80–81		
Watts, Rikki E.	11, 14, 20, 39		

Subject Index

abortion, 121, 169
Abraham, 170
Agathe, Ummidia, 140, 144
agency, 49, 117, 122, 138, 186, 187, 216, 248–49, 252, 266, 269
   absence of, 150, 187
Agrippa, Marcus, 120
Agrippa I, 92
Agrippina, 113, 123
Ahenobarbus, Gnaeus Domitius, 212–13
Akmonia, 198
Alexandria, 80, 95, 184
   death of Jews by famine in, 174
   synagogue of, 92
altars, 98, 100–101, 112, 141–42
Antioch, 80
Antonia, 113
Antonia Minor, 213
Anullina, epitaph of, 134
Aramaic language, 50, 63, 82, 87–88
   Aramaisms, 81–83, 85
architecture, 8, 101, 111, 148
   domestic, 184, 262
Ariadne, 209
Aristotle, 248
Arria, 117, 123
Augusta (daughter of Nero), 135, 140, 144
Augustus, 98, 112–14, 118, 120, 124, 126, 128
aurality, 47, 69, 78, 258
authority, Jesus as figure of, 43, 62, 64, 198, 213–24, 226, 230, 238, 240, 242, 246, 248–49, 250, 252, 264–65, 268
Babylonia, 166

Bar Kokhba Revolt, 82
Bartimaeus, 58, 63, 66–67, 69
Blake, William, 1
bleeding, gynecological, 13–14, 16–17, 21, 24
bleeding woman, story of, 2–4, 6–7, 9–10, 12, 15–16, 19–20, 22–23, 25–27, 29–31, 33–34, 36, 41–42, 46, 48, 50–51, 56, 63, 69, 106, 200, 204, 214, 225, 246–47, 249, 250–52, 255–56, 267
body
   of children, 164–83
   and emotion, 57–60
   female, in Judaism, 147–95
   female, in the Greco Roman world, 109–45
   illness in, 47–51
   importance of the, 43–47, 74–75, 255, 257–59, 264–67
   in Mark's Gospel, 43–74
   senses of, 60–74
   suffering of, 51–57
breastfeeding, 119, 121, 160, 221
burial rites, 54, 61, 99, 129–30, 149–50, 153–54, 168, 189, 192, 200–201, 205
cannibalism, 177–79
Ceres (deity), 119
Chariton, 97, 134, 138, 140–41, 145, 209–10, 261
chastity, 116, 137–38, 145, 183, 185–86, 261–63
child abuse, 33, 168, 187, 206, 269
childbearing, 13, 34, 119–21, 135–37, 140, 142–43, 145, 157, 160, 165, 183, 207, 261. *See also* pregnancy

Subject Index

childbirth, 17, 122, 126, 137–38, 140–41, 145, 149, 235, 240
children
  bodies of, 164–83
  deaths of. *See* mortality, infant
  female, 5–8, 33, 35, 42, 73–75, 96, 105, 109–10, 116, 134–39, 141, 144–45, 147, 183, 195, 205, 207, 242, 259–60, 267
  images of, 124–34
  value of, 166–68
Christology, 23–24, 85
Cicero, 96, 109–10, 113, 115–16, 122, 130, 135, 142, 144, 201, 204, 233, 260
circumcision, 161, 164, 166, 188, 221
Clement of Alexandria, 78
coins, 8, 89, 98, 100, 102, 109, 111, 118, 124, 203, 240–41, 261
commands, 37, 50, 51, 61–64, 68, 83, 214–15, 220–22, 238, 244, 258, 264–65
concubines, 161–62, 172
Connor, Noel, 1
corpses, impurity of, 16–19, 44, 46, 190
corruption, 68, 74, 120–22, 138, 227, 234–35, 238
crucifixion, 52–53, 58, 63–64, 67, 79–80, 172, 258
Cupid (deity), 128
Dalmanutha, 82
dancing, 73–75, 186, 236–38
daughters, 26, 96–98, 110–11, 113, 115, 127, 134–36, 139–42, 145, 149–51, 154, 157, 163–64, 166, 195, 199, 202, 205, 210, 217–18, 220, 223, 235–36, 238, 256, 261–64
  deaths of, 189–94
  sexual violation of, 186–89
  virginity of, 183–86
David, king, 94, 164, 171
Deborah, 157, 208
  hymn of, 158, 170
Decapolis, 50, 63, 83
deification, 144
demoniac, Gerasene, 16, 48, 50, 63, 66, 70

desire, female, 137, 138–39
diaspora, Jewish, 99, 154, 165, 166
Dinah, 155, 157, 187–89, 263
Dionysius of Alexandria, 17
disease, 3, 12–14, 23–24, 33, 41, 45–46, 49, 56, 60, 63, 122, 129, 168, 206, 247, 248, 255, 258
divorce, 64–65, 112, 118, 153, 189, 227, 235
dowries, 150, 187
Drusus, 113, 128
Egypt, 79, 151, 157, 169, 208
Eleazar, 175–76, 177
Elijah, 37, 180–82, 211–12
Elisha, 37
Eluma, 159
emotion, 8, 43, 55, 57–60, 70, 74, 104, 123, 130, 159, 177, 179–80, 191, 193, 203, 207–8, 215, 218, 220, 231, 258, 268–69
epilepsy, 244
epitaphs. *See* inscriptions, funerary
Essenes, 94
Esther, 185
Eucharis, Licinia, epitaph of, 237
Eusebius, 78
exorcism, 65, 67, 69, 241, 245
exposure (of infants), 169–70
faith, 3, 12, 14–16, 21, 24–26, 28–29, 39, 40–41, 51, 57, 62, 64, 70, 218–19, 233–34, 244, 249–50, 256
family, 224–50
  adult females within, 115–24
  central image in the Roman Empire, 111–15
  children within, 124–34
  in Judaism, 148–53
  representations of in Mark, 226–42
  young females in, 134–39
famine, 33, 173–74, 177–78
Fannia, 135–36
fasting, 64
fathers, role of, 27, 32–34, 45, 60, 97, 110, 114–15, 128, 134–35, 139–42, 150–53, 155, 169, 171, 175, 183, 187, 189–90,

fathers, role of (cont.)
　195, 199–200, 202, 203–6, 212, 214, 216–17, 219–21, 224, 229–30, 237–39, 243–44, 246, 262, 265
　paterfamilias, idea of, 32, 110–11, 115, 151, 249
feminism, 11, 15, 22, 23–24, 105, 107
fertility, 33–34, 46, 119–21, 138, 142, 144–45, 158–60, 162–64, 183, 195, 207, 221, 255, 262
　Nero dedicates temple to, 135
first-fruits, 167–68
Flavian dynasty, 93, 111
Florius family, 212
Florus, 172
Fundanus, 140–41, 143, 144, 204
Gaius (Caligula), emperor, 98, 118, 124, 128, 165, 212
Galilee, 5, 23, 54–55, 78, 81–83, 94, 184, 245
Galilee, Sea of, 83, 228
games, secular, 120, 126
Gamla, 173, 176
gender, 3, 6, 8, 12, 14, 23–24, 26, 33, 45–46, 103, 105, 122, 180, 183, 211, 221, 245, 255
genealogies, 155–57, 166, 199, 234
gentiles, 80–81, 83, 85–86, 93–94, 163, 242, 245–46, 252, 260
Gerasa, 16, 83
Germanicus, 113–15, 123, 127–28, 213
grief, 41, 58–60, 74, 109, 117, 122–23, 130–31, 135–36, 141–42, 144–45, 150, 171, 179–80, 181–82, 187, 191–92, 195, 202, 204–5, 207–8, 211, 216, 223, 252–53, 258, 261, 263, 266–67
hands, 44–47, 49, 55, 67, 71–72, 100, 125–26, 160, 175, 192, 203, 212–14, 233, 240–42, 244, 261
Hannah, 159–60, 209
Haterii monument, 120, 122, 202
healing, 10–12, 16, 19, 21, 23–25, 27–28, 30, 33, 39–41, 43–46, 49–51, 59, 63, 69–71, 75, 206, 213–14, 227, 238, 242–43, 246, 248–50, 252, 255, 257

healing (cont.)
　role of faith in, 14–15
hearers, 5, 8, 15, 68, 86–87, 90, 145, 207, 210, 222, 233–34, 241, 259–60
hearing, 43, 50, 61, 68–69, 70–71, 74–75, 77, 90, 258–59
hellenization, 5, 86–87, 94, 156, 260
Herculaneum, 101
Herod, 40, 54, 58, 64, 67–68, 74–75, 234–38
Herodians, 64–65
Herodias, 35, 56, 58, 64, 67–68, 73–75, 234–36, 238, 269
Hippo Regius, 97
Hippocratic Corpus, 14
HIV/AIDS, 15
hope, 1, 6, 26, 31, 40, 82, 110–11, 126–28, 130–31, 135, 142–45, 167, 202, 207, 218, 222, 240, 243, 250, 252–53, 261, 264, 265–66, 267, 270
household, 6–7, 45, 100–102, 120–22, 128, 151, 165, 173–74, 180, 184, 189, 198, 200, 207, 215–16, 229–30, 231–32, 238, 240–43, 244, 245, 246–47, 267–69
　imperial, 96, 114, 119
　reordered by Jesus, 24, 217–26, 249–50, 252–53, 264–66
hysteria, 23, 44
identity, Jewish, 103, 147–48, 151, 153–54, 156, 160, 164, 166, 188, 194–95, 227, 234, 263
idolatry, 163–64, 168, 200
Ilythia (deity), 120, 126
impurity, ritual. *See* corpses, impurity of
incest, 185–86
infanticide, 169–70
infertility, 13–14, 41, 158–59. *See also* fertility
inscriptions, funerary, 89, 99–101, 109–11, 117–18, 126–27, 129, 131, 134, 141–42, 145, 148, 149–50, 153–54, 164, 165, 168–69, 189–90, 198, 200, 205–6, 237, 261–62
intertextuality, 10–11, 14, 33, 105

Subject Index

Isaac, 159, 170, 193
Ithaca (concubine), 172
Jair, 31, 199–200
Jairus, 14–16, 24–34, 39–41, 62–63, 67, 70, 199–202, 203–5, 213–20, 222–23, 226, 238, 244, 245, 249, 256, 264
Jephthah, 33, 94, 190–94, 204, 211, 263
Jericho, 99, 148–49, 153, 168, 189, 200, 205, 234, 262
  Damascus Gate, 169
  Goliath family tomb, 164, 169
Jerusalem, 82, 87, 92–93, 99, 148, 153, 168, 173, 189, 198, 205, 234, 262
  temple of, 79, 81, 85, 94, 177, 179, 193–94
Jerusalem, church of, 80
Jewish Revolt. See Jewish War
Jewish War, 81–82, 92–93, 173, 175–77, 179
John Chrysostom, 79
John of Gischala, 177, 180
John the Baptizer, 53–54, 58, 64, 66–68, 81, 234, 236
Joseph, 186
Joseph of Arimathea, 53, 58
Josephus, 91, 92–93, 95–96, 147, 157, 160–61, 164, 171–73, 175–83, 185–87, 190–91, 195, 199–200, 204, 211, 239, 262
Jotapata, 179
Judaism, Second Temple, 5–7, 91–95, 147, 155, 166, 182, 190, 195, 227, 233, 261–62, 268
  images of the family in, 148–53
  material culture of, 99
Judas, 32, 52
Julia (daughter of Julius Caesar), 138, 140–41, 144
Julia, 118
Julia Livia, 236
Julia Minor, 125
Julia Severa (synagogue patron), 198
Julia Victorina, epitaph of, 134, 140
Julio-Claudian dynasty, 111, 118
Julius Caesar, 118, 140, 145

Juno (deity), 120
Juvenal, 97, 116, 122, 260
law, Jewish, 17–18, 20–23, 25, 29, 41, 64, 81, 151–52, 160, 169–70, 185–86, 191, 219
law, Roman, 13
leprosy, 17
Liber Antiquitatum Biblicarum. See Pseudo-Philo
liberation theology, 26
Livia, 112–13, 128
Livillia, 236
Lucius, 118, 124, 212
Lycurgus, 137–38
Magdala, 82
Marcellae, Minicia, 140–41, 204, 261
Markan sandwich, 2–3, 10–11, 25, 30, 41, 249–51, 255–57, 265, 267
marriage, 13, 34, 44, 117–18, 120, 132, 136–40, 142–45, 150–51, 156, 161, 163–64, 167, 185–86, 189, 207, 212, 220, 227, 234–35, 261–63
  endogamous, 156, 164, 189, 263
  levirate, 64
  remarriage, 112
martyrdom, 192, 211
Mary, mother of James, 54, 57, 82
Mary, mother of Joses, 53, 204–5
Mary Magdalene, 53–54, 57, 82, 204
Masada, 175–77
material culture, 8, 87, 99–102, 128, 134
Menimani and Blussus, stele of, 116, 132
menstruation, 13–14, 16–18, 20, 22–23, 255. See also bleeding, gynecological
Messalina, 120
miscarriages, 158, 163, 179
modesty, feminine, 116, 135, 137, 143, 145, 184, 185
monuments, funerary, 8, 89, 98, 100, 102, 109–15, 117–18, 122, 124–25, 131–34, 139, 141, 145, 202, 212, 261
mortality, infant, 33, 122, 127, 128–31, 133, 168–70, 261
Moses, 157–58, 166, 168, 192, 208–209
motherhood, 118–20, 157, 162, 233, 235

mourners, 40–41, 53, 122, 201–2, 207–8, 211, 214–16, 218, 223, 241, 264
mutilation, 52, 55, 162
Nazareth, 16, 40, 233
Nero, emperor, 79, 96, 118, 128, 135, 140, 144, 236
Noah, 157, 167
Numa, king of Rome, 136
Octavia, 118
Oppianicus, 130
Optatus, Quintus Caecilius, epitaph to, 129, 131
orality, 47, 61, 258
ossuaries, 148–49, 153–54, 168, 169
Paetus, Aulus Caecina, 117
Papias, 78
parables, 56, 68, 232
paralysis, 48, 51, 70
patriarchy, 22, 105, 190, 229, 230
patronyms, 149–50, 189, 200, 205, 228, 262, 264
Pauline traditions, 81, 85–86
Paulina, 117
pericopes, 9, 15, 34, 36–39, 44–45, 244
persecution, 16, 71, 79–84, 229
Peter, 58, 62, 65, 78–79, 82, 201, 215, 220, 229, 239, 265
Pharisees, 31, 64–65
Philo, 91–92, 95, 147, 150–53, 158, 163, 165, 167, 169–71, 174–75, 180, 183–87, 195, 221–22, 228, 239, 261–62
Philostratus, 12, 44
physicians, 13, 27, 37, 48, 247
Pilate, Pontius, 52–53, 58, 64–65, 67
Pliny the Younger, 97–98, 117, 123, 135–36, 140–41, 143–44, 204, 260, 261
Plutarch, 96, 116, 122–23, 136–38, 140, 143, 234–36, 260
Pompeii, 101
Pompey, 138, 140, 145, 235
possession, demonic, 48, 50–51, 213, 231, 243–45. *See also* spirits, unclean
postcoloniality, 11, 15
pregnancy, 56, 158, 162, 172, 179, 235, 239. *See also* childbearing

priests, Jewish, 52–53, 57, 64–65, 67–69, 92, 94, 144, 151, 159, 160–61, 176, 185, 239
Primigenius, Publius Ummidius, 140, 144
Priscus, Neratius, 135
procreation, 110, 137–38, 151, 157–58, 163, 221–22, 248
Procula, Iunia, 134, 140–42
provenance (of Mark's Gospel), 5, 77–85, 90, 94–95, 259, 267
Pseudo-Philo, 94, 156–57, 163–64, 182, 193, 208–9
Ptolemy Physcon, 171–72
puberty, 34
punishment, 44, 152, 162
Quintillian, 96, 98, 130–31, 235–36, 261
rape, 161, 186–89, 263
resurrection, 3, 25, 31, 36–39, 40, 45, 54–55, 64, 209, 219, 222, 256
resuscitation, 3, 32, 36, 37–38, 256
Roma (personification), 240
Rome, 5, 78–81, 84, 92–93, 95–98, 100–101, 110, 112–14, 116, 124, 128, 131, 133, 203, 212, 241, 268
  Ara Pacis, 100, 112–13, 119, 124, 212
  Campus Martius, 112
  Capitoline, 120, 144
  Capitoline Venus, Temple of, 128
  Circus Flaminius, 114
  Germanicus Arch, 112–14
  Horologium, 112
  Jupiter, Temple of, 127, 142
  Mausoleum of Augustus, 112
Rufus, Servius Sulpicius, 142, 144
sacrifice, 33, 44, 120, 147, 170, 178, 190–94, 210, 263
Sadducees, 64
Salome, 54, 57, 82, 204
Satan, 65, 71, 227, 232, 240–42
Scopus, Mount, 149
scribes, 53, 64–65, 69, 231, 232–33, 239
sects, Jewish, 81, 85
seed, 158, 163, 221–22, 265
Seila (Jephthah's daughter), 94, 191–94, 211

Sekella, 171
Seneca, 117, 184
Sertorii relief, 126, 131, 212
Seruili relief, 132
sexuality, 13, 33, 41, 44, 136–37, 142, 145, 160, 163, 188–89, 194, 222, 255
sicarii, 176–77
Sidon, 83
sight, 43, 47, 50, 52, 63, 68–71, 132, 208, 258–59
Silius, 120
Simon of Cyrene, 82
sin, 55, 162, 231
slaves, 52, 56, 101, 110–11, 119, 140, 162–63, 168, 185, 236
sleep, 3, 36–37, 40–41, 101, 201, 206, 208–10, 218, 256, 263
Solymius, 186
Soranus, 12
Spartans, 136
Spencer, Stanley, 1
spirits, unclean, 32, 47–51, 62–63, 65–66, 213, 245, 258
statues, 89, 109, 113–14, 128
status, children as symbols of, 131–33
Suetonius, 97–98, 127–28, 261
suffering, 48, 51–57
suicide, 55, 173
supplication, 159, 203, 241, 245
synagogues, 22, 29, 66, 92, 198, 219–20, 233, 256
Syria, 5, 78, 80, 81–82, 84, 171
Syrophoenician woman, 32, 36, 47, 50, 56, 67–69, 104, 201, 205, 242, 245
Tacitus, 96–98, 114–17, 119–21, 123, 127, 134–35, 140, 144, 236, 260
talitha, 28, 34, 206
Tamar, 162, 187
taxes, 65
Tellus (deity), 119, 233
temple, Jerusalem. *See* Jerusalem: temple of
Tertullian, 79
Thessalonica, 135
Tiberius, emperor, 98, 113, 128, 165, 172

Tiepolo, Giovanni, 1
Timoxena, 143
Titus, emperor, 80, 177, 180
tombs, 48, 50–51, 53–55, 57, 82, 98, 99–101, 113, 148–49, 150, 154, 164, 168–69, 189, 192, 195, 200, 204–5, 223, 234, 258, 262
touch, 11, 18–19, 20, 24, 28, 43–47, 49–50, 53–54, 61, 68, 71–72, 75, 124–26, 185, 211–13, 222, 238, 244, 257–59, 261
transfiguration, 68, 220
Tusculum, 109
Tullia, 96, 109–10, 135, 142, 144, 204
twelve, number, 12–13, 20, 40
Tyre, 83
underworld, 134
Valerius Maximus, 127
Venus (deity), 119, 128
Vespasian, emperor, 80, 203
Vettius, C., relief of, 133
Victorina, Julia, epitaph of, 134, 140
Villa Doria Pamphili monument, 134
Violence, 33, 43, 47, 51–53, 55, 56–58, 60, 64, 74, 92, 121–22, 145, 148–49, 158, 161–62, 164, 169, 171–72, 174–75, 179, 186–87, 195, 206, 239–40, 258, 263, 266
sexual. *See* rape
virginity, 127, 136, 150–51, 161, 183–89, 192–94, 262
wives, expectations of, 97, 116–18, 121, 137, 155, 194, 234
wombs, 12–13, 44, 56, 59, 158–60, 163, 168, 178–79, 221, 262

www.ingramcontent.com/pod-product-compliance
Lightning Source LLC
Chambersburg PA
CBHW030300010526
44108CB00038B/839